THE FACE OF THE ANCIENT ORIENT

PROFESSOR SABATINO MOSCATI was born in Rome, and studied in the Pontifical Biblical Institute and in the University of Rome. Since 1954 he has been Professor of Semitic Philology in the University of Rome. He is at present Director of the Centre of Semitic Studies in that University.

THE FACE OF THE ANCIENT ORIENT

*A Panorama
of Near Eastern Civilizations
in Pre-Classical Times*

BY

SABATINO MOSCATI

Translated from the Italian original

Anchor Books
Doubleday & Company, Inc.
Garden City, New York

The Face of the Ancient Orient was originally published in Italy by Edizioni Radio Italiana. The first translation was published in London by Routledge & Kegan Paul, Ltd. and by Vallentine, Mitchell & Co., Ltd. in 1960, and in the United States by Quadrangle Books, Inc. in 1960. The Anchor Books edition is published by arrangement with Routledge & Kegan Paul, Ltd. and Quadrangle Books, Inc.

Anchor Books edition: 1962

To
PROFESSOR JACK FINEGAN
*and to my American students
in grateful remembrance*

Contents

Contents

FIGURES

List of Plates

Foreword

This book had its genesis in 1955. Of late years the extensive archaeological discoveries made in the Near East had acquired an importance that extended far beyond specialist circles, in my country as elsewhere. Historians, men of letters, philosophers, and people of education generally had all come to realize the need for more direct and up-to-date acquaintance with this cultural sphere, because of the contributions it could offer to their own culture. The organizers of the Scientific Programme of the Italian Radio sought to meet this need by asking me to give a course of lectures aiming at the presentation of a complete, although summary, account of the civilizations of the ancient Orient.

The planning of this course called for a great deal of thought. Needless to say, one could have confined it to a summary of the outstanding events of political and cultural history; but this would have taken more time than had been allotted to the series. Nor was there much point in such an approach, since a number of books on the subject already existed. Moreover, I have never been greatly interested in exposition as such, whereas I am strongly attracted by the tasks involved in assessing a cultural epoch as a whole. For this reason I chose a more difficult and more risky approach, one not previously tried: namely, of attempting a comparative study of the essential and characteristic features of the ancient Oriental civilizations.

How was such a project to be carried through? To begin with, it was necessary to define the spatial and temporal limits of the subject. Then its outstanding historical personages had to be identified, and the distinctive cultural genres and attitudes successively reviewed. Thus I would be dealing not with history, but with the historical outlines; not with religion, but with the religious structure; not with literature, but with the literary genres; not with art, but with the artistic types. Finally, it would be necessary to draw together the threads, to gather up the results of the investigation in a synthesis which alone could give them meaning and coherence.

The next problem was that of the material; in other words, the objective content of the history and the culture. Systematic exposition was out of the question, for the reasons already given. On the other hand one could not omit the material altogether, or take it for granted, for that would have involved continual references to source material, making the course extremely difficult to follow, and so frustrating its object. I adopted the principle of treating the material as typifying ideas, expounding it extensively within the framework of my general assessment as its justification, but not aiming to present it fully. For example, the Egyptian historical romance could be dealt with by way of a description of the Sinuhe tale, without analysing all the other material available. Thus the picture would acquire organic form without being in the least exhaustive.

Finally, I could not help thinking that all too often in our presentation of the ancient cultures the frame is more conspicuous than the picture. Since we are describing literary works, why not give actual quotations from them? We draw upon the judgements of other scholars, so why not quote their very words? And when lectures are published in book form, why not reproduce works of art? Such a method would convey some idea of the actual life of the cultures under discussion.

My lectures, as I gratefully recall, aroused a lively interest in my listeners; and this book owes its origin to that interest. But only its origin; for, as is only right for a printed work, the subject matter has been recast, and appropriate modifications and additions and annotations have been included. But I have left intact its essential character: namely, that of a panoramic survey of the ancient Oriental civilizations, or rather, of the ancient Orient as a whole: a survey which any member of the educated public can read, but which embodies a number of personal judgements which will, I hope, be of interest to specialists. I trust reviewers and readers will demand neither more nor less of this book. I neither wanted, nor was I able, to avoid schematic treatments or subjective interpretations. But have I accentuated the right essential features? Have I emphasized the right values? And are my judgements, is even the outline of what has not been outlined before, correct? I think these are the fundamental problems.

Because of its basic unity, such a study as this could not but be the work of a single author; but the wide scope and variety of the source material called for the special competence of a large number of scholars. I tried to solve this problem along the following lines: first I made a draft of the work; then I submitted those sections which were more remote from my own special subject to various specialists for revision; then, making use of their suggestions and criticisms, I proceeded to the final editing. For their generous assistance I am sincerely grateful to the Rev. Prof. E. Bergmann, for the Sumerian section; the late Rev. Prof. R. Follet, for the Babylonian and Assyrian section; Prof. S. Donadoni and the Rev. Prof. A. Massart, for the Egyptian section; Prof. J. Friedrich, for the Hittite and Hurrian section; and the Rev. Prof. G. Patti, for the Persian section. Many valuable suggestions in regard to the work as a whole were made by Prof. G. Levi Della Vida; and I owe particular thanks to Dr. R. D. Barnett, who has carefully read through this English translation from my Italian original.

My thanks are also due to the scholars and institutions who have assisted me to collect the illustrations and have given me permission to reproduce them: to Dr. R. D. Barnett and the British Museum; the Rev. Prof. H. Cazelles, and the Musée du Louvre; Prof. K. C. Seele, and the Chicago Oriental Institute; Miss F. E. Day, Dr. C. K. Wilkinson, and the Metropolitan Museum of New York; Dr. F. Rainey, and the University of Pennsylvania Museum; and all the other scholars and institutions mentioned in the list of sources given in the Italian original of this book.

One final word of dedication. In token of my profound gratitude, this book is offered to Prof. Jack Finegan of the Pacific School of Religion, who invited me to give a course there as visiting professor in 1956, and to all the students who took part in the course. To the warmth of their enthusiasm and friendship I owe one of the happiest memories of my scientific career. They are many — too many to be mentioned by name; but I wish each one to accept this dedication, and this expression of my grateful remembrance, as addressed to him.

SABATINO MOSCATI

University of Rome.
January 1958.

THE FACE OF THE ANCIENT ORIENT

PART I

The Conditions

THE ORIENTAL RENAISSANCE

I *The Orient in a New Light*

For some years now a profound transformation has been going on in our knowledge of the ancient Near East; a transformation for which the history of European culture suggests the apt name: the Oriental Renaissance.

The transformation has been based fundamentally on archaeological data, but from archaeology it has naturally extended to literature, to religion, to art, and to the entire cultural sphere. It had its beginning in April 1928, when a Syrian peasant, ploughing in his field, ran his share into the remains of an ancient tomb, and so discovered Ugarit.[1] True, the earlier years of the present century had seen other important discoveries; but that of Ugarit, and those which followed, have a significance reaching beyond their own local limits, and have transformed a whole historical and cultural area. These finds are equalled only by those which in the second half of the nineteenth century first revealed the previously almost unknown peoples of the ancient Orient.

In the Oriental Renaissance we may distinguish three archaeological key discoveries: Ugarit, Mari, and the Dead Sea Scrolls. In all three cases the discovery was made by chance: at Ugarit, a peasant was ploughing; at Mari, some natives were burying a dead man;[2] near the Dead Sea, a Beduin was looking for a stray sheep.[3] In all three cases, the additions to our knowledge were revolutionary in their effect. Ugarit proved to be the site of an ancient city which had flourished for four

thousand years, and had been the centre of fertile cultural
exchange between the Near East and the Mediterranean islands; hundreds of texts, new in language and in script, revealed the beliefs and mythology of the peoples who preceded
the Hebrews in Palestine and Syria.[4] Mari disclosed another
city of like antiquity, the centre of a state which in its heyday
had held sway over a great part of northern Mesopotamia. Its
diplomatic archives, containing over 20,000 documents — still
in course of publication — are leading to a rewriting of the
history of Western Asia in the first half of the second millennium B.C.,[5] and they have revolutionized our chronology by
advancing our dates for ancient Western Asia by about two
centuries.[6] The Dead Sea Scrolls are older by several centuries
than the earliest Hebrew manuscripts hitherto known; their
Biblical texts are especially valuable to scholars in the field of
textual criticism, while the non-Biblical texts throw a new,
vivid light upon the beliefs and the ritual of the Hebrew
world on the eve of the Christian era.[7]

In addition to these, there have been many other significant
discoveries. For example, in the field of pre-history the American excavations in the Kirkuk region[8] furnish material covering the Mesopotamian palaeolithic and mesolithic periods,
and have yielded new information on the neolithic and chalcolithic periods. In the historical field, the documents found
at Alalakh[9] and a further collection from Ugarit[10] enable us
to verify and fill out from local sources our knowledge of the
policies pursued by the great empires in Syria after the middle
of the second millennium. In the field of law, ancient codes
have now been discovered[11] which lay bare the foundations
of the work of the great king Hammurabi, and indicate the
tradition to which he and the other oriental legislators belong.
Finally, in the sphere of art, the excavations at Nimrud,[12] together with those at Ugarit and Mari, are bringing to light
works so remarkable and significant as to call for revision of
the accepted opinions on much of Near Eastern art.

Obviously, all this new information affects certain regions
more directly than others, and the same applies to the various
periods. However, paradoxically yet understandably, this fact
rather increases than diminishes the changes in our knowl-

edge. For it is not sufficient to consider only the areas and the periods immediately affected by the recent discoveries; when we have done this we still have to determine the relationships between the new and the old. And this process necessitates new judgements on much that was regarded as well established. For example, the chronology of ancient Anatolia has had to be revised not so much because of finds in that region but rather in order to harmonize it with data from Mesopotamia; while many modifications in our knowledge of ancient Egypt arise from the fact that Asiatic parallels have now taken on a new aspect.

Our comparison with the Classical Renaissance is based, of course, not on the kind or the manner of the discoveries themselves, but on the nature and the intensity of the transformation which they achieve. Taking the comparison further, we might suggest that the present phase in our knowledge of the ancient Orient is still that of an incipient Renaissance, a Humanism in which scholarly activity is almost entirely absorbed in the discoveries, their publication, and their analysis. To fit the individual results into the general picture, and to reorganize our knowledge accordingly, remain tasks for the future. When these tasks are accomplished — but it is impossible to foretell when that will be — we shall see the consummation of the Oriental Renaissance. Its main significance will certainly lie in the reconstruction of the foundations of classical civilization, which hitherto have been only partially and imperfectly determined. When Greece and Rome have been assigned their proper place in the historical process, when the premises and conditions of that process have been defined, we shall see how extensive, varied, and at times decisive was the influence which the ancient Orient which preceded them exercised on those civilizations.

II *The Area*

An attempt to outline the main features of the ancient Oriental civilizations is without precedent, so we must briefly consider its conditions and prerequisites: the area and the time, the personages, and the pre-history. All these may possibly be the subject of controversy, and the solution of that controversy might play a decisive part in our investigations, or the questions involved may have been raised anew by the latest discoveries, and so may provide new bases for our investigations.

First, then, the question of the area. The 'Ancient Orient' has come, by a widely accepted scholarly convention, to mean the ancient Near East. This is justified by the indubitable general unity of the different components of that region. Its history begins at a very remote period in time, with documents that mark the dawn of history itself in the Mediterranean basin, and then continues uninterruptedly within an area enveloped, for much of the time, in the obscurity of peoples lacking written documents, and therefore lacking history. The Eastern Mediterranean basin constitutes the common centre of attraction or gravity for its peoples, who all, sooner or later, turn towards that basin and find on its coasts places of meeting and intercourse. For this reason we can use another apt term: the 'Mediterranean East'; this separates it from the cultures of India, and even more of China, which have different centres of gravity and developed in substantial independence. Nor is it simply a matter of separation — the Near East, with its trends towards the Mediterranean, played an important part in the task of laying the foundations of classical civilization, to which India and China made a much more limited contribution.

Passing from West to East, the ancient Oriental world includes Egypt, Palestine, Syria, Arabia, Anatolia, Mesopotamia, and Iran. Viewing this area as a whole, we may take as its nucleus the Arabian desert with its wastes of sand. Around it the 'Fertile Crescent' extends in a great arc, consisting of the Mesopotamian and Egyptian river valleys, with the Syro-Palestinian region which links them together. This crescent is the most fertile expanse in all the Near East. Beyond it to the North and the East curve the table-lands of Anatolia and Iran, agriculturally poorer, but possessing notable natural resources, from timber to stone and metals.

However, this demarcation of the extent of the ancient

Orient involves us in certain difficulties. In the first place, ought we to include the Iranian civilizations in the scope of our argument? Opinions on this point are divided; but we incline to think we should, precisely because of the criteria of interdependence and gravitation towards the Mediterranean which we have just specified.

It is harder to decide the question of the more outlying cultures of Crete and the Indus. Although many historians are of the contrary opinion,[13] we consider it best not to include these cultures within our survey. The ancient civilizations of the Indus lie outside the main Mediterranean area, and cannot be co-ordinated with the organic development of the region. And although the Cretan and Mycenean civilization undoubtedly had a great influence upon and was greatly influenced by our area, it had its roots in a soil which was, and constantly remained, geographically and ethnically distinct.

Finally, the ancient Southern Arabian civilization constitutes a case apart. From the viewpoint of area and time it is hard to exclude it from the general picture of the ancient Near East; but the desert encompasses it with a protective girdle, which cuts it off both from continuity with the other regions, and from gravitating together with them towards the Mediterranean. This gulf was bridged only by Islam; hence, if it be permissible to judge by the historical rather than the geographical factor, it will be as well to ignore the Southern Arabian civilization, which more properly belongs to Arabian history or Islamic pre-history. But we must add that this decision may have to be modified in the light of further knowledge, and that if the sporadic information now available concerning relations between Southern Arabian colonies in the north and other Near Eastern states increases in extent and importance we may find a decidedly different picture emerging.

Within the limits thus defined, we may resort to subdivision for various quite intelligible considerations, but not for any positive, historical reason. This applies especially to Egypt, which, because it is a specialized subject, is mainly treated independently of Western Asia,[14] even though Western Asia lacks any intrinsic historical unity which might be counter-

posed to that of Egypt. For either we must deal with the
history of the various separate regions and of the peoples who
dwelt within them, namely, the Egyptians, the Sumerians, the
Babylonians and the Assyrians, the Hebrews, and so on, or we
must visualize a wider historical entity. If we do so, that entity can only comprise the entire Near East, including Egypt.
It is the broad outline of this entity, as a clearly defined,
composite whole, despite the variety of its component parts,
which is the true subject of our historical research.

III   *The Time*

With the problem of area is associated the no less controversial problem of time. The history of the ancient Orient begins
with the first documents shortly before 3000 B.C. But how far
are we justified in extending it?

On this point, three views are expressed; or rather, since
they are not explicitly discussed, three views are followed in
practice: the later limit may be set at 538 B.C., or soon after,
when Babylon fell and the Achaemenid empire under Darius
began its contact with the Greeks;[15] or at 330 B.C., the date
of Alexander's decisive victory over the Persians;[16] or at the
time of Christ, in which case ancient Oriental history is regarded as the prologue to that of the Christian era.[17]

Of these three views, we consider that the first and last
do not withstand scrutiny. On the one hand, why wholly or
partly exclude the Achaemenid empire, which has an incon-
testable claim to belong to ancient Oriental history? On the
other, why include the history of the Hellenistic states, which,
though established in the East by conquest, were western in
their origins and their government?

Therefore the only satisfactory later limit would seem to be
the victory of Alexander the Great. Down to that date we
have an Orient under the government of Oriental empires;
after it, an East subject to Western domination. Moreover,
this transition from independence to subjection is amply reflected in the more varied forms of culture, and so we shall
take its beginning as our limit in time.

IV *The Personages*

Within the bounds of area and time which we have posited we find a complex of peoples differing in origin and in constituent elements; the intercourse and combinations of these peoples in varying organic groups determine the course of Oriental history. Looking at that history as a whole, we can distinguish no permanently predominant people or group, but each in turn assumes the principal rôle, and leaves its mark upon one phase — its own phase — of history, but not upon the whole of it. Hence ancient Oriental history is complex, and its unity is one of synthesis. This synthesis finds its complete realization and expression in the universal rule achieved by the Persian empire on the eve of its fall.

We may roughly classify the various peoples according to the different geographical zones of the Near Eastern area; these involve differing conditions of existence, and therefore differing impulses and laws governing the movements of the peoples.

The nucleus of the area, the Arabian desert, is the homeland of the Semites,[18] pastoral nomads, whom the aridity of their home forces out again and again towards the fertile surrounding regions. The concept of the Semites as a unitary and individual group of peoples is founded not upon dubious racial characteristics, but upon historical community of origin, and, above all, on the close linguistic affinity which subsists within the group.

In the regions which stretch in an arc about them — the 'Fertile Crescent' — from the beginnings of history or even before, the desert Semites come into contact with various peoples, and commingle with them, forming different ethnical complexes in different areas. To the West, in the Nile valley, Semitic and Hamitic elements come together to compose the Egyptian people, and this commingling is reflected in the Egyptian language. From the ethnic viewpoint the concept of Hamites has less consistency than that of Semites; linguistically, too, it lacks the unity of the Semitic tongues.[19] Nor is it easy to fix the time or the manner of the fusion in Egypt, because of the Hamito-Semitic linguistic relationship which is being increasingly recognized.

At the other end of the crescent, in the Mesopotamian valley, the Semites meet with the Sumerians. This people's origin is uncertain, and their language, agglutinative in type, reveals no genetic affinity with any other known to us. Uncertainty exists even with regard to their ethnic types, since the results of anthropological research are at variance with those drawn from art.[20] It is difficult to say how far ethnic fusion took place between the Semites and the Sumerians. The two languages continued to be used side by side, but neither was exclusive to its own proper people. It is commonly asserted that the history of Mesopotamia is the product of an opposition between the two peoples; but this judgement does not agree with the known facts;[21] it seems more likely that they peacefully coexisted, co-operating in deciding policy, and in economic and social life.

In the Syro-Palestinian coastal strip, which joins the two river valleys, from pre-historic times the Semites found peoples of whom we can make only one statement: their place-names indicate that they were not Semitic. In this area the Semites gained the predominance; in the various phases of penetration successive Semitic groups took control, but always Semites dominated the history of the region and its literary documents. However, owing to the peculiar nature of the area as a place of meeting and interchange, it reflected the successive great political changes of the environment, and so increasingly complicated the already complex ethnic situation.

Beyond the 'Fertile Crescent', on the table-lands of Anatolia and Iran, we again find nomad peoples, not pastoral like the nomads of the desert, but hunters and horse-breeders. They are of different stock, but are linked together by one important fact: their large-scale intervention in Near Eastern history is bound up with the migration of Indo-European peoples, who constitute at least a part of their ruling classes. Thus here, too, an element of unity — once more recognizable and definable in essentially linguistic terms — exercises a levelling influence upon a mass of peoples, and justifies their inclusion within a general concept despite the variety of their component elements.

V *The Prologue*

A discussion of Near Eastern pre-history[22] in an outline confined to history is to the point only if, firstly, it is no more than a preliminary sketch; and, secondly, if attention is concentrated not so much on the details as on the main lines of development of civilization, and the form which it assumed in the area under consideration. In that case there is no break in continuity between history and pre-history, and without prehistory history would be neither intelligible nor significant.

The Near Eastern geographical area must have been considerably more fertile in the Glacial Age than it is now. The pressure of cold air over Europe drove the Atlantic storms southward to pass over northern Africa and western Asia. This explains why tools and rock carvings have been found in places where life is impossible today. The most ancient human skeleton in the Near East is still the one which Miss Garrod found some time ago in a cave on Mount Carmel.[23] But more numerous and more ancient palaeolithic sites have recently been discovered, from Shanidar to Palegawra, in Mesopotamia. The Braidwood expedition in particular has found a number of centres in which cave dwellers lived on the spoils of their hunting;[24] human bones deliberately split to extract the marrow suggest that cannibalism was practised.

In the Mesolithic period, roughly between 10,000 and 6000 B.C., the climatic conditions of the Near East were transformed. The course of the rains was changed, and the fertile prairies became steppe land and desert. The population now concentrates along the valleys of the great rivers, where they can still find water, and so life can survive. Miss Garrod discovered traces of this cultural phase in the caves of a small torrent called Wadi Natuf,[25] to the north-west of Jerusalem; hence the term 'Natufian' applied to the men of that age. The Natufian civilization brings two principal innovations: the harvesting of wheat and barley, and the beginnings of the

domestication of animals.[26] The main significance of these innovations is that they mark the start of a transition to a settled
form of life; in the Near East the next advance, in which food
is not merely harvested but is cultivated, must have taken
place during the Natufian period or shortly after.

The Neolithic Age, for which the usual approximate dating
is from 6000 to 4000 B.C., reveals still further development.
Villages appear, and even cities; tangible evidence is found of
both religion and art.[27] The picture of this period is constantly
changing as discoveries progress: so far the most ancient village found seems to be Jarmo[28] in Mesopotamia; and the most
ancient city, Jericho,[29] in Palestine. Both date back to about
5000 B.C., a date well established by the application of the
modern radio-carbon test.[30] The village of Jarmo had houses
with rooms, and they were built of compressed mud; their
floors likewise were of packed mud over a reed foundation;
there were ovens and stoves, and cisterns excavated in the
ground. Animal bones found here show that domestic animals
were in the majority. The existence of religious and artistic
activity is indicated by crude clay statuettes, the principal
subject being a seated woman with marked signs of preg-
nancy: she is the mother-goddess, symbolizing the fertility of
the earth, and her worship will spread progressively over the
whole of the Near East. In Jericho the houses were built of
hand-formed bricks, and the walls were covered with a thick
coat of plaster; the doorways are broad, and the rooms rec-
tangular and quite large. But the most interesting feature is
the massive city wall, built of great blocks of stone, which
constitute Jericho the most ancient city not simply of the
Near East but, so far as we know at present, of the whole
world. Several plaster models of heads, with particularly
delicate and vivacious human features, witness to the remarkable development which art had attained; and a little sanctuary, with apse and altar and a small pillar, indicates the
existence of an organized religious cult.

Towards the end of the Neolithic era pottery begins to appear, providing us with a fundamental means of fixing chronology. At present the most ancient specimens have been found
at Jarmo and the recently explored sites of Tell Hassuna[31] and

Matarra,[32] also in Mesopotamia. The technique is primitive: the vessels are hand moulded and fired on an open hearth; their decoration includes geometrical designs scored or painted, or both.

The potter's art continues to develop during the Chalcolithic period, which lasts approximately from 4000 to 3000 B.C., and is distinguished into phases according to types of pottery, their diffusion, and influence.[33] Speaking generally, we now observe a further concentration of culture in the river valleys, in Egypt and in Mesopotamia; and the various types of pottery to be found in them are often scattered through the surrounding regions, so testifying to the cultural and political irradiation of the peoples of these valleys. Pottery technique is progressively perfected: the closed furnace comes into use to maintain the requisite temperature and to avoid smoke, and hand-moulded ware is supplanted by pottery turned on the wheel, with its greater regularity and precision. The decoration also evolves. Simple geometrical designs are succeeded by drawings of men and animals, which thus provide a new and invaluable source of information concerning their creators' living conditions. For instance, the pottery found at Samarra in Mesopotamia, with its designs of birds, wild goats, and stags, reflects a society in which hunting is still predominant.[34]

The evolution so far traced follows different lines in the two great centres, Egypt and Mesopotamia. But at a certain moment, on the eve of the historical era to be precise, there are signs of a number of interchanges which, though their importance should not be overrated, do indicate an historical relationship presaging consequences of the utmost significance.[35] In these interchanges Mesopotamia exerts a variety of influence on Egypt: cylinder seals of Mesopotamian origin appear there, and soon new features develop; a number of artistic themes — such as figures of composite animals, or animals intertwined, or symmetrically arranged in pairs, or scenes of heroes overcoming lions, or ships with the characteristic curved extremities — find their way from the Valley of the Two Rivers to that of the Nile; and even the Egyptian script, in its origin and development if not in its final forms, is seen to have been influenced by that developed earlier in

Mesopotamia. Moreover, a trend of influence in the opposite direction, from Egypt to Mesopotamia, has recently been noticed: Gilbert has found Mesopotamian seals bearing reliefs of houses with double doors, decorated above the lintel with intertwined flower motifs which seem drawn from Egyptian themes and symbols;[36] and for the moment we pass over the complex problem of the relationship between the pyramids and the Mesopotamian temple-towers. On the whole, however, the impression is left that, at the decisive moment of the transition to the historical era, within the substantially independent development of the two cultures, Mesopotamia played the preponderant rôle.

In the Near East history does not emerge all at once. For several centuries written documents exist, but they are not yet sufficiently numerous, or extensive, or clear to enable us to make a coherent reconstruction of the course of history. After its initial phase the development of writing is more or less parallel in the two valleys: from drawings, pictography, to conventionalized figures, ideography; from word values, ideograms, to phonetic values, in the form of a syllabary, although ideograms remain in use. In Egypt a further advance occurs by the principle of acrophony, that is, the pronunciation of only the first element of the syllable, so that alphabetic values are reached. But this principle is not generalized, and the syllabic or ideographic values persist side by side with the alphabetic.[37] The next great step forward will be the invention of a systematic alphabet; but at least a millennium has yet to pass before this comes about.

Thus, at the dawn of history, the ancient Orient already has a long life of experience behind it, indeed, the greater part of its life: from cavern to village and city, from hunting to pastoral and agricultural existence, its social, political, religious, and artistic activities have undergone a vast process of evolution. At this point history takes over the narrative and carries it on to its conclusion.

PART II

The Components

THE SUMERIANS

I *Mesopotamian Civilization*

It could be said, paradoxically, that our knowledge of Sumerian civilization[1] has come about by chance. The archaeologists who began to explore Mesopotamia about a century ago had an entirely different object in mind, namely, to discover the remains of the Babylonians and Assyrians, of whom much was known already through the Bible and classical authors. In Babylonia, however, what came to light was the existence of not one but two peoples, not one but two civilizations. They did indeed find the Babylonians; but they also found the monuments and documents of a people hitherto unknown, a people who had preceded the Babylonians and Assyrians, and who had created the most ancient of the historical cultures known, that of the Sumerians.

The two cultures were found in close association; but the difference of language furnished a clear criterion, and although there was no rejection of the close relationship, the distinction was extended to the field of culture, so that experts spoke, and still usually speak, not only of two peoples but of two cultures. Is this entirely justifiable? Examination of the historical documents, especially those dating from the earliest period, reveals that the two languages were not always and everywhere used strictly in accordance with the ethnic membership: there were Sumerians who wrote in the Semitic tongue, and *vice versa*. The distinction in the use of the two languages can more accurately be regarded as dependent upon locality, period, and subject matter: in general Sumerian was the older language and the language of learning, and it persisted in religious and literary texts even after the eclipse of the corresponding ethnic element, only gradually giving way to the spoken language that finally prevailed: Babylonian and Assyrian.

Hence the distinction between the two cultures is justified only in part. Despite the difference in their origin and their initial phases, they are closely connected. Thus the civilization which one finds is not so much either Sumerian or Babylonian and Assyrian: it is first and foremost Mesopotamian.

II   *The Historical Outlines*

First, then, to determine the bounds of area and time.[2] The Sumerian civilization first appears in history during the third millennium B.C. However, this is not the true starting point, for it is simply the beginning of the historical period; everything points to the conclusion that, if the documents were forthcoming, we should be able to trace this people much farther back.[3]

However that may be, at the dawn of history the Sumerians are already established in the land which saw the development of their civilization. They are already organized in small urban communities; the situation resembles that of the Greek city states, and the later Italian communes.

It would appear that at first the city communities were governed by assemblies presided over by groups of elders. An American scholar, Jacobsen, has called this system 'primitive democracy', and says of it:

> Our material seems to preserve indications that prehistoric Mesopotamia was organized politically along democratic lines, not, as was historic Mesopotamia, along autocratic. The indications which we have, point to a form of government in which the normal run of public affairs was handled by a council of elders but ultimate sovereignty resided in a general assembly comprising all

members — or, perhaps better, all adult free men — of the community. This assembly settled conflicts arising in the community, decided on such major issues as war and peace, and could, if need arose, especially in a situation of war, grant supreme authority, kingship, to one of its members for a limited period.[4]

Possibly this account overestimates the power of the assembly, which frequently acted only in a consultative capacity to the ruler of the city state; but undoubtedly it did impose certain limitations on the ruler's authority.

The institution of the assembly did not last long. The need for speedy and unchallengeable decision in times of emergency leads by a natural process to the concentration of power in the hands of a leader. The Sumerians call him *lugal*, 'great man', or more simply *ensi*, 'governor'.[5]

The important point to be noted is that this leader is regarded as only the earthly representative of the true sovereign, namely, the tutelary god of the city. From the very beginning Sumerian government is theocratic in character. The city belongs to one god, even though other gods may also be worshipped in it; and this one god is an absolute lord, who expresses his incontrovertible will by means of portents and presages. The earthly king's task consists in interpreting the will of the heavenly king, and keeping him content and well disposed, so that he may not cease to protect his faithful citizens. Hence the human honours the divine ruler by erecting temples, and gratifies him by bringing prosperity to the people by the excavation of canals to control the waters of the great rivers, to prevent floods, and to irrigate the sandy soil. The ideal which the Sumerians set themselves is one of peace ordered by faith and labour; and they remain constant to this ideal through all the vicissitudes of their long history.

We may ignore the lists of the ancient kings, with their fabulously long reigns, which are intended to associate the reigns of humans with those of gods and heroes; the Sumerian king list has no historical value, even though it may include the names of historical personages.[6]

The oldest surviving Sumerian inscriptions date from the reign of Mesilim of Kish, who lived about 2600 B.C.; he has left us a few lines reporting the construction of a temple for the god Ningirsu.[7] We have more knowledge of the city community of Lagash, which has left many documents.[8] Here the founder of a dynasty, Ur-Nanshe, also built a temple to Ningirsu, so evidently the erection of temples is not a casual labour, but appears to have been regarded as the first duty of a Sumerian sovereign. To build temples and dig canals: these were the works of peace which were the kingly ideal from the beginning.

It is useful to consider the character of the oldest royal inscriptions we possess. In no way can they be regarded as contributions to history in the modern sense of the word, as narratives of events interpreted in terms of causes, characteristic features, and consequences. They are simply chronicles recording important religious or political incidents, chronicles relating to the various cities and composed and developed in the temples, as part of the service to the gods. They are simply strings of facts, and, apart from the religious terms in which they are expressed, there is no attempt at interpretation. The processes of generalization, definition, and judgement would appear to be alien to Sumerian thought; this view finds confirmation in the religious literature by the beliefs which are attested, but are never theoretically formulated; in the literature of law by the case law, which is not based on any general legal principles; and in the literature of natural science by the long lists of plants and animals of various kinds, quite unclassified.[9] Nor do the Sumerians appear to have had any clear conception of the historical process; on the contrary, for them everything that happens is predetermined by divine decree. This aspect of the Sumerian mentality has been brought out very well by Kramer:

> Bound by his particular world-view, the Sumerian thinker saw historical events as coming ready-made and 'full-grown, full-blown' on the world scene, and not as the slow product of man's interaction with his environment. He believed, for example, that his own country

Sumer, which he knew as a land of thriving cities and towns, villages and farms, in which flourished a well developed assortment of political, religious and economic institutions and techniques, had always been more or less the same from the very beginning of days — that is, from the moment the gods had planned and decreed it to be so, following the creation of the universe. That Sumer had once been desolate marshland with but few scattered settlements, and had only gradually come to be what it was after many generations of struggle and toil, marked by human will and determination, man-laid plans and experiment and diverse fortunate discoveries and inventions — such thoughts probably never occurred to the most learned of the Sumerian sages.[10]

In these city communities the course of Sumerian existence was by no means free from strife. There were internal dissensions, between sovereigns and priests for example; and there were external conflicts, between one city and another. Once more Lagash furnishes us with the earliest instance of internal strife. The bureaucratic administration gets the upper hand and begins to exploit the people; the citizen is burdened with taxes, and even death involves payment of duties. Then a king, Urukagina, arises, to restore order and justice. In an inscription he has left us his account of the reforms he made:

> When Ningirsu, the hero of Enlil, had given to Urukagina the kingship of Lagash, and had made his power dwell in the hearts of thirty-six thousand men, he made a decree from that time. He spoke the word his king Ningirsu had spoken. From the boat he released the boatmen, from the ass and the sheep their shepherd. . . . In the irrigated land of Ningirsu, out to the sea, the overseer was no more. . . . When the house of a great man stands near a house of the king's estate, and that great man says 'I wish to sell it', if the king buys he shall pay money to his heart's satisfaction. . . . (The king) will protect the mother that is in distress, the mighty man shall not oppress the naked and the widow: this decree has Urukagina made with the aid of Ningirsu.[11]

Dating as it does from such a remote past, this edict has an undeniably impressive moral tone. We shall meet with that same quality again in later times, in the utterances not only of Mesopotamian rulers but of others, and the 'protection of the widow and the orphan' will become a formula expressing the determination to ensure impartial justice.[12]

But storms gather around this royal law giver. Another inscription relates that the sovereign of the nearby city of Umma attacked him, shed blood in the temples, overthrew the sanctuaries and the statues of the gods, and carried off silver and precious stones. In his indignation Urukagina appeals to the gods:

> The men of Umma, after destroying Lagash, committed mortal sin against Ningirsu. The power which has come to them shall be cut off. Mortal sin on the part of Urukagina, king of Girsu, there was none. But Lugalzaggisi, prince of Umma, may his goddess Nisaba bear his mortal sin on her head.[13]

As so often in history, there are two sides to this story. If we are to believe the other source, no sin was committed at all. The invader, Lugalzaggisi, has left inscriptions which affirm that the god Enlil, who is supreme over all other gods, supported him in his enterprise:

> When Enlil, king of countries, had presented to Lugalzaggisi the kingship of the country, when he had established full justice before the land, when his might had overthrown the countries, from the sunrise to sunset, he imposed tribute upon them. At that time, from the lower sea, the Tigris and the Euphrates to the upper sea Enlil took for him as a possession. The lands reposed in safety, the country was irrigated with the water of joy. . . . May (the god Anu) advance my life as life, cause the country to repose in quietness, may he increase the people abundantly like the grass. . . . May he be for ever the shepherd who lifts up the head of the ox.[14]

We find a new and significant quality in these words. Whether he was a bloodthirsty ravager or a peaceful builder of temples — or possibly both — this new sovereign has a different political outlook from his predecessors. He has enlarged his horizon, and he looks far beyond the walls of his city: from the southern to the northern sea, in other words, from the Persian Gulf to the Mediterranean, from the lands of the East to those of the West, he aspires to dominion over the whole of the known world. Thus the idea of universal monarchy makes its first appearance in Mesopotamia, and there is another gigantic stride forward in the evolution of society. The date is about 2350 B.C.

Now a new element appears in the story. Foreign dominion is established over the area. First the Semites, who have been steadily infiltrating from the neighbouring Arabian desert, set up a kingdom over all the world known to them (about 2350–2150 B.C.); then the Gutians, savage peoples from the East, spread destruction far and wide, and earn themselves the name of 'mountain dragons' (about 2150–2050 B.C.). It takes several centuries for the Sumerian cities to recover, and their evolution towards unity is checked. Then, little by little, they pick up again. Lagash once more becomes the focus of our interest. About 2050 B.C. Gudea, the greatest sovereign the Sumerians ever had, reigned in Lagash; his calm, pensive figure has survived in a number of statues, and his works are attested by many inscriptions. In the true Sumerian tradition this king's activity is concentrated upon the works of peace and the building of temples.

He himself has told how the god Ningirsu called him to his labours. There is a drought in the land, rain does not fall, and the rivers do not flood to fertilize the fields. In his anxiety the king turns to the god for counsel. Ningirsu bids him build a sanctuary. Then plenty will return to the earth:

When Gudea the faithful shepherd puts his right hand to Eninnu my royal house, it will cry to heaven for wind and water; then will there come to thee from heaven abundance, the abundance shall triple the land. When the foundation of my house is laid, abundance shall come. Enlarged fields shall bear for thee. . . . In Sumer oil shall be produced in abundance, wool shall be weighed in abundance. . . . When thou shalt set thy right hand to my temple, I will set my foot upon the mountain where the storm dwells; from the dwelling of the storm from a very high peak, from the holy place, abundant rain shall pour for thee, it will give the heart's life to the land.[15]

Gudea has left inscriptions giving a detailed account of the great enterprise: timber, marble, bronze and gold are brought in from the surrounding areas for the building of the temple. These accounts give us a picture of not only the royal builder but an entire people toiling in the service of their god.

However, this labour bears no resemblance to the forced labour which, rightly or wrongly, classical authors tell us was used for the building of the Egyptian pyramids. In full accord with the traditions of his people Gudea is a peaceful and benevolent monarch, under whom 'the lash struck not, and none was oppressed with blows'. There is no mention of tears, or contentions; no tax gatherer enters the citizens' homes; 'to Ningirsu, their king, they have joyfully offered their labour as a gift'.[16]

After the death of Gudea, Lagash yields its predominance in the land of the Sumerians to another city: Ur. The third dynasty of this city assumes the title: 'king of the four quarters of the earth', and thus renews the aspiration to rulership over all the known world which we have already noted in Mesopotamia. But the kings of Ur bear another title which is worth noting: they are 'king of Sumer and Akkad'. Henceforth this is their normal appellation, and it expresses the fusion of the two elements, Sumerian and Semitic, in Mesopotamian civilization. There are many other characteristic indications of this fusion, such as the names of sovereigns, partly Sumerian and partly Semitic; their divine appellatives, testifying to an approach towards that apotheosis of the monarch which had been a feature of the Semitic interlude; the retreat of the religious power before the political one, part of the trend towards the bureaucratic state for which the Semites had also furnished the model.

Not long ago a code of laws was discovered and published which dates from the sovereign who founded the third dynasty of Ur, Ur-Nammu. It is the oldest code known at present. It, too, expresses the tone of social morality which we find so impressive even four thousand years later. The king declares he has got rid of the dishonest officials, or, to use his own expression, the profiteers on the citizens' oxen and sheep and asses; he has established just and unchangeable weights and measures; he has taken care that the orphan and the widow shall not fall victim to the mighty, and that the man who possesses only one small coin shall not be victimized by him who possesses a coin of greater value.[17]

For about a hundred years, towards the end of the third millennium B.C., the city of Ur is the centre of a splendid civilization, with great monuments and copious literature,[18] which archaeologists have brought to light. But these years are in the nature of a swan-song: a fresh invasion from the Arabian desert ends the political power of the Sumerians for ever.

III *The Religious Structure*

The religion of the Sumerians[19] is a naturalistic polytheism, worship of the great natural forces of the universe, the forces which govern the fertility of the earth. Alongside and above the gods of the city there are cosmic gods; and frequently the functions of these two classes of deities overlap and blend.

But what is the conception of the universe at the base of this religious outlook? In view of what has been said concerning the Sumerian view of history, one can understand that the cosmos consists of a complex of laws instituted by the gods, an order which is identical with existence.[20] The gods speak, and their word becomes deed. To ensure the constancy of the established order separate gods are put in charge both of cosmic forces and of the earthly organisms, the cities. Where does man come in this cosmos? Men are the executors of the divine will, they are instruments created in order to enable the divine will to be effected. To what end? To put the divine decrees rigorously into force, to institute an order which shall ensure the fertile life of the earth.

The most important functions in the pantheon are exercised by the divine forces presiding over the major cosmic elements. Thus Anu, the highest of the gods, is the god of heaven, which spatially dominates the visible universe. The region between heaven and earth, the air, is presided over by Enlil, the lord of the wind and the storm; from his sanctuary in Nippur he exercises a kind of lordship over the various city gods. The earth is the domain of Enki. These three compose the cosmic trinity. As time passes Enki also comes to be known as Ea, 'house of water', since the earth is also the ever-lasting source of the life-giving waters of the canals, rivers, and sea. The comparatively late date at which the name Ea is introduced, becoming established only in the second phase of Sumerian civilization, suggests that the concept of the earth god underwent a change in which the 'Semitic interlude' possibly played a part; we get a slight glimpse of a possible evolution in a world which appears static and immutable in its elements.

The foregoing are the principal cosmic gods. A second trinity consists of the gods of the celestial bodies which by their light govern the course of earthly life: the moon (Nannar), the sun (Utu), and the morning star Venus (Inanna). Inanna also stands for Mother Earth, as the source of fertility, whose cult reaches far back into pre-history; indeed this aspect may be fundamental, while her astral aspect may be only a secondary attribute, Semitic in origin. In her function as Mother Earth Inanna is often associated in myth and lyric with the figure of a young god, Dumuzi, who dies and is reborn, a symbol of the death and rebirth which occurs in nature every year.[21]

How are the gods represented? Although they stand for natural forces and elements, in monuments and inscriptions they are given the likeness of men. They have human figures, are sexed and have families; they dress and feed like earthly creatures, though they wear far more precious garments and dine on much rarer food; finally, they have their loves and their hates, just as men have, only much more violent. Thus, in the last resort, the only features distinguishing them from men are their immortality and their divine powers. The macrocosm is modelled on the microcosm. In this respect the Homeric epics offer fairly accurate, and, be it noted, closer parallels than those to be found in some other parts of the ancient Orient.

The relations between the gods are after the manner of human parentage, and are early embodied in a theology. Thus, Anu is the progenitor of the gods; Ningirsu, the god of Lagash, is Enlil's son, and his wife is Baba, daughter of Anu; Nannar, the god of the moon, has Ningal for wife, and his son is the sun god, Utu. The list could be extended, but here we need only note the tendency to organize a system, for which the priesthood is probably responsible, and which provides a model for the much more thorough system that arises during the later Mesopotamian era.

Below the gods is the realm of the demons. There are good demons, who take temples, houses, and human beings under their protection; but for the most part the demons are wicked, restless spirits of the dead, living in tombs, in darkness, and in the desert, from which they sally forth to bring terror and torment upon the earth. The most fearsome of them all are the seven Udugs, who are insatiable in their greed and relentless in pursuit. They can be overcome only by incantations and the magical arts practised by the priesthood. These arts constitute a true learning, and many of their formulas have survived. Here is one:

> Wicked Udug, that wanderest impiously over the earth,
> Wicked Udug, that bearest disorder over all the earth,
> Wicked Udug, that hearest not supplication,
> Wicked Udug, that transfixest little ones like fish in the
>   water,
> Wicked Udug, that bringest down the great in heaps,
> Wicked Udug, that smitest the aged man and woman,

Wicked Udug, that crossest the broad streets,
Wicked Udug, that makest desert the great steppes,
Wicked Udug, that leapest thresholds,
Wicked Udug, that overthrowest the buildings of the
    lands,
Wicked Udug, that upsettest the earth . . .
I am the spell-casting priest, the high priest of Ea,
The lord has sent me . . .
Behind me thou art not to howl,
Behind me thou art not to shout,
By a wicked man thou art not to cause me to be taken,
By a wicked Udug thou art not to cause me to be
    seized.
By the heavens be thou exorcized! By the earth be thou
    exorcized![22]

To magic must be added divination, also practised by the priesthood. In such a troubled world, confronted by such mighty higher powers, man seeks to peer into the future, to interpret the gods' will and foresee their actions. This is his first step towards doing something to defend himself, by religious or by magical means.

The worship of the gods takes the form of a complex and highly developed system of ritual, celebrated in the temples by a correspondingly numerous priesthood. We learn from the inscriptions that there is a detailed division of functions among the priests, which indicates a remarkable degree of development; we have here not the incipient stages, but the maturity of an organization. The religious property is administered by civil rather than clerical officials — if such a distinction can be made in this case. More strictly liturgical functions are allotted to the anointers, cantors, wailers, sorcerers, magicians, and diviners. The female element is also well represented: there are temple prostitutes, singing women, wailing women, sorceresses, and divining women.

The religious cult is based on the sacred calendar. There are two classes of festivals: the fixed feasts, of which the principal are the New Year and the New Moon, and the movable. These latter vary either because separate days are dedicated to the gods of particular cities, or because they are associated with special occasions, such as the dedication of temples, the erection of statues, the accession of kings, or the celebration of victories.

The central feature of the festival is the sacrifice. This is attested by numerous surviving texts, though the essential purpose of the sacrifice is not clear: did only the smoke ascend to the gods, or was the entire offering burnt for their benefit? However, the information provided by the texts is extensive: we learn that sheep, goats, oxen, swine, birds, and fish were sacrificed, also grain, flour, bread, cakes, dates, figs, oil, honey, milk, wine, and beer, as well as garments and perfumes. The presentation of votive-offerings is a typical feature: these take the form of vases, jewels, and above all of statues and statuettes, which the faithful set up in the temples in order to commend themselves to the divine protection. The statuettes frequently represent the donors themselves, who by this recourse to what is intrinsically a magical ritual place themselves in the care of the gods.

The fundamental aim of the cult is the conservation of life — of earthly life, be it noted: the Sumerian prays for fertility and plenty; the naturalistic nature of the religion is clear.

Not that the Sumerians know nothing of a future life: the profusion of offerings set beside the dead in their tombs proves the contrary, and confirmation is found in the myths dealing with life beyond the tomb. Above all, we have the evidence of the cult of nature's continual rebirth, and it is difficult to think that man does not participate in this rebirth. In the royal tombs at Ur the dead sovereigns are accompanied by their retinues. Does this indicate death voluntarily accepted in the assurance of a life to come? There is much to suggest this.

However, the future life, as the Sumerians conceive it, is in strong contrast with that of Egyptians, for it is wretched and unsubstantial, with poor possibilities and overshadowed with gloom. One text makes this very clear:

I am no more a man to enjoy life.

> *The place of my resting is dust of the earth; I lie among*
>   *the wicked,*
> *My sleep is anguish; I dwell among foes.*
> *O my sister, from where I lie I can no more arise!*[23]

All the literature, and the hero epic in particular, expresses this same mood. It is strikingly different from the serene, cheerful tomb pictures which have survived from ancient Egypt.

The temple is more than the centre of religious life. In Sumerian society there is a characteristic symbiosis of activities, and so the temple is also the centre of economic and commercial activity. Jacobsen has written the following account of the origin and structure of this social system:

> Central in the city-state was the city, and central in the city was the temple of the city god. The temple of the city god was usually the greatest landowner in the state, and it cultivated its extensive holdings by means of serfs and sharecroppers. Other temples belonging to the city god's spouse, to their divine children, and to deities associated with the chief god similarly had large land holdings, so that it has been estimated that around the middle of the third millennium B.C. most of the lands of a Mesopotamian city-state were temple lands. The larger part of the inhabitants were accordingly earning their livelihood as sharecroppers, serfs, or servants of the gods.
>
> In this situation lie the economic and political realities expressed in the Mesopotamian myths which state that man was created to relieve the gods of toil, to work on the gods' estates. For the Mesopotamian city-state *was* an estate, or rather — like the medieval manor with which we have compared it — it had an estate as basis. That basic estate, the main temple with its lands, was owned and run by the city god, who himself gave all important orders.[24]

The guiding rule of the temple community is that the individual should labour in the service of the group. We find the citizens organized in corporations, headed by men assigned the task of apportioning and supervising the work to be done; they distribute food to the members of their groups as recompense. The various trades are clearly distinguished: there are shepherds, farmers, hunters, fishermen, lumbermen, carpenters, smiths; there are also merchants to look after foreign trade. In time of war, and when great public works have to be carried out, the citizens are mobilized; after doing their service they return to their everyday tasks.[25]

Such was the life of the Sumerians. The general impression it leaves is of the profound unity of all its forms, under the dominant force of religion. Every human activity, whether of peaceful works or warlike enterprise, was performed for the benefit of the gods; man's every step depended on the gods, not only those activities connected with the cult but those of economic and commercial life which we regard as quite remote from religion. This harmony within the faith, characteristic of the Sumerian conception of the universe, remains a potent and typical feature of all the civilizations which succeed them in the ancient Orient.

IV *The Literary Genres*

Beyond all doubt the discovery of the Sumerian literature[26] has been one of the most significant scientific achievements of recent years. Rather one should say its rediscovery, for most of the texts had been known for several decades; but their fragmentary state, the great difficulties of deciphering the script, and, it must be admitted, the imperfections of the copies which scholars had made of those scripts, had rendered it almost impossible to make sense of them. Today the situation is very different, thanks to the patient and persistent labours of a number of scholars, notably the American Kramer. Kramer spent years working over the material discovered fifty years ago at Nippur, which provides the most important nucleus of the surviving Sumerian writings. He re-examined the texts, recopied and compared them, and finally succeeded in scientifically establishing a number of fresh interpretations, which throw new light on the thought, the beliefs, and the manner of life of the Sumerian people.

The literature which has survived consists of tens of thousands of clay tablets, inscribed with cuneiform. This is an ideographic script of mainly syllabic character, incised in the clay with a stylus. The dissemination of Sumerian civilization extended the use of this script both among the other peoples of Mesopotamia and over a wide surrounding area, and so it became an outward sign of a well-defined cultural zone. There is great variation in the state of preservation of the tablets, and in their dimensions; the script also varies in size. Some tablets carry a dozen columns numbering hundreds of lines, while others have only a single column and a few lines. A single literary tablet rarely provides a complete text: the great poetical works in particular cover several tablets, and this fact accounts for one of the fundamental problems in reconstructing Sumerian literature, namely the order in which the various parts of a given text are to be read.

Sumerian literature has certain features which strike our modern minds as remarkable. It is as well to mention these features before turning to an analysis of the various literary genres, since they condition the nature and the contents of those genres. To begin with, the works are anonymous: we do not know the name of the author of any of the many great works which have come down to us. Nor can this be ascribed to chance: the copyists' names are so frequently and so carefully recorded that the authors' names would have been preserved too, if they had been considered of importance. Secondly, we cannot distinguish any historical development in style or subject matter such as we can observe in our own western literatures.[27] The objection that our knowledge is too limited to do so is not valid. The material which has survived leaves no doubt whatever that the Sumerian men of letters regarded the imitating of earlier models, and the copying and summarizing of ancient texts as one of the most highly esteemed of occupations, regularly practised, whereas they seem to have had no aspirations whatever towards originality or innovation.

These two characteristics are combined in and explained

by a conception of art which differed profoundly from ours. They sought not the subjective and original creation of the individual, but the objective and changeless expression of the collectivity. Hence the artist is strictly speaking a craftsman; he does not trouble to sign his works, any more than an artisan does in our own day, nor does he aim at free invention. On the contrary, his greatest aspiration is to copy every detail of the model before him. This being so, the artist's personality — and without doubt these artists had 'personalities' — eludes us, and the process of artistic evolution, which must have occurred in some form or other, however slight, is concealed beneath the accumulation of copies, of adaptations, of combinations of past models.

Yet even this collective and static art must have had its object, though the artists of the time had not the impulse to free aesthetic self-expression of our civilization. This object has to be sought in the realm of practical spirit, in the practical expression of the life of the community. And since, as we have already pointed out, the dominating and unifying feature of that life is religion, art, too, is religious in its essence. It is art despite itself, or at least, art without a positive intention as such: it is a practical and constant expression of the concept of divinity and man's relations with divinity.

Among the various literary genres, mythological poetry is predominant.[28] These poems tell of the adventures of the gods and their inter-relationships, and in doing so express Sumerian beliefs concerning the universe, its origin and destiny. They reveal the people's view of life, and reflect its conditions and customs.

A striking example of a myth dealing with the origin of things is the poem of Enki and Sumer, which tells how the god Enki brought order to the earth and organized its cultivation.[29] Enki makes his way to the banks of the Tigris and Euphrates, the two rivers which fertilize the sandy Mesopotamian valley, and pours the foaming waters into them. Then he stocks the waters with fish and lays down laws for the sea and the wind. He sets a special deity over each place and each element. Then he turns his attention to the cultivation of the earth: he creates cereals and other plants, and entrusts the plough and the yoke to the god 'of canals and ditches', and the hoe to the god of bricks. Then it is the turn of houses, stables, and sheepfolds: the god lays their foundations and builds upon them, while filling the valley with animals. This myth reflects the agricultural character of the ancient Sumerian civilization, and it is dominated by the specific conception of order as inseparably bound up with existence, so that 'create' and 'set in order' are synonymous.

From the beginnings of things, we turn to the life beyond the tomb. The most exhaustive expression of Sumerian beliefs on this subject is the myth of Inanna's descent into the underworld. This myth is of significance from more than one aspect; for it is a picturesque formulation of the vegetation cycle, a theme which dominates all the thought of the ancient Orient. Inanna, the goddess of Mother Earth, decides one day to visit her sister Ereshkigal, queen of the underworld. But she is afraid of treachery, and leaves instructions that if she does not return within three days her people are to come in search of her. The poem is in verse, and it must be pointed out that ancient Oriental verse is based not so much upon metre (although metre exists, and is more and more being identified) as upon what is known as the parallelism of members, in other words, the presentation of an idea in two or even three phrases, the second of which (and the third, where there are three) parallels the first by repeating the idea in different words, or by completing it, or by presenting an idea in contrast with it. Thus a specific form of harmony is achieved. So Inanna goes down to the underworld:

> When Inanna reached the palace, the mountain of lapis
>   lazuli,
> At the gate of the Underworld she acted in unfriendly
>   manner,
> In the palace of the Underworld she spoke in hostile wise:
> 'Open the house, gatekeeper, open the house,
> Open the house, O Neti, open the house; and I will enter
>   alone.'
> Neti, the chief gatekeeper of the Underworld,

Answers the pure Inanna:
'Who art thou?'
'I am Inanna, of the place where the sun rises.'
'If thou art Inanna of the place where the sun rises,
Why art thou come to the land of no return?
On the road whose traveller comes not back, how has thy
          heart led thee?'[30]

Inanna explains that she wishes to visit her sister Ereshkigal, and she is admitted. But as she passes through each of the seven gates of the underworld the gatekeepers deprive her of one of her jewels or garments:

At her entering
The crown was taken from her brow.
'What, pray, is this?'
'Be silent, Inanna, the ordinances of the Underworld are
          perfect,
Question not, O Inanna, the rites of the Underworld.'
At her entering the second gate
The sceptre of lapis lazuli was taken from her.
'What, pray, is this?'
'Be silent, Inanna, the ordinances of the Underworld are
          perfect,
Question not, O Inanna, the rites of the Underworld.'
At her entering the third gate
The little lapis lazuli beads were taken from her neck.
'What, pray, is this?'
'Be silent, Inanna, the ordinances of the Underworld are
          perfect,
Question not, O Inanna, the rites of the Underworld.'[31]

This happens at gate after gate, and the goddess enters naked and dejected into the presence of the terrible judges of the underworld. They regard her with their death-dealing eyes, and she falls lifeless to the ground. Three days pass, then Inanna's messenger appeals to the supreme gods to rescue her. After various unsuccessful attempts, he finally appeals to Enki:

Before Enki he weeps:
'O father Enki, let not thy daughter be put to death in the
    Underworld,
Let not thy good metal be covered with the dust of the
    Underworld,
Let not thy good lapis lazuli be broken up into
    stoneworker's stone,
Let not thy boxwood be cut up into woodworker's wood,
Let not the maiden Inanna be put to death in the
    Underworld.'[32]

The prayer is heard; Enki pours the 'food of life' and the 'water of life' over the dead goddess; she returns to life, and rises from the realms of death, accompanied by a horde of demons great and small, who threaten at every step to drag her back into the abyss.

There are numerous other myths of the gods, of varying significance,[33] but we must pass on to a literary genre which is frequently treated as distinct from the myth, but which has many essential links with it: namely the hero epic. This celebrates the great figures of the Sumerian golden age, who lived before the dawn of history; the connection with mythology arises from the fact that the gods are continually intervening in the hero's life, while, on the other hand, the heroes play their part in the god mythology. In this branch of literature the outstanding figure is Gilgamesh,[34] the Sumerian Hercules, who performs remarkable feats. The great problem raised in his story is that of death, the tragic fate that awaits all mankind, and from which not even Gilgamesh can escape, with all his strength. The figure of the hero is completely overshadowed by the mournfulness of his lot, and many of his feats are performed in order that at least his name may survive for ever, though he himself may not.

In the poem commonly known as 'Gilgamesh and the Land of Life', the hero sadly contemplates the fate of mankind, and appeals to the god Utu to allow him to undertake the long and perilous journey to 'the Land', for thus he will be assured everlasting fame:

'O Utu, a word would I speak to thee, listen to my word,
I would have it reach thee, that thou give ear to it.
In my city man dies, oppressed is the heart,
Man perishes, heavy is the spirit.
I looked over the wall,
And I saw corpses . . . floating on the river;
I too will end thus; that is certain.
No man, however tall, can reach to heaven,
No man, however broad, can cover the earth.
But not yet has the fated end arrived,
And I would enter the Land, and set up there my name,
In the places where names have been raised up, raise up
        my own,
In the places where names have not been raised up, raise
        up those of the gods.'
Utu accepted his tears as an offering,
Like a man of mercy, he showed him mercy.[35]

Accompanied by his faithful friend Enkidu, Gilgamesh sets off on his enterprise. After crossing seven great mountains they see their goal, with its vast cedar forests. But it is guarded by a fearful monster, Huwawa. In vain does Gilgamesh's friend warn him of the magnitude of the peril:

O my master, thou who hast not seen that being art not
        terror-stricken,
But I who have seen him am terror-stricken.
He is a hero with dragon's teeth,
His face is as that of a lion,
. . . is the onrushing flood-water,
From his brow which devours trees and reeds, none
        escapes.
O my master, go thou into the Land, I will return to
        the city;
I will tell thy mother of thy glory, and she will cry out,
I will tell her of thy death, and she will weep bitter
        tears.[36]

But Gilgamesh is not to be deterred by these gloomy forebodings:

For me another shall not die; the loaded boat will not
    sink;
The three-ply cloth will not be cut . . .
House and hut shall not be destroyed with fire.
If thou help me and I help thee, what can happen to us?[37]

The monster is attacked and overcome, and his body is
borne off to the gods.

Another text has the death of Gilgamesh for its theme. It
begins with a passage informing the hero that the god Enlil
has not granted him immortality:

Enlil, the great mountain, the father of the gods
— O lord Gilgamesh, this is the meaning of the dream —
Has destined thy fate, O Gilgamesh, for kingship, not for
    eternal life . . .
Be not aggrieved, be not depressed . . .
The light and darkness of mankind he has granted thee,
Supremacy over mankind he has granted thee . . .
Battle from which none may retreat he has granted thee,
Onslaughts unrivalled he has granted thee,
Attacks whence none may escape he has granted thee.[38]

This is followed by a description of the hero on his death-
bed, in a passage typical of Sumerian poetry, with its series
of verses all ending with the refrain: 'he lies and rises not'.
Thus: the destroyer of evil lies and rises not; he who has set
up justice on the earth lies and rises not; he who was mighty
of muscle lies and rises not; he who was wise in his features
lies and rises not; he who climbed the mountains lies and
rises not. These verses may, perhaps, offend our literary taste,
but there is no denying their rugged impressiveness.

The Sumerian hero overshadowed by tragic fate recalls
certain characters of Greek tragedy; beyond doubt he is one
of the most eloquent figures of this ancient literature.

A considerable amount of Sumerian literature consists of
hymns and prayers.[39] There are various types of hymns, but
two are predominant: the praise of gods and the praise of
heroes. Some of these are expressed in the third person, and
others in the first, like the following song of Inanna:

My father has given me heaven, has given me earth: I am
*   the Lady ruler of heaven.*
Is there any one, any god, that can match me?
Enlil has given me heaven, has given me earth: I am the
*   Lady ruler of heaven.*
Rule over men he has granted me, rule over women he
*   has granted me,*
Battle he has given me, skirmish he has given me,
The hurricane he has given me, the whirlwind he has
*   given me,*
Heaven has he set as crown upon my head,
Earth has he put as sandals for my feet,
In the shining mantle of godhead he has wrapped me,
The glittering sceptre he has set in my hand . . .
Is there any one, any god, that can match me?[40]

The king Shulgi, of the third Ur dynasty, is singled out for
special praise. In one hymn he speaks of himself in the following terms:

I, the king, from my mother's womb was a hero,
I, Shulgi, from birth was a mighty man.
I am a lion fierce of eye, born of a dragon,
I am the king of the four quarters of the earth,
I am the guardian, the shepherd of the Sumerians,
I am the hero, the god of all the lands . . .
Good do I love,
Evil do I despise,
Hostile words do I hate.
I, Shulgi, am the mighty king, the leader of all . . .
The foreign lands have I subdued, I have made my
*   people dwell in security,*
In the four quarters of the earth men utter in their
*   dwellings*
For days on end my name . . .
Shulgi, who destroys every foe, who makes the people live
*   in peace,*
Who possesses the divine strength of heaven and of earth,
Who has no equal,
Shulgi, the son whom the god of heaven has protected![41]

One hymn, also addressed to a sovereign, appears at first sight to be of quite a different character, being neither more nor less than a love song:

> Bridegroom, dear to my heart,
> Goodly is thy beauty, honeysweet,
> Lion, dear to my heart,
> Goodly is thy beauty, honeysweet . . .[42]

And so the song continues, in the language of love. But on examining the text more closely one discovers that the singer is a priestess of Inanna, and the beloved is the king Shu-Sin; in all probability it is a ritual song, a hymn for the ceremony presenting the marriage of Dumuzi and Inanna, which was performed in the temple every New Year, the performers being the king and a priestess.

Not many Sumerian prayers have survived. Their literary genre is similar to that of the hymns, which they resemble in content and form. The following prayer is addressed by Gudea to Gatumdu, goddess of Lagash:

> My Queen, fair daughter of the holy heaven,
> Heroine that suppliest all needs, goddess that holdest
>   high the head,
> That grantest life to the land of Sumer,
> That knowest what is good for thy city,
> Thou art the queen, the mother that hast founded
>   Lagash!
> When thou turnest thy gaze upon thy people, plenty
>   comes to them of itself;
> The pious young man whom thou guardest lives long
>   thereby!
> I have no mother, thou art my mother,
> I have no father, thou art my father!
> My seed hast thou received, in holiness thou hast
>   engendered me:
> O Gatumdu, how sweet is thy pure name![43]

Another genre similar to that of the hymns is that of the lamentations. These are songs of mourning, composed in memory of cities and houses destroyed by the enemy; they can be regarded as the predecessors of the Biblical lamentations. Thus, the goddess Ningal laments over the ruins of Ur:

> *In the rivers of my city dust has gathered, truly they*
> *   have been made into fox-dens;*
> *In their midst the foaming waters no more flow, the*
> *   workmen have deserted them;*
> *In the fields of the city there is no more grain, the*
> *   farmer has departed . . .*
> *My palm-groves and vineyards, that abounded with*
> *   honey and wine, have brought forth the*
> *   mountain thorn . . .*
> *Woe is me, my house is a ruined stable,*
> *I am a herdsman whose cows have been scattered,*
> *I, Ningal, like an unworthy shepherd on whose flock*
> *   the weapon has fallen!*
> *Woe is me, I am an exile from the city, that has found*
> *   no rest;*
> *I am a stranger dwelling in a strange city.*[44]

One extremely interesting group of texts consists of didactic or sapiential works, cast into various forms.[45] They include proverbs and maxims, often expressing a profound wisdom.[46]

Here are some reflections on poverty:

> *The poor man is better dead than alive:*
> *If he has bread, he has no salt;*
> *If he has salt, he has no bread;*
> *If he has a house, he has no stall;*
> *If he has a stall, he has no house.*[47]

At times a remarkable psychological insight is revealed:

> *Praise a young man, and he will do whatever you want;*
> *Throw a crust to a dog, and he will wag his tail before you!*[48]

And here is an exhortation to self-control:

> *In a place of brawling, do not show signs of annoyance;*
> *When wrath is burning up a man like fire, know how to*
> *   extinguish it.*
> *If he speaks to thee, let thy heart take counsel wisely;*
> *If he insults thee, do not answer him in like manner!*[49]

Another type of didactic composition is the fable; unfortunately only a few examples have survived. But we know the characters of a number of them: bird and fish, tree and reed, pick and plough, iron and bronze. The fables often take the form of dialogues or disputes concerning the good and bad qualities of the various characters, such as we find in the later fables of Aesop. Characters include not only animals and plants, minerals and tools, but also men and trades; when this occurs the literary class varies a little, and the intervention of the gods brings the story closer to the mythological type. There is a good example in the contest between Dumuzi the shepherd and Enkimdu the farmer for the hand of Inanna. The goddess favours the farmer:

> *The shepherd shall never marry me,*
> *Shall never drape me in his garment of carded wool . . .*
> *Me, the maiden, shall the farmer marry,*
> *The farmer, who raises plants,*
> *The farmer, who cultivates grain.*[50]

But the shepherd defends himself energetically:

> *Enkimdu, the man of the canals, the ditches and the*
>   *furrows,*
> *The farmer, what advantage has he over me?*
> *Let him give me his black garment,*
> *In return I will give him, the farmer, my black ewe;*
> *Let him give me his white garment,*
> *In return I will give him, the farmer, my white ewe;*
> *Let him pour for me his finest beer,*
> *In return I will pour for him, the farmer, my yellow milk;*
> *Let him pour for me his sweet beer,*
> *In return I will set before the farmer my curdled milk . . .*
> *After I have eaten, after I have drunk,*
> *I will leave for him the extra fat,*
> *I will leave for him the extra milk:*
> *The farmer, what advantage has he over me?*[51]

In the end, Inanna chooses the shepherd. But — and here is a highly significant point — the two rivals are reconciled, and the farmer also bears his gifts to the goddess. This is completely in conformity with the natural order which is simultaneously the aspiration and the characteristic feature of Sumerian thought.

The didactic genre includes numerous school compositions, one of which, recently deciphered by Kramer, is singularly interesting.[52] It tells of a boy who went to school, was diligent in his lessons, prepared and wrote out his exercise. On returning home he tells his father of all he has done, and then asks for his supper:

> I am thirsty, give me to drink! I am hungry, give me bread! Wash my feet, make my bed, I want to go to sleep. And wake me early in the morning, I must not be late or the master will punish me.[53]

Next morning the boy gets up, takes two rolls his mother has prepared for him, and runs off to school; but he arrives late, and his encounters with authority earn him a caning. When he returns home he suggests that his father should invite the schoolmaster home and placate him with gifts. The story continues:

> The father gave heed to the schoolboy's words. The master came from the school, was taken into the house, and seated in the place of honour. The schoolboy served him, sat down before him, and recounted to his father all that he had learned of the art of writing. Then his father, glad of heart, said to the master: 'My boy opens his hand and you put wisdom into it, you show him all the fine points of the art of writing.'[54]

After praise, the gifts are presented: wine, a copious supply of oil, a new garment, a ring. Won over by this generosity, the master turns to his pupil and praises him:

> 'My boy, because you have not neglected my words, and have not forgotten, may you rise to the pinnacle of the scribal art, and achieve it completely! Since you have given me what you were not obliged to give me, since you have offered me gifts over and above my earnings, may the goddess Nidaba, queen of the guardian deities, be

your patroness . . . May you be the leader of your brothers, the chief of your companions; may you rank the highest of all the schoolboys.'[55]

This tale is remarkable for its freshness and spontaneity, and at times it is highly amusing. It is a student satire? One might be tempted to think so, if it were not for the solemn gravity of Sumerian literature generally.

Before we pass from this survey of didactic and aphoristic writings, we must mention a theme first found in this literature, but which in later days is extensively diffused in the ancient Orient: the sufferings borne by the righteous man. Why are men who live good lives ill used by fortune? In the Sumerian poetic composition known as 'Man and his God' the problem is posed in the following terms:

> I am a man, a discerning one, yet who respects me
> prospers not,
> My righteous word has been turned into a lie,
> The man of deceit has covered me with the Southwind,
> I am forced to serve him,
> Who respects me not has shamed me before you.
> You have doled out to me suffering ever anew,
> I entered the house, heavy is the spirit,
> I, the man, went out to the street, oppressed is the heart,
> With me, the valiant, my righteous shepherd has become
> angry, has looked upon me inimically,
> My herdsman has sought out evil forces against me who
> am not his enemy,
> My companion says not a true word to me,
> My friend gives the lie to my righteous word.
> The man of deceit has conspired against me,
> And you, O my god, do not thwart him![56]

It must be noted, however, that these words do not express any sense of resentment against the god. On the contrary, the Sumerian view is that, whatever suffering may come, and however unjust it may seem, man's only course is to glorify his god, to confess his sins, and to await the liberation from suffering which is indicated at the end of this poem:

The man — his god hearkened to his bitter tears and
weeping,
The young man — his lamentation and wailing soothed
the heart of his god,
The righteous words, the pure words uttered by him, his
god accepted . . .
The evil fate which had been decreed for him, he turned
aside,
He turned the man's suffering into joy,
Set by him the kindly genii as a watch and guardian,
Gave him . . . angels of gracious mien.[57]

Apart from literature in the strict meaning of the word, the
Sumerians have left an enormous quantity of written material
which cannot be discussed here. But it is of interest to have
some idea of its comparative extent: suffice to say that it accounts for about 95 per cent of the surviving Sumerian texts.[58]
Most of these documents are of a commercial nature: receipts,
contracts, lists of persons and things. But they also include
linguistics (lists of signs and words); scientific writings, such
as interesting medical prescriptions;[59] private and official letters; the votive inscriptions which have already been discussed and which provide a great deal of historical information; and, finally, a body of juridical writings.

We must devote a little space to this last group, for it is
progressively revealing a society founded and organized on
justice. We have already mentioned the Code of King Ur-
Nammu, who lived about 2050 B.C. The word 'code' must not
be allowed to obscure the size of this document: in fact it
consists of a few analytical dispositions, particular solutions to
individual cases and not derived from any formulated general
principles; in this respect it reflects the Sumerian mentality,
as that of a great part of the ancient Orient. None the less,
the Code is built up on certain principles, and has an incipient literary form. It begins with a prologue, in which the
king recounts his victories over his foes and sings the praises
of the social reforms achieved in the country. We do not
know whether there was an epilogue too; we do find one in
the other code, also in Sumerian, which was promulgated by

Lipit Ishtar, king of Isin, who lived about 1900 B.C. In this Code the individual dispositions are more numerous, and, with its prologue and epilogue dedicated to the presentation and exaltation of the sovereign's labours, it is a model of the literary genre which later achieves its most highly organized formulation in the laws of Hammurabi of Babylon.

The Code is not the only surviving type of juridical document, nor is it the most common. Even more numerous are the documents relating to legal actions or individual cases: many of these come from the Lagash archives.[60] These documents may be dated about the end of the third millennium B.C., so they are an excellent source of information on Sumerian law, even if the laws of Lagash were not always identical with those of other cities, and although, because of their late appearance in Sumerian history, it is possible that some of their elements are of Semitic origin.

The legal documents are called *ditilla* (Judgement) and are composed according to a fixed formula: heading, subject of the action, list of witnesses, signatures of the royal 'commissioner' and the judges, date. Here is an example:

> *Ditilla.* Whereas Niurum, son of Urnumushda, presented himself and made declaration: 'I swear in the king's name that Gemeigalima, daughter of Lugalkigalla, shall marry Urigalima, my son and heir'; this is witnessed to by Lugaligikhush, son of the overseer Urbaba, and Lushara, son of the musician Niurum; Niurum has admitted the declaration of Lugalkigalla; whereas the son and heir of Niurum has married Inimlugala, Niurum shall pay one mina of silver to Gemeigalina. Ursatarana, son of Nimu, was commissioner. Lushara, Luebgala, Ludingirra and Ursatarana were judges in this affair. The year in which the vessel 'Abzu's Goat' was caulked.[61]

The gist of this involved statement is as follows: Two fathers, Niurum and Lugalkigalla, had made an agreement under which the former's son was to marry the latter's daughter. But Niurum's son has married someone else, so Niurum has to pay damages to the rejected bride.

This affords us a glimpse into the life of Sumerian society.

The collation of 'ditillas' gives us quite a detailed picture of that life. Society is divided into three classes: free men, slaves, and, intermediate between these, the partially free men, who have been pressed into palace service and reduced to the status of royal dependents.

The head of the family is the father. As we have already seen, matrimony is entered into by agreement between the fathers of the parties. It is monogamic, and may be dissolved given adequate cause, either by the husband, who utters a formula of repudiation, or by the wife, who 'renounces her wifely capacity':

> Ninkhilisu, daughter of the tailor Luna, married Lunin-shubura, son of the tailor Urbaba. Since Ninkhilisu wished to remain in the house of her father, and said to herself 'I may cause harm to Luninshubura in his position', she has renounced her wifely capacity.[62]

It is obvious that women hold a high position in Sumerian society. This is further indicated by the fact that they have the right to demand compensation if repudiated by their husbands. Women are ignored only in respect of inheritance, which passes through the male line; but this may have been only a formality, since a woman's father could give her a dowry.

A large number of documents relating to guarantees, securities, and buying and selling witness to the high development of Sumerian commerce, and therefore of the society practising it.

Finally, penal legislation is remarkably mild by comparison with that which comes into force some centuries later in Semitic legal practice: the chief punishment is payment of damages, as is confirmed by the few legible articles in the Ur-Nammu Code. So far as can be judged at present, only in the event of insolvency does the guilty party become the slave of the injured party. All of which goes to show that the principle of retaliation, 'an eye for an eye, a tooth for a tooth', which is found in the Hammurabi Code, is an innovation, most likely introduced by the new Semitic dynasty.

We have already dealt with court procedure. But we must add that the relevant documents so far published do not appear to confirm the impression of the private character of judicial procedure which the later Semitic texts convey. According to these, it would appear that a trial was not held unless some individual brought an action against the guilty party; but in Sumerian practice the public authorities could bring a man to trial for offending the rights of society, even though no plaintiff presented himself; moreover, unlike the corresponding Semitic documents, the 'ditillas' are not simply certificates for the use of the parties concerned, but are preserved in the public judicial archives.

This still further confirms the great maturity of the Sumerian legal system, by comparison with which, indeed, a number of later developments can only be regarded as retrogressive. And what is true of the legal system is true of literature in general; for in the complexity and subtlety of its themes, and in the maturity and profundity of the thought which dominates them it has reached a stage of advanced development amounting perhaps even to a certain decadence. In any case, it reflects a society which has achieved an organized conception of the universe, and has succeeded in creating the means to express this conception.

We are still a thousand years and more from the time of the Bible and the Homeric poems. So we cannot charge the discoverers of the Sumerians with misjudgement or conceit when they declare their discovery to be one of the most important contributions made in our day to our knowledge of humanity.[63]

V   The Artistic Types

When we turn from consideration of the written documents to study the artistic monuments[64] we find remarkably similar characteristics. For art, in the widest sense of the term and in its most diverse manifestations, is always self-consistent, no less in the ancient Orient than in the present-day Western world.

Yet the art of these two worlds differs profoundly in regard to its sphere of activity, in the exigencies which give birth to it, and the end which it pursues. Sumerian art — and we shall see that this holds true for a great part of the world around it — does not come into existence as a free and subjective expression of the aesthetic spirit, and its exigencies and ends are not the pursuit of beauty for its own sake. On the contrary, it is a manifestation of the religious, and hence of the practical spirit; it is an integral part of religious life, and therefore, since religion permeates all things in the Orient, of political and social life. Its rôle is definitely an active one, that of a stimulating and integrating force essential to the ordered development of existence: temples are built so that the gods may be duly honoured, and to avoid offending them lest they withdraw fertility from the earth; statues are modelled in order to be set up in the temples and so ensure divine protection for the persons they represent and serve, as it were, as those persons' representatives in the gods' presence; reliefs are carved in order to perpetuate and renew the memory of the events they depict. One of the facts which most clearly emphasize the difference between this type of art and our own is that various monuments, such as statues and reliefs, are set up in places where they cannot be seen; for instance, buried in the foundations of a building. Those who put them there are satisfied that the gods will see them; it does not matter that they will not be seen by mortal eyes.

Such an art has subjects and typical forms which can be readily understood: they consist of temples, votive statues, and commemorative reliefs. So it is a public art, concerned with the official celebration of religious beliefs and political power; subjects drawn from private life are of little or no interest. The style is official too, and so it is impersonal, collective. There is no place for attempts to express individuality, and the artist is no more concerned than the writer with recording his name. In art, as in the literature, the producer is more craftsman or artisan than artist in our modern sense.

Associated with this collective impersonality and anonymity is a remarkable static quality. The negative aspect of this phenomenon, the absence of any tendency towards innovation, has its corresponding positive aspect, consisting of the

deliberate intention to imitate the ancient models, which are
regarded as perfect and unsurpassable. This accounts for the
fact that in the major arts, as in literature, it is difficult to
trace any definite process of historical development. On the
other hand the minor arts, especially the production of seals,
supply a profusion of specimens and subjects which do afford
some possibility of tracing a course of evolution, though only
on a restricted scale, based more on the subjects than on the
style of the specimens available.

At the close of our introductory remarks on Sumerian art,
we may question whether we do have to resign ourselves to
the impossibility of identifying individual masters. We would
hesitate to go so far as that. There are certain monuments,
and statues in particular, which definitely afford a glimpse of
the artist's personality and creative powers. But it remains
true that this personality and creative force slip in despite the
artist's efforts, as it were, or, at least, without any deliberate
and conscious intention on his part.

As we have seen when dealing with their history, the main
and fundamental activity of the Sumerians is the erection of
great temples, centres of the city's life.[65] The building material is determined by the nature of the soil, and in turn deter-
mines the architectural style. The material is sun-dried clay
brick. The bricks are built up into walls which, naturally, look
thick and massive. Columns are non-existent, or at least they
have no structural function, wooden beams being employed
in their place. The monotony of the wall is broken only by
alternating projections and depressions in the surface, so
effecting an interplay of light and shade; but the principal
break in the continuity of the wall is that of the great entrance gateway.

The central feature of the Sumerian temple,[66] distinguishing it from the palace or the house, is the altar with its offerings table. In the pre-historic period the temple consists of a
single chamber, the altar being set against one of the short
sides, with the table before it (Fig. 1). Later, two divergent
developments are to be noted: in the south the altar and the

table are erected in a courtyard which has parallel chambers usually along its long sides, or less frequently along the short

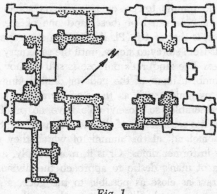

Fig. 1

ones; in the north the altar and the table remain in the primitive chamber, which is extended and completed with supplementary chambers.

A further development takes place in the Sumerian temple when the courtyard ceases to be used as the place of worship. Then the courtyard is arranged at the side of the temple, usually by one of the long sides, and in its turn it is surrounded with chambers, used as rooms for the priests and officials. Thus a *temenos*, a sacred precinct, gradually comes into existence, setting the complex of temple buildings apart from the other city edifices. An excellent example of this type is the oval temple brought to light through the excavations of the Chicago Oriental Institute at Khafaje (Pl. I). The reconstruction shows a double surrounding wall, a series of buildings for the temple personnel, a broad courtyard, a terrace at the foot of the sanctuary, reached by steps, and finally the sanctuary itself, with walls regularly buttressed, and the entrance in one of the long sides.

The terrace on which the Sumerian temple is built serves

as the starting point (we do not know whether in terms of logic or history) for the development of a kind of monument which remains typical of Mesopotamia: by the superimposition of several terraces of decreasing area one on another the temple tower, or ziqqurat, is achieved.[67] One of the most celebrated of these, and one of the easiest to reconstruct, is that of Ur (Pl. II). Here a succession of stairways leads from storey to storey, until the sanctuary is reached at the apex. The ziqqurat's purpose is still unknown. Is it an ancient tomb, a tomb of the gods or deified kings, like the Egyptian pyramids such as the step pyramid at Sakkarah, which it resembles so closely? We have no proof that this is so. Or is it a recollection of the mountains of the Sumerians' original homeland, at the summit of which they celebrated their rites in former times? Or is it, more simply, an outward expression of man's desire to approach the divine, allowing him to draw as close as possible to the gods, and offering the gods in turn a dwelling place and a pathway down to earth?

Sumerian civil architecture is parallel in its forms (with the exception of the sanctuary, of course) to those of the temple: there is a central courtyard, with rooms grouped around and opening on to it; there is only one means of communication with the outside world, through the entrance gateway. In the case of palaces this plan may be extended into a series of courtyards, each with its own surrounding chambers. Normally the buildings are of only one storey; their windows open on to the flat roof terrace, where the inhabitants are accustomed to walk in the evening, refreshing themselves after the heat of the day.

Unlike what we shall find in Egypt, in Mesopotamia little importance is attached to the tomb. This accords with the Mesopotamians' different character, and their different beliefs as to the nature of life beyond the grave. The Egyptian has full and consistent faith in a future life similar to that of this world; in Mesopotamia there is a vague and unelaborated belief in a realm of shadows and sadness. Even the most celebrated of the tombs, the royal ones of Ur, are interesting not so much for their architecture — they consist of chambers hollowed out in the ground — as for the rich harvest of archaeological finds they have provided, and especially for the interesting indications already mentioned, of a voluntary sacrifice of life.

Among the Sumerians there is only a limited development of statuary, and this is subject to certain conditions. There is an objective reason for this, in the difficulty of obtaining stone. But a subjective factor, arising from the Sumerian view of art and the aim of the artist, has to be taken into consideration: the statue is regarded as a substitute inside the temple for the person represented, and so, except for particularly important individuals, there is no need for it to be of large size. This explains the prevalence of statuettes and also the particular care taken in modelling the features, to permit the identification and recognition of the person represented. The rest of the body is neglected, and is often on a smaller scale than the head; the Sumerians are not interested in modelling the nude, and the body is concealed beneath the standard style of attire.

The best way of conveying what a Sumerian statue looks like is by citing examples. We begin with one of the oldest and crudest: a Tell Asmar statuette (Pl. III). The figure is erect, rigid, and solemn. The face is too large in proportion to the body, and is striking for its great eyes; the eyeballs are of shell and the pupils of lapis lazuli. The hair is parted in the middle and falls on each side of the face, to mingle with the great beard: in the parallel lines of the curls the striving for harmony and symmetry leads to stylization. The rigidly carved body has the arms folded over the chest, the hands being joined in the typical attitude of prayer. From the waist downward the body is simply a truncated cone, ending in a carved fringe to represent clothing.

Obviously this art is dominated by a geometrical canon. Comparing it with the art of Greece and Egypt, Frankfort has put the case well in the following passage:

In pre-Greek times it was not organic unity, but abstract, geometric unity that was sought. The main masses were arranged in approximation to some geometrical form — the cube or cylinder or cone; and the details were stylized in harmony with the ideal scheme. The clear three-dimensional character of these geometrical bodies was reflected in the figures composed under this rule. And it is the dominance of the cylinder and the cone which imparts unity and corporeality to the Mesopotamian figures: note how the arms, meeting in front of the bodies, and the fringed lower edge of kilts, emphasize the circumference, and thereby the depth as well as the width. This geometric approximation establishes the figures emphatically in space.

It also explains the spellbound appearance of all pre-Greek sculpture in the round. Only the choice of the ideal form differs: in Egypt it is the cube or oblong rather than the cylinder or cone. Once chosen, the formal ideal remains dominant; throughout all changes of style Egyptian sculpture is squared, Mesopotamian sculpture is rounded.[68]

There is much greater artistic maturity in a group of statuettes dating from a rather later period. Among these the figure of a priest, found in Khafaje (Pl. IV), is particularly significant. It reveals a great step forward in the observation of reality, without detriment to the principles of proportion and harmony. Instead of contrasting masses there is delicate modelling, with much less geometrical abstraction and symbolism. Possibly the figure is less expressive of strength, but there are certainly more delicacy and expression in it.

The principles and conventions which dominate human statuary in Sumer do not hold to the same extent for animal figures. Hence a greater degree of realism is possible in these, and consequently a greater artistic effectiveness, as is evident in the fine effigy of a bull, discovered at Khafaje (Pl. V). But even the animals are not free from the symbolism, which is essentially religious in its nature. Thus, a highly effective bull mask adorning a harp found at Ur is provided with a remarkable stylized beard; and, whatever may be its significance, this is certainly not realism.

The characteristic and predominant form of Mesopotamian plastic art is relief carving, and this is as highly developed as free-standing carving is limited in scope. Relief carving has its own peculiar problems, and on their solution depend its characteristic features; so we must consider how the Sumerians conceived and solved these problems.

First among them is perspective. Whereas the modern artist reduces the size of his figures in relation to their distance, representing them as they appear to the eye, the Sumerian craftsman keeps them all the same size, and so represents them as they appear to his mind's eye, so to speak. For this reason Sumerian art has been called 'cerebral',[69] the term being intended to convey the predominance of thought over the physical impression.

However, there is a further reason for variations in the size of the figures, namely, their relative importance. And so the god is carved larger than the king, the king is bigger than his subjects, and they are bigger than the conquered enemy. Here 'cerebralism' passes into symbolism and defies reality.

The compositional elements of the figures are governed by a number of conventions: the face is generally presented in profile, but the profile face is given a frontal eye. The same applies to the shoulders and the torso, given frontal presentation, where the feet are in profile; some attempt is made to indicate a slightly twisted torso by positioning the arms.

There are three main types of Sumerian relief carving: the stele, the plaque, and the seal. The 'stele of the vultures' (Pl. VI) is a good example of the first. Its main fragment represents the god of Lagash, Ningirsu; his stylized beard, and the relative attitudes of the face, torso, and arms, exemplify the features we have just mentioned. In his left hand the god holds what appears to be his emblem: a lion-headed eagle grasping two lion cubs in its talons. His other hand grips a mace with which he is striking the head of a conquered foe enmeshed with others in a net, symbolizing their status as captives: in accordance with the symbolism above mentioned they are all of diminutive size by comparison with their conqueror. Thus this stele brings together and exemplifies many typical features of Mesopotamian relief.

Another widely diffused type of relief carving is the square stone plaque, with a hole in the centre, probably to enable it to be fixed to a wall (Pl. VII). One subject predominates in the carvings of these plaques: a banquet scene, with a male and female figure surrounded by servants and musicians; subsidiary scenes include foodstuffs and animals destined for the table. Frankfort, who has made a special study of this type of relief carving, maintained that this scene depicts the solemn New Year rite celebrating the marriage of the fertility goddess and the vegetation god who dies and rises again.

The third principal type of relief carving is found on the seal, a form of identification, impressed on raw clay as a kind of signature. The seals are conical or hemispherical in shape at first, but they soon evolve to a cylindrical form, which finally predominates. When rolled over the flattened clay, the scene carved on the convex surface of the cylinder is reproduced (Pl. VIII). Certain subjects appear very frequently on these seals: there is the hero among subdued wild beasts; the defence of the flock; the ruler's victory over his foes; rows of sheep or oxen; intertwined figures. Harmony and symmetry dominate, even to the extent of what is called 'brocade style', in which the ornamentation is more important than the subject. As has already been observed, seals form one of the very few sectors of Sumerian art in which close investigation makes it possible to establish an evolution in both style and subject matter.[70]

We cannot dwell on this point, nor can we discuss the other minor arts, despite all their richness and variety. They include the metal statuettes, reproducing the features already mentioned in connection with the stone statuary; and jewels — some of those found in Ur are examples of fine and delicate workmanship which it would be difficult to surpass (Pl. IX). It is in this field, much more than in the major arts, that the achievements of the ancient world approach those of our own time; with freedom from restricting and differentiating conventions the gap grows smaller and less important.

Here we must leave our consideration of ancient Sumerian culture. But before doing so we must testify to the profound impression it makes. Over four thousand years ago, before civilization had been born in Europe, in Mesopotamia a rich and powerful culture, surprisingly highly developed and marvellously varied in forms, emerges from the shadows. Its creative and driving force is indeed outstanding: its literary works, its laws, and its artistic creations provide the basis for all the succeeding civilizations of Western Asia, in which we shall find them copied, adapted, and worked over, often being marred rather than improved in the process. Thus the rediscovery of the Sumerians is a great contribution to our knowledge not only for its own sake, but equally because it has enabled us to identify the point of origin of a great wave of culture, which spread over the ancient Oriental world and even further, into the Mediterranean basin.

THE BABYLONIANS AND ASSYRIANS

I 'Graecia Capta'

A history extending over more than two thousand years;[1] a political power that spread all through western Asia and even into Egypt; an intense and rich religious life; a copious literary, artistic, and scientific output: such are the main features of the civilization of the Babylonians and Assyrians, or, to give them their collective name, the Akkadians.[2] But during the past few years a problem of fundamental importance has arisen in regard to the origins and the constituent elements of that civilization: it is questioned whether it was original or derivative, an independent creation or a reworking over of material already in existence.

At the beginning of this century, when the theory of 'pan-Babylonism', which derived all the elements of ancient culture from Babylonia, was in fashion, who would have thought that the tables would be turned so completely? But in fact the rediscovery of the Sumerians is more and more clearly showing that the Babylonian and Assyrian religious conceptions, the content of their literary works, and the themes of their arts and sciences have their precedents in the Sumerian civilization. Inevitably one asks whether even that which still seems original may not sooner or later be attributable to prototypes at present unknown.

In consequence, the relationship between the Akkadians and the Sumerians is growing more and more like that which exists between the Romans and the Greeks: in Mesopotamia, too, the newer people is permeated with the older and superior culture, and, so to speak, makes a cultural capitulation at the very moment of its political victory. It must be added — and here the parallel with the Greeks and the Romans still holds — that the newcomers do not fail to make their own contribution of elements and attitudes, whether during the initial phase of their civilization or in the course of its development. But the sorting out of these elements and attitudes will long remain an extremely difficult task.

II *The Historical Outlines*

The Babylonians and Assyrians are Semitic peoples.[3] They originate in the movements of the nomads who periodically pressed outward from the desert expanses of Arabia and tried to infiltrate into the Mesopotamian valley. This origin deserves closer attention: while providing the link which connects Mesopotamia with other Semitic civilizations, it may again and again afford hints or clues to the identification of distinctive cultural features which, as we have just remarked, is as difficult to achieve as it is necessary for a proper understanding.

Semitic personal names are found in Mesopotamia as early as the first half of the third millennium B.C.; so it is probable that a peaceable mingling with the Sumerians was occurring from at least this early period. Then, about 2350 B.C., the Semites come to power with the advent of Sargon the Great, who unites Mesopotamia under his rule and presses into Syria and Asia Minor.[4] Thus for the first time is achieved the kingdom of all the known world, of the 'four quarters of the earth', and this will remain a constant element in the conceptions and aspirations of the Semitic peoples, causing a substantial modification in the political outlook of the Sumerians, which found practical realization in the city state. The figure of the ruler also acquires a new quality: he is no longer only a man in the service of the god, but a man who by his deeds becomes a god himself, as is proved by the attributes which are associated with him. The heightened importance of the monarch decides the old rivalry between king and priesthood in his favour, and the priests are relegated to the ranks of the bureaucracy which surrounds the king, and is responsible to him.

The figure of Sargon is quickly incrusted with legends, which tell how his mother abandoned him, when he was a baby, in a reed basket on the river, how he was miraculously rescued, and how through the love of the goddess Ishtar he began his great enterprises. But for information as to the facts we shall do better to refer to the chronicle which has come down to us:

> Sargon, king of Agade, overseer of Ishtar, king of Kish, appointed priest of Anu, king of the country, great *ensi* of Enlil: he defeated Uruk and tore down its wall; in the battle with the inhabitants of Uruk he was victorious. Lugalzaggisi, king of Uruk, he captured in the battle, and brought by a halter to the gate of Enlil. Sargon, king of Agade, was victorious in the battle with the inhabitants of Ur: he conquered the town and tore down its wall. He defeated E-Ninmar and tore down its wall and conquered its entire territory from Lagash to the sea; then he washed his weapons in the sea. In the battle with the inhabitants of Umma he was victorious, he conquered the town and tore down its wall. Enlil did not let anyone oppose Sargon, the king of the country. Enlil gave him the land from the Upper Sea to the Lower Sea.[5]

This curt military prose reflects the rough customs of the conquerors: the civilized and peaceable mentality of the temple-building Sumerians has not as yet taken full possession of them. Yet undoubtedly it is to this roughness, and the weapons that go with it — the bow and arrow which overcome the Sumerian lance and shield — that Sargon owes his success and the foundation of a dynasty which continues to hold sway firmly over the area for some two centuries. It will take even rougher peoples and finally the savage Gutians from the eastern mountains, to put an end to that dynasty,[6] and in the subsequent reaction the Sumerian city states will acquire a new lease on life. But not for long: about 2000 B.C. the Semites victoriously return to power.

The new conquerors are known as Amorites,[7] because they

come from the Amurru land, the 'West'. They are not the only people to be given this name, but we may retain it as a conventional designation for these invaders. Their conditions of life are also those of the nomadic beduin. A Sumerian myth says:

> The Amorite, who digs for truffles at the
>   foot of the mountains,
> Who bends not the knee,
> Who eats raw flesh,
> Who in his lifetime has no home,
> Who after death has no burial. . . .[8]

Much light is now being shed on the states founded by these new Semitic peoples by the documents which French archaeologists found in the city of Mari.[9] This was one of the main Amorite centres, and its archives contain its sovereigns' correspondence with those of the other states, with governors, generals, and envoys. More than thirty kingdoms, most of them unknown hitherto, are referred to in these archives, and we can follow all the course of their alliances, rivalries, and political manoeuvres. For example, Hammurabi, king of Babylonia, writes in the following strain to Bakhdilim, the 'Master of the Palace' of King Zimrilim of Mari:

> To Bakhdilim, say: thus speaks Hammurabi. I have sent a detachment to Zimrilim. As thou knowest, the distance these men have to cover is long. Concerning the wellbeing of Zimrilim and that of his troops, and that of the troops I have sent to Zimrilim, concerning the city of Razama and the enemy forces besieging it, continue to send me information! And let thy information reach me regularly![10]

In passing, we may point out that this letter is an example of the epistolary style of the time: we shall be dealing with other examples which reveal its elements and characteristic features. But the principal interest of the letters lies in the fact that they are free from the stereotyped language of the annalists and afford us an insight into the characters of the sovereigns concerned, as well as into their private and intimate life.[11] Thus their figures take on more vividness, losing the generic uniformity which the official accounts confer on them. For example, the great king Shamshi-Adad of Assyria thus expresses his opinion of the differing abilities of his two sons, both of whom are governors of important provinces. One of them is brave and energetic, the other indolent and unwarlike. To the latter son his father writes:

> How long shall we have to guide thy every action? Thou art still a child, thou art not a man, there is no beard on thy chin! How long wilt thou continue to neglect the administration of thy house? Dost thou not see how thy brother commands great armies? So govern for thyself thy palace and thy house![12]

Sometimes the tone of the correspondence is unconsciously comic, as in the case of an official serving the king of Mari. He has found a lion in the granary of a house, and is at a loss to know what to do, for the king has strictly forbidden the slaughter of lions, since he wishes them preserved for hunting. The official can do no other than write to the king:

> A lion has been taken in the granary of a house in Akkaka. If this lion is to remain in the granary until the arrival of my lord, let my lord write to tell me so; if on the other hand I ought to have it brought to my lord, let my lord write to tell me that.[13]

The king does not reply, the official's perplexity increases, and in the end he comes to a decision and writes again to the king:

> Now I have been awaiting letters from my lord, and the lion has remained five days in the granary. A dog and a pig have been sent in to him that he may eat. I said to myself: 'Perhaps this lion will get away!' I was afraid. I have had the lion put in a wooden cage, loaded on a boat, and sent to my master.[14]

One of the various Amorite states gains the ascendancy, and unites all Mesopotamia under its rule. This is the kingdom of

Babylonia, which reaches the zenith of its power about 1700 B.C. under the great king Hammurabi.[15] As is well known, this king has achieved fame chiefly for his legal code, in which he collated and ordered his people's laws.[16] The Code follows the Sumerian precedent in having a prologue and an epilogue which set forth its objects. The prologue has a solemn opening:

> *When lofty Anu, king of the Anunnaki[17]*
> *And Enlil, lord of heaven and earth,*
> *The determiner of the destinies of the land,*
> *Determined for Marduk,[18] the first-born of Enki,*
> *Dominion over all mankind . . .*
> *Then did Anu and Enlil name me,*
> *Hammurabi, the devout, god-fearing prince,*
> *To make justice rule in the land,*
> *To destroy the wicked and unjust,*
> *That the strong might not oppress the weak;*
> *To rise like Shamash[19] over the Mesopotamian people*
> *And to light up the land,*
> *To promote the wellbeing of the people.[20]*

The epilogue is in an equally exalted strain:

> *I made an end of war,*
> *I promoted the welfare of the land.*
> *I made the peoples rest in friendly dwellings,*
> *I did not allow trouble-makers in their midst.*
> *The great gods called me,*
> *And I was the beneficent shepherd of righteous sceptre,*
> *And my benign shadow spread over my city.*
> *I took to my bosom the peoples of Sumer and Akkad,*
> *And they prospered under my protection;*
> *I have governed them in peace,*
> *I have sheltered them with my wisdom,*
> *That the strong might not oppress the weak,*
> *That justice might be done to the orphan and the*
>   *widow . . .*
> *Let any oppressed man who has a cause*
> *Come into the presence of my statue as king of justice,*

Read my inscribed stele,
And give ear to my precious words;
And may my stele make clear to him his cause,
Show him his rights,
And set his mind at rest.[21]

These lines express the ancient ideal of the Sumerian rulers: an ideal of inviolable peace, founded on law and order. The weak are to be protected, justice is to be done to the orphan and the widow. . . . Under Hammurabi the two cultures which compose Mesopotamian civilization achieve complete and harmonious fusion. The deification of the kings which is characteristic of the first Semitic dynasty has disappeared. For centuries to come the inscriptions left by the sovereigns of Babylonia are distinguished by the paucity of their reports of warlike enterprises and their ample recordings of the works of peace.

Hammurabi's dynasty comes to an end about 1530 B.C., and Babylonia enters on a long period of decadence, during which power is in the hands of the Kassites[22] who come from the nearby Iranian mountains. In the meantime the ascendancy in the Mesopotamian area passes more and more to the northern power, Assyria.[23] Already established as a powerful state in the times of Mari — we may recall our mention of King Shamshi-Adad — Assyria begins its gradual rise to power over the other states of the Near East in the fourteenth century. About 1100 B.C. Tiglath-pileser I invades Anatolia in the north, conquers the district of Nairi, and reaches the Black Sea; in the West he penetrates into Syria and crosses it to the Mediterranean:

(I am) Tiglath-pileser, the legitimate king, king of the world, king of Assyria, king of the four parts of the earth, the courageous hero guided by the oracles of Ashur and Ninurta, the great gods his lords; he who has overcome his foes. . . . At the command of my lord Ashur, my hand conquered from beyond the lower Zab river to the upper sea that lies towards the west. Three times did I march against the Nairi countries . . . I made bow at my feet thirty kings of the Nairi countries, and took hostages from them. I received as tribute horses broken to the yoke. I imposed upon them tribute and gifts. Then I went to the Lebanon. I cut cedar timber for the temple of Anu and Adad, the great gods my lords, and brought it away. I set upon the Amurru country. I conquered the entire Amurru country. I received tribute from Byblos, Sidon and Arvad.[24]

This military prose reveals that Assyria has a character of its own, rough and warlike, which is reflected not only in the manifestations of public life but also in those of literature, law, and art. The royal annals, a typical and clearly defined literary form, express it most clearly. They present the figure of a ruler who, following the Semitic rather than the Sumerian tradition, concentrates in his own hands an absolute sovereignty with a military basis. He is not a god, but rather the representative of the nation's war-god; in his person political and religious authority are united, so that the dualism is once more resolved in the unity of the single head of a bureaucratic state.

We must not take all the victories announced in the annals entirely at their face value. We have proof that, by a process not unknown to any state or epoch, these military bulletins exaggerate the successes and minimize the defeats. But it is certain that the expansion of the Assyrian empire pursues an inexorable course along the main lines of its military advances. In the eighth century, Tiglath-pileser III is victorious everywhere; after defeating the powerful state of Urartu in the north,[25] now at the height of its power and organizing alliances against him, he penetrates into Asia Minor, Syria and Palestine, and into Babylonia. Under the name Pulu he assumes the governorship of Babylonia, thus initiating the singular institution of the union of two crowns in the person of one ruler bearing two different names. This procedure reflects a prudence and a political delicacy not usually to be found in the ruthless Assyrian power. But its explanation is to be seen in Babylonia's exalted cultural tradition, which the Assyrians recognize as their own; and so, apart from certain times of crisis, they are careful to represent themselves not as conquerors but as liberators, going so far as to recognize and venerate the gods of Babylonia.

The reign of Sargon II (721–705 B.C.) is famous for his conquest of a number of Syro-Palestinian cities. In the royal annals we read what happened to Ashdod:

> Aziru, king of Ashdod, had schemed not to give tribute any more and had sent messages hostile to Assyria to the kings his neighbours. On account of the ill done by him I took from him the government of his people and named Ahimiti, his younger brother, as their king. But the Hittites, ever scheming evil, hated his rule and raised to power over them a Greek who, without any claim to the throne, had no more respect for my authority than they had. In my wrath I did not wait to gather the whole force of my army or prepare a camp, but I set out for Ashdod with only those soldiers who even in peaceful regions never left my side. That Greek, however, learned betimes of the advance of my expedition, and fled into Egypt, to the borders of Ethiopia, and could not be discovered. I besieged and conquered the cities of Ashdod, Gath, Asdudimmu; I declared as booty his gods, his wife, his children, all the possessions and treasures of his palace, and also the inhabitants of his land. I reorganized those cities and settled there people from the eastern regions, whom I myself had conquered. I set my own officer as governor over them and declared them Assyrian citizens. . . .[26]

This passage reveals one of the most typical features of Assyrian conquest: the mass deportation of conquered populations. Certain pages of the Bible, which we shall be quoting later, describe the sorrow of the Hebrews forcibly carried off to Babylonia, far from their own land.

Assyrian expansion reaches its highest point in the seventh century B.C., when the armies of King Esarhaddon penetrate into Egypt and take possession of the country. This is in 671 B.C., a memorable year; for the first time in their thousands of years of rivalry one of the two great valleys conquers the other; for the first time, though only for a brief period, the ancient Orient, from the Tigris to the Nile, is united in a single empire, and, from being an aspiration, the lordship of the 'four quarters of the earth' becomes a reality. The resulting exultation is clearly expressed in the annals of Esarhaddon:

> From the town of Ishhupri as far as Memphis, the royal residence, a distance of fifteen days' march, I fought daily, without a break, the bloodiest battles against Tirhakah, king of Egypt and Ethiopia, the one accursed of all the great gods. Five times I dealt him incurable wounds with the points of my arrows. I laid siege to Memphis, his royal residence, and conquered it in half a day with mines, breaches and assault-ladders; I destroyed it, I tore down its walls, I burned it with fire. His wife and the women of his palace, his heir Ushanahuru and his other children, his possessions, his horses, his cattle in immense quantity I bore away as booty into Assyria. All the Ethiopians did I deport from Egypt, leaving not even one to do homage. Everywhere in Egypt I appointed new kings, governors, officials, maritime overseers, officers and scribes. I instituted sacrifices for Ashur and the other great gods my lords, for all time. I laid upon them the tribute due to me as overlord, to be paid annually without a break.[27]

This occupation of Egypt lasts less than twenty years. Then, as rapidly as she has achieved power, Assyria is overtaken by the final crisis: an Iranian people, the Medes, allied with the renascent power of Babylon, assails the Assyrian empire from the rear. In 612 B.C. Nineveh, its capital, is taken. Assyria falls.

The crisis of Assyria is followed by the renascence of Babylonia under the Chaldaean dynasty, a brief meteoric episode. At the beginning of the sixth century the great Nebuchadnezzar presses once more along the road to the West, overthrows Jerusalem, and reaches the Egyptian border. Until a few years ago we had to resort to foreign sources for information concerning his warlike enterprises, for the royal inscriptions represented him as occupied in the works of peace, in accordance with the best traditions of his people. Nowadays the situation is rather different: the chronicle which Wiseman published in 1956[28] shows that the Babylonians also put their wars on record; so the contrast which used to be drawn so drastically with the Assyrians proves to be based more on the limitations of the material available at the time than on the facts of the case. Nevertheless, we must recognize that there is a genuine difference in emphasis. Moreover, in Babylonia military expeditions are often connected with the works of peace, and seem to aim rather at collecting material for temples than at defeating an enemy:

> Under the power of my lords Nabu[29] and Marduk, I organized an expedition of my troops to the Lebanon. I rendered that region happy, everywhere dislodging my foes. I gathered together the scattered inhabitants and brought them back to their homes. I did what no king in the past had achieved: I cut through steep mountains, I split rocks, I opened passages and I built a road for the transport of the cedars. For my lord Marduk, I caused mighty cedars, high and strong, of precious beauty and excellent dark quality, the abundant yield of the Lebanon, to float like reed-stalks on the Arahtu[30] even into Babylonia. I made the inhabitants of the Lebanon dwell in security together, and did not suffer any to disturb them.[31]

The Iranian power presses hard on Babylon. Cyrus's Persians invade it in 538 B.C. And then the history of the ancient Mesopotamian empires is ended for ever.

III *The Religious Structure*

Nowhere, perhaps, is the nature of the relationship between the Sumerians and the Semites more clearly exemplified than in their religious beliefs and practices.[32] In the Babylonian and Assyrian pantheon we meet once more with the three great cosmic gods of the Sumerians: Heaven, Air, and Earth. Their names also remain the same: Anu, Enlil, and Ea (Enki). There is also the astral trinity: the Moon, the Sun, and Venus the morning star; but the names are different: Sin, Shamash, and Ishtar. We may ask: is the difference confined to a change of name? The answer is not so simple. For instance, we cannot exclude the possibility that the special emphasis laid on Ishtar's warlike as distinct from her astral aspect, is due to the influence of the Semitic element in the population. But her status as a fertility goddess remains unchanged, and she is still associated with the young god Tammuz (an adaptation of the Sumerian name Dumuzi) who dies and rises again as an expression of the annual vegetation cycle.

The national gods present a different picture, for by their very nature these are not easily transferred from one people to another. Babylonia and Assyria each have their own gods, to whom great honour is accorded. In Babylonia the Hammurabi dynasty exalts the national god, called Marduk, and henceforth he retains his place at the head of the heavenly hierarchy, being regarded as the creator and orderer of the universe. In Assyria the name of the national god is the same as that of the people and their capital: Ashur; and he possesses the same warlike attributes that are characteristic of his people.

Moreover, because a long existing religious life is dynamic in its nature, there is the possibility of establishing autonomous beliefs by another road; and the main reason for the distinctive features of the Babylonian and Assyrian religious beliefs has to be sought in this dynamic quality, as well as in their diversity of origin. Now divinities appear which hitherto have been almost or entirely unknown, such as the god of writing and wisdom, Nabu, who is the minister and secretary of the gods; while others are peculiar to a separate group of the population, such as Adad, the god of the Amorites; or they are borrowed from neighbouring peoples, like Amurru, the god of the West. So, too, in the hierarchical organization of the pantheon, which grows more and more detailed and complex as state centralization develops, particular circumstances determine differences in development: for instance, the ascendancy of Marduk, and his assumption of the attributes proper to other gods, are a consequence of the political ascendancy of the first Babylonian dynasty.

Besides the qualitative differences, the religious documentary material left by Babylonia and Assyria is distinguished, also and above all, by its quantity. It must not be forgotten that the Semitic far surpass the Sumerian texts both in number and in the possibility of interpretation. In consequence we have a far larger and more detailed picture of religious life, and categories which were barely hinted at in the days of the Sumerians acquire a more definite content and more clearly defined characteristics.

Together with faith in the gods there is a no less lively belief in demons. These are maleficent spirits, often the souls of the dead who have not been properly buried. Their bodies are part human and part animal. Like the ghosts of our own stories, they appear particularly in dark and lonely spots. Worse still, they have the power both to render themselves invisible, and to invest themselves with all kinds of forms. Hence there is no escaping from them, as one text tellingly puts it:

> *Doors and bolts do not stop them;*
> *High walls and thick walls they cross like waves;*
> *They leap from house to house . . . ;*
> *Under the doors they slip like serpents.*[33]

It is a feature of the Mesopotamian religious outlook (as of others, it must be added) to attribute the ills that befall mankind to the activity of the demons. Here, for instance, is a description of the demon called *ashakku*, the bearer of one of the ills most feared by the people of Mesopotamia, namely, headaches:

> *The wicked ashakku comes on like a hurricane,*
> *Clad in splendour, he fills the broad earth,*
> *Wrapped in fearful noise he spreads terror,*
> *He prowls about the ways, he clutters the roads;*
> *He stands at a man's side and none sees him,*
> *He sits beside a man and remains unperceived;*
> *If he enters a house, none knows his design,*
> *If he goes out of it, he is still unnoticed.*[34]

Demonic intervention is in turn regarded as being brought about by man's own sins. Similar ideas are not unknown to us of later days; but a typical feature of the ancient Mesopotamian religion is that even good deeds do not necessarily save a man from the demons: there is always the possibility that they will take possession of a man's body as the result of a spell, or even of a mistake.

So the demons have to be driven out. This task is undertaken by an entire class of the priesthood, who resort to all manner of exorcism.[35] Here is an example of a formula to be said against demons:

> *Thou art not to come near to my body,*
> *Thou art not to go before me,*
> *Thou art not to follow after me,*
> *Where I stop, thou art not to stop,*
> *Where I am thou art not to sit,*
> *My house thou art not to enter,*
> *My roof thou art not to haunt,*
> *Thou art not to put thy foot in my foot's imprint,*
> *Where I go thou art not to go,*
> *Where I enter thou art not to enter.*[36]

A meticulous ritual complements the work of the formulas: religion links hands with magic, and medicine also is pressed into service. One prescription gives the following singular procedure for treating a headache:

> When the sun returns to his abode, cover thy head with a garment and cover also the wild cucumber that has grown by itself in the desert. Then set around it a ring of flour. Next morning before sunrise, pluck it from its place and take its root. Then take the fleece of a virgin she-goat and tie it on the head of the sick man, tie it to the neck of the sick man, in order that the headache which is in this man's body may be driven forth and be unable to return, like straw scattered afar by the wind. By heaven be thou exorcized! By earth be thou exorcized![37]

One of the most significant of the Babylonian and Assyrian rites is that of substituting an animal for the sick man. In order to deceive the demons the animal is laid out on top of the patient; then the demons will set on the animal, and the man will be rid of them. The prescription governing this rite reads:

> Take a sucking-pig and set it level with the head of the sick man. Tear out its heart and put it over the sick man's heart. Sprinkle the sides of the bed with its blood. Dismember the sucking-pig and lay the parts on the sick man's members. Then purify this man with pure water. . . . Offer the sucking-pig in his place. Let its flesh be as the flesh of the sick man, his blood as the blood of the sick man![38]

The texts relating to magic are impressive by their very quantity. The same may be said of those dealing with divination, which constitutes another sector of religious life, and is served by a separate class of the priesthood.

The most widespread method of divination is based on scrutiny of animal livers. A very large number of clay models of livers have been found, each carefully marked out according to the various parts, and with annotations on the significance of each. But prognostications were drawn from practically everything. Here, for example, are some omens connected with dogs:

> If a dog stops in front of a man: an obstacle will check him.
> If a dog stops at his side: the god's protection will be upon him.
> If a dog lies on his bed: the god's wrath will be against him.
> If a dog lies on his chair: his wife will follow him into disaster . . .
> If a white dog enters a temple: the foundations of the temple will be stable.
> If a black dog enters a temple: the foundations of the temple will not be stable.

If a brown dog enters a temple: prosperity for that temple.

If a yellow dog enters a temple: prosperity for that temple.

If a parti-coloured dog enters a temple: favour of the gods for that temple.[39]

Ants, too, are of significance: when found near a city gate, for instance, by their numbers and the direction of their movements they will indicate the fate of that city.[40] Even from his own sufferings a sick man can deduce what the future holds in store for him:

If the nerve of his left lip hurts him: he will have a good son.

If the nerve of the sole of his left foot hurts him: he will become rich.[41]

And so on: a blister on the forehead indicates danger; one on the right side of the lower lip, poverty; one on the left side of the same lip, riches. There are many hundreds of texts dealing with such matters, which indicates the intense interest shown in this aspect of religious life.

Divination contributed greatly to the success of a science which placed the whole world in debt to the Babylonians: namely, that of astronomy. The position of the stars at the moment of a child's birth, their movements and their conjunctions, even their precise hues were regarded as affording indications of the future, and so were diligently studied. Observatories were established at the top of the temple towers, and their astronomers accurately recorded the courses of the stars, and even predicted eclipses. Together and in association with astronomy went mathematics, providing the means of making measurements and calculations. The Babylonians were able to calculate with all the four arithmetical rules, to raise to powers, extract roots, and solve equations; in geometry they could measure areas and volumes.[42] But all this scientific activity was on a restricted scale, being subordinated to the requirements of religion, of divination; consequently there was no separation between astronomy and astrology:

If the moon occludes Jupiter: a king will die within the year or there will be an eclipse of moon and sun. . . .

If Jupiter appears to enter into the midst of the moon: prices will be low in the land.

If Jupiter emerges from behind the moon: there will be strife in the land. . . .

If Mars is visible in the month of Tammuz: the bed of the warriors will remain empty.

If Mercury lies to the north: there will be corpses; the king of Akkad will invade a foreign country.

If Mars approaches the Twins: a king will die and there will be enmity.[43]

The Babylonians also had an oracular literature connected with divination. The king would consult the oracle before setting out for war, and would regulate his conduct in accordance with the answer. For example, the Assyrian king Esarhaddon is given encouragement in the following message:

Esarhaddon, king of the countries, fear not! . . . I am the great lady, I am Ishtar of Arbela, who has destroyed all thy foes before thee. Which of the words that I have said to thee has not been fulfilled? I am Ishtar of Arbela. I will lie in wait for thy enemies, I will give them into thy hands. I, Ishtar of Arbela, will go before thee and behind thee. Fear not! . . .

Esarhaddon, fear not! I, the god Bel, speak to thee. The beams of thy heart do I strengthen, like thy mother who brought thee into being. The sixty great gods stand with me and protect thee. The god Sin is at thy right hand, the god Shamash at thy left hand. The sixty great gods stand about thee, ranged for battle.[44]

Babylonian and Assyrian ritual practice is extremely rich and very fully documented.[45] The minutely particularized details provided in extensive passages reveal an unmistakable tendency towards formalism, and also the predominant rôle which religious practice plays in everyday life. As we have seen, the priesthood is organized in several distinct categories, which continue and further develop those which existed among the Sumerians. The religious calendar repeats the Sumerian sacred seasons, also with further extensions and developments. New Year's Day is still the central point of the religious year, and the New Year celebration in Babylonia, of which we have a detailed description, exemplifies the nature of the celebrations: for twelve successive days there are purifications of sanctuaries, sacrifices, and prayers; the main features of the ceremonies are the king's homage to the god, the great procession of the statutes, and the prognostication of destinies for the coming year, which the gods determine at this season. The ancient Sumerian conception of order is still the basis of existence: the determination of events in advance is an indispensable condition of life's progress along its due course. But the Babylonian New Year has yet another, ancient significance: the celebration of the resurrection of Marduk is an expression of the primeval cult of the earth's life cycle. Thus, along with the constant accretion of new religious elements, the ancient features persist and acquire new life.

The account of the great Babylonian festivals may give a wrong impression of the religion of which they were a particular expression, for it might suggest a people serene and joyful in the cultivation of their fertile land and the cult of their patron gods. But we must not forget the great quantity of magical and divinatory texts, with their ceaseless and always uncertain effort to foresee and influence the dreaded course of fate, the ills which threaten all existence. We must bear in mind the dismal prospect of a squalid life beyond the tomb, when the soul will wander wearily in search of remembrance. For the Babylonians, like the Sumerians, believe in life after death, but, as with the Sumerians, this belief is not associated with any views on retribution for the good and evil deeds of this life. The abode of the dead is situated beneath the earth and is enveloped in darkness. Its inhabitants drag out a wretched existence, eating dust and drinking dirty water. Only the offerings of the living can sometimes alleviate their condition; and when the living forget them, or, worse still, when they do not bury the dead bodies, the dead wander about restlessly, and return in the form of demons to molest the living.

So the religious life of the Babylonians is fundamentally an extremely gloomy one. There is no guarantee that one can escape from the assaults of evil; no hope that evil will one day be decisively overcome and good will triumph; no belief that good works will be rewarded in another life. Here is the tragedy of a civilization that was yet so massive and powerful. We shall find that tragedy reflected in the themes of a vast and flourishing literature, which ponders again and again on the question to which it finds no answer: What is the meaning of today and the nature of the morrow?

IV The Literary Genres

Babylonian and Assyrian literature[46] covers a wide and rich range of subjects, including discussion of man's fundamental problems and their solution in terms of the predominant religion. So much at least we can say. In respect of the originality of the subject matter, and the discussion and solution of the problems, we find ourselves confronted once more with the old question of Mesopotamian civilization, with the additional factor that the dependence of Babylonian and Assyrian upon Sumerian culture can be especially well evaluated and documented in the field of literature. We shall therefore not be surprised to find the same anonymity, the same imitation of ancient models and consequent diminution of historical perspective,[47] in a word, the same collective and practical art, reflecting the religion and the civil authority.

So we need only traverse the old ground, and, fitting the new material into the old categories, note whenever possible any contribution that may have been made by the Semitic newcomers.

In the field of mythological poetry there is one poem of fundamental importance, since it deals with the creation of the world. It is called *Enuma elish* ('When on High') from its opening words.[48] The account is probably based on Sumerian sources, but it owes its unity to the glorification of Marduk, the god of the first Babylonian dynasty; the original version of the poem must date back to the period of that dynasty, about the beginning of the second millennium B.C. The text, which is very long and is in a good state of preservation, tells of the conflict between primeval chaos personified by the goddess Tiamat, and cosmic order, of which the god Marduk is the incarnation. The struggle between the two forms one of the most authentic and telling epic passages which have survived from Mesopotamian literature:

> *He fashioned a bow, and made it his weapon,*
> *Fitted to it the arrow, and fixed its string.*
> *He lifted the mace, and took it in his right hand,*
> *Bow and quiver he hung at his side.*
> *Lightning he set before him,*
> *With a blazing flame he filled his body.*
> *He made a net to enfold Tiamat;*
> *The four winds he took that nothing of her might*
>   *escape . . .*
> *Tiamat cried out aloud in fury,*
> *Her legs trembled to their roots;*
> *She recited a charm, and cast her spell,*
> *While the gods of battle sharpened their weapons.*
> *They joined issue, Tiamat and the wisest among the gods,*
>   *Marduk;*
> *They went to battle, they drew near for the struggle.*
> *The lord spread out his net to enfold her;*
> *The Evil Wind, which followed behind, he let loose*
>   *before her;*
> *When Tiamat opened her mouth to destroy him,*
> *He sent in the Evil Wind, so that she could not close*
>   *her lips.*
> *The raging winds filled her belly,*
> *Her body was distended and her mouth gaped.*
> *He loosed an arrow, it tore her belly,*
> *Cut through her insides, and split her heart,*
> *And so, having conquered, he slew her.*[49]

The victorious god divides the body of the dead goddess into two: with one part he forms the heavens, with the other the earth. This is an expression and a good example of the mentality of the ancient Orient: the divine person and the cosmic element coincide, the one and the other being animated by the same life, for Tiamat is both goddess and part of the universe.

This establishment of heaven and earth marks the beginning of Marduk's creative activity, which, be it noted, is creation in the Sumerian and Akkadian sense of the word. Hence it is not the production of entirely new matter, but the ordering and bringing about of the transition from chaos to cosmos. This concept pervades all the rest of the narrative, which continues with a description of the origin of the stars:

> He constructed stations for the great gods,
> Fixing their astral likenesses as constellations.
> He determined the year by designating its zones;
> He set up three constellations for each of the twelve
>   months.
> After defining the days of the year with celestial
>   figures,
> He founded the station of Nebiru[50] to determine their
>   zones,
> That none might go too far or fall short.
> Alongside it he set up the stations of Enlil and Ea.
> He opened up gates on both sides,
> And set on them strong bolts to left and to right.[51]

So creation is a work of forming and ordering. From the stars the story turns to plants and animals (or so it would seem, for at this point the text is mutilated) and finally to man. The task assigned to man, the very reason for his creation, is explicitly stated and of great significance: he is to serve the gods. The poem closes with the triumph of the all-conquering Marduk, whom the other gods exalt to the head of the celestial hierarchy. Thus the Babylonian dynasty grafts the glorification of its own god on to the traditional story. But there is more to be said than this: the conflict between chaos and cosmos is only another aspect of the annual cycle of the universe, which causes nature to flower anew after being overthrown by the storms of winter. Thus the ancient Oriental myth finds new expression, being revived and understood as

actual reality. With the recital of this poem every New Year
the Babylonians express their faith in the renewal of Nature;
life will succeed death, and order, synonymous with existence,
will follow chaos, synonymous with non-existence.

Passing from one pole of the god-mythology to the other,
from legends concerning the beginning of things to those concerned with the farther side of the grave, we find in Akkadian
form a poem already discussed, the descent of Inanna (now
Ishtar) to the underworld.[52] We do not need to dwell further
on this subject, beyond mentioning it as an example of the
characteristic reformulation of ancient themes which we have
already discussed. Instead, we shall consider another underworld myth, so far known only in Semitic, though a Sumerian
prototype may yet come to light: we refer to the myth of
Nergal and Ereshkigal.[53] This latter deity has already appeared in Sumerian mythology as the goddess of the underworld. The poem relates that Ereshkigal, being prevented by
her duties from attending a banquet of the gods, is invited
to send one of her ministers as her representative. She does
so, and at the same time bids him bring down to the underworld any god who does not rise in homage on his arrival.
The god Nergal refuses to rise, and so he is carried down to
the underworld; but when he arrives there he attacks and
overcomes the guardians, then turns on the goddess herself:

> Inside the house he seized Ereshkigal,
> By her hair he brought her down from the throne
> To the ground, to cut off her head.
> 'Slay me not, O my brother! Let me speak a word to
>   thee!'
> When Nergal heard this, he set her free.
> She wept and abased herself:
> 'Be thou my husband and I will be thy wife!
> I will let thee hold dominion over the vast Underworld.
> I will place the tablet of wisdom in thy hand.
> Thou shalt be the master, I will be the mistress.'
> When Nergal heard these her words,
> He took her and kissed her, wiping away her tears:
> 'All that thou hast for months desired of me
> Shall now come to be.'[54]

The myth seems intended to justify Nergal's assumption of lordship over the underworld. Nothing could be more natural: there is here a procedure common to all the ancient world.

Among the poems concerned with the heroes, we find Gilgamesh once more in the centre of things: but now he is in Semitic garb. And there is a connection between the various episodes, and a general coherence, which are lacking in the Sumerian sources. And, of course, there are elements which at present at least would appear to be new in the story.[55]

Gilgamesh, the hero who has seen everything, and who knows the secret of wisdom, passes from feat to feat. The goddess Ishtar herself is filled with admiration for him and proposes to take him as her lover. The dialogue which ensues embodies a literary theme which we shall find in other Oriental mythologies, namely, an offer to a man to raise him to the level of the gods, and the man's refusal because of his knowledge that this is impossible, and that the attempt can only lead to misery:

> 'Come, Gilgamesh, be thou my lover!
> Grant me the gift of thy love.
> Be thou my husband and I will be thy wife.
> I will harness for thee a chariot adorned with lapis-lazuli
>   and gold,
> With golden wheels and with horns of precious stone.
> Thou shalt harness to it storm-demons for horses,
> Amid the fragrance of cedars shalt thou enter our house!
> And when thou enterest our house,
> The threshold and the dais shall kiss thy feet.
> Before thee shall bow down kings, governors and princes,
> The produce of mountain and of plain shall they bring
>   thee as tribute.'[56]

The goddess details the prospect of happiness that is opened to the hero; but he is well aware of the other side of the picture: Ishtar is fickle and will soon abandon him. So he replies:

> 'But what must I give thee, if I take thee in marriage?
> Am I to give thee oil and garments for thy body,

Bread and victuals,
Food for thy godhead,
Drink for thy queenship?
What do I gain from marriage with thee?
Thou art a brazier that goes out in the cold,
A door that withstands not the wind and the storm,
A palace which collapses upon heroes . . .
Whom of thy lovers hast thou loved for ever?
Who of thy swains has been pleasing to thee always?
Come, I will tell thee the tale of thy lovers . . .
Thou didst love a lion, marvellous in strength,
And didst dig for him seven pits and yet seven.
Thou didst love a stallion, splendid in battle,
And didst ordain for him whip, spur and lash;
Seven leagues didst thou bid him run . . .
Thou didst love the shepherd of the flock
Who ever gathered fuel for thee
And daily slaughtered kids for thee;
Thou didst smite him and turn him to a wolf;
His own sons now hunt him down,
His own dogs snap at his legs . . .
If thou lovest me, thou wilt treat me like them.'[57]

The hero's tragedy is that he cannot escape death. In all his feats he is haunted and troubled by this knowledge. We have already seen that this theme dominates the Sumerian text of the poem; now we find it in the Semitic text, expressed in striking verses of remarkable artistic quality:

Gilgamesh, whither rovest thou?
The life thou pursuest thou shalt not find.
When the gods created mankind,
For man they set aside death,
Life they retained in their own hands.
O Gilgamesh, fill thy belly,
Make merry by day and by night,
Of each day make a feast of rejoicing,
Day and night dance thou and play;
Let thy garments be sparkling fresh,
Thy head be washed; bathe thou in water;

> *Pay heed to the little one that holds thy hand,*
> *Let thy spouse delight in thy bosom:*
> *For this is the task of mankind.*[58]

And again:

> *Do we build houses for ever?*
> *Do we seal contracts for ever?*
> *Do brothers share out the inheritance for ever?*
> *Does hatred persist for ever in the land?*
> *Does the river rise and flood for ever? . . .*
> *How alike are the sleeper and the dead,*
> *Do they not compose a picture of death,*
> *The commoner and the noble,*
> *When they are near to their fate?*[59]

The elevated tone of this expression of human misery gives the poem of Gilgamesh a vitality which we could regard as almost modern, and places it in the foremost rank of Babylonia's and Assyria's rich and ample literature.

Besides the poems concerned with myths of the gods and heroes there is a flourishing lyric poetry,[60] which is completely dominated by religious themes. As with the Sumerians, hymns to gods and sovereigns are predominant. A hymn to the sun-god Shamash reads:

> *O Shamash, king of heaven and earth,*
> *Who orderest all things high and low,*
> *Shamash, the wakening of the dead to life*
> *And the freeing of the captive is in thy hand.*
> *Incorruptible judge,*
> *Who orderest mankind,*
> *Exalted scion*
> *Of the Lord Namrassit,*
> *Most mighty and noble son,*
> *Light of the lands,*
> *Maker of all that is in heaven and on the earth,*
> *Thou art, Shamash.*[61]

In addition to hymns, there are penitential psalms and simple prayers; these do not constitute a distinct literary genre, but are expressions of the fundamentally unitary religious life. We may quote a fine evening prayer. A ritual act, a sacrifice, is in progress. There is silence. The great gods of the day are asleep. To the stars shining in the heavens ascends the invocation:

> *They are lying down, the great ones;*
> *The bolts are fallen, the fastenings are placed;*
> *The noisy crowds are quiet,*
> *The open gates are closed.*
> *The gods and the goddesses of the land,*
> *Shamash, Sin, Adad and Ishtar,*
> *Have betaken themselves to sleep in heaven.*
> *They are not pronouncing judgement,*
> *They are not deciding disputes.*
> *Veiled is the night.*
> *The palace and the fields are quiet and dark . . .*
> *The great gods, the gods of the night . . .*
> *Stand by . . .*
> *In the divination which I am performing,*
> *In the lamb which I am offering,*
> *May the truth be revealed to me.*[62]

The didactic and wisdom literature reproduces the forms which we found among the Sumerians.[63] Some of the proverbs are especially pointed:[64]

'My cistern is not dry, so I am not very thirsty' — which means that we do not fully appreciate the value of a thing till we are deprived of it.

'The net is loosened, but the fetters were not remiss.' This seems to correspond to 'Out of the frying-pan into the fire'.

'If I myself had not gone, who would have gone at my side?' Compare our 'If you want a thing done properly, do it yourself'.

'He consecrated the house before starting it.' As we would put it, 'He counted his chickens before they were hatched'.

'You go and take the enemy's field, the enemy comes and takes your field' — a reflection on the futility of war.

Wise counsels are not lacking:

> *As a wise man, let your understanding shine modestly,*
> *Let your mouth be restrained, guarded your speech.*
> *Like a man's wealth, let your lips be precious.*
> *Let affront and hostility be an abomination to you.*
> *Speak nothing impertinent, give no unreliable*
>   *advice ...*
> *Unto your opponent do no evil,*
> *Your evildoer recompense with good,*
> *Render justice to your enemy ...*
> *Pay homage daily to your god,*
> *With sacrifice, prayer, and offerings of incense ...*
> *Reverence produces wellbeing,*
> *Sacrifice prolongs life,*
> *Prayer expiates sin.*[65]

We turn now to the fables, the dialogues between animals, which revive the ancient Sumerian genre. Here, too, as in the case of the Sumerian fables, our material is sparse and fragmentary, but not so much so that we are unable to quote any example. Here is the charming story of the ox and the horse.[66] It opens with a cheerful picture of spring:

> *The fenlands are in bloom, the fields are green,*
> *The uplands are drenched, the dykes are watered;*
> *Ravine and slope carry down the mountain-torrents*
> *That rush into the dykes, watering the fields.*
> *The soil, without cultivation, becomes a plantation,*
> *The grass grows in wood and in meadow,*
> *The bountiful womb of the earth is opened,*
> *Giving plenteous food for cattle and abundance for the*
>   *homes of men.*
> *An ox and a horse struck up a friendship.*
> *The rich pasture had sated their bellies,*
> *And glad of heart they lay resting.*
> *The ox opened his mouth to speak, and said to the horse,*
>   *glorious in battle:*
> *'I seem to have been born under a lucky star:*
> *From beginning to end of the year I find food;*

I have fodder in abundance and spring water in
*　　profusion . . .*
Change thy way of life and come away with me!'

But the horse has no liking for a comfortable life:

'*Strong brass to cover my body*
Have they put upon me, and I wear it as a garment.
Without me, the fiery steed,
Nor king nor prince nor lord nor noble fares upon his
*　　way . . .*
The horse is like a god, stately of step,
Whilst thou and the calves wear the cap of servitude.'

The dialogue continues in this vein of argument and counterargument, but we can follow its course only to a very limited extent, for the text is mutilated. We do not know the outcome, whether the ox or the horse had the better of the debate. The significant factor is that the poem is a moral fable, opposing the peaceful to the warlike life, the modest tranquillity of the labourer to the perilous glory of the warrior. Later on this literary form is represented by Aesop in Greek, and we are thoroughly justified in suspecting that he had Oriental inspiration, though the paucity and fragmentary state of our material make it impossible to investigate the question thoroughly at present.

In the field of wisdom literature we meet again with the theme of the sufferings of the righteous,[67] which we have already noted in Sumerian literature. Now it acquires Akkadian dress. Here is the lamentation of the Mesopotamian Job:

I have now reached the borne of life and have passed
*　　beyond it;*
I look about me: evil upon evil!
My affliction grows, I cannot find justice . . .
Yet I thought only of prayer and supplication,
Invocation was my care, sacrifice my rule;
The day of the worship of the gods was my delight,
The day of my goddess's procession was my profit and
*　　my wealth;*

The veneration of the king was my joy,
Music for him my pleasure.[68]

After stating the problem, the poem attempts its solution. Why is it that the righteous man suffers? To begin with, a reservation of principle has to be made: how is one to judge whether a thing is good or evil? Man is a fragile and mutable creature:

What is good in a man's sight is evil for a god,
What is evil to a man's mind is good for his god.
Who can comprehend the counsel of the gods in heaven?
The plan of a god is deep waters, who can fathom it?
Where has befuddled mankind ever learned what is a
*   god's conduct?*
He who was alive yesterday is dead today;
In an instant he was darkened, in a moment he was
*   crushed.*
One moment he is singing a happy song,
In a moment he will wail like a mourner.
Like day and night their mood changes.
When they are hungry they are like corpses,
When they are sated they rival their god;
In good fortune they talk of mounting to heaven,
When they are afflicted they grumble about going down
*   to the underworld.*[69]

As compared with the Sumerian treatment of the subject, this agnostic approach is a new feature, at least so far as our present knowledge allows us to judge. The conclusion, however, is the ancient one: the gods will draw out the suffering righteous man from the depths of his misfortunes, he will be restored to life from the grave, and will be liberated from destruction.

But even this last hope cannot be said to be constant. In a magnificent dialogue on the miseries of the human state a master and his slave discuss the pros and contras of life.[70] The master formulates a proposition, and the slave commends it for its good points; then the master rejects the idea, and the slave condemns it for its bad points. The conclusion is that there is no ground for any certain judgement on this earth:

'Servant, hear me!'

'Yes, my lord, yes!'

'A woman will I love.'

'Yes, love, my lord, love. The man who loves a woman forgets pain and trouble.'

'No, servant, a woman I will not love.'

'No, do not love, my lord, do not love: woman is a well, woman is an iron dagger, a sharp one, that cuts a man's neck.'

'Servant, hear me!'

'Yes, my lord, yes!'

'I will do something for the good of my country.'

'Yes, do, my lord, do: the man who does something for the good of his country, his good deed is placed in the bowl of Marduk.'

'No, servant, I will not do something for the good of my country.'

'No, do it not, my lord, do it not: climb the mounds of ancient ruins and walk about them; look at the skulls of late and early men: which of them was wicked, and which a public benefactor?'

And so the dialogue continues, demonstrating the futility of all human activity, until the dramatic conclusion is reached:

'What then is good? To break my neck and yours, to cast the pair of us into the river, that is good!'

But no, there is a doubt about even this proposition. The master once more changes his mind: first he will kill the slave, will send him on ahead. At this point the slave turns the lesson of the dialogue to his own account. He is to die first? Well and good. But if there is no point in life, if everything is vanity, why wait at all?

'Then would my lord wish to live even three days after me?'

These verses express the speech of a society in decline. After so much creation and construction, it has come to know doubt, discouragement, crisis.

The poetic literature has an abundance of prose writings as its complement. These consist above all of historical texts, especially annals, such as we have already mentioned. In addition there are records and reports and commemorative stelae; texts dealing with linguistic subjects, from lists of signs to vocabularies; scientific writings, especially on mathematics and astronomy. By far the most numerous group of all consists of letters, texts relating to economics, and juridical documents, all of which afford an insight into the outlook and structure of Babylonian and Assyrian society.

We cannot deal with all this material, but we must discuss the legal writings, if only summarily and by way of example. They illustrate one of the most typical forms of Mesopotamian thought, one which permeates every branch of life.[71] In this field the situation is diametrically contrary to that in Egypt: the Egyptians have no code of laws; but in Mesopotamia everything is law, in both public and private life, and religious law at that, for the omission to perform a rite is placed on the same level as the commission of theft or murder, in accordance with that unity of religious faith which is characteristic of Mesopotamian thought and action.

This can be exemplified by reference to the Hammurabi Code.[72] As we now know, this code is not the only, nor the oldest one in Mesopotamia, and we can no longer count on its originality; but it still remains the most complete and organic synthesis of law that we possess, and therefore it most fully documents its epoch and environment.

In its literary form, the Code follows the scheme of Sumerian times: prologue, laws, epilogue. The laws still have that analytic, piecemeal quality characteristic of the Sumerians; we find enunciated not general principles, but individual cases with their appropriate solutions. But considerable differences are to be noted in the content of the laws. Those relating to persons reveal a society divided into three classes, which approximate to the conceptions embodied in the modern terms: patricians, plebeians, and slaves. Patricians and slaves correspond to the two classes already found among the Sumerians, but the concept of plebeians is new, in that the distinctive feature of their state is no longer dependence upon the palace, as in the case of the 'partly free' Sumerians, but a different legal status:

> If a patrician put out another's eye, his eye shall be put out. If he break another's bone, his bone shall be broken. If he put out the eye or break the bone of a plebeian, he shall pay a mina of silver.[73]

The law relating to the family treats the father as its head. Marriage is preceded by a betrothal gift from the bridegroom to the bride, the so-called 'acquisition price', something of which there is no evidence in Sumerian law. A further innovation, or, at least, something that cannot be traced back to Sumerian times, is the written contract:

> 'If a patrician has taken a wife, but has not made a contract with her, that woman is not his wife.'[74]

Polygamy is permitted, whereas Sumerian marriage was monogamic. Divorce is granted for an adequate reason. For example:

> If a patrician has been taken prisoner and there is not sufficient in his house to live on, his wife may enter the house of another; that woman shall incur no blame at all.[75]

The law of inheritance is based on legitimate succession. The inheritance is divided between the male heirs, and daughters have no rights except when there are no sons; but they do have the right to share in usufruct, and to a dowry. Wills are not made, but their place is often taken by contracts of adoption.

Property rights are highly developed and organized, as one would expect in an evolved sedentary society. There are deeds of sale and purchase, hire and lease, commercial partnerships, loans on interest, and so on.

The penal law is dominated, so far as patricians are concerned, by the law of retaliation. We have already noted the application of this law: an eye for an eye, a tooth for a tooth; and we have observed that the most recent discoveries lead us to regard this law as of Semitic introduction; at any rate, it is unknown to the more ancient Sumerian legal provisions, which explicitly stipulate the payment of damages. An interesting feature of the Hammurabi Code is the punishment inflicted on medical practitioners for any ill consequences arising from their operations:

> If a surgeon has operated on a patrician with a bronze knife, and has killed him . . . his hands shall be cut off.[76]

The penalty prescribed for negligence in an architect is more in line with our own legal conception:

> If a builder has constructed a house for anyone and has not made his work solid, so that a wall has fallen down, that builder shall repair the wall at his own cost.[77]

Judicial proceedings take place before judges, to whom the litigants apply when they cannot reach a private solution of their dispute. Thus the law is subjective, not objective: if there is no private plaintiff there is no trial. During the hearing, both documentary and oral evidence is admissible. In the absence of evidence, recourse is made to trial by ordeal, the river test, already known to the Sumerians: the accused plunges into the water; if he survives, he is acquitted; if he succumbs, he is adjudged guilty:

> If a patrician accuses another of sorcery, but has no proofs, the accused man shall go to the river and plunge into it. If the river bears him away, the accuser shall take possession of his house. If the river shows him to be innocent and he comes forth safe, the accuser shall be slain, and the other shall take his house.[78]

The Hammurabi Code is only a stage in the juridical tradition of Mesopotamia, but it is a particularly significant one. In the Babylonia of the great kings, under the aegis of a prosperous and powerful state, literature, art, and economic and social organization flourish as never before; and, as never before, the Sumerian heritage and the Semitic contribution achieve a harmonious synthesis. For this reason, the times of Hammurabi constitute the acme of Babylonian and Assyrian

civilization; and the great king, warrior and diplomat, builder
of temples and digger of canals, personifies this civilization
better than any other.

V *The Artistic Types*

On the Sumerian foundation the Babylonians and Assyrians
give life to an art[79] which faithfully preserves the outlook and
general characteristics of the older tradition. But the longer
period of development and the wider geographical extension
allow of the rise of notable independent elements in the
practical realization of the various forms of art; and these
elements can be ranged along a line of historical development,
at least to some extent. This applies, in fact, not so much to
the major arts (a point we have already noted in regard to the
Sumerians) as to the minor ones, which reveal a definite process of change in their subjects. Moreover, we can establish a
chronology of type succession, in so far as definite artistic
types come into being and are established in definitely determined periods.

Area also affects these distinctions. Babylonia and Assyria,
the two regions of the Mesopotamian bloc, are clearly enough
distinct in the characteristics of their respective art. Assyrian
culture is of more recent origin, and its relationship to Babylonian can be formulated in terms singularly akin to those we
found to apply to relations between the Babylonians and
Sumerians: a coarser and inferior culture takes a superior
culture as its model, thoroughly assimilates its elements, making them its own, and reproduces and develops them within
the framework of its own natural conditions and historical
environment. Once more the comparison with Greece and
Rome is valid.

Thus, in the earliest Assyrian period, there is a substantially
undifferentiated imitation of Babylonian models. Later, with
the beginning of the imperial phase, local peculiarities come
gradually into prominence. Some are of a material nature,
such as the possibility of using columns as functional elements
in architectural construction, arising from the existence of

supplies of stone; some are of a thematic nature, such as the prevalence of martial scenes; and some are conceptual, such as the greater alienation of the human from the divine, observed in the absence of representations of deities, or in their reduction to symbols. The history of Assyrian art still has to be written, but the foregoing observations, together with others that will be made as we proceed with our study, sufficiently indicate that such a history, with its elements of an independent cultural cycle, can certainly be written.

In the architectural field the construction of temples and temple towers continues as before, and the latter even add to the number of their storeys and their colours; but from the thematic aspect the type of building which is given the greatest impetus, and which wherever present becomes the determining and characteristic feature of the great cities, is the royal palace. Developing the Sumerian layout still further, the palace multiplies its courtyards and the surrounding chambers, and these chambers accommodate not only the sovereign and his household, but a host of officials, scribes, servants, and priests.

This last category is the most significant of all, primarily because of the indubitable fact that some of the palace chambers were used as sanctuaries. Thus there is a progressive shift in the centre of gravity of society: originally it was the temple with its sacred precincts; now it is the palace, of which the sanctuaries have come to form a part.

All the great kings of Assyria have palaces of the type just indicated in their capitals, and we do not need to refer to a late age to find them. Already at the beginning of the second millennium B.C. Mari had a palace with rooms and courtyards numbering altogether more than two hundred and sixty, grouped within an area of over six acres (Fig. 2).[80] Mari goes back to the initial phase of Semitic civilization in Mesopotamia: in this sector will further evacuations bring Sumerian models also to light, showing the same degree of development which we have just noted among the Semites?

One characteristic feature of architecture in Assyria, though it is developed only to a very limited extent, is the structural use of columns, which we have already mentioned. Stone was much more abundant in northern Mesopotamia than in the south, and this factor is responsible for its greater employment and for the architectural forms associated with it. In general the columns are arranged to support an open forecourt; the Assyrians called this type of building *bit khilani*. Can this feature be regarded as original? Probably not; we shall see later that its provenance may be attributed to other peoples. This kind of situation is not infrequent in Assyrian civilization: its own is not new, and the new is not its own.

Babylonian and Assyrian statuary reproduces the static,

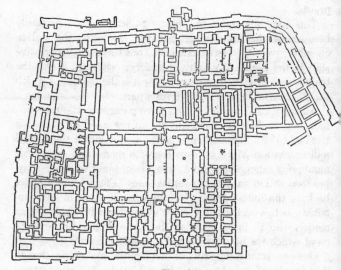

Fig. 2

solemn, almost impersonal figures of god and kings and officials which we found in Sumerian art; their reduced numbers and proportions indicate that it is not extensively resorted to as an art form. But the Mari excavations have modified this view to some extent by uncovering an abundance of statues. As an example of these we select that of the overseer Ebih-Il (Pl. X), which clearly shows the persistence of characteristic Sumerian features during the earlier phase of Semitic art in Mesopotamia. At the other extreme of Akkadian civilization, towards its close, the continuity of tradition is revealed in the finest of the Assyrian statues, that of Ashurnasirpal II: traces of development can be discerned in the proportions of the parts, but the general characteristics remain unchanged.

On the other hand, there was a great development in animal statuary. The great realism of non-human as compared with human figures was continued, but a new type of monument developed and grew common especially in Assyria. This is the orthostat, which consists of a statue inserted into the wall flanking the great entrance gate of a palace, and so combining features both of statuary and of relief carving. The orthostat also has its distinctive range of subjects: lions, bulls, and especially fantastic winged bulls with human heads. This is the predominant type found in the great gateways, and in the grandeur of its form it combines a realistic care for details with unreality in the composition as a whole (Pl. XI). Unquestionably this figure has a religious significance, as guardian of the entrance; and so, as always in Mesopotamia, religion constructs and asserts a higher reality.

However, the triumph of Babylonian and Assyrian art, the form in which it reaches its fullest and highest development, is relief carving. The Sumerians also showed some preference for this type of art, but it became the predominant form among the Babylonians and Assyrians; new kinds were added to the older ones, and were developed to the height of artistic perfection.

Commemorative stelae continue in use. Some of them are of importance to the history of art, for example that of the Akkadian king Naram-Sin, in the third millennium B.C.; this presents the human figure with a vivacity and sense of movement which were quite unknown to the Sumerians. A variant form of the stele is the obelisk, which in Assyria becomes an established form. It achieves its finest expression in the famous black obelisk of Shalmaneser III, whose four faces are carved with reliefs and inscriptions illustrating the king's military expeditions.

The use of seals also continues. Their fine workmanship and choice of subjects enable us not only to trace in detail the history of this type of art but to formulate elements of comparison for a fuller history of the art to which it belongs. We cannot here undertake an examination of individual features of style or theme, but it is important to note the specific and fundamental function which they fulfil.[81]

One type of relief which is not found among the Babylonians and Assyrians, and which may therefore be classified as Sumerian, is the perforated plaque. On the other hand, a new type comes into existence and is established in Assyria, exceeding all others in its extensive application and artistic importance; this type is peculiar to an epoch, to a region, and even to a distinctive mentality, and so can be individualized with great precision: we refer to mural decoration.

The walls thus decorated are those of the rooms in the great palaces. Here the sovereign's exploits, in particular those of war and the chase, are illustrated in bas-relief on a continuous series of stone plaques. An impressive quantity of these reliefs has survived, and this fact, together with their distinctive feature of continuity, indicates that they performed not merely a decorative but also a documentary function. It would seem that these mural reliefs are to be regarded as the counterpart in art of the annals in literature; to both contemporaries and posterity each form bears extensive testimony to the king's activities. These activities, be it noted, are no longer in the tradition of the Sumerian and also the Babylonian rulers: the peaceful builder of temples has been succeeded by the warrior; and combat, previously regarded as a necessary evil, has now become a subject of boasting and enjoyment, even forming the favourite sport of the monarch's leisure hours.

As we have said, the main subjects depicted in these reliefs are battle and hunting scenes, though other themes are found, such as banquets and sacrifices. The scenes go so far as to represent crowds of figures, intricately juxtaposed and superposed, and as there is no sense of perspective the impression of confusion is intensified. Of the human and animal figures, the former are still undoubtedly the stiffer, after the Mesopotamian tradition, but the animal figures have a remarkable naturalness and effectiveness. The most perfect examples of this type of art are the hunting scenes from Ashurbanipal's palace (Pl. XII). A series of pictures depicts the life of wild boars, of birds among reeds, fish and crabs in water, and wild beasts in the fields. The king, on horseback and armed with bow and arrows, gallops with his attendants in pursuit of lions, antelopes, and wild asses. Transfixed by arrows, the beasts drop down dead. In these reliefs, harmony of composition is at least successfully combined with a high degree of subjectivism in the details. Every figure lives its own intense life. The sculptor, like all great artists, has transcended the bounds of his own time.

Other subjects are also found in Assyrian mural reliefs: the winged bull with human head, now reproduced on the walls instead of serving as an orthostat at the gate; the very ancient theme of the hero overcoming wild animals, a significant example of the conservative force of tradition; and, also based on ancient models, but with new elements, the cult of the sacred tree which is the source of life, performed by winged genii with eagle heads. The religious significance of this last subject is associated with the general conception of renascent fertility which has its fullest expression in the Babylonian literature.

A distinctive feature of the representation of the sacred tree is an accentuated stylization, and this merits our attention because it reappears in various forms but with unfailing constancy all through the art of relief sculpture. It has been said that Mesopotamian art is dominated by style, and that even the strongest claims of reality are powerless against it. We have seen that this is true of the statuary; but the same phenomenon recurs in the reliefs. Typical examples are the small whorls which symbolize water, or the pile of three stones which stands for a mountain. These are traditional motifs, and the artist makes no attempt to free himself from them, any more than he escapes from that combination of fantasy and reality which for his milieu is simply the most authentic reality.

The Assyrian type of mural relief has a counterpart, equally circumscribed in area and time, in the Babylonia of the last, Chaldaean dynasty:[82] the coloured relief in enamelled brick (Pl. XIII). But by its very nature, this type of relief is more suitable for exterior decoration: in Babylonia it adorns the gates and streets. Moreover, its function is purely decorative, and so, instead of scenes with several figures, we find the figure of some animal — a lion or bull or fantastic dragon — repeated at regular intervals and surrounded by a geometrical design as border. Against the blue brick ground the animals, and the borders too, stand out in white or yellow or red. This is a refined and elegant form of art, an excellent example of the final splendours of Mesopotamian civilization.

Thus painting makes its appearance as an accessory to relief; but it also has an independent existence, though the perishable nature of its materials has left us very scanty documentation, insufficient to enable us to obtain any general idea of the style or the subjects. However, Babylonian and Assyrian painting is better documented than the Sumerian, and certain tentative conclusions can be drawn. In general, painting appears to have been used to decorate the walls of the rooms in the great palaces, and then it has a similar function to the reliefs. The motifs also must have been analogous. The best preserved specimen found so far (though it is by no means perfect) comes from Mari: it is a large painting portraying the investiture of the sovereign (Pl. XIV). At least, this is the most probable interpretation: the king, standing, is receiving the insignia of rulership from the hands of the goddess Ishtar; the scene has a fantastic setting of palms, winged beasts, and overflowing vases, the symbols of fertility.

Finally, the minor arts also flourish exceedingly; there are statuettes and reliefs in metal, such as those on the great memorial gates of the Assyrian king Shalmaneser III, which reproduce the themes of the mural reliefs in a different material; there are jewels and ornaments of the finest workmanship; there are ivories, carved and engraved: a form of art found in the Sumerian period, but now brought to its greatest perfection by the Assyrians. A rich collection of ivories discovered at Nimrud[83] may serve as our example: it includes remarkably vivid reliefs of female figures, such as the 'lady at the window' (Pl. XV) or the face whose pleasant and mysterious smile has earned it the name 'Mona Lisa'; and also animal figures of remarkable realism and precision, of which a good example is an inlay of ivory, gold, lapis-lazuli and cornelian, representing a lion slaying a negro in a field of lotus blossoms.

Thus, on the eve of the final political crisis, an artistic production imposing by its extent and intrinsic value achieves its consummation. By their fertile union Akkadians and Sumerians, linked together in three thousand years of history, bring to birth one of the greatest cultures mankind has known. Aided by favourable geographical conditions permitting a prosperous and organized economic life, bound together by the peaceable conjunction of peoples of different origin and stock, and nourished by a political power which reaches constantly beyond its frontiers, Mesopotamian culture flourishes impressively in the forms of faith and worship, of letters and law, of science and art. All these are held in equilibrium and harmony by the all embracing unity of religious belief. The vital presence of subjectivity in culture has not yet arrived, and philosophic, scientific, and aesthetic thinking have not achieved existence independent of one another; but this culture is marked by a profound and greater cohesion, such as few future civilizations will be capable of creating.

4

THE EGYPTIANS

I *Oasis Civilization*

Hail to Thee, O Nile, that gushest forth from the earth
and comest to nourish Egypt![1]

These are the opening words of an ancient Egyptian
hymn, and they may be said to epitomize the essence of an
entire history and culture.[2] For, as Herodotus so expressively
puts it (and even if the expression is hackneyed it has not
ceased to be felicitous), Egypt is a gift of the Nile. This river,
which comes down from the mountains of Ethiopia, cuts its
way through many hundreds of miles of African sands, until
it reaches the Mediterranean. Thanks to its water, life flourishes on both its banks.

This is the 'Black Land', as the Egyptians called it: the
river's periodical floods, disciplined by ceaseless human labour,
endow it with an agricultural wealth that has become pro-
verbial: as many as three harvests a year. But all this applies
only so far as the waters reach: beyond that mark lies the
'Red Land', an arid waste of sand.

Egyptian civilization has with justice been likened to that
of an oasis: an immense oasis, far longer than it is broad,
enclosed and protected by the desert. Its history unfolds
autonomously and organically, and its inhabitants remain
substantially one and unchanged. In this oasis we witness the
flowering of the longest cultural period in human history:
three thousand years in history, following an incalculable

period of pre-history; a continuous cultural tradition uninterrupted by the changes and stratifications that are characteristic of the other civilizations of the ancient Orient.

Perhaps that is why ancient Egypt represents a human
experience more serene, more joyful, and more vivacious than
any other that we have had or will have occasion to study
in this survey. After the world of the Mesopotamian civilizations, with their gloomy solemnity, we cannot but be conscious of a great change of climate. Not that anything is
definitely subtracted or added: yet everything is coloured by
a sense of freedom from fear, a positive and confident outlook
upon life.

One of the most penetrating of modern Egyptologists, J. A.
Wilson, has admirably comprehended and summarized certain aspects of this human experience:

> An element in the Egyptian psychology which we have
> stressed was confidence, a sense of assurance and of spe-
> cial election, which promoted individual assertiveness, a
> relish of life as it was, and a tolerance for divergences
> from the most rigid application of the norm. The Egyp-
> tian was never introspective and was never rigidly de-
> manding of himself or of others, because he was free
> from fear. As yet he had been the architect of his own
> destiny, had achieved a proud, rich, and successful cul-
> ture, and had survived one period of inner turmoil with
> a return to the full, round life. This feeling of security
> and of unimpaired destiny may have been the product of
> geographical isolation; it may have had its roots in the
> fertile black soil; it may have been warmed by the good
> African sun; it may have been intensified by the contrast
> of the harsh and meagre life in the deserts that bordered
> Egypt. Or its origins may be too subtle for us moderns to
> penetrate. Yet it was there, and it gave to Egyptian civili-
> zation its characteristic cheerful urbanity. The dogmatic
> expression of this special providence was the belief that
> Egypt alone was ruled by a god, that the physical child
> of the sun-god would govern and protect Egypt through-
> out eternity. What was there then to fear?[3]

What attitude does this conception of life connote in the presence of death? This is a crucial question, and it is around it that the difference between Egyptian and Mesopotamian ways of thinking shows up most clearly, even to the point of contrast. At the centre of Egyptian thought is the belief that beyond the tomb the forms of our present existence are renewed in more perfect forms. Recall for a moment the picture which Mesopotamia has presented of its dead as wretched eaters of dust and drinkers of dirty water, abandoned and restless spirits haunting living men; then consider the Egyptian picture, painted for us by the artists who decorated the ancient tombs. We see the dead man seated among his intimates, surrounded by servants and friends. His toilet is being attended to by the manicurists and pedicurists. His wife and he play games similar to our draughts. Musicians and dancing girls minister to his pleasure. In other scenes he is fishing from a canoe, or hunting antelopes or gazelles with his bow. The round of everyday life continues in the villages and fields: peasants sow and reap, craftsmen manufacture their wares, artists carve statues or engrave jewels. Nor is a note of comedy lacking from these tomb-pictures: while a herdsman's attention is distracted a thief stealthily leads away one of his cows; a monkey is swiftly seizing the servant's hand extended towards a basket of figs; elsewhere a crocodile is patiently waiting for the birth of a baby hippopotamus in order to make a meal of it.[4] So in scene after scene the ancient Egyptian projects beyond the tomb the gay and prosperous life of his own world.

II   *The Historical Outlines*

Throughout all its lengthy course ancient Egyptian history[5] reveals the simultaneous existence of two opposing tendencies: a disruptive one, which can be attributed to the country's extreme length, and a centralizing one, arising from the single river, the conditions it creates, and the organization enforced by its presence.

So far as we can establish, the most ancient phase of Egyp-

tian history is marked by a movement away from differentiation and towards unity. Before the emergence of written
documents the region is divided into agricultural districts; and
these will exercise a constant influence on subsequent events,
they will constitute a recurrent element actively making for
local autonomy. But these districts manifest a tendency to
organize into confederate groups. Thus, about 3000 B.C., on
the threshold of history, we find two such confederations, two
antagonistic kingdoms: one in the north, covering the enormous delta which divides the Nile waters before they reach
the sea; the other in the south, comprising the long, narrow
strip of land bounding the river course as far as the first
cataract. This division, also, is fundamental in Egyptian history, and will remain one of its decisive factors. For the two
regions have differing geographical and historical conditions:
the north, turned towards the Mediterranean, is open to intercourse and interchange with the other great cultures that lie
around the sea; the south, facing the African continent, is
more enclosed within it and drawn into its civilization.

Moreover, when the monarchy is unified, the distinction
between the two kingdoms does not remain simply as an
intrinsic condition of history; it also persists in the consciousness of the people and in the external trappings of sovereignty.
The royal crown is a combination of the red crown of the
north and the white one of the south; and the Pharaoh's official title is 'King of Upper and Lower Egypt'.[6]

This title deserves consideration for yet another reason. It
persists throughout Egyptian history, even in the time of the
country's greatest expansion, and thus provides a significant
contrast to the Mesopotamian title of 'King of the four
quarters of the earth'; it points to and symbolizes the difference between a policy of definite assertion of universal monarchy and one which aims rather at strengthening and securing
the frontiers. This is to be understood, of course, in the sense
which includes supremacy over surrounding countries, though
in terms of overlordship rather than domination and total annexation. In this different outlook we have the key to the
policy which Egypt pursues all through her long history.

It is usual to distinguish three great periods of Egyptian history: the Old, the Middle, and the New Kingdom. This is not a purely formal distinction, since the three kingdoms correspond to three distinct periods of great prosperity, which are interspersed with more or less brief periods of crisis, and are finally followed by inexorable decadence. The chronological division into dynasties which was formulated by the ancient historian Manetho,[7] may also be retained for intrinsic reasons: in spite of all its inexactness and imperfection, it indicates a definite succession of phases, which were accepted by the people who were contemporary with them.

At the dawn of history the two kingdoms are united by a great sovereign whom Manetho calls Menes. Certain doubts still exist as to his identity.[8] The one certainty is the union which he achieves, so determining the beginning of the Old Kingdom (about 2850–2200 B.C.).[9] Henceforward there is only one capital for Egypt: at first it is This, and later Memphis, in the north.

During this period the conception of kingship takes definite shape, and we may stop to consider its characteristic features, as compared with those which are proper to Mesopotamia.[10] In Mesopotamia the sovereign is the god's representative on earth, and only rarely is he given divine attributes; but in Egypt the Pharaoh is himself a god, who has become incarnate in order to govern the world. Consequently the dialogue between god and king, which in ancient Mesopotamian history finds such intense expression, even to the point of anguish, is silenced and eliminated by a higher unity. It is no longer necessary to seek to know the will of heaven; that will is naturally expressed through the lips of the Pharaoh, and one has only to obey it.

Rulership based on such principles cannot but be absolute and centralized. The Pharaoh is at the summit of the bureaucratic pyramid, and the most exalted member of the bureaucracy is the vizier, an active and impressive figure, the human executor of the will of the incarnate god. From the Pharaoh also the life of the community derives its origin and significance. Mesopotamia presents a picture of diggers of canals and builders of temples, headed by the king himself. In Egypt the picture is partly similar and partly different: similar in regard to the excavation of canals essential to the country's agricultural life; but here the temple is rivalled in importance by another structure, also religious in function but with quite a different purpose: namely, the pyramid. This is the god-king's sepulchre, in which he will continue his immortal life; and the king is not only the subject but also the object of the building activity. The period most famous for its pyramids is the Fourth Dynasty, and then they become so mighty and grandiose as to be in very truth the result of the collective labour of generations. To the Greeks the sight of these immense masses suggested harsh, forced labour imposed by a hateful tyrant. But to believe this is to misunderstand the mentality of the milieu. The tomb was indispensable to the cult of the Pharaoh who had returned to the company of his fellow gods, and it had to be of a magnitude befitting his divine dignity. What devout Egyptian would have wished to shirk his part in such a task?

The wealth of monuments left by the early dynasties is not matched by a comparable wealth of historical documents. The fragmentary annals which have survived show that this class of literature existed, but do not provide adequate documentation.[11] Even so, we can establish three main directions of military activity: southward to Nubia, westward to Libya,[12] and eastward to Palestine. In this last direction the Egyptians have left abundant archaeological traces; already in the Second Dynasty an inscription refers to the Pharaoh Peribsen as 'he who ravages Asia'. Our most detailed information, however, is derived not from the royal inscriptions, but from the long description of his achievements which an officer of King Pepi I of the Sixth Dynasty had carved on his tomb. This document is interesting both because it is remarkably informative and because it is of a new type. It is not the king who is writing to put his feats on record, but a subject laying bare his personality — that of a private individual: a thing unheard of in Mesopotamia; and he does this in order to acquire adequate claims both on posterity and, above all, on the life to come. Our officer writes:

His majesty wished to punish the Asiatics who dwell in the sands, and mustered an army of many tens of thousands of men from the whole of Egypt. . . . His majesty sent me at the head of this army. . . . It was I who drew up the plans, though my office was that of Supervisor of the Palace Domain, because I was so capable that none quarrelled with his neighbour, nobody stole even a lump of dough or a wayfarer's sandals, nobody took even a piece of stuff from any town, nobody stole another's goat. . . .[13]

Thus the object of this enterprise was to punish the rebels, those who resisted the Pharaoh's authority. This purpose will turn up again and again in Egyptian history, as the expression of a policy which regards imperial expansion as a means of securing the frontiers.

From the Fifth Dynasty onward a slowly developing crisis is to be noted in the structure of the Old Kingdom. The priesthood of Heliopolis, the 'City of the Sun', situated not far from Memphis, is steadily increasing in importance; in the religious sphere this leads to the ascendancy of the sun god Re, and in the political sphere to a number of fiscal exemptions and donations in favour of the priests, which cannot but have repercussions upon the Pharaoh's supreme authority. We must also note the tendency of the office of district governor to become hereditary, so leading to what is known as the 'feudal state'. This is initiated with the Sixth Dynasty, and likewise tends to undermine the royal authority. Thus we come, about 2200 B.C., to the first period of decadence and transition, 'the first illness' as it has been called, which lasts until about 2000 B.C.[14] The unity is broken, the empire disintegrates into a number of petty states; insecurity and poverty are rife; the social classes are overturned. A telling picture of this state of affairs can be drawn from the literary writings of the age, and especially from the so-called 'prophecies' of Ipuwer, in which we read:

> Why really! Poor men have become the possessors of treasures. He who could not make himself sandals now possesses riches . . .

Why really! The desert is spread over the land. The provinces are destroyed. Barbarians are come into Egypt from without . . .

Why really! Laughter has disappeared for ever. It is wailing that fills the land, mingled with lamentation . . .

Why really! The roads are no longer guarded. Men sit in the bushes till a benighted traveller comes, to take away his burden and steal what he has. He is received with beatings and wrongfully slain . . . Ah, would it were the end of mankind, no more conception, no more birth! Then there would be no more turmoil and wrangling on earth.[15]

State unity and the authority of the sovereign are restored by the Pharaohs of the Eleventh Dynasty, about 2000 B.C. This begins the Middle Kingdom, and the foundations are laid of the great internal and external prosperity which Egypt attains during the Twelfth Dynasty. The Pharaohs of this Dynasty have to be credited with the great work of reclaiming the Fayyum, the marshy region to the south of Memphis; this is the practical expression of a long term internal policy aiming at the consolidation of the agricultural prosperity which is the country's chief asset. These Pharaohs are also responsible for a vigorous military policy, which carries Egyptian arms into Northern Nubia and Syria. Another official, Khu-Sebek, has left a funerary stele recording his achievements as one of the retinue of Pharaoh Sesostris III:

When His Majesty the King of Upper and Lower Egypt, Sesostris the Triumphant, appeared with the crowns of Upper and Lower Egypt upon the Horus-throne of the living, His Majesty had me as a warrior behind him and at his side, with seven men of the court. I showed zeal in his presence, and he made me an Attendant and gave me sixty men. His Majesty proceeded southwards to overthrow the nomads of Nubia . . . His Majesty proceeded northwards, to overthrow the Asiatics, and reached a region called Sekmem . . .[16] It fell, together with the wretched Syrians.[17]

Archaeological discoveries have confirmed that Egyptian domination extended along the Syro-Phoenician coast:[18] statues of Pharaohs, scarabs, and pottery have been found in such cities as Byblos and Ugarit, in the extreme north of the area. We must draw a distinction as to the manner in which this domination was exercised. In Nubia, Egyptian policy begins to be one of annexation, because of the general geographical continuity between that country and Egypt, the riches to be extracted from it, and, not least important, its lack of any great degree of independent cultural tradition. In Syria, on the other hand, Egypt is content with appointing its own officials to exercise control over the local petty sovereigns and to extract periodical tribute from them.

The prosperity which the Twelfth Dynasty develops fails to last. About 1800 B.C. comes the second intermediate period, the second 'illness'; and this illness is aggravated by the greatest humiliation that Egypt can suffer: she falls under a foreign domination, that of the Hyksos.

The rise to power of the Hyksos,[19] towards 1700 B.C., forms part of the general upheaval in ancient Near Eastern history which follows the intervention of the peoples of the mountains. The origin and ethnic composition of the Hyksos are still the subject of controversy; it is certain that they came from Asiatic regions and arrived as nomads, possessing cultural standards far below those of the country which they occupied. Their assumption of power is their greatest success, and simultaneously the greatest blow inflicted upon Egyptian pride. The Egyptians react violently; a new national dynasty arises in Thebes, and its first task is to liberate the country. An historical inscription left by the Pharaoh Kamose relates how he set to work to recover power. The inscription has survived in the form of an exercise for school children, copied out on a school tablet; this is another characteristic type of document, providing information of all kinds and of varying importance. The wording reads:

> The mighty king in Thebes, Kamose, given life for ever, was a beneficent king. Re himself had made him

king and given him strength in truth. His Majesty spoke in his palace to the council of nobles who were in his retinue: 'I would like to know what use to me is my strength! One prince rules in Avaris, another in Ethiopia, and here I am, associated with an Asiatic and a negro. Each has his slice of Egypt, dividing up the land with me . . . None can rest in peace, despoiled as all are by the imposts of the Asiatics. I will grapple with them, and cut open their belly! I will save Egypt and overthrow the Asiatics!' [20]

We are told the result of the enterprise:

I went north victoriously to repulse the Asiatics through the command of Amon, the just of counsel. My valiant army marched before me like a blast of fire . . . When day broke I pounced on the foe like a falcon; at breakfast time I attacked him, I broke down his walls, I slew his people, I captured his women. My soldiers were as lions with the spoils of the enemy: slaves, flocks, fat and honey. They shared out their property with merry heart.[21]

Once more Egypt rises from the depths of misfortune, and goes on now to climb to the most powerful period of her history: the New Kingdom lasts approximately from 1600 to 1100 B.C.[22] The experience of the past leads the Pharaohs to intervene in Palestine and Syria with the intention of firmly establishing their power in those countries; and as during the same period the forces of the mountain peoples and the Mesopotamian valley powers are also concentrated on this area, the history of the Near East changes from the story of isolated blocs to that of a gigantic struggle between rival powers. Not one of them achieves lasting predominance, and as the result of the fluctuating balance of power there is for centuries a varied and fruitful intercourse and interchange of cultural elements.

The builders of the Egyptian empire in Asia are the Pharaohs of the Eighteenth Dynasty: while continuing the conquest of Nubia in the south, Thutmose I penetrates into Syria as far as the Euphrates. His successes are consolidated by Thutmose III, who in the course of seventeen campaigns subjugates the entire Syro-Palestinian coastal strip, and even crosses the Euphrates to inflict defeat on the Mesopotamian states.[23] Now we have ample documentation of the royal activity in the shape of the annals which the Pharaoh has carved in the walls of the temple at Karnak in order to perpetuate his memory. We also have biographies of his officers, and some important stelae, such as that of Barkal, which gives a good summary account of the sovereign's victories:

> Hear, O people! (The god) entrusted to me the foreign countries of Syria, in the first campaign, when they came to give battle to My Majesty with millions and hundreds of thousands of men, the pick of all the foreign lands, standing in their chariots: three hundred and thirty princes, each with his army.
>
> When they were in the Qina valley . . . I had a great success against them. My Majesty attacked them, and at once they fled or fell slain. They entered Megiddo, and My Majesty besieged them there for seven months, till they came out, pleading to My Majesty and saying: 'Give us breath, Our Lord! The lands of Syria will never again rebel against thee!'
>
> Then that enemy and the princes who were with him sent me great tribute, borne by their children: gold and silver, all the horses they possessed, their great chariots of gold and silver and painted, all their coats of mail, their bows and their arrows, all their weapons. With these had they come from afar to give battle to My Majesty, and now they were sending them to me as tribute, while they stood upon their walls, praising My Majesty and begging that they might be granted the breath of life.[24]

We may complement this survey of the varieties of historical literature produced during this great king's reign — varieties which serve as excellent specimens of this kind of ancient Egyptian literature — by quoting his hymn of victory. It is the prototype of others to follow. The god is speaking to the Pharaoh:

I am come to make thee trample on the great ones of
    Syria,
I have strewn them under thy feet in their countries;
I have caused them to see thee as the lord of radiance,
When thou shinest upon their faces in my likeness.
I am come to make thee trample on the Asiatics,
To make thee smite the chiefs of the Syrians;
I have caused them to see thee wrapped in thy
    adornment,
When thou takest thy weapons in the chariot . . .[25]

And there follows a list of the conquered peoples and the
royal victories. At the death of Thutmose III the empire
extends from Nubia to the Euphrates. From one end to the
other it is under the control of Egyptian officials. Strongholds
containing military garrisons are set up at strategic points. The
petty local rulers are laid under tribute, their heirs are brought
up in Egypt, their princesses enter the Pharaoh's harem.
Temples devoted to the Egyptian religion are built everywhere. This empire is the maximum ever attained by the
kingdom of the 'Two Lands'. But, for all its long reach, the
Pharaoh's hand rests only lightly on his foreign subjects;
Egyptian rule is mild, especially in comparison with the treatments which the same areas later endure at the hands of the
Assyrians: local dynasties are not suppressed, and, above all,
there is no mass deportation of conquered peoples such as has
earned the Mesopotamian powers so grim a renown.

At the height of the empire's triumphs a sudden internal
crisis develops and checks its prosperity for several decades;
it is a strange crisis, for the sovereign is not its victim but its
cause: it arises from the attempt which a Pharaoh of un-
doubted genius, Amenophis IV, makes to carry out a religious
reform. In opposition to the ascendancy of the Theban priesthood and their god Amon,[26] Amenophis restores the ancient
cult of the sun, giving it practical expression in the worship
of the solar disc, Aton. Moreover, he insists that the worship
of Aton must be exclusive, and repudiates all the other gods
and their temples. This is an astonishing and perplexing step:

is it to be regarded as true monotheism? And did it have any influence on the monotheism of the neighbouring people of Israel? Whatever the answers, Egyptian religion, broadly polytheistic in nature, is subjected to a powerful unifying and spiritualizing pressure.[27] The Pharaoh changes his name to Akhenaton, 'Pleasing to Aton', and hymns his one god in the following lines:

> Thou appearest in beauty on the horizon of heaven,
> O living Aton, the beginning of life!
> When thou risest on the eastern horizon
> Thou fillest the earth with thy beauty.
> Thou art gracious, great, glistening, high over
>   every land,
> Thy rays encompass the earth to the bounds of all
>   thou hast made . . .
> Egypt is in festivity,
> Awake and afoot,
> Because thou hast roused it.
> When they wash their bodies, when they take their
>   clothes,
> Their arms are raised in worship at thine appearance;
> Throughout the world men go to work.
> All beasts are glad of their pasturage,
> Trees and plants are flourishing;
> Birds take flight from their nests,
> Spreading their wings to adore thee . . . ;
> The fish in the river dart before thy face,
> And thy rays are in the midst of the great green
>   sea . . .
> Thou art in my heart
> And none knows thee as does thy son, Akhenaton,
> Whom thou hast made wise with thy designs and thy
>   strength.[28]

The priests resist this reform, the laity do not understand it. Within a few years after Akhenaton's death his memory is execrated and the capital he founded is destroyed. Meanwhile, when the internal crisis has passed, the strong military policy is resumed in Asia. About 1300 B.C. Ramses II, the Pharaoh of the long reign and the abundant monuments, comes to the throne. In Syria, the Egyptian conquests are threatened by the Hittites moving down from Asia Minor. Ramses intervenes with a strong force, meets the Hittites at Qadesh,[29] and imposes on them a peace treaty which has survived in both Egyptian and Hittite texts. It is an important document of nascent international law, based above all on the historical outlook of the Hittites, and so it will be considered in more detail when we deal with that people. The Pharaoh takes the daughter of the enemy king for wife, and this event is joyfully recorded on an Egyptian stele:

> The daughter of the Great Prince of Hatti marched to Egypt, escorted by the infantry, chariotry, and officers of His Majesty, mingling with the Hittite infantry and chariotry . . . The Hittite people were mingled with the Egyptian, together they ate and drank, with one heart, as brothers, without shunning one another, because peace and brotherhood prevailed . . . Then they led the daughter of the Great Prince of Hatti, who had come to Egypt, into the presence of His Majesty, and very great tribute followed her, without limit . . . His Majesty saw that she was fair of face like a goddess . . . So His Majesty was glad of her, and loved her above all things.[30]

The truce established in the Oriental world by this treaty between the two principal rival powers does not last for long. About 1200 B.C., after repeated preliminary skirmishes, the coasts of the eastern Mediterranean are overrun by a new invasion, that of the 'peoples of the sea', who put an end for ever to the Hittite empire, and place the Egyptian world in mortal peril. The Pharaohs repel the attack, but their power in Asia is shattered, and the internal vitality of their state is impaired beyond recovery. Henceforth Egypt will be a 'broken reed', to use the Assyrians' contemptuous expression.[31]

The 'broken reed' continues to vacillate for centuries in successive crises and recoveries, but Egypt's prestige is ended. An official named Wenamon, who was sent into Syria about 1100 B.C. in quest of timber for the sacred barque of the god

Amon, has left an account of his distressing adventures, and especially of the disrespectful treatment meted out to him by the Syrian princes, who openly assert their independence:

> If the ruler of Egypt were the lord of mine, and I were his servant, would he have sent me gold and silver, saying: 'Carry out the commission of Amon'? . . . Am I thy servant? Am I the servant of him who sent thee?[32]

Contrast this with the language of the princes who, less than three centuries before, had written to the Pharaoh, saying that 'they prostrate themselves seven times and seven at his feet' and 'are the dust on which he walks'.[33] And how humiliated is Egyptian pride, which in this period of decadence attempts to assert its ancient glory and cannot adapt itself to the changed conditions. As soon as circumstances permit, the Pharaohs — Sheshonq and Necho may serve as examples of them all — march once more into Palestine in the endeavour to revive the old expansionist policy and to counterbalance the Mediterranean powers; but their efforts are fruitless and their successes shortlived. In any case, henceforth Egypt is turned in on herself, at grips with her own crisis. The religious authority secedes and opposes the political authority; feudal autonomy is re-established in the districts; the old constitutional weaknesses reappear and gain the upper hand. Mercenary troops lord it over the people and even establish dynasties of their own. Then Egypt is conquered:[34] first by the Assyrians, who in the seventh century B.C. unite the whole of the Near East from the Euphrates to the Nile under their rule, and maintain their occupation of Egypt, with various vicissitudes, for several years; then by the Persians, who conquer the Pharaohs in 525 B.C., and remain in Egypt for over a century. They return a second time, shortly before Alexander the Great puts an end for ever to the ancient Egyptian civilization, in 332 B.C.

III The Religious Structure

The Egyptians are an extraordinarily religious people, much more so than the rest of mankind, wrote Herodotus,[35] who journeyed through Egypt when the Pharaonic civilization was in decline. Such was the first impression which the Egyptian religion made upon the father of Western history; and we may well take his judgement as our own, for in Egypt we find a truly vast and exuberant world of belief, and a profound and intense religious life.[36]

If, however, we examine this religious world more thoroughly, and seek with our modern eyes to discern its essential features, it repels and baffles us with the endless multiplicity of its forms, the obscurity which is characteristic of so many of them, and its many contradictions. It can be likened to a kaleidoscope, with an immense range of colours which shift and turn in perpetually changing juxtaposition and superposition. There is nothing more difficult than to describe and define them. The contemporary American Egyptologist already quoted, J. A. Wilson, has written:

> But to return to the Egyptian's concept of the world in which he lived. We are going to try to give this in a single picture, which will have only partial justification. In the first place, we are concerned with something like three thousand years of observed history, with the vestiges of prehistoric development partially visible; and there was constant slow change across this long stretch of time. In the second place, the ancient Egyptian left us no single formulation of his ideas which we may use as nuclear material; when we pick and choose scraps of ideas from scattered sources, we are gratifying our modern craving for a single integrated system. That is, our modern desire to capture a single picture is photographic and static, whereas the ancient Egyptian's picture was cinematic and fluid. For example, we should want to know in our picture whether the sky was supported on posts or was held up by a god; the Egyptian would answer: 'Yes, it is supported by posts or held up by a god — or it rests on walls, or it is a cow, or it is a goddess whose arms and feet touch the earth.' Any one of these pictures would be satisfactory to him, according to his approach.[37]

So we meet with a remarkable variety of conceptions even in respect of the same gods and the same phenomena. The ancient Egyptian does not see any contradiction in leaving them all to co-exist, he even sets his ingenuity to work to combine them, instead of proceeding by elimination. History dawns upon an Egypt in which each region has its own god, and the cities in those regions have yet other gods. Later, during the process of unification, when a chief conquers several cities he does not reject their divinities, but prefers to combine them with his own in bonds of kinship, generally in trinities composed of father, mother, and son. Sometimes fusion is achieved: thus, when the Theban dynasty comes to power, its god Amon is assimilated to the previously supreme Re, and the result is Amon-Re. There are instances of even more subtle syntheses, arising from the theological speculation of the priesthood: we shall consider these later on.

Behind all this lies the spirit of benevolent tolerance which we have already noted as characteristic of the Egyptian mentality, a spirit completely opposed to the violent obduracy which distinguishes other peoples of the ancient Orient, and especially the Assyrians. Because of this trait in the Egyptian character, we shall find their world less unitary and coherent in form, and less forceful in its achievements; but far more human, and so more highly civilized.

Moreover, the unity which is not to be found in Egyptian beliefs is found in the cult. Here, even in the most archaic forms of religious life, there is a remarkable coherence, a basically organic relationship. From the structure of the temples to the religious ceremonies, from the formulas used in prayer to the categories of the priesthood, apparently neither the immense distances nor the passing millennia had any but a superficial influence upon a society which conserved and exalted the common patrimony.

The outstanding feature of Mesopotamian religious beliefs is their substantially static quality; that of the Egyptian beliefs is their intense dynamism. This in itself is a profound difference, even ignoring the differing constituent elements: in

Mesopotamia, only a few gods can be ascribed to chronological dates, and even then the dating is doubtful; in Egypt all is history, and even the treatment of religion can only be historical.

This being so, let us begin by adopting the viewpoint of a foreign observer, which is usually the most objective one, if only by way of contrast. The first thing to strike the travellers of ancient times is the Egyptian worship of animals. In astonished and occasionally scoffing tones they report that oxen, sheep, dogs, cats, and birds are accorded divine honour, and that no distinction is made between good and bad animals, or tame and wild ones, since even crocodiles and serpents are included in the list.

To some extent these travellers' impressions are correct. The animal cult has its roots in the most remote times of Egyptian pre-history. In those days the groups of people who sought their sustenance on the banks of the Nile must each have had its totem:[38] some object, some plant, or, above all, some animal guardian. Cemeteries of sheep, bulls, jackals and gazelles have been found in the pre-historic archaeological strata, and the fact that the dead animals were carefully wrapped in mats or linen shrouds indicates that they were objects of a cult. In any case, there are other proofs: the agricultural districts into which pre-historic Egypt was organized before the political unification have distinctive standards, of which pictures have survived; and these standards, mounted on poles, consist largely of animal figures.

With the beginnings of history[39] the standards evolve until the human image prevails. But the new figures bear the ancient symbols on their heads, or even retain some part of an animal, as an indication of their origin. Thus Horus, the god of the western Delta, is represented with a human body and falcon head; Hathor, the goddess of Aphroditopolis and Denderah, has a cow's body and a woman's head; Set, the god of Ombos, has a man's body and the head of an animal that cannot be definitely identified; Anubis, the god of Cynopolis, has a man's body and the head of an ibis. It must be noted that the images are not always the same, and in the case of certain gods the animal form is sometimes left entire.

Beside the divinities partly or completely animal in form, others begin to appear that are entirely human. This is an indication of an already completed evolution, and so probably of a less remote epoch. This category of gods includes Min, the ithyphallic god of Koptos, symbolizing fecundation;[40] the famous Amon, god of Thebes, who during the Middle Kingdom, with the political ascendancy of that city, rises to the top of the heavenly hierarchy;[41] also Osiris and Isis, who belong to the Delta area, and are the principal characters of one of the most famous myths. This myth, even in its local variants, contains readily recognizable elements: Osiris is the god who teaches mankind agriculture, and Isis is his faithful wife; Set, the god already mentioned, here represented as the brother of Osiris, is jealous of his power, and treacherously slays him. In her despair Isis persuades the gods to resurrect her dead husband; but his new life has to be passed in the realm of the dead, as their righteous king. So the myth is only a new version of the ancient vegetation cycle. Furthermore, Horus, the son of Osiris, gives battle to Set[42] and, after a long series of adventures, slays him. Horus is endowed with solar attributes, and so his victory reflects the triumph of the sun over hostile forces. Finally, in this moving story the Egyptian people see the triumph of those ideals which they hold most dear: justice and loyalty, the victory of good over evil, and profound faith in survival.

Our survey of the Egyptian pantheon is completed with mention of the cosmic deities. The Egyptians conceive the earth on which they live as being in the shape of a dish, with their fertile valley as its centre, while its raised edges are the mountainous foreign lands. The dish floats on a stretch of water which supports and surrounds it. This water is the primordial element of life and of the universe, the element from which the first hillock of earth emerged at the beginning, and out of which every day the sun rises, and into which he sinks. The Nile gushes forth from under the earth through various openings, bringing fertility to the land. Above the dish of earth is the air, which supports the vault of heaven.

In accordance with the mentality of the ancient Orient, the various parts of the universe are personified in the divinities.

The Egyptians, too, have their cosmic gods, although these are perhaps less ancient, and certainly are less prominent, than those of the Mesopotamian and other Near Eastern peoples. The earth, Geb, is conceived of as a god lying down; heaven, Nut, as a goddess with her body arched, her feet and hands resting on the edges of the earth; or as a cow standing on its four legs; the air, Shu, is a god standing erect on the earth and holding up the sky with his arms to prevent it from falling.

The stars also have their cult, the principal among them being the sun, Re. Each morning he rises out of the ocean, and traverses the sky in his great barque. Each evening he descends once more into the waters, and crosses them in another barque during the night. But this period is full of danger: a great serpent lies in wait for the sun on his setting, with the intention of overturning his barque and engulfing him; only after a bloody struggle does the god prevail.

During his absence from the sky the sun leaves the moon as his deputy. This is none other than the god Thoth, whom we have already mentioned as represented with the head of an ibis. It is worth noting that here, in contrast with what we have found hitherto, the moon's position in the cosmic economy is decidedly inferior to that of the sun. An ancient Egyptian text relates how the sun god assigns his functions to the moon god:

> Then His Majesty the god said: 'Pray, summon Thoth!' He was brought immediately. Then His Majesty the god said to Thoth: 'Behold, I am here in the sky in my place. As I am going to take the light to the Underworld . . . thou shalt be in my place, as a substitute, and thou shalt be called, the substitute of Re . . . Moreover, I will make thee to extend thy power over the primordial gods, though they are greater than thou . . . I will make thee to encompass the heavens with thy beauty and thy rays . . . Thou shalt be my substitute, and the faces of all who look upon thee shall see by thee, so that the eye of every man shall praise god through thee.'[43]

Attempts to organize the pantheon are made by the educated elite, the priesthood, who apply themselves to the task of introducing order into the wide variety of existing beliefs. They also provide an organized account of the origins and laws of the universe. Thus the great theological systems come into being. At Heliopolis, the supreme gods are arranged in order of descent and relationship in an Ennead, which begins with the waters of the ocean, then sets the sun and the other divinities in mated couples. At Hermopolis, on the other hand, the priesthood creates an Ogdoad, namely, a group of eight divinities from whom the sun emerges as the final result. Then, at Memphis, it is the local god, Ptah,[44] who creates the others, they being only parts of him: his tongue, his heart, his thought.[45]

The particularly interesting feature of these theological reconstructions is the level of speculative faculty they reveal, higher than that of other peoples of the ancient Orient, who are more tied down to the immediate, practical content of their images. Speculative capacity is also reflected in the conception of certain abstract deities, outstanding among whom is Maat (Truth).[46] Thus Egypt, though not emancipated from myth, provides certain prerequisites for such an emancipation. In many respects that is her destiny, to indicate the way of progress, and to achieve its elements; but then, because of her own benevolent spirit of tolerance, to fail to isolate and specify them completely.

On a lower level than this religious speculation, which we may call learned, is the palpitating life of popular religion,[47] with its cult of more modest local demigods or guardian spirits. Here we find Tueris, with a crocodile head, hippopotamus body, human arms, and lion's feet; this deity protects pregnant women and wards off evil spirits. And here, too, is Bes, a grotesque dwarf with luxuriant beard, a leopard's tail, and crooked legs; he, too, watches over the birth of children, and he also presides over music, dancing, and attire.

Magic is very highly developed,[48] its fundamental purpose being once more to ward off evil. Thus a mother drives away a spirit that would trouble her child's sleep:

Be off with thee, thou that comest in the darkness and
enterest by stealth, with thy nose turned backward and
thy face turned backward, without achieving that for
which thou hast come! Art thou come to kiss this child?
I will not let thee! Art thou come to silence him? I will
not let thee silence him! Art thou come to harm him? I
will not let thee! Art thou come to take him away? I will
not let thee! I have protected him from thee with a spell
of clover, which repulses thee, of onions, which injure
thee, of honey, which is sweet for men but bitter for the
dead . . .[49]

Also associated with magic are the curses levelled at the
violators of tombs. For example the tomb of a magistrate
under the Old Kingdom has the inscription:

As for this tomb which I have made in the necropolis
of the West, I made it in a clean and central place. As
for any noble or any official or any man who shall remove
any stone or brick from this tomb, I will be judged with
him by the great god; I will seize his neck like a bird,
and make all the living who are on earth fear the spirits
who are in the far-off West.[50]

An interesting example of magical practice is provided by
the 'execration texts': the names of foreign princes or states
are inscribed on clay statuettes, and these are smashed; thus
by sympathetic magic their fortunes are shattered.

Special importance is attached to names; and in this respect
we are once more reminded of the Mesopotamian conception
that to utter the name is to create, and the possession of a
name means the possession of life. An Egyptian papyrus
prefaces a spell against scorpions with an account of the contest between Re and Isis, in which Isis is determined at all
costs to learn the name of the supreme god, and mercilessly
poisons him until she obtains the knowledge.[51]

However, even this magic is influenced by the Egyptian
mentality, and so by a cast of thought different in its nature
from that of the other peoples. So it is not surprising that we
miss the dominant note of sorrow which we noted among the

Mesopotamians. Indeed, at times, intentionally or otherwise, Egyptian magic is amusing. We may cite one practice of this nature. The idle rich were afraid that when they entered paradise Osiris might assign them to labour in the celestial fields. So they had recourse to the system which served them so well in this life, of getting others to do their work for them. To this end they prepared and placed in their tombs statuettes in the form of mummies, provided with agricultural implements, and with an inscription reading: When I am called upon to carry out the labours of the other world, to cultivate the fields, to irrigate the banks, then it is up to you!

We have already remarked that however varied and at times contradictory the Egyptians' beliefs may be, the body of their religious practices is equally marked by its unity. These practices centre round the temple, where an inner chamber contains the statue of the god. The temple is the seat of a numerous and highly organized priesthood,[52] in no way inferior to that of Mesopotamia in the specialized character of its various classes: readers, purifiers, sacrificers, prophets, musicians. There is a female personnel too: singing women, women musicians, and the god's 'concubines'. This priesthood is organized hierarchically, and in the New Kingdom it acquires a clearly defined primate, the First Prophet of Amon, the High Priest of Egypt. But the temple is also the centre of cultural life: it is there that the scribes foregather, their business being to compose, to copy, and to interpret texts. The Pharaoh often appeals to their wisdom for advice. Thus priests and scholars make the temple the centre of religious and intellectual activity alike, earning for it the expressive appellative: 'House of Life'.

To complete the picture it must be added that the temples also contain the storehouses, with their administrative personnel. This naturally evokes a comparison with the Sumerian temple, but there is a difference, subtle yet essential: the Sumerian temple is the power house of the citizens' economic activity, whereas the Egyptian temple is simply an independent and well-organized economic centre, lacking the centralizing and directive function which is characteristic of its Sumerian counterpart.

The ritual begins with the daily ceremony, which it is possible to reconstruct in some detail.[53] It is an act performed by the priest alone, the public does not participate. After a preliminary purification he enters the sanctuary, scattering the scent of terebinth from his censer. Then he breaks the seals of the Holy Place, unlocks it, and stands before the statue of the god. He prays before it, then proceeds to wash, perfume, and clothe it; he offers it a meal, which is consumed by fire. Finally he withdraws, locks and seals the doors, and the ceremony is over.

In addition to the daily worship there is that of the great festivals, which vary from centre to centre and from god to god. But they have a fundamental unity in their seasonal and agricultural character, which exalts the fertility of the earth. During these festivals the statue of the god is brought out of the sanctuary and carried in procession through the city and its environs. These solemnities draw crowds from all over the country. Herodotus saw boats laden with pilgrims sailing along the Nile on their way to Bubastis, where the feast of the cat goddess Bast was celebrated. He has left this striking description:

> When they go to the city of Bubastis, this is what they do: men and women sail in company, a great crowd of persons of both sexes on each boat; some of the women carry rattles and shake them, some of the men play the flute during the whole of the voyage. The rest of the men and women sing and clap their hands . . . When they reach Bubastis they celebrate the feast by offering great sacrifices; and more wine is drunk during this festival than in all the rest of the year. According to the report of the inhabitants of the place, as many as seven hundred thousand persons congregate there, both men and women, without counting the children.[54]

During one of these festivals, in the district of Papremis, Herodotus witnessed a remarkable scene: one group of believers rallied to the defence of the god's statue, while another group attacked them with maces; heads were broken in earnest, he says, though the Egyptians assured him that nobody was killed. What was the object of this performance? The believers were enacting episodes in the life of the gods, and in particular the conflict between Osiris and Set, this being the subject of the scenes. They presented the murder of Osiris, the mourning of Isis, and the resurrection of the murdered god. This reflects a fundamental phenomenon in the history of culture, namely the sacred play, from which the theatre was born.[55] Unfortunately, only a few fragments of these plays have come down to us, but enough to confirm the fact of their existence. For that matter, how much of what we give the generic name of literature is not in fact drama, either directly or indirectly? That there was a definite class of artists to perform the plays is proved by the stele which one of them left in Edfu:

> I accompanied my lord in his journeyings and did not fail to recite. I gave the responses to my lord in all his recitals. If he was the god, I was the king; if he slew, I restored life.[56]

If we were called upon to sum up Egyptian civilization in terms of a single monument, a tomb would be the inevitable choice. The great pyramids are tombs. Connected with the tombs are the funerary temples. From the tombs has come a great part of the archaeological discoveries and documents which enable us to reconstruct the culture of ancient Egypt. But all this association with tombs must have a specific significance, namely, the overriding importance which the future life had for the ancient Egyptians.[57] Of them, far more than of any other Oriental people, it can be said that the problem of the future life pervades all their thought. Moreover, and even more important, for the first time this problem is given a definite and organic solution, because of the Egyptian belief in retribution for the deeds of this life, and the fixing of the limits within which that retribution is to operate. After death the dead man appears before the tribunal of the god of the other world, Osiris. Before him he recites a 'negative confession' of sins, a formula which has come down to us in the celebrated 'Book of the Dead':

> Hail to thee, O great god, lord of the Two Justices! I have come to thee, my lord, I have been brought that I might see thy beauty. I know thee; I know thy name and the names of the forty-two gods who are with thee in the Hall of the Two Justices . . . I have come to thee, I have brought thee justice, I have banished deceit for thee.

I have not done evil to men.
I have not illtreated animals.
I have not sinned in the temple.
I have not known what is not . . .
I have not blasphemed the gods.
I have not done violence to the poor.
I have not done what the gods abhor.
I have not defamed a slave to his master.
I have not made anyone sick.
I have not made anyone weep.
I have not slain.
I have not given orders to slay.
I have not made anyone suffer.
I have not stolen temple property.
I have not harmed the food of the gods . . .
I have not falsified the measure of grain . . .
I have not added weight to the scales . . .
I have not taken the milk from the mouth of children.
I have not driven cattle from their pasture.
I have not hunted the birds of the gods.
I have not caught fish in their marshes.
I have not held up the water in its season.
I have not dammed running water.
I have not put out a fire that should have stayed alight.
I have not neglected offerings to the gods.
I have not stolen their cattle.
I have not held up a god's procession.
I am blameless.[58]

After this declaration has been read, the dead man's heart is weighed in the balance before Osiris. If he is found to be sinless, he is admitted into the kingdom of the blessed; but if he bears any guilt, he is handed over to forty-two judges, whose names constitute a programme of what lies in store for him: Devourer-of-entrails, Eater-of-shadows, Breaker-of-bones, etc.

In Egyptian religion we find, as is usual, not one single conception of the kingdom of the blessed, but several. Sometimes it is represented as situated in caverns below the ground, in the midst of the desert; sometimes, and more often, it is in the heavens, where there are fertile fields for the blessed to cultivate; at night, each of them lights his lamp: these are the stars.

The cult of the dead is derived from and explained by the view of the future life. The Egyptians have quite a clear conception of the distinction in man between the corporeal and the spiritual elements. Indeed, the latter splits up into the soul, the spirit, the name, the shadow, and above all the untranslatable ka,[59] the divine and indestructible vital principle. Although it leaves the body at the moment of death, the spiritual part of man has the power and the desire to return to it from time to time. In order that it may do so the body has to be prevented from decomposing. Hence recourse is had to embalming, one of the most characteristic of Egyptian customs.[60] Herodotus has given us a description of this process:

First of all with a crooked piece of iron they draw out the brains through the nostrils. . . . Then with a sharp Ethiopian stone they make a cut along the flank and extract all the intestines, and after purifying and washing them with palm-wine, wash them once more with pounded spices. Then after filling the belly cavity with pure finely powdered myrrh, cinnamon, and other spices, except frankincense, they sew it up again. After this they put the body in salt, covering it with natron for seventy days; they must not leave it in the salt any longer. When the seventy days are over, they wash the body and wrap it around from head to foot with strips cut from a sheet of fine linen, smeared with gum. . . . Then the relatives take it and have a wooden coffin made shaped like a man, and shutting the body up in it they place it in the sepulchral chamber, setting it upright against the wall.[61]

This is rather a crude picture, certainly; but it accounts for the manner in which another characteristic element of Egyptian civilization, the mummy, came into existence.

Offerings of all kinds are placed in the sepulchre, beside the sarcophagus. Thus the dead man will be able to go on living in tranquillity, and will not be tempted to come back to earth and haunt the living: for even in this civilization, more serene and cheerful than any other of the ancient Orient, a certain fear of the mysterious power of the dead is not lacking. The living have recourse to them to obtain favours, to renew remembrance, to ask for justice. A typical Egyptian literary genre is the letter to a dead person; and one of the more striking examples of this kind is the one sent by a high official to his wife, whose spirit gives him no peace. The official writes: What wrong have I done thee? What have I done that I should conceal? I married thee when thou wast young. I was with thee in my employments. I did not neglect thee, I did not cause thee pain. I always acted in accordance with thy wishes. I made thee presents of every kind. I took care of thee when thou wast sick. I wept over thy tomb. No, thou canst not tell good from evil![62]

IV   *The Literary Genres*

Egyptian literature[63] has come down to us partly in the form of monumental inscriptions — on temples, statues, stelae, and tombs — and partly in ostraca and papyri. While the monumental inscriptions predominate in the historical sphere, the ostraca and papyri are pre-eminent in the sphere of literature in the strict sense, and condition our knowledge of that literature: the texts have reached us for the most part in single fragmentary copies, and their discovery has been due to chance. So we have reason to believe that what we know of Egyptian literature is only a small and fragmentary part of the original heritage: the reconstruction which we offer is only a collation of the known elements, involved as they are in considerable obscurity.

One might observe that the same also applies to Mesopotamian literature; but the situation is not exactly the same. In the first place, in Mesopotamia the copying and adaptation of ancient texts was practised more than in Egypt, so that there is a greater possibility that important texts have been preserved. Moreover, there is some 'canonization' of religious literature in Mesopotamia, principally during the Kassite period, so that it is included in the great libraries, and is more carefully preserved. We have therefore reason to think that the proportion of ancient Mesopotamian literature which has failed to survive is probably smaller and less important than that of Egypt.

When we consider the intrinsic features of Egyptian literature, as compared with the other literatures already examined, our first impression is of a great richness and variety. We come across new literary genres, such as the love song and the banquet song, the romance and the tale of fantasy; and these genres have the common characteristic that they complement the religious literature with a production essentially profane in content and object. On the other hand, certain genres are no longer so extensive or so independent as they were in Mesopotamia. This applies to the mythological literature, whose elements, short, fragmentary, and frequently inconsistent, have to be sought within the bounds of a different literary genre. This genre, consisting of funerary texts, is typical of ancient Egypt, and is as uniform in its intention as it is varied in content.

Another impression derived from a comparison of Egyptian with Mesopotamian literature is that the former is less uniform and less static. To begin with, we know the names of several Egyptian authors, though not many; and then, as time passes, we can see certain literary genres coming to maturity while others decline, and we see new themes and conceptions evolving.

Drawing a general conclusion from these observations, we may say that in Egypt there seem to be gaps in that profound unity in religious faith which is characteristic not only of Mesopotamian, but of all the other literatures of the ancient Orient. Not that this phenomenon is the result of any positive cogitation: it derives from a broader and more varied mentality, rich even in incongruous elements, and these elements cannot all be reduced to religious terms.

Mythological literature, as we have said, is embodied largely in the funerary texts, which bring together the most disparate themes with the single aim of assisting the dead man. As an example we may take the celebrated 'Book of the Dead', a collection of hymns, prayers, and magical formulas, which contains various traditions concerning the origins of the universe and the doings of the gods.[64]

It is in line with the characteristic mode of Egyptian religious thought that it provides not one single account of the origins of things, but several, and that these exist simultaneously; nor is there any sign of attempts to bring them into harmony with one another. However, one theme does turn up with especial frequency, and it must be mentioned because it is deeply rooted in Egyptian life. This is the theme of the primeval hillock, which emerges from the chaos of waters, and which originates the sun god, who is destined to give life to the other gods. One can hardly avoid associating this conception with the salient features of nature. At the time of the Nile floods the ancient Egyptian saw the swirling waters covering the soil, saw the waves slowly recede and the first hillock emerge, rendered fruitful by the fertilizing waters. Then the sun with its warmth caused the vegetation to spring up. The Egyptians' mythic-religious imagination transferred this essential phase in the life of nature to the plane of cosmic origins, seeing in it a picture of the primordial phase of the world's existence.

The most striking of the myths concerning the deities is undoubtedly that of Isis and Osiris, not only because of its significance in regard to the religion, but because it served as the source of certain dramatic representations of which records have survived. However, once more we have no complete version of the myth; indeed, the surviving elements are so fragmentary that in order to piece them together we have to rely on the account given by the Greek historian Plutarch.[65] Although some reservations have to be made in regard to its content, this account is at least continuous, and from it we can gather how the vegetation cycle came to be fixed in certain definite forms, and can compare and contrast those forms with others known to us. Osiris is the king who establishes peace on the earth and teaches men the art of agriculture; Isis is his wife; Set, his jealous brother. Set has recourse to a trick: he has a marvellous coffer made to the exact measurements of Osiris; at a banquet he exhibits it and promises to give it to anyone who fits it exactly when lying inside it. After various guests have tried in vain, Osiris in his turn lies down in the coffer, which fits him to perfection. Then Set's followers rush in, close the coffer, and throw it into the river. According to the Greek version, the waters sweep it away to the sea and thence to Byblos. Brokenhearted with grief, the murdered man's wife sets out in quest of the corpse, and when, after many journeys, she finds it, she lifts up her voice in a lament to the gods. The gods are moved. The body of Osiris is laid out and swathed with bandages. Taking the form of a kite, his consort hovers over it with flapping wings. The inert body begins to stir, and its breath slowly returns to it. But Osiris is not to pass his new life among the living: he is to rule over the dead, bringing them the justice which he had formerly established on earth.

The Osiris myth has a sequel, and we have this from a good Egyptian source. Isis gives birth to a posthumous son, the falcon god Horus. As soon as he is old enough, Horus seeks out his father's murderer in order to avenge his memory. The struggle between Horus and Set continues for decades, and is told in a series of episodes of craft and violence, which take place before the tribunal of the gods. Here, for instance, is one detail of the struggle:

Set made a great oath to the gods, saying: 'The office should not be given him till he has been sent forth with

me: we will build stone ships and have a race, and the
one who beats his opponent shall have the office of
ruler.' Then Horus built himself a ship of cedar and
covered it with plaster and launched it in the evening
without any man in the country noticing. Set saw Horus's
ship and thought it was of stone, and he went up the
mountain and cut off a peak and made himself a stone
ship of 138 cubits.[66] Then they embarked on their ships
in the presence of the Ennead, and Set's boat sank.[67]

With this and other tricks Horus at last succeeds in overcoming his antagonist, and the gods proclaim him worthy to
hold the position formerly occupied by his father.

There is no denying that the text makes an impression of
coarseness. Its connection with the Osiris myth, which was
inspired by far more elevated religious conceptions, is purely
formal. One wonders whether its author is ingenuous or scep-
tical. His gods are certainly on a much lower level than those
of Mesopotamia.

Before passing from this survey of Egyptian mythological
literature, we wish to draw attention to the fact that it does
not offer any counterpart to the figure of the semi-divine hero,
which is characteristic of Mesopotamian and, later, of Greek
epic poetry. The absence of the theme of the vain hankering
after immortality which animates that figure is even more
noteworthy. But how could it be otherwise, since the Egyptian
is sure that he will renew his own existence in the next world?

Lyrical poetry,[68] both religious and secular, flourishes in the
New Kingdom. As in Mesopotamia, the religious lyric is represented by hymns to gods and kings. We have already
quoted the magnificent hymn of Amenophis IV when we dealt
with Egyptian history. A new feature in this hymn is that it
goes beyond the usual religious formulas and makes a living
exploration of nature: so full and joyous a feeling for nature
can be said to have been unknown to the peoples of Mesopotamia. This literary genre is not confined to the period of the
reformer king; its characteristics and its qualities are to be
found even before, as is shown by this hymn to Amon-Re:

Thou art the sole one, who made all that is,
The solitary one who made what exists;
From whose eyes mankind came forth,
Upon whose mouth the gods came into being;
He who made herbage for the flocks,
And fruit-trees for mankind;
He who made that on which the fish live in the water,
And the birds in the heavens . . .
Jubilation to thee for every foreign land,
To the height of heaven, to the breadth of earth,
To the depth of the great green sea!
The gods bow down to thy majesty,
And exalt the might of him who made them,
They rejoice at the approach of him who begot them.
They say to thee: 'Welcome,
O father of the fathers of all the gods,
Who hast raised the heavens and founded the earth,
Who hast made what is and created what exists,
Thou king and chief of the gods!'[69]

We have already quoted an example of the royal hymns, when we were writing of Thutmose III; penitential psalms and prayers are also found. But we must go on to consider the most distinctive, indeed the unique feature of the Egyptian lyric: its secular poetry. To begin with, there are fresh and tender love songs. As we listen to the voice of this maiden we hardly seem to be in the ancient Orient:

My heart beats fast
When I think on my love for thee;
It will not let me walk as other people do,
And leaps in one spot;
It will not let me look for a garment,
Or take up my fan.
I am no longer capable of making up my eyes
Or perfuming myself.
Do not flutter, O my heart!
The beloved comes to thee,
But so do people's eyes;
Don't let them say of me

> *'That woman is fallen in love!'*
> *Hold firm when thou thinkest on him,*
> *O my heart, and flutter not!*[70]

And here is the lament of a young man who has not seen his beloved for a whole week:

> *For seven days to yesterday I have not seen my*
>   *beloved,*[71]
> *And a sickness has come upon me:*
> *My body is become heavy,*
> *Forgetful of my own self.*
> *If the physicians come to me,*
> *My heart is not satisfied with their medicines;*
> *Nor do the magicians find any solution,*
> *Because my illness is unfathomable.*
> *But to say to me: 'she is here!' — that revives me;*
> *Her name puts me on my feet again;*
> *The coming and the going of her messengers gives new*
>   *life to my heart!*
> *My beloved is for me the best of all remedies,*
> *The greatest of medical treatises.*
> *My health is in her coming,*
> *When I see her I am cured.*
> *If she opens her eyes my body is young again,*
> *If she speaks, my strength returns.*
> *When I embrace her, she drives off every ill,*
> *But she has been away, alas, for seven days.*[72]

There is a similar originality in the convivial poetry. The invitation to make merry is reinforced by consideration of the uncertain future: *carpe diem!* The following song is from a New Kingdom tomb:

> *Follow thy desire as long as thou shalt live,*
> *Anoint thy head with myrrh and put fine linen on thee,*
> *Perfume thyself with the genuine marvels of divine oils!*
> *Enjoy thyself as much as thou canst,*
> *Let not thy heart flag . . .*
> *Fulfil thy desire upon earth, as thy heart bids thee,*
> *Until the day of mourning come . . .*

Wailing does not save a man's heart from the
        underworld!
Make holiday, and weary not therein:
For a man can not take his property with him,
For of those who depart not one comes back again![73]

Such words recall the grief of Gilgamesh; but how different
is the setting! Even the psychological background is different:
in the Gilgamesh poem there is a desperate clinging to life;
here, a detached expectation of death.

This review of the Egyptian lyrical poetry must be ended
with the remark that the lamentation, in the strict sense of
expressing sorrow over a destroyed city, which was a distinct
literary genre in Mesopotamia, and will be again in Israel, is
not found in Egypt. Some authorities have sought to classify
the dialogue between a disillusioned man and his own soul,
which we shall be discussing later, among this form of poetry.
But the likeness is only superficial, for the embittered man's
dialogue is subjective, a poetic expression of human sadness,
whereas the lamentation is based on a precise objective fact:
the destruction of a city. In this respect we think that there
is a greater affinity with the Mesopotamian and Hebrew lamentation to be found in the 'prophecies' of Ipuwer, which we
have cited when considering Egyptian history. These are
called 'prophecies' only through an inexact employment of
Biblical terminology. It is not without significance that the
situation to which Ipuwer refers is one of the few in which
Egypt experiences crisis and destruction, before rising again
triumphant. But Egyptian civilization has little time to brood
on disaster: during the period of its grandeur it scarcely experiences it, and when it does, the experience comes too late.

Didactic and wisdom literature is practised in Egypt from
ancient times.[74] Collections of maxims are scattered over the
whole period of Egyptian civilization, and the names of the
authors, whether true or fictitious, have been handed down as
paragons of wisdom.

From the time of the Old Kingdom we have the precepts of
Ptah-hotep, who when old and weary begs the Pharaoh to give

him his son to support him, promising in return to educate him. Here are some of his teachings:

> Be not puffed up with thy knowledge, be not proud because thou art wise. Take counsel with the ignorant as well as with the wise. There is no limit to art, nor any artist who possesses the whole of his craft. Good speech is more hidden than emeralds, but it may be found among the maidservants at the grindstone . . .
>
> If thou be a guest at the table of one greater than thyself, take what he gives thee when it is set before thee . . . Cast thy gaze down till he addresses thee, and speak only when thy speech is called for. Laugh when he laughs, and it will be pleasing to his heart, and all that thou doest will be acceptable to him . . .
>
> If anyone makes petition to thee, listen calmly to the petitioner's words. Do not put him off before he has said what he came to say. A petitioner wants attention to be paid to what he says, even more than to be granted what he asks . . .
>
> If thou art a man of standing, found a family, and love thy wife at home as is fitting. Give her plenty to eat, clothe her back; ointment is the prescription for her body. Make glad her heart as long as thou livest. She is a rich field for her lord . . .
>
> Bow to thy superior, to him who is above thee in the royal administration: thy house and thy property will endure, thy reward will be what it should be. It is a bad thing to go against a superior: one lives as long as he is well-disposed.[75]

At a later period of Egyptian civilization, indeed, when it is already in decline, another collection of maxims adds the inspiration of an intense moral feeling to this expression of wisdom. These are the precepts of Amenemopet; their importance is enhanced by the fact that they served to some extent as a model for the writer of the Biblical Book of Proverbs:[76]

> *If thou findest a debt against a poor man,*
> *Make it into three parts:*
> *Forgive two of them and let the third stand.*

Thou wilt find it like the ways of life:
Thou wilt lie down and sleep well,
In the morning it will be like good news.
Better is praise as one who loves men
Than riches in a storehouse;
Better is bread, when the heart is glad,
Than riches with sorrow . . .
Do not laugh at a blind man or tease a dwarf,
Or do harm to the lame.
Do not tease a man who is in the hand of the god,
Nor be severe with him if he errs,
For man is clay and straw,
And the god is his builder:
He is tearing down and building up every day.[77]

Because of the innumerable traces which have been found, it is as certain that the fable existed in Egyptian literature as it is scantily documented. The only definite example which has survived is, however, a very significant one: it is a debate between the head and the body, which it is easy to see was a prototype of one of Aesop's fables, as well as of the celebrated allegory of Menenius Agrippa.[78] In the Hellenistic era the situation is different, for then we find Egyptian fables in Greek translation, and we are able to go deeper into the question of Egypt's influence upon Greece.[79]

Our discussion of wisdom literature must end with consideration of the poetry of *Weltschmerz*, world weariness, which achieves its highest expression in the dialogue already mentioned, between a disillusioned man and his soul. It was probably written during the period of crisis which preceded the Middle Kingdom.[80] It has many points of contact with the Mesopotamian and Hebrew treatments of the theme of the sufferings of the Righteous Man, but in the Egyptian text the suffering is only implicit and is not emphasized, so that there is not in that sense a problem demanding to be solved. Instead, the accent is on the suffering, on the incentive to suicide, and the doubt whether even this has any point:

To whom can I speak today?
One's fellows are evil,

The friends of today do not love one.
To whom can I speak today?
Hearts are grasping,
Every man seizes his fellow's goods.
To whom can I speak today?
The gentle are no more,
But the violent have access to everybody.
To whom can I speak today?
Even the calm of face is wicked,
Goodness is everywhere rejected . . .
To whom can I speak today?
Hearts are grasping,
None has a heart on which to rely.
To whom can I speak today?
There are no righteous,
The land is left to those who do wrong.
To whom can I speak today?
There are no more friends,
One must have recourse to an unknown to complain . . .
To whom can I speak today?
The sin which stalks the earth
Has no end![81]

And then the writer turns to praise of death:

Death is in my sight today
Like recovery for a sick man,
Like coming out into the open after being confined.
Death is in my sight today
Like the odour of myrrh,
Like sitting under an awning on a breezy day.
Death is in my sight today
Like the scent of lotus-blossoms,
Like sitting on the bank of drunkenness.
Death is in my sight today
Like the passing of rain,
Like coming home from an expedition . . .
Death is in my sight today
Like the longing to see one's home
After many years spent in captivity.[82]

But is it true that death at least is good? Or is not even
death torment and futility? This doubt, formulated in the dis-
course of the world-weary man with his soul, recalls the one
expressed in the Mesopotamian dialogue between master and
slave. In the conclusion likewise there is a singular parallelism:
the lot of the two speakers, whatever it is, will be shared by
both.

Narrative is widely developed in Egypt, both in the form
of the romance with an historical background, and in that of
the tale of fantasy.[83] To the former class belongs a work of
the Middle Kingdom which, classical in its language and style,
is rightly regarded as the most important and significant of its
kind in Egyptian literature. This is the tale of Sinuhe.[84]

Sinuhe is a nobleman who is forced by a palace intrigue to
flee from the court and take refuge with a beduin tribe in
Asia. The author possesses descriptive powers of the highest
order:

> It was a good land, named Yaa. It produced figs and
> grapes. It had more wine than water. Its honey was
> plentiful, its olives abundant. Every kind of fruit was on
> its trees. Barley was there, and corn, and innumerable
> beasts of every kind. And great privileges accrued to me
> because of love for me.

Sinuhe is elected chief of a tribe, and gains the esteem and
goodwill of his tribesmen. But the chief of another tribe, a
man universally feared, challenges him to battle. Then follows
the epic passage:

> A mighty man of Asia came to challenge me in my
> own camp. He was a hero without peer, and had con-
> quered all the land. He said he would fight me, he pur-
> posed to despoil me, and planned to plunder my cattle
> . . . During the night I strung my bow and shot my
> arrows, I gave free play to my dagger and I polished my
> weapons. When day broke, the Asiatics were there. They
> had rallied their tribes and collected a good half of their
> country. They thought only of this fight. Then he came
> to me as I was waiting, set against him. Every heart

burned for me; men and women groaned. Every heart was sick for me. They said: 'Is there another strong man who could fight against him?' Then he took his shield, his battle-axe, and his armful of javelins. But after I had escaped his weapons I made his arrows pass by me uselessly, one close to another. Then he charged at me, and I shot him with an arrow, which stuck in his neck. He cried out, and fell on his nose. I felled him with his own battle-axe and raised my cry of victory over his back.'

With this feat, Sinuhe's prestige is consolidated. But, as the years go by, he is seized with a longing for his homeland. Here there is an elegiac note:

O thou god, whoever thou be, that didst ordain my flight, be merciful, bring me back to the court! Wilt thou grant me to see once more the place where my heart has not ceased to dwell? What matters more for me than to be buried in the land in which I was born? Come to my aid! Lo, a joyful thing has happened: the god has borne witness to me of his mercy. May he act in like manner to bring to a happy end him whom he made wretched! May his heart be moved by him whom he drove forth to live in a strange land! If today he be disposed to show mercy, let him hear the exile's prayer!

Sinuhe's dream comes true. The Pharaoh recalls him and receives him with great honour. He knows once more the comfort of Egyptian life:

Years were made to pass away from my body. I was plucked and my hair was combed. A load of dirt was left to the desert and my clothes to the beduin. I was clad in fine linen and anointed with precious oils. I slept on a bed. I gave up the sand to those who are in it, and wood-oil to him who is anointed with it. . . . There was built for me a pyramid of stone in the midst of the pyramids. The stonemason took over the ground reserved to him, the draughtsman designed it, the chief sculptor carved it, and the overseers of works in the necropolis made it their concern. All the materials which need to be placed in a tomb were put in mine. . . . A statue was made for me overlaid with gold, and its skirt was of fine gold. His Majesty had it made. There is no other man for whom the like has been done. And I was in the king's favour until the day of my death.

Here the romance ends. Sinuhe has realized the Egyptian's highest aspiration: to die in peace in his own land, after preparing a worthy sepulchre for himself. With its assertion and exaltation of the ideals which shape Egyptian thought, it is not surprising that the story became a national epic.

Among the tales of fantasy, that of the shipwrecked sailor is one of the most ancient and amusing.[85] It is of interest for more than one reason. An Egyptian thus describes his adventures:

I had gone down to the sea on board a ship 120 cubits long and 40 broad. It had a crew of a hundred and twenty sailors, the finest in Egypt. Whether they looked upon the sky, or whether they looked upon the earth, their hearts were more resolute than a lion's.

But a tempest arises and the ship is wrecked. Only the narrator reaches safety on an island, where he finds all manner of fine flowers and fruits. Suddenly there is a noise as of thunder; the trees creak, and the earth trembles:

It was a serpent that was coming towards me. He measured thirty cubits and had a beard more than two cubits long. His members were covered in gold . . . He opened his mouth, as I lay prostrate on the earth before him, and said: 'Who has brought thee hither, who has brought thee hither, little one? If thou delayest to tell me who brought thee to this island, I will reduce thee to ashes, and thou wilt find that thou art no more.' I answered: 'Thou speakest, but I do not understand. I am before thee and I have lost my senses.' Then he took me in his mouth and carried me to his cave and put me down without hurting me, safe and sound, without being maimed in any way. He opened his mouth to me as I lay before him, and said: 'Who has brought thee hither, little one, who has brought thee? Who bore thee to this island of the sea, whose two shores are in the waves?'

The castaway relates his adventures, and the serpent goes on:

> Fear not, fear not, little one. Let not thy face be downcast now that thou art come to me. God has surely let thee live, since he has brought thee to this isle of life, which lacks nothing, but is full of all good things. Thou shalt spend four months here. Then a ship will come from thy country, sailed by mariners whom thou knowest; with them thou shalt return home, and thou shalt die in thy own city. Blessed is he who can relate what is past, once sad happenings are over!

In his gratitude the castaway promises to send the serpent rich gifts from Egypt; but the serpent laughs: those gifts are the produce of his own island; it is he who supplies Egypt with them. No, there is no need for the gifts, the only thing the castaway can do for the serpent is to make his name known and respected:

> I prostrated myself with arms extended before him. And he gave me a cargo of frankincense . . . , of black eye-salve, giraffe's tails, terebinth-resin, sticks of ivory, hounds, apes and baboons, and all manner of fine and precious products. I loaded it all upon that ship. Then, when I prostrated myself to thank him, he said to me: 'Thou wilt reach thy land in two months, thou wilt clasp thy children to thy breast, there thou wilt recover thy youth and there thou wilt be buried.' Then I went down to the shore near the ship and greeted the crew that was in it. On the shore I gave thanks to the lord of the isle.

Thus the castaway, like Sinuhe, can return to his native land and there prepare a fitting tomb for himself.

As we have said, this tale presents many points of interest. In the first place, it is not isolated as a story complete in itself, but set within a framework: a captain has returned deeply discouraged from an enterprise, and is afraid to say anything to the Pharaoh; the castaway encourages him by telling his own story as an example of how speech may save a man. It is probable that this was not the only tale told, for the captain was still downcast after hearing it, and there may well have been a succession of such tales within the same framework. This technique will be adopted by other Oriental story-tellers, and later by western authors.

Another point of interest in the mariner's tale is its coherent directness, even in handling the fantastic elements. This does not apply to other stories, in which the straining after the wonderful and stupendous overcomes all question of consistency. Take, for instance, the celebrated tale of the two brothers Anubis and Bata, written during the New Kingdom.[86] It is an involved story of miracles and metamorphoses, which possibly had some influence on later novel writing. It would be an arduous task to go into this tale in detail, but we may glance at its first part, which is the most coherent and the least fantastic. It provides us with the oldest model of a theme which in time becomes remarkably diffused:

> Now they say that once there were two brothers, of one mother and one father; Anubis was the name of the elder, and Bata was the name of the younger. Now Anubis had a house and a wife, and his younger brother lived with him as if he were his son.

But Anubis's wife is consumed with desire for Bata, and, profiting by her husband's absence, seeks to seduce him:

> Then she stood up and took hold of him and said to him: 'Come, let us pass an hour lying together. It will be of advantage to you, for I shall make fine clothes for you.' Then the lad became like a raging leopard at this wicked suggestion which she had made to him, and she was frightened, very frightened. Then he reasoned with her, saying: 'See, you are like a mother to me, and your husband is like a father to me; for being older than I he brought me up. What is this great wrong you have said to me? Do not say it again!'

The wicked woman plans to take a terrible revenge for this rebuff:

> Her husband came home in the evening according to his daily custom, and when he came to the house he found his wife lying down pretending to be sick. She did not put water on his hands after her custom, nor did she light a light for him, and his house was in darkness, and she lay vomiting. So her husband said to her: 'Who has been talking evil to you?' Then she said to him: 'Nobody has been talking evil to me except your younger brother. When he came to take the seed to you he found me sitting alone and said to me: "Come, let us spend an hour lying together . . ." So did he say to me; but I would not listen to him: "Am I not as your mother? — and your elder brother is like a father to you." So did I say to him. But he was afraid, and beat me, so that I should not tell you.'

Anubis resolves to kill his brother, but Bata's friends the cows warn him in time for him to escape. He embarks on the marvellous adventures of which we have spoken above.

In addition to the strictly literary texts there are a large number of others, which we shall not discuss in detail. There are the historical writings already mentioned. There are lists of names and objects, but not the more thorough linguistic works such as we found in Mesopotamia, from sign lists to vocabularies. There are school exercises, important to us because they conserve texts which otherwise would have been lost. There are letters, giving us an insight into private and family life. There are scientific works, in the limited, hardly self-sufficient sense which we can give the word in this context. These include works on astronomy and mathematics,[87] which did not reach so high a level as in Mesopotamia, and medicine.[88] Here, even among the formulas for resort to magic we meet with some particularly vigorous diagnoses:

> When you examine a man with constipation, pale face, and palpitating heart, and on examination you find that

he has a hot heart and a swollen belly . . . he has eaten heating food. Prepare a potion to wash away the heating things and free his bowels. . . .[89]

Finally, there are legal writings,[90] which we shall consider for a moment, for we think that they provide one of the most striking points of contrast with the rest of the Near Eastern world. In Mesopotamia, as we have seen, law is based on the 'code' which the king receives from his god and promulgates to his people. In Egypt not one code of laws has yet been found. If this is not pure accident — and that does not seem likely — we must assume that justice was based on the Pharaoh's own decisions, together with custom.[91] We have documents relating to legal practice. Thus we may note the exemptions granted to temples and their personnel in the period of antiquity, such as the following dating from the Fifth Dynasty:

> I do not permit any man to take any of the prophets who are in the District in which thou art for the corvée or for any other work of the District, except to do service to the god himself in the temple in which he is and to conserve the temples in which the prophets are.[92]

We also find accounts of trials, such as that of a group of conspirators in the time of Ramses III. The accused are brought one at a time before the judges:

> The great enemy Paibakkamen, who had been Great Chamberlain: he was brought in because he had been in collusion with Tiye and the women of the harem. He had made common cause with them. He had begun to take their words out to their mothers and brothers, saying: 'Gather people and stir up enemies to make rebellion against their lord.' He was set in the presence of the great officials in the court of justice. They examined his crimes. They found him guilty. His crimes laid hold on him. The officials who examined caused his sentence to come upon him.[93]

It is obvious, therefore, that juridical procedure is a normal activity; but if we inquire into the source material for the judgements we cannot trace any conception of an objective codification on which magistrates could base their decisions independently of the sovereign. Being god in person, he is the permanent source of law, which without him has neither validity nor meaning.

Thus, at the close of our review of Egyptian literature, we make a significant return to those characteristics which we recognized as the essential features of ancient Egyptian civilization. Of the three constituent elements of the cosmos — the gods, the king, and the people — the second rises to the level of the first and has his identity therein. Thus there is no dialectic between the first two elements, and the third, the human one, has only one objective: to bring itself into harmony with the single superior order.

V The Artistic Types

In respect of the principles from which it draws its inspiration, Egyptian art[94] is fundamentally at one with the rest of the ancient Orient. In Egypt, too, the artist is moved by eminently practical aims, within the framework of religious life: the building of dwellings or of tombs for gods or kings, the carving of statues in order that the dead man's soul may be able to return in definite form, the evocation of the future life by means of sepulchral reliefs and paintings. Moreover, in Egypt, too, art is understood as craftsmanship, and so is collective and anonymous. If, for example, the artist had been allowed to put his name or his portrait on the wall of a tomb, the magic power of evocation involved in such a proceeding would have given him an undeserved share in the dead man's new life and in the offerings made for him, even in the comfort and the pastimes prepared for him.[95]

So far as the broad principles are concerned, therefore, Egyptian art fits into the general scheme of its environment; but beyond that the parallel no longer holds. To begin with, there are other features in which Egypt reveals a noteworthy difference. Thus, whereas representations of private or family life are almost entirely missing from the artistic subjects of the remainder of the Oriental world, Egyptian art finds one of its most constant and rich sources of inspiration in this aspect of life. But above all the Egyptians have an instinctive feeling for art, which often leads them to transcend the limitations of conventional schemes and to achieve an immediate and telling vivid quality, intensely subjective, profoundly and elegantly harmonious. The faithfulness to reality and the dynamism of the elements are such that it is only by contrast that they can be compared with the clumsy and static productions of the rest of the Oriental world. A French scholar, Desroches-Noblecourt, has well said that in the course of producing commissioned works the humble Egyptian artist has nobly overcome the limitations imposed by his subordination to his employers and his environment:

> Only by way of rare exception do we know who the artist was: professional pride was for him an impossibility; but he most nobly succeeded in overcoming the fact that no self-ostentation was permissible to him. Even if his masters wished them to be as stiff as mummies, he contrived to breathe into his statues a life which affects us all the more powerfully for being profound, and thus unveils to us the innermost feeling and grace of his soul. It is this wealth of inner feeling which, despite the lack of variety in the subjects set him, and the conventions of the design, will permit the artist to give his reliefs an unexpected fidelity to truth in attitude and gesture, an unparalleled subtlety of observation, a very exact portrayal in its shades of detail of everyday life, with its comic and joyous features; and in his painting, new themes full of spontaneity, drawn from the freshest and free inspiration, to such an extent that private art will almost come in the end to exercise in turn an influence upon official art.[96]

Even the static quality characteristic of the rest of Oriental art is eliminated in this more immediate and realistic inspiration. Undoubtedly there is an Egyptian style, clearly marked and unmistakable; and there is a cohesion, a coherence in it which is the continuation of a tradition for which the long and almost unchanging course of Egyptian history affords the most favourable of environments. But within the limits of this organic frame, artistic types and subjects evolve and succeed one another in a clearly distinguishable historical process; indeed, one can expound Egyptian art only in terms of history.

The culminating phases are two: the Old Kingdom, the age of the pyramids, in which art flourishes almost unexpectedly yet is already monumental in its forms and mature and refined in its elements; and the New Kingdom, the age of the great temples of Thebes, which supplements, develops, and completes the traditional heritage with a wide range of fresh motives. So there is no evolution in the sense of a development from a lower to a higher level, from simplicity to complexity; but a history, in which a civilization makes its appearance in full vigour, and of which the factors are modified and succeed one another within the organic bounds of tradition.

In Mesopotamia the fundamental problem of architecture is the temple; in Egypt, it is the tomb,[97] which has the function of assuring the dead man, and in particular the god king, a full and untroubled existence in the next world.[98] We must consider the genesis of the tomb structure. The most ancient type, from which the others are progressively evolved, is the mastaba, a low truncated pyramid, beneath which a vertical shaft driven into the earth leads to the sarcophagus chamber. One or more chambers are hollowed out in the edifice itself, and these include the chapel and the niche to contain the dead man's statue. On one of the outer walls is the outline of a false door, with a table in front of it for offerings; it is held that the vital essence of the dead man emerges at the call of those who make the offerings. From the very beginning the inner walls of the mastabas are richly decorated with bas-reliefs and paintings, portraying the dead man's life in the next world.[99]

The superposition of several mastabas of decreasing size produces the step pyramid, of which the most celebrated example is that at Sakkarah, dating back to the Pharaoh Djoser, of the Third Dynasty. The resemblance between this type of pyramid and the Mesopotamian ziqqurat is complete: when discussing the Sumerians, we saw that one of these two architectural forms influenced the other, though one can hardly be more explicit than that, and though the influence may have concerned the form rather than the function of the edifice.

However, the development of the two types of building is not the same. Whereas the Mesopotamian ziqqurat persists for thousands of years in ever increasing perfection of form, during the Fourth Dynasty the step pyramid evolves into the type which thenceforth remains constant: the true pyramid with smooth walls, in the form of isosceles triangles on a square base.[100] The most celebrated specimen, which we may take as an example of them all, is that of Cheops: the sides of the base are 130 metres in length, and the height is 145 metres. The funerary chamber is built into the pyramid, and access to it is by a system of corridors. The pyramids usually form part of an architectural group, which includes a funerary temple and a covered arcade leading down to the river valley and ending in a vestibule.

As time passes the pyramid decreases in size and importance. In the New Kingdom the prevalent type of royal tomb is the hypogaeum hewn out of the virgin rock. The hidden entrance and the maze of corridors confirm what the new type of tomb suggests at first sight: it owes its origin to the fear of tomb riflers. The texts show that their depredations were quite frequent. The same motive leads to the choice of remote spots, places difficult of access; one such spot is the Valley of the Kings, to the west of Thebes, where the tomb of Tutankhamen with its wealth of treasure,[101] and many others were discovered; another site is the Valley of the Queens, a little farther south, where the tombs of the Pharaohs' wives and children are situated.

With the first specimens of the Egyptian tombs we come upon a new feature: the large-scale use of stone as a building material. This marks its first employment in the ancient Orient.[102] This phenomenon, which by its very nature sets Egyptian art in contrast to the early art forms of Mesopotamia, acquires a widely differentiated function in the temple and the palace. In Mesopotamia, and in Egypt too, there is a feeling and desire for the grandiose; but in Mesopotamia the absence of columns having a functional purpose necessitates the predominance of unbroken, massive walls, whereas the

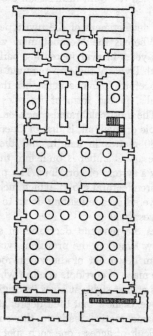

Fig. 3

extensive functional use of the column in Egypt endows the edifices with a lithe and slender outline, a skilful use being made of empty space.

By an evolutionary process whose elements can be identified only partially, the temple reaches its classic form in the New Kingdom (Fig. 3). It is approached by an avenue flanked with sphinxes. Two obelisks stand before the gate, and there is a tower on each side. The gates open on to a great roofless courtyard, surrounded by a portico with a single

or double row of columns. The courtyard leads to a hypostyle
chamber, on a higher level, and divided into five naves by
parallel rows of columns (Pl. XVI). The chamber gives access
to the third section of the temple, on a yet higher level, which
contains the sanctuary of the god, with his statue; around it
are other rooms for associated divinities and the priests. As we
have indicated, the level steadily rises as the seat of the god
is approached; and there is a parallel increase in obscurity,
from the full daylight of the open courtyard to the total
shadow of the sanctuary.

The architectural scheme just described has several associated elements. In the first place, there are the sphinxes,
which we shall discuss in the section devoted to sculpture.
Then there are the obelisks, a distinctive type of granite
pilaster with inscriptions carved on the four faces; these have
been made familiar to us through the specimens which have
been carried away to adorn European cities. There are two
main types of column: the palm type with smooth surfaces
and with capitals of spreading palm leaves; and the lotus type,
with fluted surfaces, and capitals of more or less open lotus
blossoms. Finally, both the temple walls and the columns are
decorated with reliefs illustrating the Pharaoh's enterprises,
and historical inscriptions describing them.

We have already mentioned the funerary temple, which is
found in conjunction with the pyramid from the time of the
Old Kingdom onward, but is also brought to its greatest perfection in the New Kingdom. The finest example – though,
unlike those already mentioned, it cannot be taken as a model
– is that at Deir el-Bahri, built by order of queen Hatshepsut.
In a rugged amphitheatre of rock two arcaded terraces rise to
give access to the sanctuary, which consists of chapels hollowed out of the mountain face.

In civil architecture we have only scanty remains of royal
palaces; but so far as is known, these must have been based
on the same scheme as the great country mansions, of which
we have many examples. They consist of three main sections:
a pillared entrance hall; a central reception hall, also pillared,
with an elevated platform on each side and a hearth in the
centre; and a third section containing the private rooms, bath-

rooms, and kitchens. In addition there are the servants' quarters, and a garden before the entrance. The houses in the cities were evidently not so commodious; such reconstruction as is possible shows, in contrast with Mesopotamia, the use of more than one storey.

In Mesopotamia statuary is developed only to a limited extent, but in Egypt it flourishes exceedingly.[103] It is no longer subject to the purely material limitation which the scarcity of stone imposed in Mesopotamia, and in any case the Egyptian artist does not disdain to use other materials, achieving excellent results in wood, for example. Nor is there the limitation imposed by convention on the representation of the human form; on the contrary, the human form predominates, within the bounds of a style which, though well defined, does not fetter or distort the artist's work.

Egyptian statuary undoubtedly has canons of its own,[104] including both the geometrical principle which we noted in Mesopotamian art (with the necessary changes) and the law of frontal representation which is characteristic of the ancient world. To these principles must be added the fact that the essential purpose of the statuary is not to represent a fact or event, but to present a person. This is particularly true of the statues of the gods and the Pharaohs, in which the very posture of the figures is restricted to a few definitely schematic types (seated on thrones, or standing erect with one leg advanced, but essentially immobile).

However, to counterpose this comparative stylistic uniformity of pose there is a great variety in the representation of the features. It has been justly remarked that behind this there is also a religious motive: being intended as an abode for the dead man's spirit on its return to this world, the statue must present the best possible and most unmistakable likeness of him. But, as always, this motive would have had little effect if it had not been reinforced by an innate artistic capacity. This capacity is present among the ancient Egyptians, and so the faces of their statues bear witness to an eager observation of reality, a marvellous multiplicity of themes, and a vivid power of expression. Nor is this all: the artist seems to be trying through the physical features to bring out the essential features of his subject's personality, sometimes by deliberately toning down salient elements into a serene and noble composition, sometimes by sharpening them into a harassed unrest. Thus in the history of Egyptian sculpture we find the combinations and alternations of two tendencies: one restrained and composed, almost idealistic; the other strongly marked by an accentuated realism. But in both cases we are far from the stiff and uniform conventionalism and stylized symbolism of Mesopotamian art.

In Egypt artistic perfection, as we already know, is not the result of an evolution. Even the Old Kingdom presents achievements of the first order. There is one work of this period which seems most perfectly to realize and exemplify the combination of the canonical geometry on the one hand and intense subjective expression on the other: the Louvre scribe (Pl. XVII). He is represented seated crosslegged, with a roll of papyrus opened out on his knees; the parts have a perfect correspondence and proportion. But when we look at the lean and clearcut features, with their prominent jawbones, the long, supple, slightly pursed lips, and the vivid eyes, we are in the presence of an individual, with all his expressive personality. As Donadoni writes in his sketch of Egyptian art:

The most abstract geometrical scheme avails itself of the most obviously naturalistic means for its realization. The artist thinks in cubes or spherical surfaces or cylinders, and composes according to mathematically proportioned schemes. This figure might quite easily be used to illustrate geometrical theorems, if we could for the moment abstract from its real significance. But it is precisely this abstraction which is denied to us, which is impossible. The sculptor's faith in the expressive possibilities of his geometry coincides so perfectly with his Egyptian faith in reality, and his Egyptian abhorrence of arabesque, that there is no possibility of mistake. He has created anew a human nature, which is our own, by giving new order to the empirical casualness of that which inanimate nature set before him; he has given it a meaning and a value. Just as a physical law does not alter the world of phenomena, but assimilates it for us, so this statue impresses the shapeless and ambiguous reality with the seal of humanity.[105]

Fundamentally, the opposition between the idealizing and the realistic tendencies does not emerge clearly until the period of the New Kingdom. Here on the one hand we find the graceful, harmonious lineaments and the calm expression, relieved by a faint smile, of such statues as that of the general, in the Cairo Museum (Pl. XVIII). On the other, we also observe the fierce striving after realism which has a religious crisis as its background,[106] and which finds expression in such works as the statue of Amenophis IV, also in Cairo (Pl. XIX). In this bony face with its fleshy lips and pointed chin the artist's labour goes beyond the bounds of reality itself.

The truth to nature which we have found to be a characteristic of Egyptian statuary should not lead to the assumption that it excludes the elements of fantasy which belong to the sphere of Egyptian beliefs. On the contrary, perhaps nowhere else is imagination more closely linked with reality, or, rather, accepted as a higher reality. In the field of statuary this is exemplified by that typically Egyptian monument, the sphinx.[107] The oldest and most monumental of these, that of Gizeh (Pl. XX), was originally a rock which was reminiscent of a lion couchant; this resemblance was accentuated by human hands, and a human head was fashioned for it, the result being a magnificent symbol of Pharaonic might. From this origin the sphinx evolved into a distinctive type of statue, and rows of sphinxes were set up as guardians of the entrances to temples; thus the sphinx became in a sense the Egyptian counterpart of the huge, fantastic animals which were set up at the gates of Mesopotamian sanctuaries.

In Egypt bas-relief and painting[108] constitute essentially a single artistic type, with overlapping techniques (for the reliefs are frequently painted) and identical subjects. Both branches are very widely developed; and while Mesopotamia can stand comparison with Egypt in respect of the quantity at least of its reliefs, in painting there is a complete contrast, since remains of Mesopotamian painting are scanty and in a poor state, while the Egyptian examples are plentiful and excellently preserved.

In this field also there is a striking correspondence with the rest of the Oriental world in regard to theoretical principles, as well as a singular difference in their practical application. In spite of certain tentative experiments, perspective may be said to be lacking, in Egypt as in Mesopotamia. The Egyptian, like the Mesopotamian artist, approaches the problem of representation objectively and not subjectively, drawing persons and things as they are, and not as they appear. Nevertheless, because of his innate artistic sense, he avoids the mechanical superposition of planes, preferring to keep to a single plane, in which he can find a solution to his problems without creating a glaring contrast with reality. Here too we find a number of conventions governing the presentation of the figure, and they are essentially the same as in Mesopotamia: the face in profile but giving a frontal view of the eye, shoulders and pelvis frontal, arms and legs in profile. But the elements are unified by a harmonious freedom which reduces or eliminates their lack of articulation. Above all, there is movement; the movement which seems to be denied to the Mesopotamian human figures is now affirmed with a fullness of achievement in no way impaired by the composure of the style.

Bas-relief and painting find practical expression in two main types of monument: temple reliefs, in which war scenes predominate, and sepulchral reliefs and paintings, where the chief subjects are drawn from private and family life. These themes reveal a prime and fundamental difference from the art of the rest of the Oriental world, which is entirely public and official. As we have seen, the Egyptians not only depict the life of individual citizens, but detail the most varied forms of that life, down to those typical of dances and games. At the beginning of this chapter we have described the scenes pictured in a tomb: these convey not only the telling realism which we found in the statuary, but an elegant freshness in the great variety of their themes, a gay and smiling outlook on life, a taste for laughter and jest which we can safely say were unknown to the other peoples of the ancient Orient.

Group scenes are common, so that we may repeat, *mutatis mutandis*, what was said about Assyrian relief, namely that it is documentary before being ornamental, that it is no less expressive of phases of life — albeit of the future life — than a written account could be. But, to illustrate the foregoing remarks, we shall select examples of isolated figures. From the Theban tombs we take the portrait of a female musician (Pl. XXI): the pure and delicate facial profile, the slender and supple lines of the body, with its suggestion of sensuous pleasure, the lightly draped garment, the graceful movement of the arms and hands holding the instrument, all express a serene gaiety and harmonious delight in life. Next, from the tomb of Beni Hasan, we have a bird among branches (Pl. XXII), showing the same fidelity to nature, the same simplicity and purity of line, the same gay serenity. It is the first impression that Egyptian civilization made on us, and it is the last as we leave that civilization.

Out of the extensive variety of products of the minor arts we should at least mention manufactures in wood, and particularly furniture, of which we have fine specimens dating from as early as the Old Kingdom; glassware, finely worked from the Middle Kingdom onward; accurately modelled bronzes;[109] and jewellery, of which a very fine and valuable collection has survived. But as we come to the end of our exposition, we would like rather to summarize the nature and the function of this art. Set on the margin of the ancient Orient, it undoubtedly shares in the general conceptions and characteristics of this world; but in its observation of living man and nature, in its capacity for modelling, in what we may call the classic rhythm of its style, and finally in its expression of subjective feeling, it forms a prelude to those features which later are proper to Greece and the West. Was there a true continuity? Was there a direct handing down and inspiration of subjects? We would not say that, and in any case

it is not the main question. Egyptian art lives a life which is
essentially its own, like that of the 'oasis civilization' of which
it is the expression. If we ask what, then, is its significance
and function, we may answer in the words with which
Donadoni closes the book which we have already quoted:

> Egyptian art did not survive the Arab conquest. It
> did not survive as an active tradition, as a tradition
> which with changing senses and values is passed on
> from generation to generation. But it cannot for that
> reason be said that Egyptian art is a dead art: for an art
> is not living only when it is the seed of another art, but
> rather when it lies open to the understanding of him who
> seeks out the reasons of its being and its problems. If
> the cycle of Egyptian art is chronologically closed in a
> sealed past, this does not prevent us from re-living it
> within ourselves and bringing it into that eternal present
> in which every human experience can become a living
> element of our own personal and active experience.[110]

PART III

The Catalysts

THE HITTITES AND THE HURRIANS

I *The Middle Ages of the Ancient Orient*

About 1500 B.C. — the date is only a very broad approximation — a profound structural modification is to be distinguished in the history of the ancient Near East. Hitherto that history has been governed by two great motive forces, the powers of Egypt and Mesopotamia. Owing to the natural conditions, in the great river valleys civilization emerges sooner, and political aggregates are formed earlier. Then, after achieving internal unity, each of these turns towards the other in a natural movement of expansion and conquest. The other regions and peoples around them, less favoured by fortune, are passive participants in events, objects and not subjects in the determination of their outcome. Now the picture changes: the people of the mountains forming the curving boundary of the north-eastern section of the ancient Orient, and, a little later, those of the desert wastes that stretch to the south of it, intensify their centripetal movement, set up solidly founded states, and enter into competition on equal terms with the valley powers. These newcomers are the catalysts of history: they are responsible for the meeting and synthesis of the opposing forces; and so, in the last resort, it is with their arrival that the ancient Near East assumes its well-defined position as an historical entity beyond and above the individual national elements of which it is constituted.

The mountain peoples who set up strong states in Western Asia about the middle of the second millennium B.C. are three in number: in southern Mesopotamia the Kassites, in northern Mesopotamia the Hurrians, and in Anatolia the Hittites. All three peoples have a history beginning long before the time we are considering. Indeed, the tracing of their origins back into the third millennium is one of the most significant achievements of our own day. But from the viewpoint of their political emergence, 1500 B.C. may still be taken as an approximate date. About this time the Kassites take over power in Babylonia, remaining there for nearly four hundred years, and assimilating the language and culture of the local civilization so completely that they come to form part of it. Also about this time the Hurrians farther to the north set up the great state of Mitanni, which expands almost to the Mediterranean, only to collapse abruptly after less than 150 years. Finally, about this same time the Hittites sally forth from Anatolia to enter the field of international politics with a raid that reaches as far as Babylonia. They will remain on the political scene for some three centuries, and have an eventful history which will soon be examined in detail because of its importance and extensive documentation; here we need only mention that these three centuries from 1500 to 1200 B.C. delimit the period to which the peoples of the mountains give their character and their name.

It is necessary to ask whether, and if so to what extent, it is legitimate to regard these peoples as interconnected, thus historically justifying their designation by a common term. Undoubtedly the similarity of their original homes and primitive conditions is a significant factor, but it does not get us very far. Their ethnical relationship is more important, for though it is only partial and varying in its nature it is worth noting. All the peoples of the mountains include an Indo-European element, varying in its extent and purity. In the case of the Hittites the upper classes of the population are Indo-European immigrants who have brought their language with them; in the case of the Hurrians Indo-Europeans constitute the dominant noble class, as is evident by their names; several of the Kassites' divinities are probably Indo-European, which suggests a corresponding ethnic element. Thus a new family of peoples, with a well-known function in the history of the Mediterranean basin, makes its appearance in the Near East and, concurrently with the Semitic populations who come from the Arabian desert, becomes a principal actor in a new phase of history.

An interesting parallel can be drawn between the situation of the ancient Orient in the age of the 'Peoples of the mountains' and that of Europe in the early Middle Ages, based on the characteristics and social organization of the new peoples, and on the general situation which results from their activities.[1]

Coming, like the barbarians, from a stage of nomadism, the peoples of the mountains bring with them a social structure based on the predominance of a limited noble class who control the means which determine military success: the horse and the chariot. Outstanding among the nobles, *primus inter pares* in war and peace, is the king: and so a type of sovereign very different from that we have previously found in the ancient Orient. After their conquest, the nobles share out the land in the feudal fashion, assuming the rights and obligations involved; their power is decisive, and that of the king is conditioned by it, at least in the very earliest phase.

The situation which results from the formation of the new kingdom prefigures that which is achieved in Europe through the Roman-barbarian states. New active forces come into play; the geographical area is widened and political organisms are multiplied; the centres of gravity shift from the ancient empires, leaving a relative equilibrium in which old and new factors work together. Thus, both through the differentiation of its forces and in spite of it, the ancient Near East, like mediaeval Europe, becomes an organic historical entity, with its boundaries defined and its elements interflowing in a combined movement.

The new equilibrium is no longer founded, as in the past, simply on the relation between the opposing forces. It is a significant fact that, predominantly as the result of action on the part of the peoples of the mountains, international law is established, based on a number of treaties with a clearly defined juridical structure. There is a parallel development in diplomatic activity, taking the form of a more advanced organization of embassies, the exchange of gifts, marriages between members of ruling houses; and, above all, diplomacy crystallizes into a single form and an organic procedure from one end of the region to the other. The system is based on the single language selected as the form of its expression, namely, Akkadian: a striking example of this is the fact that correspondence between the Pharaohs and their vassals on the Syro-Palestinian coast is conducted in this language, which is foreign to both parties.

Here we may make a further observation on this phase of Oriental history. In the course of establishing themselves, the new peoples thoroughly absorb the great cultural tradition already existing. In this process of absorption, Mesopotamian seems to prevail over Egyptian influence; and, indeed, because of the new lines of communication it extends to and asserts itself even over Egypt, as the case of the diplomatic language just mentioned proves. But obviously the effect on the peoples of the mountains is stronger and more direct, with the result that those most exposed to it, the Kassites, yield completely; and although the same cannot be said of the others, they largely assimilate the forms and the content of Mesopotamian civilization. Thus the cuneiform script is extended over all the Near East, the deities and religious beliefs and practices of Mesopotamia are diffused over a wide area, its great literary works are transmitted in translations, summaries, and adaptations, and its artistic motifs and the concepts which inspire them are taken up and repeated.

Thus the new civilization has neither victors nor vanquished. Like Rome in the Middle Ages, despite its political decadence Mesopotamia in the age of the peoples of the mountains celebrates the triumph of its culture.

The parallel between Europe's Middle Ages and this period of Near Eastern history is so striking that there is a danger of losing sight of certain profound differences between them. It is well to draw attention to these differences, not with the object of weakening the parallel, but in order to make it more precise and satisfactory. The dissolution of the Roman Empire has a Near Eastern counterpart in a crisis of the great powers; but that crisis is only temporary, the powers continue to exist, and, in contrast to events in Europe, recover their dominion.

Moreover, in the Near East there is no religious phenomenon comparable with Christianity; it is true that the Mesopotamian religion has an influence over the surrounding peoples, but it is only limited and within the framework of the general expansive force of culture, and has no oecumenical drive. The Near Eastern scene also presents no phenomenon analogous to the Holy Roman Empire, and so the longing for equilibrium does not become a longing for unity, nor is there any effective centralizing element at work on the various political and spiritual forces. Thus, in Europe there is a phase of development, in the Near East there is a parenthesis and a temporary halt: the ancient motive forces will soon recover their ascendancy and will maintain it until the close of ancient Oriental history.

II *The Historical Outlines*

Three main phases, each with its distinctive characteristics, can be identified in the history of the Hittites.[2] The first phase, the Old Empire, covers the establishment and consolidation of the state in Anatolia; the second phase, the New Empire, is distinguished by a determined intervention in international politics, with success and sudden collapse; the third phase, the Neo-Hittite one, is, so to speak, the empire's posterity, with its ethnic elements persisting in the area of expansion beyond its frontiers.

This division into three phases is based on more than superficial distinctions; there is a parallel and connected development of intrinsic characteristics: whereas at first the political structure is marked by the predominance of the hereditary autonomy of the mountain peoples, later on the elements proper to the milieu penetrate and become established, and in the end it is these elements that predominate. There is a process of assimilation and synthesis fully based on the course of events.

The task of tracing the history of the Hittites will therefore connote the following of an evolution along two lines: that of the persistence of original characteristics, and that of the infiltration of environmental factors. From first to last these two lines run parallel, as they shift from the extrinsic to the intrinsic history of the ancient Near East.

It is difficult to say when the Indo-European element was superposed on the native peoples of Anatolia and the fusion was initiated of which the Hittite people was the product. Nor is it necessary, as in other cases, to presume that there was a single overwhelming conquest, rather than a repeated and prolonged penetration. Many indications suggest that the original division of the invaders into tribes was paralleled in the occupied territory by a division into city states, which were not drawn into a centripetal movement of political organization until later. If the information conveyed by a later inscription is exact, the beginning of this process occurs in the times of the kings Pitkhanas and Anittas of Kussara, who subjugate a series of neighbouring city states at a period which is conjectured to be about 1800 B.C. In any case, the process is completed some time later, in the days of another king, Labarnas, whom Hittite tradition regards as the true founder of the Old Empire: it is told of him that he subjugated enemy lands, extended the frontiers to the sea, and made his sons governors in the great cities. There is no reason to suspect any exaggeration in this statement, and, even if there were, all that really interests us is the fact that the empire is now established.

The military drive beyond the frontiers of Anatolia begins under Labarnas's successor, Hattusilis I. He is unsuccessful in his expedition against the city of Aleppo, but he has opened the way and pointed the direction. At home he is faced with a hostile court, and is obliged to change his choice of successor: facts not significant in themselves, but rendered highly important by their formulation in a document, the so-called 'Testament', in which the king sets down the causes, the circumstances, and the effects of these events. This is to be noted as the first appearance of that capacity to think and write as an historian (in the modern sense), of which we shall find even clearer examples among the Hittites later. Furthermore, the discussion on equal terms between the king and his nobles reveals a typical feature of Hittite monarchy, not previously found in the Near East; while the direct and spontaneous vigour of the narrative has a literary style as new as it is significant. Here is the great king Hattusilis speaking to the assembly of nobles and dignitaries:

> Lo, I fell sick. I had presented to you the young Labarnas as he who should sit upon the throne; I, the king, called him my son, I embraced him, I exalted him, I cared for him without cease. But he proved himself a young man not worth looking upon: he did not shed tears, he did not sympathize, he is cold and heartless. Then I, the king, called him and made him come to my bedside. So no longer can I go on treating a nephew as a son! To the king's words he paid no heed, but to those of his mother he paid good heed, the serpent! Brothers and sisters spoke evil words to him, and to those he paid heed. But I, the king, learned of it; and then I met strife with strife. Now it is finished! He is no longer a son. Then his mother lowed like an ox: 'They have torn my bosom in my living flesh! They have destroyed him, and thou wilt kill him!' But I, the king, did I ever do him any harm? Did I not make him a priest? Always I honoured him, thinking of his good. But he did not follow the king's will with love. How could he, following his own will, feel love for Hattusas? . . .[3] Behold, Mursilis is now my son! Him you must acknowledge, set him upon the throne. In his heart god has put rich gifts. . . . In time of war or insurrection, be at his side, O my servants, and you, chiefs of the citizens . . . Hitherto no one (of my family) has obeyed my will. But do thou obey, O Mursilis, thou who art my son. Follow the words of thy father![4]

Which of the other oriental kings we have met so far would have made such an appeal? Which of them would have so openly admitted that his family was insubordinate? It has been conjectured[5] that the 'Testament' is really a *Fürstenspiegel*, a work composed for the edification of princes, and attributed to the king only at a later date. This does not seem a very likely hypothesis; but even if it were correct, the features would only be all the more typical.

Thus the Hittite king is a *primus inter pares*, a chief with limited powers and controlled by an assembly of nobles which confers his authority on him and can deprive him of it. For the first time in the ancient Near East, we meet with a right of human investiture: the king of the Hittites is neither god as in Egypt, nor god's representative, as in Mesopotamia; he is closer to the mediaeval Germanic chief than to the oriental sovereign. Similarly, the Hittites have a different conception of political dominion corresponding neither to the Mesopotamian idea of universal kingship nor to the Egyptian system of colonization. The Hittites make treaties with the peoples they conquer, and use this political form to bind them to themselves.[6] Hence, on the political plane we have the outcome of another characteristic of Hittite thought: its attitude to international law. Their internal feudalism is projected into the sphere of external politics, in a kind of federalism which to some extent reproduces the characteristics of that feudalism.

The second phase of the Hittites' drive beyond their borders takes place under Hattusilis's successor, Mursilis I: about 1530 B.C. he sends an expedition on a raid as far as Babylonia. This episode is significant in several respects. Militarily, it indicates that good bases have now been established in Upper Syria, the expedition's starting point. Politically, it is the newcomers' first success in the very heart of the areas of the older culture; it is only a temporary success, but it brings about an upheaval from which other peoples of the mountains, the Kassites, will profit ere long in order to establish their own domination of Babylonia. It would perhaps be an inexact comparison to parallel Mursilis's march on Babylon with those of the Germanic kings on Rome;[7] but it undoubtedly indicates that the mountain peoples are asserting themselves against or alongside those of the valleys, and so it is legitimate to regard this raid as initiating a new era.

The peculiar character of the Hittite regal power — its limitation and control by the assembly — renders it ill adapted to the pursuit of political expansion: Mursilis is assassinated, and this deed is followed by a number of conspiracies and political crimes, with the king and the nobility as opposing forces in a struggle which appears to have no solution. In the end it is the royal power that prevails, but not without the intervention of outside influences. The outcome of this development is a constitutional reform, achieved by king Telipinus at the beginning of the fifteenth century B.C. He secures the adoption of the hereditary principle of succession to the throne, and so blunts the edge of the assembly's most dangerous weapon.

Now by various means the foundations have been laid for the period of the state's greatest development. The Old Empire ends, and after a time of obscurity[8] which recent chronology has reduced from centuries to decades, the New Empire arrives, reaching its zenith of power under the great king Suppiluliumas (1380–1346 B.C.).[9] At the time Egypt is passing through a crisis as the result of Akhenaton's religious reform, and so the conditions for Hittite expansion are at their most favourable, and it reaches out to Upper Mesopotamia and Upper Syria, as far as the Mountains of Lebanon. Thus the way is prepared for a future clash between the empires. The age of Suppiluliumas is important also in the internal sphere: the concept of kingship evolves in the direction of that of the great oriental monarchies. We have already noted the prelude to this evolution. The king's title is changed, and he is now addressed as 'my Sun', a winged solar disc being incorporated in his standard. This indicates direct or indirect Egyptian influence. Further, still under the same influence, the sovereign is deified, though this takes place only after his death: hence the phrase 'to become a god' comes to be simultaneously a reference to the king's demise.

The victorious campaigns continue under Mursilis II, and the annals of his reign give us documented details. These annals are an historical text of prime importance both because they are the first of their kind (the Assyrian annals are later in date) and because they thoroughly develop the Hittite capacity for thinking in terms of cause and effect which we have noted in the 'Testament' of Hattusilis I. A striking feature of these annals is, in fact, that they mention the motives for the actions taken by the king and others, and inquire into the thoughts and reflections lying behind events.[10] For example, Mursilis describes the situation when he came to the throne in the following terms:

> When Arnuwandas, my brother, had become a god, even those enemy lands which had not yet begun war began it. The enemy countries round about us thought as follows: His father, who was king of the Hittite region, was a heroic sovereign and had the upper hand over enemy countries; but he became a god. His son, who sat on the throne of his father, was also at first a hero; but he, too, fell ill and became a god. Now, however, he who sits on the throne of his father is a child and will not save the Hittite region and its territory.[11]

Mursilis, who understands the meaning of these prognostications, takes steps with the aid of his patron goddess to prove them false.

A further example of this feature of the annals is drawn from the narrative of the expedition against Carchemish, in the ninth year of Mursilis's reign. The account is prefaced by a thorough survey of the motives for the attack: the Assyrians have attacked Carchemish, and Mursilis has to choose between two expeditions, against the Assyrians or against Hayasa. The king would like to deal with Hayasa first, but then he reflects on the effect that would have on the Assyrians, for they would think he had abandoned Carchemish to its fate. So he decides in favour of that city. Furlani has brought out excellently the historical value of this passage:

> In this passage the *Annals* of Mursilis once more rise to the height of a truly historiographical work. We can see into the king's very mind and follow his thoughts and reflections on the events which were taking place before his eyes, and whose course he himself, at least in part, directed and determined. The king further tells us the motives which led his adversaries to act in this way or in that . . . As may be seen from what we have set forth, the more closely we study these *Annals* of

Mursilis, the more clearly do they reveal their true character as a historiographical work of the highest value, whose importance is truly exceptional among the historical works of ancient Western Asia. This is perhaps the first true historiographical work of the ancient civilizations which preceded that of Greece.[12]

Of course, we have not overlooked the crudity and unsystematic nature of parts of these narratives, which puts them on a lower level than the finer passages of Hebrew prose, for example. But if history differs from simple chronicle by supplementing the account of events with an estimate of their importance, then Mursilis's work is no less history than the later Biblical writings.

Mursilis's victories hasten the great clash with Egypt, which has now recovered from its crisis. Under his successor, Muwatallis, a battle is fought at Qadesh (1296 B.C.), but without decisive outcome,[13] and so Hattusilis III is able to sign a treaty which establishes peace and a balance of power in the Near East. Hattusilis III is a usurper, and he has left an account of his internal politics which is unique in the ancient Near East. It is an autobiographical *Apologia pro vita sua*, justifying his accession to the throne by a revolt against his nephew Urhi-Teshub. Here an historical sense equal to that revealed in the annals is accompanied by a lively and direct narrative spontaneity which takes the form of an intimate conversation with the reader:

> For seven years I conformed. But he, at the bidding of his deity and of his council, sought to destroy me . . . Then I no longer conformed, but broke with him. All the same, in breaking with him, I did not do so treacherously, rebelling against him in chariot or in house; instead I declared war on him: 'Thou hast picked a quarrel with me. Thou art the Great King, whereas I possess only the one stronghold which thou hast left me. Well, the goddess Ishtar of Samuha and the storm-god of Nerik will decide between us!' When I wrote thus to Urhi-Teshub, someone might have said to me: 'Why didst thou in the first place set him on the throne, and now

thou writest to him to depose him?' But if he had not picked a quarrel with me, would the gods have permitted a Great King to be defeated by a little king? It is because he picked a quarrel with me that the gods by their judgement brought him to defeat at my hands.[14]

Hattusilis dies about 1250 B.C., and the Hittite empire survives him by only a few decades. Its end is brought about not by a slow and progressive decline, but by a sudden mortal crisis. About 1200 B.C. the 'peoples of the sea', armed with the new and powerful weapons of the Iron Age, pour into the Near East from Greece and the Aegean Islands; the Hittite empire collapses before their onslaught, and the Egyptian and Assyrian empires are driven back within their home frontiers. The Oriental Middle Ages are ended.

However, the Hittites leave behind an epilogue, which lasts for several centuries. In the region of the Taurus and in Upper Syria, petty states formed during the centuries of Hittite imperialism live on after the death of the empire, and share the small-scale political history of the rising Hebrew and Aramaean kingdoms.[15] True, they are only partly Hittite, namely, in certain strata of their people, and for this reason some of them, Sam'al, Aleppo, and Hama, for instance, in which the Aramaean element is prominent, will be considered elsewhere. Their language, written in a script which is not cuneiform, and which has only recently been deciphered, is now recognized as related to Hittite but not identical with it. The culture also is a typically hybrid one.

The most important document left by the Neo-Hittites is one recently discovered at Karatepe in Cilicia. This is a long inscription in Phoenician and in hieroglyphic Hittite, recounting the activities of the local king Asitawandas:[16]

> I am Asitawandas, servant of Baal, vassal of Aurik, king of the Danuna. Baal has made me father and mother of the Danuna. I have exalted the Danuna. I have broadened the territory of the plain of Adana from the east to the west. In my days there has been every kind of

wellbeing, plenty and wealth for the Danuna. I have
filled the storehouses of Pahri, have added horse to horse,
shield to shield, army to army, thanks to Baal and the
gods. I have put down the mighty, have destroyed the
evil which was in the land, have established the wellbeing of the clan of my lord and done good to his line-
age. I have sat on my father's throne and have made
peace with all the kings: all the kings have regarded
me as a father because of my justice, my wisdom, and
the goodness of my heart. . . .

The history of the petty Neo-Hittite states, like that of the
Upper Syrian states generally, is passive, expressing the negative aspect of the growing Assyrian expansion. When the
principal centre, Carchemish,[17] falls in 717 B.C., and Malatya
eight years later, that history is completed.

III *The Religious Structure*

A definition of Hittite civilization and an identification of its
fundamental characteristics seems to us to be possible only if
we accept a notable renunciation in principle: not to seek a
common denominator, a unifying factor. On the contrary, we
have to regard the plurality of the components as the typical
feature: not, of course, simply because we find this plurality,
for every culture reacts to innumerable stimuli; but because
in this case there is no consistency of reaction, and the various
elements remain in simple juxtaposition rather than becoming
fused into a single complex.

The Hittite religion provides a typical example of this:[18] it
includes the beliefs of the earlier, native peoples, those of the
Indo-European superstratum, and those of other mountain
peoples, of the Hittites' Anatolian neighbours, of the Mesopotamian peoples, and of the Egyptians. Moreover, each god
retains his own temples, his own priesthood, his own cult, and
even his own religious language. There is, in fact, some attempt to organize the pantheon, resulting rather from the
political unity of the state than the theological initiative of the

priesthood; but this does not affect the core of the religious life, and although it brings about processes of fusion and inter-connection in the realm of theory, the texts show that these are tolerated only superficially in practice.

The German authority, Moortgat, is right to speak of 'spir-itual federalism', and to see in this a parallel with the politi-cal federalism which is characteristic of Hittite civilization:

> The religious life of the Hittite Empire is distinguished by a general spiritual tolerance, and even veneration for foreign gods, to whom, as to foreign visitors to their land, they accorded full hospitality, as later did the Persian Achaemenid rulers. Not fusion of the cults or myths of the gods, but what one might call a spiritual federalism corresponds to the feudal conception of the civil constitution. The various cultural and biological strata of the Hittite people, which never grew into a real unity, had not only their own gods with their own temples in the locality, but also their own priests, and the convenience of worshipping in their own local lan-guage. It is true that veneration was shown primarily to one's own particular supernatural powers, those closest to one's own being, and to which one had always been accustomed, as a child is to its own parents and fore-bears; but it was realized that other peoples and tribes worshipped similar forces, and that each valley should have a different mountain-god, or river-god, or storm-god, enthroned on a mountain-peak. These were the Hit-tites' thousand gods, who can no longer be cited by name: an exaggerated form of polytheism, which offers the sharpest internal contrast to the fervent exclusive faith in Yahweh which is soon to exercise its activity in West-ern Asia.[19]

The mountain peoples have a characteristic deity[20] in the storm god, for here is represented the natural force which makes the most direct impression in regions of cloud and rain such as those from which these peoples came. But, in con-formity with the traits just discussed, Hittite religion has not one, but several, storm gods, varying from place to place; and these gods are sometimes native, sometimes imported from abroad, like the Hurrian god Teshub or the Luvian Dattas.

Among the deities associated with cosmic forces, the Mesopotamian trinity, Anu, Enlil and Ea, are widely welcomed. Of the astral elements, the sun is regarded as of the greatest importance, yet not so much its male divinity, though he exists, as its female one, whose most important personification is the goddess of Arinna. But, as usual, there are others too, foremost among them the Hurrian Hebat, while Mesopotamia provides a further figure in the Hittite pantheon, namely Ishtar, with her Hurrian variant, Shaushka.

The well-known Oriental vegetation god is also present, and his Hittite incarnation in Telipinus does not appear to be a foreign importation; his adventures, which will be considered when we come to the literature, are to be set beside those of the Mesopotamian Dumuzi (Tammuz) and the Egyptian Osiris.

So far as we can tell, the Hittite conception of the gods is the same as in Mesopotamia: similar to man in all things, they are mightier than men, and enjoy immortality. *similar to Mes*

We have said that the pantheon was subjected to an attempt at organization, albeit partial and superficial. This organization places the sun goddess of Arinna, coupled with the storm god, at the summit of the heavenly hierarchy; they give birth to Telipinus, as well as other storm and sun gods. But variety and contrast dominate these relationships from one period to another and one locality to another, so that it is these qualities, rather than organization and harmony, that distinguish Hittite theology.

The foregoing seems to indicate clearly enough the predominance of Mesopotamian influence in Hittite religion. Even the foreign gods, though independent in themselves, come to be incorporated in forms of worship and ritual of Babylonian or Assyrian, and thus often of Sumerian, inspiration. Mesopotamian also, but with a religious background which may well be autonomous, is the belief in demons as disturbers of human life, causes of the evils which are the result of sin, but which may also be the effect of sorcery. And so there is a corpus of magic literature, which often reproduces the forms already met among the Babylonians and Assyrians.

There is, for instance, a rite directed against family quarrels. If a father quarrels with his son, a husband with his wife, or a brother with his sister, the following steps have to be taken to reconcile them:

> They drive up a black sheep, the witch[21] presents it to them and speaks as follows: 'For your heads and all the parts of your bodies the black sheep is a substitute. The tongue of cursing is in its mouth and its tongue.' She waves it over them. The two sacrificers spit into its mouth. They slaughter the sheep and cut it up. They kindle the hearth and burn it. They pour honey and olive oil over it. She breaks a sacrificial loaf and throws it on to the hearth. She also pours out a libation of wine.[22]

Once more we have a procedure embodying the idea of substituting an animal for the man, which we have already noted as a characteristic concept of the Babylonians and the Assyrians.

Mesopotamian divination[23] exerts a similar influence on the Hittites. But here we find a group of texts with a distinctive literary structure. The object is to consult the omens when a god is angered: a set of questions is asked the oracle concerning the cause of his anger, and by a long process of eliminating the negative replies the cause is identified. For instance, the god Hurianzipas is angry. The temple priests are asked their opinion, and they reply that the sacrificial offerings have not been made punctually. So the omens are consulted:

> Is the god angry because the sacrifices have been made belatedly? If so, let the omens be unfavourable. Unfavourable. If this is the sole reason, let the omens be favourable. Unfavourable.[24]

Thus a reason for the god's anger is now known, but it is not the only reason. The priests' opinion is sought once more:

We asked the temple officials again and they said: 'A
dog came into the temple, it shook the table and the sacrificial loaves fell down. They reduced the daily ration
of sacrificial loaves considerably.' Is the god angry for
that reason? Unfavourable. If the god is angry only because of the offences we have so far established, let the
omens be favourable. Unfavourable.[25]

And so on, from one hypothesis to another, until the final
solution is reached and all the causes of the god's anger are
identified.

The cult is still dominated by Mesopotamian influence, but
it exhibits variants fully justified by the people's independent
origin and tradition. The priesthood is well organized, and
divided into categories according to their character and function: sacrificers, cantors, sorcerers, diviners, attendants, or
vergers; nor are female personnel missing. As representative
of the community, the king has an essential part to play in
divine worship, and — a new feature — the queen also plays a
distinctive part, and even has certain functions reserved to
her. This fact indicates that Hittite women have a much more
prominent and active position than those of the other Oriental
peoples, and exert an outstanding influence in the life of the
court, as certain documents have already shown.

Festivals of years, seasons, and months, form the basis of
the religious calendar, and the celebration of the annually
renewed fertility of the earth is given particular prominence.
The procedure of the sacrifice, the cardinal feature of the celebration, is governed by a complex casuistic system which the
texts faithfully document; food and drink, selected and puri-
fied in accordance with detailed and meticulous rules, form
the offering. There is not much novelty in this by comparison
with what we have already seen elsewhere; but occasionally
our attention is attracted by details, such as hints at human
sacrifice,[26] which provide a glimpse of a religious attitude
which is not official, and so is more independent and original
in its forms.

One Hittite rite is of quite outstanding interest because it is unique in the ancient Orient: the kings are cremated after death.[27] The rite lasts several days. On the first day a funeral pyre is lit, and the body burned on it. Then:

> On the second day, at daybreak, the women go to the pyre[28] to gather up the bones, and they extinguish the fire with ten flagons of beer, ten of wine and ten of *valhi.*[29] A silver amphora weighing half a mina and twenty shekels is filled with refined oil. They then take up the bones with a silver *lappa*[30] and put them in the refined oil in the silver amphora; then they take them out of the refined oil and put them on a *gazzarnulli*[31] linen cloth, under which is set a fine web. When they have finished gathering up the bones, they wrap them up along with the linen in the web and put them on a chair, but if it is a woman they put them on a stool. Around the pyre on which the body was burnt they put ten loaves, and on the loaves they put a pie of fat. The fire has already been extinguished with the beer and the wine. In front of the chair on which the bones are lying they place a table, and offer warm loaves and sweet loaves[32] to be broken. The cooks and the attendants of the table serve the dishes and take them away. To all those who have come to gather up the bones they give to drink.[33]

This cremation rite is a new phenomenon in the Near East, and in many respects it recalls the *Iliad's* description of the cremation of Patroclus and Hector. Is there possibly a historical connection? Undoubtedly, if we remember that Troy was situated on the verge of Anatolia. But there is more to it than that. The Hittite texts contain many names, both of regions and of peoples and persons, which are closely similar to Achaean and Trojan ones. Are the Ahhiyawa, whom the Hittites encounter in the West, the Achaeans?[34] Is the city of Truisa Troy? And is the vassal king Alaksandus of Wilusa Alexander of Ilion? We can make a number of tentative hypotheses, of all which it can be said, after the long discussion on the subject,[35] that nothing is certain, and nothing ruled out; but the very quantity of the indications available sufficiently justifies our accepting them at least as working hypotheses.

We cannot follow this description of the funeral rites with an adequate treatment of Hittite beliefs concerning the next world, for they by no means attain the importance and extension they have in Egypt, and do not even reach the modest level of the Mesopotamian conceptions. The allusions in the texts are few and restricted in scope; and, even more significant, they are mainly found in literary works whose inspiration not only is clearly Mesopotamian, but belongs rather to the realm of literature than to the inner realm of religious life. Nor does the little we do know — the belief in a kingdom of the underworld, and in survival after death — depart from its models.

So it is not in this direction that we must seek the autonomous elements of Hittite religious life and thought. And yet, when closely examined, with all their often incoherent multiplicity of factors, and their subjection to predominant foreign influence, that life and thought do reveal the indelible traces of an independent origin and tradition.

IV *The Literary Genres*

More than any of the literatures previously considered, Hittite literature is affected by the reservation that our judgement is conditioned by the limits of our knowledge. This may seem trite, but it is not really so, if it be remembered that our documentation is so incomplete and uncertain that it is not possible to present even on a small scale the literary patrimony and the conceptions by which it was governed. This is indeed the case in regard to Hittite literature, for all we know of it is derived from a single library, that of the capital city Hattusas, and from only a part even of that. In Mesopotamia the documents are at any rate derived from a number of localities, and this gives some guarantee that our presentation of the literary genres will not be far from the truth, at least so far as the construction and the quality of the literature are concerned. But as we have only a single, and partial, source for Hittite literature, there is no guarantee that many aspects and genres of literary activity are not still hidden from us.

In regard to content, Hittite literature, like Hittite religion, is clearly under predominantly Mesopotamian influence. Even so, it is significant that this influence is for the most part not direct, but is exercised through the medium of another of the mountain peoples, the Hurrians, who because of their geographical situation act as a bridge between the two civilizations. Simultaneously the Hurrians themselves prove to be the creators on their own account of a broad cultural cycle, a corpus of traditions and literary genres which the Hittites take over more or less faithfully and make their own. Generally speaking, this is done amazingly crudely, and with a primitiveness in striking contrast with the high degree of evolution and elaboration found in the literary genres which had existed in Mesopotamia ever since the days of the Sumerians.

These remarks apply, of course, only up to the point at which the Hittites themselves begin to create; for then — as we have already seen to some extent — original and independent literary forms do exist, the annals and political treaties being the most outstanding. At this stage, Hittite literature becomes a positive force: it creates new literary genres and raises them to the highest level hitherto achieved in the ancient Orient.

The most extensively exploited genre is that of the mythological epic, the narration of the activities of the gods, their conflicts and adventures. But unlike the Mesopotamian parallels, this is for the most part in crude prose, or at least, we cannot detect that it contains any poetic structure.

If we classify the myths according to their origins, two outstanding cycles are apparently Hittite, at least their chief characters are Hittite. One of these deals with the slaying of a dragon, and the other with the disappearance of a god. They both have their roots in the religious and literary patrimony of the ancient Orient: the former reproduces the tale of the divine hero conquering the forces of evil, in other words, the Mesopotamian myth of Marduk's victory over the dragon

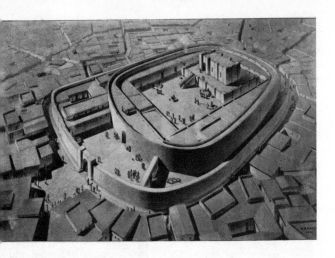

I. Temple oval at Khafaje: reconstruction

II. Ziqqurat of Ur: reconstruction

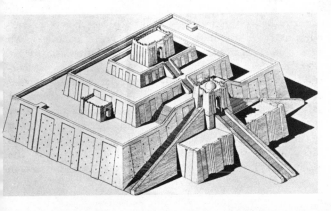

III. Statuette from Tell Asma

IV. Priest of Khafaje

v. Bull's head from Khafaje

vi. Stele of the Vultures; detail

VII. Perforated plaque with banquet scene

VIII. Sumerian seals

IX. Jewellery from Ur

X. The overseer Ebih-il

XI. Winged bull
with human head

XII. The hunt of Ashurbanipal

XIII. Relief in glazed tiles from Babylon

XIV. Wall painting from Mari

xv. Ivory from Nimrud

xvi. Hypostyle hall at Karnak

XVII. The Scribe. Louvre

XVIII.
Statuette of a general

XIX. Amenophis IV

XX. Sphinx of Gizeh

XXI. Egyptian musician

XXII.
Painting
of a bird

XXIII.
Lion from Malaty

XXIV. Procession from Yazilikaya

xxv. Relief from Karatepe; detail

xxvi. Gods of Ugarit

XXVII. Golden dish from Ugarit

XXVIII. 'The Goddess of wild beasts'

XXIX. Ivory from Samaria

XXX. Remains of palace of Persepolis

XXXI. Rock tombs and fire temple

XXXII. Winged bulls of Persepolis

Tiamat and the Egyptian myth of the sun vanquishing the serpent Apophis; the latter is the Hittite version of the Mesopotamian cycle of Dumuzi (Tammuz) and the Egyptian cycle of Osiris. But the relationship is conceptual, not literary: the Hittite versions differ considerably from the others, showing that they arose and were developed independently.

As we are explicitly told at the beginning of the text, the dragon cycle, brought together in two versions by a priest of Nerik, was recited on the feast of Purulli, which probably coincided with the New Year. This information is of great interest: it constitutes one of the elements from which we draw the conclusion that in the ancient Orient there was a very close connection between mythology and ritual, and that some at least of the 'literary' texts are in reality the scripts of religious ceremonies. We shall come back to this problem later, after accumulating the relevant data. Confining ourselves for the moment to the cycle under consideration, we have the storm god as its protagonist, and the main purpose of the narrative is to exalt his victory. According to the more ancient version, the dragon Illuyankas has the better of the encounter at first. In order to avenge himself, the storm god arranges a great banquet, to which he invites his enemy; he makes the dragon eat so much that he is no longer capable of returning home:

> The dragon Illuyankas came up with his children, and they ate and drank. They drank every amphora dry and quenched their thirst. Thereupon they were no longer able to descend to their lair . . . The storm-god came and killed the dragon Illuyankas, and the gods were with him.[36]

We can recall few parallels to such a crude and ingenuous tale: one might, perhaps, adduce the story of the struggle between Horus and Set. But that was by way of exception, and here it is the rule and characterizes the artistic level. The later version of the myth provides another example: now the dragon, after its initial success over the storm god, removes his heart and eyes; the god is anxious to recover them, and avails himself of his son's marriage to Illuyankas's daughter to gain his end:

> The storm-god told his son: 'When thou goest to the house of thy wife, ask them for my heart and my eyes.' When he went there, he asked them for the heart and they gave it to him. Later he asked for the eyes and they gave him those too. He brought them to the storm-god, his father. Thus the storm-god got back his heart and his eyes. When his frame had been restored to its old state, he went to the sea for battle. When he engaged the dragon Illuyankas in battle, he came close to vanquishing him.[37]

The mythological cycle of the Missing God[38] calls for attention from more than one aspect. To begin with, it appears to be the fullest and most immediate literary expression so far met with of the vegetation cycle conception which is common to all the ancient Orient. Secondly, the ritual connection is explicit and direct, in the complicated magical procedure of the purification and resuscitation of the god which occupies the concluding part of the narrative. The cycle has one principal version, in which Telipinus plays the part of the missing god; but the existence of other versions with other actors indicates that the essential and original element of the myth is the event which it relates, and not the actors taking part in it.

The story goes that Telipinus (to confine ourselves to the principal version) is angry and vanishes from the earth; there follows an impressive description of the dying off of all life:

> So grain and spelt thrive no more. So cattle, sheep and man no longer breed. And even those with young cannot bring them forth. The vegetation dried up, the trees dried up and would bring forth no fresh shoots. The pastures dried up, the springs dried up. Famine arose in the land, man and gods perished from hunger.[39]

The significance of the god's disappearance could not be stated more explicitly. In any case, it is confirmed by the words which, in his distress, the storm god addresses to the other gods:

The storm-god became anxious about Telipinus, his son: 'Telipinus, my son,' he said, 'is not here. He has flown into a rage and taken off every good thing.' The great gods and the lesser gods began to search for Telipinus. The sun-god sent out the swift eagle, saying: 'Go, search every high mountain! Search the deep valleys! Search the watery deep!' The eagle went, but could not find him.[40]

After various ineffectual attempts, it is the bee who at last succeeds in finding Telipinus, and it would be of interest to dwell for a moment on the significance of this motif in folklore. But we must proceed: Telipinus returns, still unplacated. The goddess of magic exorcizes his wrath with a magic ritual, and finally he is restored to tranquillity, and he consents to the revival of fertility. Once more there is an explicit description:

> Telipinus came home to his house and cared again for his land . . . The altars were set right for the gods. He put the log on the hearth. He let the sheep go to the fold, he let the cattle go to the pen. The mother tended her child, the ewe tended her lamb, the cow tended her calf. Also Telipinus tended the king and the queen and provided them with enduring life and vigour.[41]

This closes the cycle, which, we may remark, is on a higher literary level than that of the storm god and the dragon or that of the one which we shall discuss now. This is a myth borrowed from a Hurrian source, and so is the first we meet of those derived from the peoples of the Hittite milieu.

In the cycle of Kumarbi, the father of the gods,[42] two main parts can be distinguished. The first, called 'Kingship in Heaven', tells how this kingship passes from Alalu to Anu, from Anu to Kumarbi, and from Kumarbi to the storm god Teshub who, born of his predecessor, apparently succeeds in depriving him of his throne:

> Once in the olden days Alalu was king in heaven. Alalu was seated on the throne and the mighty Anu, first among the gods, stood before him. He would sink at his feet and set the drinking-cup in his hand.

Nine in number were the years that Alalu was king in heaven. In the ninth year Anu gave battle to Alalu and vanquished him; he fled before him and went down to the dark earth. Anu took his seat upon the throne. Anu was seated on the throne and the mighty Kumarbi would give him his food. He would sink at his feet and set the drinking-cup in his hand.

Nine in number were the years that Anu was king in heaven. In the ninth year Anu gave battle to Kumarbi and like Alalu, Kumarbi gave battle to Anu. Anu could no longer withstand Kumarbi's eyes, he struggled forth from the hands of Kumarbi and fled, like a bird he moved in the sky. Kumarbi rushed after him, seized him by his feet, and dragged him down from the sky.

He bit off Anu's genitals, and his manhood went down into his inside. When it lodged there, when Kumarbi had swallowed Anu's manhood, he rejoiced and laughed. But Anu turned back to him and began to speak: 'Thou rejoicest over thine inside, because thou hast swallowed my manhood. Rejoice not over thine inside! In thine inside I have planted a heavy burden. To begin with I have impregnated thee with the noble storm-god . . . !'[43]

Note the affinity which this myth reveals with the Theogony of Hesiod:[44] the succession Anu-Kumarbi-Teshub corresponds to that of Uranus-Kronos-Zeus; and elements such as the emasculation of the god seem to confirm the existence of something stronger than a general affinity, namely a direct connection. In that case the Greek myth would have sprung from the soil of the Near East: the Hurrians seem to have been the first to formulate it, and the Hittites to have transmitted it.

The second part of the cycle, called the Song of Ullikummi, relates that Kumarbi does not resign himself to his defeat, and launches a counter-attack, generating Ullikummi, the monster of the rocks, and sending him to assail the storm god in his own home at Kummiya:

Let him mount to heaven . . . Let him vanquish Kummiya, the beautiful city! Let him attack the storm-god and tear him to pieces like a mortal! Let him tread him under foot like an ant! . . . Let him bring down all the gods from the sky like birds, and shatter them like empty pots![45]

To this end Ullikummi is set on the right shoulder of Upelluri, a giant who holds up the universe; and from there he grows and grows until he touches the heavens. Only the wise Ea succeeds in averting the peril, by having the monster severed from the giant's shoulder and so deprived of his strength.

Listen, ye olden gods, ye who know the olden words! Open the ancient storehouses of the fathers and forefathers! Let them bring the olden seals of the fathers and let them seal them up again with them afterwards! Let them bring forth the olden copper knife with which they severed heaven from earth! Let them cut through the feet of Ullikummi, the man of diorite, whom Kumarbi has fashioned as a rival to oppose the gods![46]

This part of the myth also has interesting, though less detailed, parallels with Greek mythology: the giant who holds up the heaven and the earth is a figure of the Atlas type; the monster who scales heaven to do battle with the gods recalls Typhon. Thus Hittite culture contains several elements which are distinct from Mesopotamian themes, and these are woven into a cycle with its epicentre in the Hurrians, and a range of action extending so far as to include Greece.

On the other hand, another group of mythological epic fragments, relating to the adventures of Gilgamesh, goes right back to the Mesopotamian tradition.[47] This demonstrates the tremendous expansive force of the Sumerian myth, which now appears partly in translation, partly in adaptation, and partly enriched with fresh details. It is true that this myth is also found among the Hurrians, and that in all probability this is the route by which it was transmitted to the Hittites; thus the cultural cycle we have mentioned is continuous, and the different civilizations are interconnected.

Hittite lyrical poetry, like that of Mesopotamia, is confined to the religious sphere. It includes hymns and prayers: not that there is a great difference between the two, for they are linked together and formally the one is often to be included in the other. But the different conception of kingship leads to the hymns being concentrated on the gods. Thus we have this hymn to Telipinus, which has come down to us as part of a prayer text:

> Thou, Telipinus, art a noble god; thy name is noble among names.
> Thy godhead is noble among the gods; among the gods art thou noble, Telipinus.
> Great art thou, Telipinus; there is no other deity more noble and mighty than thou.
> Thou art lord of judgement; thou watchest over kingship in heaven and on earth.
> Thou settest the bounds of the lands, thou hearkenest to prayer.
> Thou, Telipinus, art a merciful god; forever thou showest thy mercy.
> The godly man is dear to thee, Telipinus, and thou dost exalt him.
> In the orbit of heaven and earth thou, Telipinus, art the light; throughout the lands thou art a god who is celebrated.
> Of every land thou art father and mother; the inspired lord of judgement art thou.
> In the place of judgement thou art untiring; among the olden gods thou art the one who is celebrated.
> For the gods thou, Telipinus, assignest the rites; to the olden gods thou assignest their portions.
> For thee they open the door of heaven; thou, the celebrated Telipinus, art allowed to pass through the gate of heaven.
> The gods of heaven are obedient to thee, Telipinus; the gods of earth are obedient to thee, Telipinus.
> Whatever thou sayest, Telipinus, the gods bow down to thee.
> Of the oppressed, the lowly . . . thou art father and

mother; the cause of the lowly, the oppressed, thou,
Telipinus, dost take to heart.[48]

The expressions used in this hymn are the usual ones, not
excepting mention of defence of the lowly. The same cannot
be said of the prayer of King Mursilis II on the occasion of a
plague, of which we quote an extract below; for it is distinguished both by its lively sense of human guilt and the liber-
ating power of confession, and by its direct and telling
descriptive force:

> Hattian storm-god, my lord, and ye gods, my lords!
> It is only too true that man is sinful. My father sinned
> and transgressed against the word of the Hattian storm-
> god, my lord. But I have not sinned in any respect. It
> is only too true, however, that the father's guilt falls
> upon the son. So my father's sin has fallen upon me.
> Now, I have confessed before the Hattian storm-god,
> my lord, and before the other gods, my lords: It is true,
> we have done it. And because I have confessed my
> father's sin, let the soul of the Hattian storm-god, my
> lord, and of the other gods, my lords, be again pacified!
> Suffer not the few to die who are still left to offer sacri-
> ficial loaves and libations![49]

So far as we can judge at present, the Hittites lack the
didactic and wisdom type of literature which is so extensively
developed among the other peoples of the ancient Orient. On
the other hand, their historical prose is truly remarkable, both
that of the annals already discussed, and that of the treaties
which we have yet to survey.[50] As we have already noted,
both these types of composition reveal a capacity to think in
terms of cause and effect, and so in a genuinely historical
fashion. And we also find conceptions of international law
based on fixed juridical principles as regards both interre-
lations among the great powers, and relations between them
and minor states.

The treaty is a clearly defined literary genre. It opens with
a preamble, which sets forth its precedents and its aims, then

lists the agreements made, and concludes with an invocation of the gods and threats for him who dares to violate the pacts. The most important specimen is undoubtedly the treaty with the Egyptians, preserved in both Egyptian and Hittite versions. After describing the past relations between the two powers, it lays down principles for the mutual renunciation of the use of force, and for the basis of the defensive alliance; it deals with the extradition of fugitives; and finally calls upon the gods to witness to the fidelity of the contracting parties and to judge him who breaks his word.[51] Perhaps even more interesting are the treaties made with minor states, in which a condition of vassalage is justified and translated into legal terms. One of these is the treaty between Mursilis II and Duppi-Teshub, prince of Amurru; the preamble sets forth the precedents as follows:

> Aziras was your grandfather, O Duppi-Teshub. He rebelled against my father, but submitted again to him . . . As he was bound by treaty, he remained bound by treaty. As my father fought against his enemies, in the same manner fought Aziras. Aziras remained loyal towards my father as his overlord, and did not arouse his anger. My father was loyal towards Aziras and his country; he did not undertake any unjust action against him or arouse his or his country's anger in any way; 300 shekels of first-class refined gold, the tribute which my father had imposed upon your father, he brought year after year; he never refused it.[52]

It is to this fidelity, Mursilis continues, that Duppi-Teshub owes his throne, since his father had commended him to Mursilis, and the latter has aided and protected him. But now let him take care to maintain the agreement and pay his tribute:

> So honour the oath of loyalty to the king and the king's kin! And I the king will be loyal towards you, Duppi-Teshub. When you take a wife and beget an heir, he shall be king in the Amurru land likewise. And just

as I shall be loyal towards you, so shall I be loyal towards your son. But you, Duppi-Teshub, remain loyal towards the king of the Hatti-land, the Hatti-land, my sons and my grandsons for ever! The tribute which was imposed upon your grandfather and your father — they presented 300 shekels of gold, first-class refined gold weighed with standard weights — you shall present likewise. Do not turn your eyes to anyone else![53]

Next the military dispositions follow, and those concerning relations with other states. Then the gods are invoked, and the treaty ends:

The words of the treaty and the oath that are inscribed on this tablet — if Duppi-Teshub fails to honour these words of the treaty and the oath, may these gods of the oath destroy Duppi-Teshub together with his person, his wife, his son, his grandson, his house, his land, and together with everything that he owns. But if Duppi-Teshub honours these words of the treaty and the oath that are inscribed on this tablet, may these gods of the oath protect him together with his person, his wife, his son, his grandson, his house and his country.[54]

As usual, we shall not enter into detailed discussion of texts which are not literary in the strict sense of the word; in any case they are few and of small interest. But, again as usual, we make a brief exception in favour of the juridical literature,[55] which reflects the structure and organization of society.

The two tablets of laws found at Hattusas, which constitute the main source of our present knowledge, and which are collectively known as the 'Hittite code', are in reality only partial counterparts to the Mesopotamian codes. It is true that they contain a number of case decisions, arranged in the form of various hypotheses, such as are characteristic of Sumerian and Akkadian laws; but they lack the prologue and epilogue, which are essential parts of the Mesopotamian literary form.

What is the documentary value of the 'Hittite code'? Several reservations have to be made: in the first place, many subjects, even of such importance as adoption, inheritance, and contracts, are not treated at all. It has been suggested that these were omitted because they did not normally lead to litigation;[56] and this may be so, though it seems unlikely. But another reservation, more important although extrinsic, is that we lack the confirmation provided by documents relating to judicial procedure and private acts: abundant in Mesopotamia, they are lacking among the Hittites, and this fact leaves it doubtful when and how the laws were applied.

The social organization once more consists of a division into free men and slaves, with hints at an intermediate condition which may be compared with that of the Babylonian plebeians. In the eyes of the law the slave, as in Babylonia, has a lower value than the free man, but he has the right of acquiring and owning property. So we may presume that the society structure was dynamic, with the citizens passing from one class to another under certain conditions.

The law relating to the family is strikingly analogous to that of Babylonia, and indicates a patriarchal system with, however, some suggestion that women had a more prominent position; we also find again that the marriage rite is preceded by a gift from the bridegroom to the bride's parents. There are detailed interdictions of marriage between blood relations; and there is a provision whereby a widow is to be taken for wife by her dead husband's brother, or, failing that, by his father or nephew; this closely recalls the Hebrew institution of the levirate.[57]

As we already know, property rights are based on a feudal system. The law distinguishes between 'feudatories', who derive their titles from the sovereign, and 'artisans', local workmen whose exact position still has to be elucidated.[58]

A characteristic feature of the penal law is that the principle of compensation takes precedence over that of retaliation. For that matter, we have already seen that this latter principle seems to be peculiar to the Semites. Among the Hittites, apart from political crimes, robbery, and sexual relations with animals, restitution and compensation are the predominant forms of punishment, and above all, monetary compensation:

If anyone blinds a free man or knocks out his teeth, he shall give twenty shekels of silver and pledge his estate as security.

If anyone blinds a male or female slave or knocks out his or her teeth, he shall give ten shekels of silver and pledge his estate as security.[59]

In some prescriptions we find that a development has occurred in the law:

If anyone steals a cow, they would formerly give twelve head of cattle; now he shall give six head of cattle; he shall give, specifically, two two-year-olds, two yearlings and two weanlings; and he shall pledge his estate as security.[60]

As for Hittite judicial procedure, in the absence of reports of trials or records of judgements we can obtain indications from another special class of texts, the instructions to priests and officials.[61] It is true that their matter consists mainly of religious prescriptions, but some of them concern the administration of civil and military justice, as in the following case of a frontier guard commander, who is ordered:

Whenever you arrive at a town, call all the people of the town together. For him who has a complaint, judge it and set him right. If a man's slave or a man's slave-girl has a complaint against a woman of the upper class,[62] judge it for them and set them right.[63]

The same text contains some remarkable instructions to respect local customs, which throw light upon the Hittite behaviour in conquered territory. These reflect the same prudence and broadness of mind that dominate in the treaties:

Furthermore the commander of the border guards, the town commandant and the elders shall judge and decide legal cases in accordance with the law. As it has been from olden days, in a town in which they have been accustomed to impose the death penalty, they shall continue to do so. But in a town where they have been accustomed to impose exile, they shall continue to do so.[64]

In conclusion to our remarks on Hittite literature, we must mention that recently a background of deliberate farce, an intention to laugh and make the reader laugh, has been found in the crudity of certain of its manifestations;[65] thus regarded, the great mythological and epic cycles would be simply grotesque fables, not taken seriously even by their compilers. This view appears to be far from the truth. Humour, as our experience teaches, is rare in the ancient Orient; indeed, if these cultures produce any one direct and spontaneous impression, it is of their profound and almost gloomy seriousness. Exceptions to this general judgement are to be found in Egypt, where the peculiar geographical and political situation favours tranquillity of spirit, and the highly refined culture facilitates the further advance consisting in a readiness to smile. But to attribute such a quality to the Hittites, to empty their literature of its religious and ritual content, is surely nothing but reading our own impressions and feelings into the literature of those times, and, however welcome and attractive the result may be, turning the entire structure of a civilization upside down.

V The Artistic Types

Before turning to a study of Hittite art[66] it is useful to refer again to Mesopotamia. This, it must be noted, is a logical and not an historical starting point, in that it does not involve any prejudgement as to the origins of this art, or, for that matter, even as to the independence of its elements. But it is beyond challenge that Hittite art comes within the sphere of influence of that great artistic centre, Mesopotamia; and one may take the forms of art that arose in that centre as points of reference (which we could not do in respect of Egypt or any other zone of irradiation) for all that concerns the general conception of the function of art, its basic features and the main principles governing its style.

This being postulated, it must be added that Mesopotamian is not the only influence at work in Anatolia, for one can trace Egyptian influence brought to bear through Syria-Palestine.

Finally, there is Hurrian influence, all the more important because it is less tangible and definable in details.

All these are environmental cultural areas acting on an unusually receptive subject, but one which none the less has a real and independent existence. The nature of the region, the customs and characteristics of the people, their ideas and beliefs, give rise to a number of elements which are peculiar to them, and which are found both in isolation and associated in new combinations with others. The identification and evaluation of these numerous factors, often juxtaposed rather than blended, just as in other aspects of this same culture, constitutes the history of Hittite art.

We cannot trace any well-defined lines of development in terms of chronology. Hittite art is rather a matter of two great phases, produced in different conditions governed by differences of time and space: there is the late period of the New Empire, from which we have the remains of the capital city Hattusas and the surrounding localities;[67] and there is also the Neo-Hittite era, involving the output of the petty states which survive the fall of the Empire in Cilicia and Upper Syria.[68] As these are closer to the centres of foreign influence, it is understandable that the external elements grow stronger and the autochthonous elements are reduced to the point of creating an art which has hybridism as its distinctive feature.

Here, as everywhere, architectural development[69] is conditioned by the terrain, and this is totally different from that of Mesopotamia or Egypt. These two countries are valley lands, the Hittite country consists of mountains. Stone is abundant, and so it is the main building material: the foundations and the lower parts of the buildings are built with rough blocks of stone, and bricks of sun-dried clay, together with wooden beams, compose the structure of the upper parts. None the less, the column is brought into use only at a comparatively late date, to a restricted extent, and, as we shall see, in a class of building which has certain features suggesting a foreign origin.

The first nucleus of Hittite organized life is the mountain stronghold, surrounded by a wall, to which a gateway with double entry gives access without breaking the line of defence. The stronghold develops into a city with temples and palaces: the principal centres of Hittite civilization were formerly fortresses.

The construction of the temple, as we can judge from several specimens in the capital city, Hattusas, is like that of the Mesopotamian temple, with its chambers grouped around one or more courtyards; but, in contrast to the Mesopotamian practice of constructing the outer walls to form a solid enclosure for protection against floods, the Hittite chambers have windows opening on to the street in order to admit light; and — an innovation in the ancient Near East — this is true even of the chambers containing the statues of the gods.

The Hittite palace is constructed on fundamentally the same lines as the temple. But, as we have already indicated, there is a particular type, found especially in the Neo-Hittite era, which is distinguished by the name *bit khilani* (Fig. 4). Its typical feature is an entrance hall with roof supported on columns. These are simple wooden shafts, but their bases have one distinctive feature: pairs of sphinxes or lions carved in stone. Beyond the entrance hall is the main hall, a parallelogram set lengthwise, with the smaller rooms arranged around it. Palaces of this type are found in many neighbouring centres, from Assyria to Syria, and they set a difficult problem

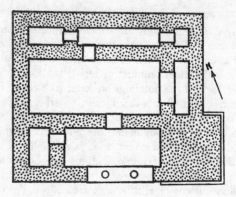

Fig. 4

of origin. Some authorities consider that the evidence points to the Hurrians as the originators, others are inclined to suggest the peoples of Syria.

Hittite sculpture is conceived and executed mainly as an adjunct to architecture. Large scale statuary of the human figure, such as is found extensively in Egypt, and to a limited degree in Mesopotamia, is entirely lacking; all that has remained are several small metal statues, interesting for their type and attire, but of comparatively crude workmanship and artistically not particularly worthy of note. The same may be said of the animal statuary; but here an artistic type intermediate between free standing sculpture and relief, namely the orthostat, contributes a widespread exception to the rule, and becomes a distinctive form of Hittite art. In the great cities the bases of the gateways are decorated with lions or sphinxes, of which the head and the forequarters of the body project, while the hindquarters are merged into the solid mass of the wall or are traced in relief on each side. These models are undoubtedly of Mesopotamian or Egyptian inspiration, but their treatment reveals decidedly independent development, as is clearly indicated by the muzzles, accurately carved and expressive with a realism which is all their own (Pl. XXIII).

As everywhere in the ancient Orient, bas-relief is highly developed. It takes here the characteristic form of carvings in the natural rock. At the open-air mountain sanctuary of Yazilikaya, not far from the Hittite capital,[70] the rock walls bear relief carvings portraying two long processions of divinities approaching each other[71] (Pl. XXIV). On one side are the female deities led by the sun-goddess of Arinna, on the other the males led by the storm god. Beneath the latter are the figures of two priests, while beneath each of the other deities is his appropriate animal. The gods wear robes and conical caps, the goddesses have crowns and long pleated tunics. Note that the female figures are shown with the bust in profile: this is a striking innovation in Oriental art, violating the established canons, and we never find it again. What is the significance of this procession? Does it represent the sacred marriage of the supreme gods? Or is it simply an illustration of the 'thousand gods' referred to in the texts?[72] No definite answer can be given to these questions.

Not far from this procession, two other Yazilikaya reliefs attract attention. One represents the king Tudhaliyas in the embraces of his god: this is a new and distinctive theme in Oriental art, and we shall come across it again on the Hittite seals. The other is that of the so-called 'dirk-god':[73] a dagger with a hilt formed by two pairs of lions surmounted by a human head wearing the conical cap proper to gods. This figure clearly indicates a gift for symbolism associated with a tendency to combine real and unreal beings or parts of beings without the fusion which is characteristic elsewhere. Another example of this is found in a Neo-Hittite relief at Carchemish; here the head of a winged lion is surmounted by another, human, head.

This example from Carchemish brings us to the Neo-Hittite period. Now relief carving grows extremely common on the blocks of stone which form the bases of city fortifications, and on the walls of palaces. The scenes are small in size, fairly crude in form, and characteristically lacking in any feeling for composition; but the human and animal types represented, the attire, and the manner in which the subjects are treated give them an easily recognizable physiognomy of their own. Among the most noteworthy specimens are the recent discoveries at Karatepe (Pl. XXV).

The Hittite seal[74] is strikingly different from the Mesopotamian in both form and design. The conical shape is more common than the cylinder, and it bears the engraving on its flat base, so that it is used simply as a stamp, and is not rolled over the clay. The design is often enclosed in one or more borders of inscription or geometrical ornamentation. The design itself may consist of symbols or figures: the royal seals bear the winged solar disc — of Egyptian origin, and corresponding to the title 'Sun' which, as we have seen, was assumed by the Hittite kings of the New Empire — set above the seal of the sovereign, or even a figure of the sovereign in the embrace of his god, similar to that of the rock reliefs already mentioned.

It is undoubtedly significant that Hittite art, which is almost non-existent in the Old Empire, suddenly flourishes during the New Empire, or rather, during one definite phase, which coincides with the victory over the Hurrians and the emergence of the Hittites as a great power in the ancient Near East. When we add that several of the elements of this art have their counterpart in the Hurrian area, and extend beyond the temporal and spatial bounds of the Hittite empire, it would seem a reasonable deduction that Hittite art is derived from the Hurrians[75] and draws its impulse and themes from them. It may seem that we have formulated our hypothesis too crudely; but in fact it has been maintained that the whole of Hittite art is really Hurrian.

This theory is open to two criticisms. The first is an external one, namely: we know too little about Hurrian art to be able to judge; the second is internal, namely: some of the themes are not exclusively Hurrian, but have their precedents in the other civilizations of the ancient Orient. Even so, however, it is not to be challenged that the Hurrian element plays a notable part in Hittite art; and we are in the singular position of locating an artistic vein and yet of being unable to define its constituent elements owing to the paucity of the evidence.

On the other hand does Hittite art achieve the decided originality, the high quality which some authorities have found in it?[76] All things considered, we do not think so. A comparative view of Hittite culture suggests that its more original and significant elements, those with more enduring and far-reaching effect, are to be found in the sphere of its political and social organization, its conception of history and international law. In this direction the Hittites are definitely outstanding, and surpass the other peoples of the ancient Orient. In the remaining spheres of civilization there is a conjunction of various foreign elements in simple association, rather than in fusion, both with each other and with the national elements which undoubtedly exist. And it is this juxtaposition which is most characteristic of the Hittite civilization, just as it is the balance of opposing factors, neither encroaching upon one another nor yielding ground, that establishes the historical and cultural character of the age that takes its name from the mountain peoples.

VI *The Problem of the Hurrians*

In the preceding pages the problem of the Hurrians has arisen again and again;[77] it is precisely as a problem that we prefer to deal with the subject, for the material on which we can draw for the reconstruction of the history and culture of the Hurrians is so far as scanty and doubtful as their importance is obviously considerable.[78]

It is a singular fact that this material comes for the most part from localities outside the area over which Hurrian political power is presumed to have extended: from Tell Amarna in Egypt, from Boghazköy in Anatolia, from Ugarit, and Mari. The interpretation of the texts, which has only recently been achieved, reveals a prevalence of ritual documents and epicomythological fragments; but some of these texts still await publication, and others are in such a fragmentary condition that full use cannot be made of them.

Beginning with history: a tablet in Hurrian telling of a certain Tisadal, king of Urkish,[79] reveals the presence of the Hurrian element in Mesopotamia as far back as about 2300 B.C.; and this fact tends to confirm that the advent of the mountain peoples towards the middle of the second millennium B.C. only marks a political success following many centuries of infiltration. About 2000 B.C. Mesopotamian documents contain many Hurrian proper names; and Hurrian texts of a religious nature, found at Mari, date from about 1700 B.C. This is the first phase of Hurrian expansion; it supplies too much material for us to ignore it altogether, and too little to enable us to write its history. As we shall see, the situation is analogous to that which, as the result of recent discoveries, has arisen in regard to the history of the Aramaeans.

Towards 1500 B.C. the Hurrians establish the state of Mitanni in Upper Mesopotamia; the site of its capital, known as Wassukkanni, has not yet been identified. The Mitanni political domination quickly extends to the surrounding areas, and in the east reaches the cities of Nuzi and Arrapkha in Assyria, and in the west that of Alalakh in Syria. The state government is in the hands of an hereditary monarchy which, however, after the manner of the mountain peoples, is surrounded by a restricted class of nobles; this class, known as *maryannu*, controls the means of warfare and shares out the land in feudal style.

The Tell Amarna letters provide extensive information concerning the rulers of Mitanni, who are on good political terms with Egypt, so much so that their daughters are given in marriage to the Pharaohs. King Tushratta, the author of a long letter written to Amenophis III, has to wage war against a certain Artatama, king of Hurri; we are faced with the queer problem of having to decide whether this was a case of dynastic conflict, or whether Artatama was the ruler of another state founded by Hurrians. In any case, Artatama's relations with the Hittites lead to a clash between them and Mitanni. The struggle has fatal results: Mitanni is defeated; Tushratta's son Mattiwaza makes a treaty with the great Suppiluliumas, and this, in Hittite terms, amounts to a genuine recognition of vassaldom. This event occurs in 1365 B.C., and it ends the history of the empire.

Turning to the Hurrian religion,[80] we find two old acquaintances in the divine couple who head its pantheon: the storm god Teshub and the sun goddess Hebat. Both these figures find their way into the surrounding world, and are established especially strongly among the Hittites. Of the other divinities, we know Kumarbi, the father of the gods and protagonist in numerous mythological stories; of Shaushka and of Simike, the sun-god, only the names are known to us. The pantheon includes numerous foreign elements, from Mesopotamian, outstanding among them Ishtar, to Aryan, such as Indra, Varuna, and Mithras, who are connected with the ruling class of Indo-European origin. Thus the very culture which possesses such a great expansive force is also highly receptive to infiltrations and outside influences.

When more light has been thrown on Hurrian literature, it will prove of fundamental importance in the cultural history on the Near East during the second millennium B.C. In the first place, it is on the path followed by several great Mesopotamian literary works — for instance, the Gilgamesh poem, which has been found in Hurrian fragments — en route to the Hittite world. Moreover, it is extensively creative in its own right: it is clear both from the fragments of Hurrian works which are coming to light, and from the general background of the texts and the names of gods and men occurring in them, that a large number of works which have survived in Hittite drew their inspiration from Hurrian sources.[81] The interpretation of these texts is still very difficult and subject to dispute. They include the tale of the voracious dragon Khedammu, who spreads general ruin until the goddess Ishtar succeeds in putting matters right; that of the hunter Keshshi, who neglects the chase for his wife's sake and thus incurs the anger of the gods; that of the love of the mountain Pishaisa for Ishtar, with a story of struggle between the storm god and the sea god which is decidedly reminiscent of an episode in the Ugaritic Baal-cycle; and finally, that of Appu, which we select as an example because we can more easily reconstruct its plot than that of others. Appu is a rich man, but he has no children:

> There is a city named Shudul in the land of Lulluwa, near to the sea, and here there dwelt a man named Appu. He was rich in the land, had many sheep and oxen . . . Nothing was lacking to him save one thing: he had no children.[82]

Here we find the theme of the longing for progeny which is so widely diffused throughout the ancient Oriental literatures, and which we shall meet with again. After many prayers to the gods, Appu at last obtains the favour he desires:

> When it was the tenth month, Appu's wife gave birth to a son. The midwife took him up and laid him on

Appu's knees. Appu began to be glad on account of the child, and to fondle him, and he gave him the name of Evil, saying: 'So long as I was young, the gods did not follow the good path, but the bad one: for this reason his name shall be Evil.'

Then Appu's wife conceived a second time, and in the tenth month gave birth to a son. The midwife raised him on high, and he gave him the name of Good: 'His name shall be Good.'[83]

As the tale indicates, one of the two sons will be good and the other bad. When they grow up, Evil suggests to Good that they should share out their possessions, and he takes the better part for himself:

Evil and Good began to share out their property, while the sun-god watched from the heavens . . . Evil took for himself a good ox, while he gave his brother Good a bad cow. Then the sun-god looked down from heaven and said: 'Let Good's cow go and become good and engender!'[84]

Another text, probably the continuation of the one we are discussing, tells how the cow begets a human child, and is so enraged that she decides to kill him; but the sun-god saves him and arranges for him to be found by a fisherman, who with his wife brings him up as their son in their own house. It has been conjectured that when he grows up the child helps his father to secure justice from his wicked brother; but the mutilated text is of no help here.

In conclusion, we may ask how we are to class this kind of literature: it has an epico-mythological touch, but it also has elements of the fantastic tale and the fable. Indeed, the tale of Appu is a very definite form of fable, recalling certain works of Egyptian literature which we have already described.

As for Hurrian art, this, as we have seen, raises the greatest of problems. There are several indications that suggest that it had considerable development and influence. But close examination does not help much in deducing its characteristics; and the difficulty is aggravated by the fact that we cannot identify the capital of Mitanni and have to gather our material from outlying localities, where the possibility that other centres and influences have their part cannot be excluded. So far, the only firmly determined characteristic element of Hurrian art is a special type of pottery with large black lines on a yellow ground, with animal or geometrical figures painted on it in white.[85] As we have already hinted, and as we shall see more clearly later, the other element which formerly was regarded as distinctive of Hurrian art, namely the *bit khilani* type of building, has recently come under question.

We have said enough to show that the Hurrians still remain a considerable problem. Even so, it may be possible to draw a general conclusion. It is probable that as our knowledge increases this people will more and more be found to hold a position vis-à-vis the Hittites analogous to that of the Sumerians in regard to the Babylonians and Assyrians. *Graecia capta:* here is yet another civilization which, after succumbing politically, survives and even dominates its conquerors.

THE CANAANITES AND THE ARAMAEANS

I *The Buffer States*

When the desert peoples, who fan out from the wastes of Arabia over the more fertile surrounding regions, intervene in Near Eastern history, they proceed not only in the opposite direction, but also in a manner structurally different from that of the mountain peoples. The latter come to the forefront in a circumscribed though large historical period; they achieve political organisms of strongly marked entity, whose driving force is equal to that of the Egyptian and Mesopotamian empires; and they collapse and disappear suddenly under the pressure of outside intervention. The desert peoples, on the contrary, are on the spot from the beginnings of history; their regular periodic movement is maintained throughout the ages; and they build up aggregates of smaller dimensions, with a driving force weaker than that of the surrounding great powers.

The main debouchment and assembly point for the desert peoples is the coastal zone of the Eastern Mediterranean, between Egypt and Mesopotamia; that is normal enough, not only because this area is the most natural and direct object of their conquest, but also because, set between the opposing political blocs, it is the point of least resistance.

The geographical conditions of this region lay down the conditions of its history. A strip of land open on one side to the desert and on the other to the sea, traversed through all its length by a series of mountains, carved up both in length and breadth by river beds and open plains, it could hardly be other than the scene of political fragmentation. Moreover, its position, halfway between Mesopotamia, Anatolia, and Egypt, at the centre of the routes of communication linking three continents, makes it the natural setting for the meeting and clash of the great powers. This explains the precarious existence as well as the disintegrated nature of the local political organisms, which are periodically subjected to contrasted influences and are often dissolved by that same foreign domination which, paradoxically enough, is the only factor that can give them unity. To use a modern term, they are 'buffer states'. Caught between forces greater than their own, they have a history which is decidedly passive, and their politics are marked by oscillations and reactions, although, as we shall see, this does not rob them of a very real individuality.

The customary division into two areas, Syria and Palestine, to which Lebanon and Phoenicia may be added, is far from satisfactory from the historian's viewpoint, since it conveys both too little and too much. Too little, because in these areas the terrain is widely varied in nature and the political history is greatly subdivided; too much, because the definition and demarcation of the areas among themselves is inadequate, with the result that one gets the impression that facts of religious rather than political significance — to be precise, the history of Israel — have created entities which could be regarded as such for only a brief period. We think it more advantageous for historical purposes to drop the division in favour of a single comprehensive term, which is to be understood as connoting a summation of numerous and frequently varying elements. If we follow the usage of classical authors and modern geographers, the only applicable term is that of Syria, taken in the broad sense, including the entire area bounded by Egypt and Mesopotamia, the Arabian desert and the Mediterranean sea. Such homogeneity as this region has is primarily geographical, but it also possesses historical significance, negative and passive perhaps, but none the less real: it is the middle zone lying between the blocs of powers, the historical objective of opposed active powers, the point of alternating union and cleavage according to circumstances.

The peoples who sweep out of the desert from time to time

into Syria (we shall henceforth use the word in the broad sense just expounded) are certainly not the only ones to converge thither; but undoubtedly they are the most outstanding, because of the part they play both in forming the ethnic complex, and in determining the course of history. These peoples are linked together by a community not only of geographical but also of ethnological origin; and this latter bond is much tighter than that between the mountain peoples, because in the latter case it is confined to individual strata or elements, whereas it extends to the entire group of desert peoples, at least in regard to their origins. This is sufficiently accounted for by the isolation imposed by desert conditions.

The desert peoples are Semites. We have already witnessed one outstanding assertion of their tendency towards expansion when they conquered Mesopotamia and formed the Babylonian and Assyrian civilization. In Syria they achieve a greater predominance ethnically, but a more restricted political objective. This is due to local conditions.

The various groups of these peoples are known by names just as varied and opposed as the geographical terms. For the title of this chapter we have chosen the names Canaanites and Aramaeans, these being the most common and comprehensive. The former broadly covers the Semitic inhabitants of Palestine and the Phoenician coast, the latter a single group which was established in the northern hinterland at the end of the second millennium. As will be seen, only the latter term is comparatively exact; 'Canaanites' is a collective term which includes a number of individual elements, and so in the last analysis it is defined rather by the negative 'other than Aramaean'. It includes the Amorites, the Moabites, the Edomites, the Ammonites, even the Hebrews. For this reason we repeat the remark made concerning the geographical situation: the division into two is inadequate, because it does not take the internal variety into account; and it goes too far, because it does not take into account the basic general unity which is impressed upon these peoples, despite the variety of the component elements, by their community of stock, origin, and habitat. So the problem posed is similar to the geographical one, and the solution is likewise similar: just as we chose the term 'Syria' to cover the entire area, so we may use the term 'Syrians' to cover its inhabitants. The preliminary reservations will also be the same, but the survey which follows brings out perfectly the need of a collective term to cover the common characteristics and conditions, and therefore to cover the historical entity which is none the less real because it consists of multifarious and changing elements.

II *The Historical Outlines*

The longest period of ancient Syrian history,[1] from its beginning until close on 1200 B.C., is under Egyptian influence. Then, for some three centuries, the crisis of the great empires makes it possible to establish local independence and even, for a brief time, a unity. Finally, from 900 B.C. onward, the expansion of Assyria gradually involves the area, first by influence and later by conquest; in the sixth century, when the Babylonians have succeeded the Assyrians, the occupation is complete, and Syria, losing its independence, passes from one empire to another as a province.

This historical summary has to be completed by a geographical distinction: even in the period of Egyptian predominance, the extreme north of the area belongs to the political and cultural sphere of the Mesopotamian and Anatolian peoples; whereas the extreme south remains under Egyptian influence even during the era of Assyrian expansion.

The policies pursued by the opposing forces in Syria find expression in different types of organization, and so they differ in the nature of their predominance. As we shall see later in detail, the object of the Egyptians is not to annex but to control the area, and they are content to impose tribute on the local princes and maintain their own overseers and collectors on the spot; they do not colonize the territory and so do not modify its ethnical structure. The Hittites follow a policy similar to that of the Egyptians, and they even give their own juridical treaty form to the vassaldom of the local sovereigns; but ethnically they penetrate the area to a striking extent, and so a neo-Hittite political and cultural sector comes into being. Finally, the Assyrians develop a policy of direct annexation, and strive to eradicate all traditions of independence by carrying out mass shifts of population. This policy, which is carried to its full lengths by the Babylonians, is responsible for the collapse of Syria as an historical entity in its own right.

We have no first-hand information concerning the first penetration of Semitic peoples into Syria;[2] so it is better to ignore the various hypotheses and dates that have been proposed. But we shall consider the indirect evidence: the mountains and rivers of the area have mainly Semitic names, and this also applies to certain cities which archaeology proves to have been built as early as the beginning of the historical period, or even before. This justifies the surmise that the Semites are already present in the area when history begins, about 3000 B.C.

Still taking archaeology as the basis, it is possible to formulate hypotheses concerning the political organization of those earliest inhabitants. The strong walls built around the towns suggest the system of city states, organized with a view to defence both against one another and against the nomads of the surrounding countryside.

Probably the cities were ruled by local sovereigns[3] from the beginning, as they were in their later history. We cannot reach any conclusion as to the nature and forms of their government. But we do know from the oldest Egyptian texts, confirmed by archaeological evidence, that Egypt enjoyed a political and commercial ascendancy over these petty states; from time to time she consolidated this ascendancy by military expeditions and the imposition of tribute. On closer examination, this fact witnesses to a local state of unrest, for otherwise there would have been no adequate reason for such action.

By the beginning of the second millennium we are provided with more data. Egyptian texts reveal a new type of proper names for the Syrian rulers: it is the type characteristic of the Amorites, the Semitic peoples who, as we have seen, penetrate into Mesopotamia and establish themselves there at about the same period. Thus, although we do not know precisely when or how it occurred, we may conclude that the movements of these peoples extended to Syria, bringing a new ethnic stratum to that area, as they do to Mesopotamia. As Egyptian and Mesopotamian testimony tends to coincide, the history of the Amorites is much better known than that of their predecessors. The Egyptian 'execration texts'[4] indicate the names and seats of the rulers, while the mural paintings at Beni Hasan give us some idea of their appearance. In addition, the Mari diplomatic archives contribute a considerable quantity of correspondence engaged in by these rulers. The two sources combined point clearly to a stratification of city, or at the most, provincial states, on the model of those previously existing in Syria, and reveal that those in the centre and south of the area fall within Egypt's sphere of influence, and those in the north within that of Mesopotamia.

From what has been said, it is obvious that the greater part of our knowledge of Syrian history is drawn from foreign sources, and these consist in the main of diplomatic archives. In fact, it is from two such sets of archives, those of Mari in Mesopotamia already mentioned, and the somewhat later ones of Tell Amarna[5] in Egypt, that we derive almost all our knowledge of the events of the second millennium B.C. Only recently has this state of affairs been modified to some extent by the discovery of the political archives at Alalakh[6] and Ugarit,[7] which prove that the petty local rulers also preserved their diplomatic documents. This predominance of archives is counterpoised by the extreme paucity of historical inscriptions or annals,[8] such as provide the main documentation for the surrounding empires. This explains the different nature of the information at our disposal: in the case of the great empires it is concerned chiefly with military exploits and the peaceful activities of internal politics; in the case of Syria we have mainly the interplay of diplomacy and relations between chancelleries.

As the 'execration texts' provide us only with names, we have to rely on the Mari archives for our documentation of the Amorite period. Three states are outstanding in Upper

Syria: Carchemish, Aleppo, and Qatna. Relations between Mari and Qatna are especially close, and the power of the latter state is indicated by the fact that twenty kings are mentioned as being dependent upon it, by the intermarriage which occurs between its royal house and that of Assyria, and by the expeditions it undertakes in alliance with Mari on an equal footing. Thus the king of Qatna invites the king of Mari to join him in an enterprise in the following terms:

> To Yasmakh-Addu say: thus says Ishkhi-Addu thy brother . . . For thy coming hither, be not negligent. This is the opportune moment for thee to come. Let thy troops enjoy the booty, that they may bless thee. Those three cities are not strong, we shall be able to take them in a single day. Come therefore at once, let us take those cities, and thy troops shall enjoy the booty. If thou art my brother, come to me at once.[9]

Note the introductory phraseology, characteristic of this epistolary style. We have another letter, also relating to Qatna, which is interesting for its private and personal tone: it is a good example of the possibilities opened up by these archives, such as we have seen when considering the Babylonians and Assyrians, of getting away from the stereotyped forms of the official inscriptions and studying the character, the subjective reactions, of these kings. The king of Qatna has sent the king of Assyria two valuable horses. In return he has received the miserable sum of twenty minas of lead. This infuriates him so much that he writes:

> To Ishme-Dagan say this: thus says Ishkhi-Addu, thy brother. This is a thing that ought not to be said, nevertheless I simply must say it to relieve my mind. Thou art indeed a great king! Thou didst ask me for the two horses thou desiredst, I had them brought to thee, and behold, thou hast sent me twenty minas of lead! . . . The price of those horses here in Qatna is six hundred shekels of silver; and thou hast sent me twenty minas of lead! What will people say if they learn that? Certainly they will be unable to put us on the same footing![10]

An outburst of this kind, with its straightforward liveliness, is rare in the ancient Orient. Still more interesting is the fact that the document was found in Mari, which means that the king of this city, who was the king of Assyria's brother, had intercepted and not scrupled to read it, and then had thought it better not to forward it.

The archives also witness to the constant pressure of the nomads against the states on the fringe of the desert, in their quest for more fertile lands. A local chief writes in these terms to the king of Mari concerning one of the most dangerous of the nomad groups, the Binu-Yamina:

> To my lord, say this: thus speaks Yaqqim-Addu, thy servant. Concerning the affair of the Binu-Yamina, about which I wrote to my lord, I sent a man to their cities to clear up the matter . . . When they are interrogated, they answer: 'There are no pasturelands, and we are making for the upper land.' That is what they told me. My militia is strong . . . Every one of the Binu-Yamina that goes from the lower to the upper land will be captured, and once he is taken will be put in prison. Let my lord deign to write to me and I will have the prisoners brought to him.[11]

The Mari era is succeeded by the Hyksos interlude. Then Egypt regains its predominance, which is balanced in the north only by the intervention of the mountain peoples, especially the Hittites. The Hittites penetrate ethnically still further and further, until in the sixteenth century B.C., as the proper names again show, the Syrian population is a mixture of pre-Amorite Semites, Amorites, Hittites, and Hurrians;[12] only the Egyptians are missing, because their dominion is characterized not by colonization but control.

We have an amplitude of data for the fourteenth century, drawn from the other archives already mentioned: those of Tell Amarna. In this capital of the reforming Pharaoh Amenophis IV was found the correspondence which he and his predecessor exchanged with the petty Syrian vassal states. Owing to Egypt's weakness, the period is a particularly troubled one. The petty kings are in conflict with one another, and inform on one another to the Pharaoh, in order to obtain his aid. For example, the king of Megiddo, Biridiya, denounces the conduct of Labaya, king of Shechem:

> To the king, my lord, and my sun-god, say: thus Biridiya, the true servant of the king. At the feet of the king, my lord, and my sun-god, seven times and seven times I fall . . . Let the king know that ever since the archers went back, Labaya has carried on hostilities against me, and we are not able to pluck the wool, and we are not able to go outside the gate in the presence of Labaya, since he learned that thou hast not given archers; and now his face is set to take Megiddo. Let the king protect his city, lest Labaya seize it! Verily, the city is destroyed by death from pestilence and disease. Let the king give a hundred garrison troops to guard the city, lest Labaya seize it! Verily, there is no other purpose in Labaya. He seeks to destroy Megiddo.[13]

Note again the characteristic phraseology of the opening. Labaya reacts to the Pharaoh's remonstrances with a protestation of his innocence:

> To the king, my lord, and my sun-god: thus Labaya, thy servant, and the dirt on which thou dost tread. At the feet of the king, my lord, and my sun-god, seven times and seven times I fall. I have heard the words which the king wrote to me, and who am I that the king should lose his land because of me? Behold I am a faithful servant of the king, and I have not rebelled and I have not sinned, and I do not withhold my tribute, and I do not refuse the requests of my commissioner. Now they wickedly slander me, but let the king, my lord, not impute rebellion to me![14]

Was Labaya sincere in his protestations? In such cases the only means the Egyptian court had of ascertaining the truth was to send inspectors to act both as supervisors and tribute collectors. However, sometimes these officials themselves began to act arbitrarily. On one such occasion king Milkilu of Gezer complains with obvious sincerity:

To the king, my lord, my pantheon, my sun-god, say: thus Milkilu, thy servant, the dirt under thy feet. At the feet of the king, my lord, my pantheon, my sun-god seven times, seven times I fall. Let the king, my lord know the deed which Yanhamu did to me after I left the presence of the king, my lord. Now he seeks two thousand shekels of silver from my hand, saying to me 'Give me thy wife and thy children, or I will smite!' Let the king know this deed, and let my lord send to me chariots, and let him take me to himself lest I perish![15]

Certain letters referring to warrior desperadoes called Khabiru[16] are of particular interest. Who were they? Were they indeed the Hebrews, as formal similarity between the two names has long led certain authorities to believe? The texts reveal that the Khabiru are men of considerable military capacity, under the control of the authorities in certain states but attacking the frontiers of other states and harassing them with guerilla activities. Their most striking feature, however is that their names vary in type and national affinity from place to place, so they would seem to be not so much an ethnic group as a social class. This indicates that it is incorrect to identify them with the Hebrews, unless the latter formed part of the Khabiru groups in certain places and times, and were given the name of Khabiru by other peoples

The history of the period immediately following the Tell Amarna age is reflected in the political archives which have been discovered at Ugarit. These relate to a period extending approximately from the middle of the fourteenth to the middle of the following century, and show that Ugarit, situated in the extreme north of the Syrian area, was under Hittite domination Written in the customary Akkadian tongue of diplomacy there is a treaty between the great king Suppiluliumas and Niqmadu king of Ugarit; its construction follows the classic model of Hittite diplomatic documents, beginning with a historical preamble, passing to the terms of the agreement and concluding with invocations to the gods. It is accompanied by a letter in which Suppiluliumas advises Niqmadu to accept the alliance:

Thus says the Sun, the great king . . . To Niqmadu, say: although the land of Nukhashshe and that of Mukish are my enemies, do thou have no fear of them, have confidence in thyself! As in the past thy forefathers were friends and not foes of the land of the Hittites, now do thou, Niqmadu, be the enemy of my enemy and the friend of my friend. If thou, Niqmadu, wilt hearken and keep these words of the great king thy lord, thou shalt see the effect of the favours which the great king thy lord will grant thee. Maintain, therefore, Niqmadu, the alliance and friendship with the land of the Hittites, and thou wilt then see how the great king will deal with the kings of Nukhashshe and of Mukish, who have abandoned the alliance and friendship of the Hittite people and become enemies of the great king their lord! Then wilt thou, Niqmadu, for the future have confidence in the words of the great king thy lord.[17]

The latest documents of the Ugarit archives date from a time a little prior to the invasion of the peoples of the sea. This invasion, preceded by numerous skirmishes, comes to the Near East about 1200 B.C.

The peoples of the sea[18] leave their political marks behind them in the form of the petty state of the Philistines, on the coast,[19] and their ethnic traces in the form of the injection of a new Indo-European element into the heterogeneous complex of peoples of the Syrian area. But the invasion is of greatest significance in the fact that it creates an historical void between the great powers, whom it destroys or drives back within their natural frontiers. This void is filled by a succession of Semitic peoples, pursuing their traditional expansionist trends; they establish their own political organisms, of limited extent, but now, for the first time, fundamentally independent. In the south the group of Israelite tribes predominates, but other groups come with and settle alongside it: the Midianites, Edomites, Moabites, and Ammonites. In the north it is the Aramaean tribal group which predominates. Both Israelites and Aramaeans have a long history behind them: that of the Israelites is given traditional formulation in the Biblical narrative, while that of the Aramaeans is now coming to light as the result of a series of references in various texts; however, these references simply establish their existence, without shedding further light on them.[20] The one certainty arising from the modern view of their history is that their self assertion in Syria is no longer to be regarded as coincident with their arrival in the area, but only with the formation of the states known to us.

The organization of the new peoples reproduces the monarchic form already existing in the area. The one exception is Israel, which is initially a confederation of tribes around a religious center. The Midianites, Edomites, Moabites, and Ammonites have their own kings, and so, too, have the Aramaeans, though these are not united, but set up a series of separate states: Damascus, Soba, Hama, Bit Agushi — with Aleppo and Arpad as its centres — and Sam'al. Nor are the Aramaeans confined to Syria: they penetrate into Mesopotamia, where they found the states of Bit Adini, Bit Bakhyani and Bit Yakini.[21]

About the year 1000 B.C., as the result of the creation of the Israelite monarchy, the existing equilibrium is disturbed to the advantage of that monarchy, and before many years have passed the Syrian area is united under its dominion or predominance. The state of the Israelites is the largest and most independent known to Syria so far, and its existence is possible because the empires between which it lies continue to be feeble. When these empires resume their drive towards expansion near the end of the tenth century and the Israelite monarchy is divided between the states of Judah and Israel, the equilibrium is restored; but it is unstable, and a threat of domination from outside growingly tends to disturb it.

From now on it is possible to follow the last phase of Syrian alliances and conflicts quite well, and from local sources. We have, to begin with, the extensive historical literature of the Israelites; the cities of Phoenicia provide various, though brief, inscriptions, and Flavius Josephus preserves and reproduces fragments of the annals of Tyre, which at this time is Phoenicia's principal city; the Moabites have left the long and important inscription of king Mesha; and finally, numerous Aramaean inscriptions enable us to identify and reconstruct various historical events. It must be noted that all these inscriptions are in alphabetic characters, and this signifies the achievement of a further great advance along the path of civilization: the invention of the alphabet. This probably comes during the second millennium B.C. somewhere in Syria, and is undoubtedly the greatest contribution which the peoples of this area have made to human progress.

The historical inscriptions invariably have the same kind of content: they celebrate victories gained over enemies. For instance, the Aramaic inscription which king Zakir of Hama, about the end of the tenth century, dedicates to his god Baalshamin, reads as follows:

> A stela set up by Zakir, king of Hama and La'ash, for El-Wer . . . I am Zakir, king of Hama and La'ash. A humble man am I, Baalshamin called me and stood by me, he made me king over Hazrak. Bar-Hadad, the son of Hazael, king of Aram, united a group of fourteen kings against me: Bar-Hadad and his army, Bar Gush and his army, the king of Que and his army, the king of Amq and his army, the king of Gurgum and his army, the king of Sam'al and his army, the king of Meliz and his army . . . and seven other kings with their armies. All these kings laid siege to Hazrak. They made a wall higher than the wall of Hazrak. They made a moat deeper than its moat. But I lifted up my hands to Baalshamin, and he heard me, and spoke to me through seers and through diviners, saying: 'Fear not, for I made thee king: I will be with thee and deliver thee from all these kings who have besieged thee.'[22]

From this inscription we can deduce a lasting independence, an outlook limited to local problems. And this holds true of the entire Syrian area. Only one group of petty states, the cities of Phoenicia, broaden their horizons, and this is achieved not by way of local politics, but through overseas colonization, which remains their distinctive feature. From at least the eleventh century, Phoenician bases are set up in the islands of the Aegean, in Cilicia, in north Africa, in Malta, Sicily, Sardinia, and Spain. The credit for the greater proportion of these colonies is due to Tyre, which also founds the most important of them all, the city of Carthage; it comes into being at the end of the ninth century, and in due course it builds up a great empire.[23]

With the beginning of the eighth century the Syrian political scene changes. Assyrian pressure intensifies, and finally takes the form of permanent annexation. From now on the sovereigns are not ashamed to admit their vassaldom, as we can see from the inscription left by Bar-Rakib, king of Sam'al:

> I am Bar-Rakib, the son of Panamuwa, king of Sam'al, servant of Tiglath-pileser, the lord of the four quarters of the earth. Through the righteousness of my father and my own righteousness, I was set by my lord Rakib-El and my lord Tiglath-pileser upon the throne of my father. My father's house has profited more than any other, and I have run at the wheel of my lord, the king of Assyria, in the midst of mighty kings, possessors of silver and possessors of gold. I took over my father's house and made it more prosperous than the house of one of the mighty kings. My brethren, the kings, are envious of all the prosperity of my house. My fathers, the kings of Sam'al, had no good house. They had the house of Kila-muwa, which was their winter house and also their summer house. But I have built this house.[24]

The petty Syrian states begin to succumb during the second half of the eighth century: in 743 it is the turn of Arpad, in 732 of Damascus, in 722 of Samaria, in 675 of Sidon. The Babylonians succeed the Assyrians, but there is no change of policy: in 586 Jerusalem falls, and so ends the ancient history of the Hebrews; in 573 Tyre is conquered; finally the southernmost states are subdued. When Babylonia is conquered by the Persians, in 538, Syria is already no more than a province of the Babylonian empire, and it is simply transferred from one conqueror to the other. Vassaldom has given place to occupation; now, the policy of mass deportation is applied and the ethnic forces which had been moulding the history of Syria are broken up and dissolved.

III   *The Religious Structure*

The characteristic features of Syrian civilization are clearly derived from the nature and conditions of its history. As this is lacking in unity, it is impossible to speak strictly of a single culture, but rather of as many cultures as there are petty political organisms in which they are formed. As Syria's history is based on the mingling of ethnic elements, its culture, too, is the product of the conjunction of highly disparate components. Finally, as foreign supremacy is the prevalent note of Syrian history, so the influence of the neighbouring great powers is predominant in the culture. These factors are joined by the almost constant state of war or invasion, which results in a situation not only unfavourable to the development of civilization, but even positively imperilling its maintenance. This explains the paucity of the remains, which is in remarkable contrast with the wealth of the Mesopotamian and Egyptian documentation.

The foregoing considerations fully apply to the religion, or rather, the religions, of Syria.[25] Here the distinction between Canaanites and Aramaeans is of some point, not in the sense of a distinction between unitary elements, of course, but in that of a distinction between two groups differentiated both subjectively by their beliefs and objectively by the nature and the period of the respective sources of information. The Canaanite sources are more extensive and older, owing to the direct evidence provided by Ugarit, and also the ample though indirect information of the Old Testament; so it is possible to describe their pantheon, and to some extent their religious life, from as early as the second millennium. In the case of the Aramaeans we have no specifically religious documents for the period we are now considering; and the few historical inscriptions, together with the Biblical data, also of an historical nature, only allow us to reconstruct their beliefs for a period restricted to the first millennium B.C., and in respect chiefly of their divinities.

The Canaanite religion, like others of the ancient Orient is a naturalistic polytheism, distinguished by the fragmenta tion and foreign influences we have already mentioned. None the less, a careful scrutiny will reveal certain features which are typical, and we may well concentrate our attention more particularly on these. To begin with, the characteristics and attributes of the gods have a disconcerting fluidity: identical functions are assigned to various gods, their relationships change, even their sex is not constant.[26] Secondly, their names are frequently common nouns, or nouns of common origin and not proper names: they give the impression that the *numen loci* prevails over the personal god, that the feeling that a divinity is present in this or that place is primary, and the feeling for his subjective individuality is only secondary Finally, Canaanite religion contains elements of remarkable crudity, such as human sacrifice and sacred prostitution These testify to some degree of barbarity, to the absence o a developed civilization such as is found among the grea peoples of the environment. In a few words, the Canaanite i a more primitive religion, and this distinguishing feature sum: up all those we have just mentioned.

For the reconstruction of Canaanite religion our principa source is the Ugarit texts.[27] But immediately the question arises whether the beliefs expressed in these texts are con fined to that city, or can provide some indication for the en vironment also. We can answer this only by comparing the Ugarit documents with those few and indirect reference. which we obtain from elsewhere; and the answer is that, so far as we can judge, the Ugarit texts reflect beliefs which were widely current in the neighbouring area. This does no contradict our previous remarks concerning the fragmenta tion of the area, for the Ugaritic literature is undoubtedly the expression of a cultivated class, whose formation and tra dition rise superior to the immediately local popular beliefs

The supreme god of the Canaanites is El.[28] The word is a common noun which simply means 'god'; but in other part of the Semitic area there are traces of a process of personali zation. El is an enigmatic figure: he may be a celestial god but appears so rarely in the mythology that, apart from supreme authority, it is difficult to specify his attributes.

The other great Canaanite god, Baal,[29] is inferior to El in authority, but is much more present and active; Baal is also a common noun, meaning 'lord', and here again we have an intelligible personalization. We are better able to define Baal's nature and attributes: he is the storm god, and is thus the Canaanite counterpart to the cosmic force we found worshipped in Mesopotamia, and which the mountain peoples set at the apex of their pantheon. Moreover, through a characteristic combination of functions, Baal is also the vanishing vegetation god, and as such he corresponds to another well defined and primary figure of ancient Oriental religions.

The female element of the vegetation cycle, the great fertility goddess, is Baal's wife Astarte: this name is simply a variant of the Mesopotamian Ishtar. This, however, does not prevent her distinctive features and functions from being sometimes attributed to other goddesses, such as Anat, the sister or wife of Baal, and Asherah, the wife of El; this is a typical example of a religion lacking in organizing and centralizing activity, with the consequence that its various elements are superimposed on one another without system, and the personal entities shift about against the common basis of belief. However, this basis is extremely vivid; the fertility goddess in particular is a dominant theme of Canaanite art, being represented by figurines with strongly emphasized sexual features, the most common and typical production of that art.

Our list of the native gods must also include the patron deities of the various peoples, such as Kemosh of the Moabites and Milkom of the Ammonites. This last name is yet another common noun, meaning 'king'; it reappears in the name of the god of Tyre, Melkart — a compound meaning 'king of the city'.

Astral divinities play a remarkably small part in the Canaanite pantheon, this being in striking contrast to the religion of other Oriental peoples. Moreover, they appear to be of foreign origin, and as such they come first in the numerous line of imported gods. Mesopotamia and Egypt make approximately equal contributions to this importation, with the result that the presence in Canaan of such Egyptian deities as Hathor, Amon-Re, Ptah, and Bes is balanced by the Mesopotamian gods Sin, Nergal, and Ninurta.

At present we can only partially reconstruct the religious life of the Canaanites, for instead of the copious ritual literature of the surrounding peoples we have only a few brief and badly preserved Ugaritic documents. Consequently the indirect information provided by the Old Testament remains our most extensive source.

The sacerdotal personnel is fairly well organized with much subdivision of functions: in addition to the High Priest and the priests there are sanctuary keepers, wailing women, and sacred prostitutes. Diviners must also exist, since the Ugaritic documents mention many practices of divination. Finally, there is a special and distinctive category of prophets: we are unable to determine the details of their functions owing to the lack of data, but they constitute the environmental basis of a religious class which will acquire primary importance in Israel.

Another new element also appears in the conception of sacred places: these are no longer exclusively, or even principally centred in the temples; very often they consist of open air sanctuaries — a more natural place of worship and one nearer to the origins — situated near trees or sources of water, and above all on hills, the celebrated 'high places' mentioned in the Bible. The constituent elements of such a sanctuary are one or more sacred stones, which the local god is considered to inhabit, an altar, and a small enclosure.

Canaanite sacrifice,[30] too, presents some novel features. There is evidence not only of animal offerings, but of the sacrifice of human beings. This takes place at times of great general calamity, for example, when it is desired to show profound homage to the divinity. But the common assertion that the Canaanites sacrificed children when important buildings were being erected is not justified: there is no certain proof of these 'foundation sacrifices', for none of the skeletons reveal any trace of death by violence.

A final distinctive feature is sacred prostitution, a rite which expresses and reproduces that conception of the recurring fertility of the earth which also forms the basis of an extensive literary production.

All over the Canaanite area there is evidence of a cult of the dead, in the tombs in which the bodies are deposited. Sometimes the sarcophagi are given a human shape, an artistic element of Egyptian origin, and offerings such as vases, dishes, lamps and jewels are placed inside them with the body. This indicates that the Canaanites believed in survival beyond the tomb, but we cannot determine their conception of the future life with any precision.

In a later epoch, and over a more restricted area, the Aramaean pantheon has one characteristic feature — none the less significant for being negative — namely, the absence of any god that can definitely be considered as its own.

One deity, Hadad the storm god, is widely distributed over the area. He is none other than the Adad which we found in Mesopotamia, provided that, as our knowledge of the Aramaeans extends further backward in time, we do not find one day that in fact he was of Aramaean origin.

As usual, Hadad must have had his female consort: the Greek writer Lucian who visited the sanctuary of Hierapolis[31] at the beginning of the Christian era, identified her as Atargatis, a new incarnation of the fertility goddess. With her he found associated a young god, Simios, who thus completed the nature cycle.

Mesopotamian elements are to be found among the Aramaeans also: we find the sun-god, Shamash, the moon god, Sin, also Nergal, Nabu, and others. As there is no evidence of a comparable Egyptian influence, we must conclude that in this area, closer to the Mesopotamian center of influence, the Mesopotamian culture was strongly predominant.

The neighbouring Canaanite world is not without its influence on this area: El and Baal reappear in several places, and even Israel's Yahweh seems to find acceptance.[32]

We have almost no knowledge of Aramaean ritual. In view of the common environmental conditions, we may assume that it did not differ greatly from that of the neighbouring

peoples, but we cannot be more precise or detailed in ou
statements until such time as new discoveries throw light or
this religious life.

IV *The Literary Genres*

When we talk of ancient Syrian literature we mean mainl
Ugaritic literature.[33] The Canaanite area has yielded no other
and the Aramaean area not even so much; the splendid fu
ture that awaits Aramaic literature is so far foreshadowed
only by the progressive spread of that language over the geo
graphical area between the Euphrates and the Nile, and by
the appearance, right at the end of the period under consid
eration, of an interesting romance, that of Ahiqar.[34]

Only one of the many literary genres found elsewhere
turns up at Ugarit: that of mythology and epic; we canno
regard the correspondence, inventories, and administrative
writings as literature in the strict sense, nor the recently dis
covered juridical documents, though these will afford us a
brief glimpse of Canaanite society. To atone for this lack, the
mythological and epic texts are quite numerous, and althougl
there is much uncertainty as to their interpretation and suc
cessive order, it can be said that they stand comparison witl
the rich literatures of the surrounding peoples.

Having said so much, we must recall what we said when
writing of the religion, namely that Ugarit exemplifies and
documents a civilization of much greater extension. So the
literature, like the religion, is not, or rather not only, that o
one city, but has a wider range of validity and inspiration
though we are not in a position to trace the precise limits o
its extension.

The longest mythological poem, or cycle, which we have
has the god Baal and his sister Anat as its principal person
ages.[35] It consists of various episodes, such as the god's
struggle with the sea god Yam and his victory over him, and
the building of a great palace in Baal's honour. But the es

sential core of the story is Baal's death and resurrection, which is yet another expression of the myth of the vanishing god. Moreover, this new presentation is very interesting, both because the myth appears in a form so explicit that it is equalled only in the Hittite version, and because it contains independent elements. Chief among these are that Baal's antagonist is personalized in Mot, the god of the underworld, and that the struggle between the two gods is the main theme of the story.

Baal quarrels with Mot, makes his way to the underworld, and there, after a desperate conflict, meets his death. His sister Anat resolves to avenge him:

> As the heart of a cow toward her calf,
> As the heart of a ewe toward her lamb,
> So is the heart of Anat for Baal.
> She seizes Mot by the fold of his robe,
> Grasps him by the edge of his garment.
> She lifts up her voice and cries:
> 'Thou, Mot, give me back my brother!'
> But the god Mot makes answer:
> 'What wouldst thou, O Maiden Anat? . . .
> I met the mighty Baal,
> And made him as a lamb in my mouth,
> Like a kid in my throat was he crushed' . . .
> A day passes, and two days,
> And after the days, the months.
> Maiden Anat draws near to him.
> As the heart of a cow toward her calf,
> As the heart of a ewe toward her lamb,
> So is the heart of Anat for Baal.
> She seizes the god Mot;
> With sword she cleaves him,
> With fan she winnows him,
> With fire she burns him,
> With mill she grinds him,
> In fields she sows him.
> Birds eat the pieces of him,
> Devour the bits of him.[36]

The terminology is explicit: Mot, who is cut down, winnowed, burnt, ground, and sown, is the god of the summer harvests, of the dry season which destroys the fertility brought by the spring rains. But then fertility returns, and Baal comes back to the earth:

> *In a dream of the god El, the kindly and benign,*
> *In a vision of the creator of creatures,*
> *From the heavens rains fat,*
> *The wadis flow with honey.*
> *The god El, the kindly and benign, is glad.*
> *He sets his feet on the footstool,*
> *Opens his mouth and laughs;*
> *He lifts up his voice and cries:*
> *'Now will I sit and rest,*
> *My soul will have peace in my breast;*
> *For mighty Baal is alive,*
> *The prince, the lord of earth still exists!'*[37]

The terminology is just as explicit: with the god's return fatness rains down from the sky, and honey flows. Here the ancient myth has been given one of its most vivid literary expressions.

Hero epic is represented by two important Ugaritic poems, that of Aqhat and that of Keret; both are new in their characters and themes to their environment, so we cannot exclude the possibility that they are based on incidents of local history transferred to the realm of legend.

Aqhat[38] is the young son of a wise king, Daniel, who has long prayed to the gods to grant him progeny; when at last his wish is fulfilled, he gives voice to his joy:

> *Daniel's face lights up,*
> *His brow shines.*
> *He opens his mouth and laughs,*
> *Sets his feet on the footstool,*
> *And lifts up his voice and cries:*
> *'Now will I sit and rest,*
> *My soul will have peace in my breast,*

For a son is born to me as to my brethren,
A scion, as to my kindred.'[39]

Note the parallels, even to the point of verbal identity, with the passage previously quoted: we are justified in concluding that already a conventional rhetoric existed with appropriate formulas for the expression of certain psychological states. And, turning to the content, note the conception, very dear to the Oriental world, that offspring is a blessing of the gods.

A divine craftsman makes Aqhat a magnificent bow, with which he goes hunting. But the goddess Anat covets the bow, and in order to obtain it promises the hero gold and silver, even immortality:

Ask for life, Aqhat the hero,
Ask for life and I will give it to thee,
For deathlessness and I will grant it to thee.
I will make thee count years with Baal,
With the son of El shalt thou count months.
When Baal gives life, he gives a feast,
Gives a feast for his chosen one, and bids him drink,
Makes music and song for him,
Sings a sweet strain;
So will I give life to Aqhat the hero.[40]

But Aqhat replies:

Deceive me not, O maiden;
To a hero thy deceit is hateful.
What further life can a mortal attain,
How can a mortal attain everlasting life?
Greyness will be poured upon my head,
Whiteness upon my pate,
And I shall die as every man dies,
I shall inevitably die.[41]

These lines evoke comparison with the epic of Gilgamesh, in which the hero rejects the advances of the goddess Ishtar and cannot avoid death. The conception of the inevitable end which men, however strong and mighty, cannot escape,

runs through the whole of ancient Oriental literature. Because of his refusal, Aqhat will be slain by Anat's emissary.
As the end of the script of the poem is damaged, we cannot
say with certainty, though one may presume it, whether the
loving care of his family succeeds in bringing him back to life.

Even more human is the story of king Keret:[42] disasters
deprive him of all his family, and in a dream he is urged by
the god El to set about the conquest of the distant land of
Udum. The king of that region will grant him his beautiful
daughter as wife. When Keret has won the victory he de-
mands not gold and silver, but only the hand of the princess:

> *What need have I of silver and yellow-glittering gold,*
> *Friendship by covenant and vassalage for ever? . . .*
> *Give me the maiden Hurriya,*
> *The fine-mannered, the first-born,*
> *Whose grace is as the grace of Anat,*
> *Whose beauty is as that of Astarte;*
> *Whose pupils are gems of lapis,*
> *Whose eyes are alabaster cups.*
> *El hath granted me her in a dream,*
> *The father of men in a vision,*
> *That a scion be born to Keret,*
> *A child to the servant of El.*[43]

This poem, too, expresses the desire for progeny in order
that the line may not become extinct. The young princess is
given to Keret and the prophecy comes true: he raises a new
family. But then the king falls seriously ill, and the ancient
lament returns once more: can man never escape death? The
end of the story is obscure; possibly Keret is saved by a divine exorcism.

These are the principal poems found at Ugarit. There are
others of minor importance, though some of these have a special interest. For instance, there is the poem of Dawn and
Sunset:[44] it tells of the birth of two divinities who bear these
two names; and — a characteristic touch — the events are accompanied by a sacred ceremony, in which various characters appear and speak; in other words, it is the script of a
religious drama. So here too there is the connection between

myth and ritual to which we have already drawn attention; doubtless this connection is much more profound than appears in the literary version, just as it must go beyond the limits which apparently confine it. Gaster has made out a strong case for this thesis, carrying it to its ultimate conclusion and extending it to almost the whole of the mythological literature of the ancient Orient:

> In the first place, much of what has come down to us as ancient literature was not, in fact, mere artistic creation, but possessed a strictly functional character within the structure of communal life. Texts which we have been wont to regard as the products of this or that author's individual fancy and genius were, in fact, the traditional 'books of words' of religious ceremonies, inspired by a goddess more practical than the Muses, and fully intelligible only if read against the background of the rituals which they accompanied. Accordingly, far more is needed for their elucidation than a mere translation of words. They have first and foremost to be placed in their appropriate cultural context — their *Sitz im Leben* — and they must be viewed as expressions and not as forms.[45]

This theory, especially in its extension, is subject to discussion; but in any case it constitutes a salutary warning to avoid criticism which seeks to explain everything in terms of literature and, instead, to go more deeply into the practical background of ancient Oriental texts, and to identify a great part of them as the product and direct expression of religious life.

On the very fringe of the period we are discussing — in the fifth century B.C. — we find an Aramaic romance aiming at edification. This is the tale of Ahiqar. Ahiqar is a wise and virtuous man, chancellor at the court of the Assyrian kings Sennacherib and Esarhaddon. Having no son of his own, he adopts his nephew Nadin, and hands over his office to him. But Nadin repays him with evil: he slanders him to Esarhaddon, and induces the king to have him put to death. However, the executioner secretly lets Ahiqar escape, and he is able to rehabilitate himself by exposing his unworthy nephew's intrigue. The tale has an appendix, a number of sayings which link up the work with wisdom literature. For instance, the wise Ahiqar says:

> My son, chatter not overmuch, utter not every word that comes into thy mind: men's eyes and ears are fixed on thy mouth. Beware lest it be thy undoing. Above all other things set a watch upon thy mouth, and over what thou hearest harden thy heart. For a word is a bird: once it is released, none can recapture it . . .
>
> The wrath of a king is a burning fire. Obey it at once. Let it not be enkindled against thee and burn thy hands. Cover the word of the king with the veil of thy heart. Why should wood contend with fire, flesh with a knife, a man with a king?[46]

The work also contains fables:

> The leopard met a goat who was cold, and he said to her: 'Come, I will cover thee with my hide.' The goat answered: 'What need have I of that? Don't take my hide! For thou greetest not, save to suck blood.'[47]

From the foregoing, can we say that the romance is one of the literary forms found in Syria? And, in conjunction with it, the didactic and fable genres? Not necessarily. The tale of Ahiqar, which is written on a papyrus found in Egypt, and which has Mesopotamia as its setting, is mentioned here because of the Aramaic language in which it is written; but the diffusion of this language beyond its own natural boundaries prevents our drawing reliable conclusions as to the origin of the text.

As we have said, the juridical documents recently discovered in the central archives of the palace at Ugarit afford us a glimpse into the organization of the city's society.[48] These documents relate chiefly to commercial transactions: sales, exchanges, gifts; and so the information they yield is mainly economic in nature; nevertheless indirect light is shed on elements of personal, family, and penal law.

The chief interest of these documents is in the manner in which they are drawn up; it is remarkably constant, and so constitutes an established genre or type. First the date is given, then the class of act (before witnesses, before the king, or, most frequently, a direct royal act), the description of the act, subsidiary clauses if any, and authentication by witnesses or, more usually, the royal seal. For example:

> This day, before Arkhalpu son of Niqmadu, king of Ugarit, Ilinergal son of Sudumu has adopted Arteshup as his brother. In future . . . if Ilinergal wishes to separate from his brother Arteshup, he shall pay 1000 shekels of silver into his hands and those of his sons and Arteshup shall quit the house. Seal of the king.[49]

As will be observed, the king plays an essential part in the formulation of these acts. He presides, directly or indirectly — but more often directly — over the administration of justice.

The law relating to persons[50] reflects the stratification of Babylonian society into three classes: patricians, plebeians, slaves. The condition of the slaves is particularly good, and freed slaves can reach high office. In the law relating to family life we are struck by the position of women: there is no proof of polygamy, in the event of repudiation the dowry is returned, juridical capacity is assured; and so we find women bringing actions, adopting sons, entering into contracts for buying and selling. The penal law seems very mild: the death penalty is reported only once in the Ugarit archives, and then for treason; otherwise the maximum penalty is exile. As Nougayrol has well written, here we have a prosperous and civilized city, where 'life is sweet for all, and for some luxurious'.[51]

V The Artistic Types

Our remarks concerning Syrian culture generally are true of art[52] in particular: we find fragmentation, prevalence of foreign influences, paucity of remains. To these must be added the absence of a definite aspiration towards great art: what

is produced in a region of such unstable conditions and such
restricted independence meets rather the needs of commerce,
of the ordinary market. Indeed, the best producers of this
art were commercially minded people, namely, the inhabitants of the Phoenician cities.

After the foregoing, one might expect a negative answer
to the question of originality. But it is not so simple as that,
for originality may find an outlet not only in the formulation
of new themes, but also in the forms in which old themes are
repeated and blended. Ugaritic art merits special attention
from this aspect: here a strongly represented Aegean component unites with Egyptian, Mesopotamian, Anatolian, and
yet other elements in a synthesis of a Mediterranean character which is both significant and new, since it cannot be said
to have been achieved to such an extent and in such a manner in any other part of the ancient Orient.[53]

The primary task of architecture in the Syrian area seems
to have been connected with the construction of fortifications,
the walls which ensured the defence of the city from its earliest days against the assaults of the nomads. Pre-Israelitic
Palestinian archaeology has identified many of these walls:
they are composed of several blocks of rough hewn stone,
placed one above another. At a later period, in the Aramaean
zone, the city fortifications are directly linked in their character with that of the neo-Hittite period, thus completing the
chain connecting Syria with Anatolia: the best example of
this is Sam'al, with its double surrounding wall and its system
of fortifications, which can be fairly well reconstructed.

Just as the Syrian area approximates to the Anatolian in
regard to the main architectural tasks and the manner in
which they were executed, so, too, the two regions have a
common basic material, stone, which is scarce elsewhere. Its
function, however (and in this respect too there is some affinity between Syria and Anatolia), remains confined to the
lower courses of walls and buildings, and the exploitation of
the column does not come until a late period. Even then, it
is only to a limited extent, and in a type of building, the *bit
khilani,* of uncertain origin.

Civil architecture has left few remains, and it is only recently that excavations at Alalakh and Ugarit have added to our knowledge. The palace follows the same general plan as those of Mesopotamia, though on a decidedly smaller scale; it consists of a series of rooms grouped around one or more courtyards. In the later period extensive use is made of the building with a frontal portico, the *bit khilani*. We have already described the structure of this type of building, and have mentioned the problem of its origin. In opposition to the former theory that it is a Hittite architectural type, recently authorities have maintained its Syrian origin.[54] In fact, the question is still undecided, both because of the paucity of data, and also because of the uncertainty of the elements which are alleged to mark the course of its development.

As we have said, the religious edifices frequently consist of simple open air precincts, with one or more sacred pilasters and an altar for the holocausts. But the more important cities do not lack closed sanctuaries, of an extremely simple structure. As an example we may take the temple of Baal at Ugarit, which dates from the beginning of the second millennium: it consists of a courtyard with an altar, an antechamber, and a principal chamber. This is inadequate to allow of comparative evaluation; yet it may be said, in negative terms, that the essential elements proper to the Egyptian temple as distinct from those of the rest of the ancient Near East are not present, and therefore that Syrian religious architecture appears to gravitate towards Asia rather than Egypt.

In the realm of sculpture large scale statuary of the human form is lacking, whereas statuettes are extremely numerous. The dominant type is a nude female figure with the sexual features deliberately exaggerated and the hands frequently raised to the breasts; this is a representation of the fertility goddess, whose significance we have indicated when dealing with Syrian religion. There are also numerous statuettes of gods, and two silver figurines found in an amphora at Ugarit may serve as examples of these (Pl. XXVI). Golden robes and collars fail to modify the crude impression left by the faces and bodies: the sign of an art which, when it is not inspired by foreign models, remains disconcertingly primitive.

Turning to animal sculpture, during the period of the neo-Hittites and in the area adjacent to them we again find the orthostats of lions and sphinxes which have already been noted as characteristic of Anatolian art and its derivatives. The latest example, a fine orthostat of a lion, comes from the Israeli excavations now being carried out at Hazor.[55] This is really only the continuation of an artistic type, and proves that it radiated southward.

Relief carving, as usual, is plentiful. On the fringes of the Anatolian area there are again the characteristic engravings of scenes on stone blocks used as wall bases. There are also reliefs in metal, of extremely fine workmanship; an example of this is a golden dish found at Ugarit (Pl. XXVII), bearing a hammered design of a lively scene in which a hunter riding in a chariot, with drawn bow and unleashed hounds, is chasing wild bulls and gazelles. The workmanship reveals remarkable artistry and skill not found in other branches of Syrian art.

The discovery of Cretan and Mycenaean art themes at Ugarit is novel, but quite understandable in view of the city's geographical position. Perhaps the best example of this feature is a female figure carved in relief on ivory, known as the 'goddess of the wild beasts' (Pl. XXVIII). She is seated, and naked to the waist, the lower part of the body being wrapped in a skirt decorated with a network of lines. She is holding stalks of grain in each hand, and on either side a goat rampant has its head level with her hand. There is no reason to assume that this object was imported: a number of other examples, including many remarkable specimens of vases with faces modelled in relief, show that the Ugaritic artists took over a wide range of art themes from overseas.

Relief carving on ivory is found in several other parts of the Syrian area[56] besides Ugarit. Perhaps the most outstanding specimens have been found at Arslan Tash, and these originate from Damascus. The style is very similar to that of Mesopotamia.

An artistic production characteristic of the Phoenician area is the stone sarcophagus with a human figure carved on its top.[57] These sarcophagi reveal first Egyptian and then Greek influence, and are found particularly in Sidon; chronologically they date from a late period, in fact later than that which we are now considering.

Minor arts also flourish extensively among the Phoenicians, who produced medallions, necklaces, bracelets, rings, and other articles, decorated with birds, wild goats, lions' heads, and palms. Glass articles and coins are common too, but these take us beyond our chronological limits.

Nor is it desirable to enter into detailed discussion of these items, for the proper task of a broad outline of ancient Oriental civilizations is to bring out the newer and more decisive elements, leaving the subordinate features in shadow. But we have to remember that whether any feature is subordinate or not is a relative problem: in its synthesis of contrasted elements, and especially in its reaching out towards the Aegean civilizations, ancient Syria takes up a foremost position, anticipating that meeting of East and West which is fully realized only at a later date in history.

ISRAEL

I The Revolution in Values

The 102nd Psalm praises the Lord in the following terms:

Of old hast thou laid the foundations of the earth,
And the heavens are the work of thy hands.
They shall perish, but thou shalt endure:
Yea, all of them shall wax old like a garment;
As a vesture shalt thou change them, and they shall be
*   changed:*
But thou art the same,
And thy years shall have no end.[1]

These words express a fundamentally new idea. We recall the conception of the universe shared by the other peoples of the ancient Orient: all without exception regard the earth as a divinity, and the sky as a divinity; the gods are immanent in nature and render it divine. The psalmist's conception is diametrically contrary: there is only one God, and this God is outside and above all nature, which He himself created. Nature is subordinate and of short life in relation to its Creator. If it has any function of its own, it is to express the glory of God. The position of man is completely analogous: he draws his origin and destiny from God.

Thus we are faced with a change in the old values and the advent of a new conception of the universe. Here we have a crisis in the forces of nature, the divine is withdrawn from them and retires into transcendence. But the God of Israel is not only transcendent rather than immanent: he is one instead of many, so the cosmos is under a single direction. And he is just and merciful, rather than animated by the human type of passions; and so there is no doubt as to the morality of that direction, there is freedom from fear, and the genesis of a confident submission.

Here, too, the thinking of ancient Israel differs from that of its environment. The people of Egypt and Mesopotamia had their cult of the pre-established order, of predetermined destinies; and every change was regarded as an evil. We recall, for instance, Ipuwer's lament over the Egyptian crisis during the first intermediate period:

> Why really! poor men have become the possessors of treasures. He who could not make himself sandals now possesses riches . . .[2]

The Hebrew song of Hannah is at the opposite pole:

> *The Lord killeth, and maketh alive;*
> *He bringeth down to the grave, and bringeth up.*
> *The Lord maketh poor, and maketh rich:*
> *He bringeth low, he also lifteth up.*
> *He raiseth up the poor out of the dust,*
> *He lifteth up the needy from the dunghill,*
> *To make them sit with princes,*
> *And inherit the throne of glory:*
> *For the pillars of the earth are the Lord's,*
> *And he hath set the world upon them.*[3]

Hence, although it is God who created the cosmic order, this does not imply that he does not alter it and renew it in accordance with his inscrutable judgement. God alone is active force: the rest, nature and man, have their existence only as a reflection of him.[4]

II   *The Historical Outlines*

In the history of Israel[5] we are faced from the outset by a problem: on the one hand there is a congenital political debility in the state, resulting necessarily from the geographical position of the area in which that history occurs; on the other we have a survival in time far beyond that of the great peoples surrounding it: a survival which is primarily a religious one, but is also ethnic. In other words, the people lives on after the death of the state.

The solution to this problem has to be sought in the particular conception which Israel itself holds of history,[6] a conception which is a direct deduction from its idea of the universe. The elements of the idea are extremely simple: Israel has its God; this God has made a pact with Israel; the working out of this pact constitutes history.

It may be objected that other peoples of the ancient Orient also have their national gods, on whose power they rely, and to whose will they entrust themselves. But the God of Israel is a universal god — this is not the place to examine when or how Israel adopted this conclusion — and therefore he is the God of all the peoples. So he is responsible not for a part only but for the whole of history, and to him must be attributed not only the people's victories and successes, but also its defeats and failures. The latter are conceived of as the consequences of its faults and its violations of the covenant, and are held to be brought about through its enemies, who thus become the instruments of the divine will.

This conception of history enables us to understand the survival of Israel beyond the final political crisis, since the human party to the covenant is not the state but the people, and the people does not disappear with the downfall of the state. On the other hand, the conception itself contains the seeds of a dual and divergent development, which we shall see taking place during Israel's politico-religious history: in one direction we have universalism, for God is the one lord of all the peoples; in the other we have nationalism, for the covenant was made with one particular people.

Just as unique as the Israelite conception of history is the tradition by which it has been handed down to us. For the first time in the ancient Near East we have not isolated documents, no matter how numerous or extensive, but entire books of continuous narrative. It is true that this is the final form achieved by tradition: but it is achieved within the bounds of ancient Near Eastern history, and well within those bounds. Moreover, the narratives apply in practice the conception of history we have just expounded; and so there is continual judgement by reference to cause and effect, motives and consequences, such as is not found in the great literatures of either Egyptians or Mesopotamians. As we have seen, only the Hittites have left proofs of a capacity to think historically; but these proofs, the royal inscriptions and the treaties, did not achieve organic fusion into a single narrative outlining and interpreting the whole of the people's history. In its final version Hebrew historiography, the Old Testament, is precisely that: a group of books collected and chosen for their documentation of sacred history, in other words, of the long intercourse between God and the people, the principles on which that intercourse was based, and the conditions in which it came into being. Of course, the collection was made after the events described, and was affected by the interpretation which was posited for them, and this fact sets the historian a number of problems; but at a certain stage the significance which Israel attributes to its own history becomes the driving force of that history itself, the law and condition of its development.

What is Israel? As a constituted entity, it is a confederation of tribes established in Palestine and held together by allegiance to a central sanctuary. But the tribes come from outside, and the confederation preserves their more ancient traditions.[7] Nowadays it is generally admitted that these have an historical foundation, although opinions differ as to the date of the events and the manner in which they occurred.

Following the order in which the accounts are presented, the earliest tradition tells of how the primitive nucleus of the people came from Mesopotamia. The patriarch Abram, with his family, leaves Ur of the Chaldees, goes up the Euphrates to Haran, and turns aside into Palestine. We are told the motive which determined this succession of events:

> Now the Lord said unto Abram, Get thee out of thy country, and from thy kindred, and from thy father's

house, unto the land that I will show thee: and I will
make of thee a great nation, and I will bless thee, and
make thy name great; and be thou a blessing: and I will
bless them that bless thee, and him that curseth thee
will I curse: and in thee shall all the families of the
earth be blessed. So Abram went, as the Lord had
spoken unto him.[8]

Here we have the earliest formulation of the covenant between Israel and its God.[9] It will be repeated constantly, as a
kind of leitmotif, throughout the subsequent narrative.

A second tradition tells of Israel's sojourn in Egypt, its
oppression at the hands of a Pharaoh, and its liberation by
the great leader Moses. He too, like Abram, is elected and
called to his mission by God:

Now Moses was keeping the flock of Jethro his father-
in-law, the priest of Midian: and he led the flock to the
back of the wilderness, and came to the mountain of God,
unto Horeb. And the angel of the Lord appeared unto
him in a flame of fire out of the midst of a bush: and
he looked, and behold, the bush burned with fire, and
the bush was not consumed. And Moses said, I will turn
aside now, and see this great sight, why the bush is
not burnt. And when the Lord saw that he turned aside
to see, God called unto him out of the midst of the bush,
and said, Moses, Moses. And he said, Here am I. And
he said, Draw not nigh hither: put off thy shoes from
thy feet, for the place whereon thou standest is holy
ground. Moreover he said, I am the God of thy father,
the God of Abraham, the God of Isaac, and the God of
Jacob. And Moses hid his face; for he was afraid to look
upon God. And the Lord said, I have surely seen the
affliction of my people which are in Egypt, and have
heard their cry by reason of their taskmasters; for I know
their sorrows; and I am come down to deliver them out
of the hand of the Egyptians, and to bring them up out
of that land unto a good land and a large, unto a land
flowing with milk and honey. . . . Come now therefore,

and I will send thee unto Pharaoh, that thou mayest bring forth my people the children of Israel out of Egypt.[10]

The third tradition relating to the earliest history of the tribes tells of the journey across the desert, en route for the Promised Land, and the event of fundamental importance which occurs during that journey: God makes a further appearance to Moses, the covenant is renewed, and laws are given for the government of the community. The manifestation of God on the mountain, amid clouds, smoke, and fire, illustrates the Israelite conception of the Divine:

> And it came to pass on the third day, when it was morning, that there were thunders and lightnings, and a thick cloud upon the mount, and the voice of a trumpet exceeding loud; and all the people that were in the camp trembled. And Moses brought forth the people out of the camp to meet God; and they stood at the nether part of the mount. And mount Sinai was altogether in smoke, because the Lord descended upon it in fire; and the smoke thereof ascended as the smoke of a furnace, and the whole mount quaked greatly. And when the voice of the trumpet waxed louder and louder, Moses spake, and God answered him by a voice.[11]

The theophany on Sinai is of fundamental importance in Israel's conception of history. By associating the body of religious, moral, social and juridical prescriptions regulating the people's life with this theophany, the Biblical text projects their origin even beyond the tribal confederation in Palestine.

In the Biblical narrative the occupation of the Promised Land develops around the figure of the great leader Joshua: after crossing the Jordan he conquers Jericho and swiftly fans out his forces towards the centre, the south, and the north of the country. The rural districts are occupied before the cities, which hold out longer: the future capital, Jerusalem, does not fall until the time of David.

However, these events, for which archaeology suggests a period about 1230 B.C., may represent only part of what actually happened. The conquest may have been partly the

fruit of a long and peaceful penetration which took different
forms in different places; and it is possible that the Israelites
who participated in the occupation found certain brother
tribes already on the spot, and entered into a close union with
them.

As we have said, at first ancient Israel is organized on
federal lines. The Biblical text speaks of twelve tribes held
together by a central sanctuary: the 'holy ark', a coffer plated
with gold, which during the nomadic period is carried about
with the tribes, but later finds a permanent resting place in the
city of Shiloh, and has its own priesthood. Shiloh is the centre
for the meetings of the confederation and the communal religious ceremonies: this system recalls the one known to us
from classical antiquity under the name of amphictyony. In
this connection a German scholar, Noth, writes:

> The Israelite twelve tribe system does not in any way
> represent a singular phenomenon, and for this reason it
> is to be traced historically neither to the fortuitous cir-
> cumstance of the association of twelve brothers as fore-
> fathers of the tribes, nor to a secondarily worked-out
> construction of the schematic subdivision of a greater
> whole; it seems rather that there are present here cer-
> tain juridical provisions, such as were usual with tribal
> confederations still lacking fixed political institutions.
> This certainly holds for all the examples known from the
> Old Testament. These bare lists do not of course tell us
> much about the sense of those provisions. We are taken
> further by the fact that such confederations of twelve
> are known to us also from ancient Greece and Italy; and
> of these we learn from various sources that a cult car-
> ried out in common constituted their focal point, and
> that for certain festivals the members of these confeder-
> ations used to foregather in the central sanctuary, and
> moreover that certain cults were carried out and admin-
> istered precisely by such confederations of twelve or six
> tribes. Here the fixed and constantly maintained number
> of twelve (or six) also seems to fit in in quite a practical
> fashion, inasmuch as the members of these confedera-

tions were to undertake the care of the common sanctuary in monthly (or two-monthly) rotation. In Greece such a sacred confederation was given the name amphictyony, the 'community of those dwelling around' (i.e. around a determinate sanctuary); and this expression may serve as a technical term for such an arrangement.[12]

In political matters authority rests with the tribe. Only at times of especial danger do occasional and temporary chiefs arise to combat the foe: these are the Judges, whose deeds are described in the Biblical book of this name. Their authority is considered to rest on divine concession made to them and accepted by the tribes. Hence, their era has been known as the charismatic age of Israel: in the last analysis it is *charisma*, God's grace, which governs the determination of authority.

The Judges are popular heroes whose feats live long in the memory of the people; and the Book of Judges contains passages of indubitable antiquity, such as the celebrated Song of Deborah:

For that the leaders took the lead in Israel,
For that the people offered themselves willingly,
Bless ye the Lord.
Hear ye, O ye kings; give ear O ye princes;
I, even I, will sing unto the Lord;
I will sing praise to the Lord, the God of Israel.
Lord, when thou wentest forth out of Seir,
When thou marchedst out of the field of Edom,
The earth trembled, the heavens also dropped,
Yea, the clouds dropped water.
The mountains flowed down at the presence of the Lord,
Even yon Sinai at the presence of the Lord, the God of
    Israel.[13]

The Judges' authority remains modest and restricted, in harmony with the democratic heritage of the tribes; but the enemy pressure on the frontiers does not allow such a political system to survive. Thus, determined by circumstances, a monarchy comes into being which, falling within the era of

the political void caused by the temporary crisis in the neighbouring empires, forms a strong and unified power. But historically this is only a brief episode, for when the empires
recover a crisis swiftly sets in. Politically, too, the unity
achieved is precarious, for the nomadic tradition of freedom
is ill adapted to the new regime, and the religious trends are
rigorously opposed to those attempts at concession to and
assimilation with the environment towards which govern-
mental practice is fatally drawn. The royal policy aims constantly to conciliate the opposed and centrifugal forces: it
succeeds for a time, but not decisively.

The first king of the Israelites is Saul. He is invested with
the kingship by the prophet Samuel, and so by a religious
authority; he proceeds to conquer the enemy and organize
and consolidate the state. But his agreement with Samuel is
shortlived, and he begins to find himself isolated, to fear
revolt everywhere, to persecute everyone who arouses his
suspicions. The episode which places him in opposition to his
young son-in-law-to-be, David, is characteristic of his reactions:

> And it came to pass as they came, when David re-
> turned from the slaughter of the Philistine,[14] that the
> women came out of all the cities of Israel, singing and
> dancing to meet king Saul, with timbrels, with joy, and
> with instruments of music. And the women sang to one
> another in their play, and said,

> > Saul hath slain his thousands,
> > And David his ten thousands.

> And Saul was very wroth, and this saying displeased
> him; and he said, They have ascribed unto David ten
> thousands, and to me they have ascribed but thousands:
> and what more can he have but the kingdom? And Saul
> eyed David from that day and forward.

> And it came to pass on the morrow, that an evil spirit
> from God came mightily upon Saul, and he prophesied
> in the midst of the house: and David played with his
> hand, as he did day by day: and Saul had his spear in
> his hand. And Saul cast the spear, for he said, I will
> smite David even to the wall. And David avoided out

of his presence twice. And Saul was afraid of David, because the Lord was with him, and was departed from Saul.[15]

The figure of the king, abandoned by God, a prey to jealousy and persecution mania, stands out from the Biblical pages in all its tragedy. Here Israelite historiography proves capable of depicting not only events, but characters and personalities. Whereas we had to seek out and deduce fragmentary features from the not strictly historiographical documents of the other peoples of the ancient Orient, here those elements are explicit in the historiography, which sets itself up as a judge of events, and provides a free and detached appreciation even of the kings.

Saul dies on the field of battle, and after various vicissitudes David succeeds him, and unites all Israel under his rule. This occurs about 1000 B.C. A number of successful wars extends the state power in all directions, and within it the policy of equilibrium among the tribes and the attachment of the priesthood to the court, involving the transfer of the Ark of the Covenant to the new capital, Jerusalem, counteracts the traditional elements making for dissension. David's house becomes the sacred interpreter of Israel's mission to the world;[16] and his reign goes down in Hebrew tradition as the type of the golden age, to be regretted for its passing.

The second Book of Samuel contains a well informed and precise historiography, close to the events narrated, of David's reign, and the sovereign's character, his human as well as his political qualities, are summed up with unequalled acumen joined to independence of judgement. By way of example we may take the episode in which by a parable the prophet Nathan brings David to repent of the wrong he has committed by his adulterous relations with Bath-sheba:

> And the Lord sent Nathan unto David. And he came unto him, and said unto him, There were two men in one city; the one rich, and the other poor. The rich man had exceeding many flocks and herds: but the poor man had nothing, save one little ewe lamb, which he had bought and nourished up: and it grew up together with

him, and with his children; it did eat of his own morsel, and drank of his own cup, and lay in his bosom, and was to him as a daughter. And there came a traveller unto the rich man, and he spared to take of his own flock and of his own herd, to dress for the wayfaring man that was come unto him, but took the poor man's lamb, and dressed it for the man that was come to him. And David's anger was greatly kindled against the man; and he said to Nathan, As the Lord liveth, the man that hath done this is worthy to die: and he shall restore the lamb fourfold, because he did this thing, and because he had no pity.

And Nathan said unto David, Thou art the man. Thus saith the Lord, the God of Israel, I anointed thee king over Israel, and I delivered thee out of the hand of Saul; and I gave thee thy master's house, and thy master's wives into thy bosom, and gave thee the house of Israel and of Judah; and if that had been too little, I would have added unto thee such and such things. Wherefore hast thou despised the word of the Lord, to do that which is evil in his sight? thou hast smitten Uriah the Hittite with the sword, and hast taken his wife to be thy wife. . . . And David said unto Nathan, I have sinned against the Lord.[17]

By comparison with the rest of Oriental historical writing, this narrative is striking in more than one respect: in its unusual theme of private life; in its account of the submission of political authority to a superior moral principle; and finally, in the expression of this principle through the mouth of the characteristic figure, the prophet, who will dominate so much of Israel's later history.

David's successor, Solomon, enjoys a long and prosperous reign. According to the first book of Kings, the frontiers extend to the Euphrates and to Egypt, and thus the whole, or almost the whole, of ancient Syria is united under a national sovereign. Wars are almost unknown. However, because of the very extent and power of the state, there is a determined attempt to copy the model of the great Oriental monarchies, through large scale economic and commercial development, great public works, and increase in the wealth and pomp of the court. In this humanization of the Israelite theocracy, a tolerant assimilation of foreign cults also comes about; and so the equilibrium is destroyed, the religious tradition reacts, and the historiography does not hesitate to become the mouthpiece of that tradition:

> For it came to pass, when Solomon was old, that his wives turned away his heart after other gods; and his heart was not perfect with the Lord his God, as was the heart of David his father. For Solomon went after Ashtoreth the goddess of the Zidonians, and after Milcom the abomination of the Ammonites. And Solomon did that which was evil in the sight of the Lord. . . . Wherefore the Lord said unto Solomon, Forasmuch as this is done of thee, and thou hast not kept my covenant and my statutes, which I have commanded thee, I will surely rend the kingdom from thee, and will give it to thy servant.[18]

In this passage the principle of judgement by cause and effect is quite obvious: political decadence is the result of moral guilt. Only the instrument of punishment remains to be determined; and this will be done beyond all possibility of error during the days of the divided monarchy.

So Solomon's reign is followed by a crisis. The kingdom is split into two: in the north is the kingdom of Israel, the larger and stronger of the two, but deprived of the religious centre, Jerusalem. In the south is the kingdom of Judah, which retains that centre, but is reduced to a shadow of the former power. The decisive factor in this split is the ancient tribal rivalry, and so, in the last resort, Israel's nomadic heritage. A general religious decline sets in, for the north establishes and re-establishes its own sanctuaries, and for reasons of expediency the kings are generally prone to continue and intensify the tendency to tolerate foreign cults which was inaugurated by Solomon. The religious tradition reacts at once; and as the official priesthood is only too often hand in glove with the court, the reaction centres round the independent and spontaneous phenomenon of the prophets.[19] The historical sources, the books of Kings, attach much importance to this movement and its manifestations, a fact which once more demonstrates, if that be necessary, the religious character and purpose of these books. With the prophets, the universalism of the historical outlook is explicit: a single moral law rules the affairs of all mankind; whether by reward or punishment they are the means whereby that law is brought into operation.

From the purely political aspect the history of the divided kingdom is dominated by the recovery of the great powers adjacent to Israel, namely Egypt and Assyria: the latter power in particular emerges from a long period of crisis and renews its westward pressure, at first with expeditions aimed at reducing the Syrian states to vassaldom, and then with a policy of outright annexation. The affairs of Israel and Judah are overshadowed by this pressure; and the shifting interplay of alliances and conflicts typical of petty states set between greater ones does not alter the main course of history, nor its inevitable conclusion.

In Israel, after the dynastic tradition is broken, the old instability of the supreme political power reappears, and a succession of revolts and conspiracies undermines that power. Not until the beginning of the ninth century does king Omri succeed in establishing a more solidly based dynasty; but concessions to foreign cults bring about another reaction and put an end to this dynasty. Meanwhile the external situation grows steadily more unfavourable. King Jehu (842–815 B.C.) is forced to cast himself down at the feet of the Assyrian king Shalmaneser III, and the Assyrian's celebrated black obelisk provides a description of the scene. Under Jeroboam II (786–746 B.C.) the state has one last period of prosperity; then crisis develops rapidly, and in 722 the capital, Samaria, falls to the Assyrian armies. The prophets see this as the logical punishment of past guilt, and the enemy as God's instrument. Isaiah fulminates against the tribe of Ephraim who dwelt in Samaria:

> Woe to the crown of pride of the drunkards of Ephraim, and to the fading flower of his glorious beauty,

which is on the head of the fat valley of them that are
overcome with wine! Behold, the Lord hath a mighty
and strong one; as a tempest of hail, a destroying storm,
as a tempest of mighty waters overflowing, shall he cast
down to the earth with the hand. The crown of pride
of the drunkards of Ephraim shall be trodden under
foot: and the fading flower of his glorious beauty, which
is on the head of the fat valley, shall be as the first ripe
fig before the summer; which when he that looketh upon
it seeth, while it is yet in his hand he eateth it up.[20]

The kingdom of Judah lasts for a further century and a half.
It, too, experiences an internal vacillation between religious
crisis and recovery, and the latter is personified in king Josiah
(640–609 B.C.), who solemnly desecrates the sites of the
pagan cult and reasserts the pure ancient tradition. But the
enemy is at the gates of Judah too: no longer Assyria, which
has been overthrown by the Medes, but Babylonia, in its last
brief period of renewed prosperity. In 586 Nebuchadnezzar
conquers and destroys Jerusalem, burns down the temple, and
deports a large part of the population. The prophets, con-
sistently with their view of history, have for long been pro-
claiming the futility of the struggle, because the divine will
is sealed. Jeremiah proclaims:

Declare ye in Judah, and publish in Jerusalem; and
say, Blow ye the trumpet in the land: cry aloud and say,
Assemble yourselves, and let us go up into the fenced
cities. Set up a standard towards Zion;[21] flee for safety,
stay not: for I will bring evil from the north, and a
great destruction. A lion is gone up from his thicket, and
a destroyer of nations; he is on his way, he is gone forth
from his place; to make thy land desolate, that thy cities
be laid waste, without inhabitant. For this gird you with
sackcloth, lament and howl: for the fierce anger of the
Lord is not turned back from us.[22]

The Babylonian exile[23] eliminates the political element from
Israelite history for the first time in that history. But the religious and national cohesion is strong, and endures. The

memory of the distant homeland does not fade, as the Old Testament bears witness more than once. A celebrated psalm says:

> *By the rivers of Babylon,*
> *There we sat down, yea, we wept,*
> *When we remembered Zion.*
> *Upon the willows in the midst thereof*
> *We hanged up our harps.*
> *For there they that led us captive required of us songs,*
> *And they that wasted us required of us mirth, saying,*
> *Sing us one of the songs of Zion.*
> *How shall we sing the Lord's song*
> *In a strange land?*
> *If I forget thee, O Jerusalem,*
> *Let my right hand forget her cunning.*
> *Let my tongue cleave to the roof of my mouth,*
> *If I remember thee not;*
> *If I prefer not Jerusalem*
> *Above my chief joy.*[24]

By a paradox which the course of Hebrew history makes perfectly intelligible, the exile is a period of great religious exaltation. The political bonds have disappeared, and the way is clear for religious universalism; now that ruin has come, the idea of resurrection and return can take shape. In 538 Cyrus conquers Babylon. The Hebrews are given permission to return to their land.

Few events in ancient Oriental history are of such great importance. Obviously this is not because of the political content of these events, which is only a small part of a much larger picture, but because of their religious import. The Hebrews return to Palestine and re-establish their community. But they do not re-establish the state, which is engulfed in the Persian empire, just as, later on, it will be engulfed in the Hellenistic and Roman empires. Here, therefore, we have the first divinity to survive his kings, and the first religious community in the ancient Orient to lack a political basis. It is maintained by two elements: a religious, and also an ethnic one, the blood relationship which remains as a bond between the members of the community. The restorers, from Ezra to Nehemiah, struggle clearsightedly against any violation of that bond. Thus the history of Israel is again subject, in the last resort, to the dualism which we have noted as characteristic of it from the beginning: its God is universal; but his followers are a people, bound to him by a covenant.

III The Religious Structure

Israelite religion[25] presents a preliminary problem which confronts us at every step: from when does this or that conception date? From when does this or that custom date?

The problem is as grave as it is difficult of solution, for Israelite religion undoubtedly underwent an evolution with time, but the texts present it already balanced and systematized into unity; and as the dating of the various texts and their respective sources is frequently challenged, the one problem comes to condition the other, forming a vicious circle.

The one thing that can be said by way of generalization is that each period of Israel's religious history has its own distinctive features, and that the salient periods may be taken as follows: the days of nomadism, the transition to settled civilization, the monarchy, and the lack of political power. The nomadic is the decisive period, because it is the one in which the fundamental elements of Hebrew religious thought were crystallized; it is also the most critical period, because the elements that compose it are more dubious and open to question. The transition to settled civilization is characterized by the definition of the fundamental beliefs and the beginning of conflict with the surroundings. The monarchy provides the history of this conflict, in which despite repeated crises the foundations hold firm. The period of lack of political power is that of the consolidation of religious thought free of political complications, and simultaneously of its codification together with the more extensive development of ritual and legal casuistics.

These are the successive steps, so to speak, in the history of Israel's religion; but their determination is a matter of hypothesis or theory according to circumstances, rarely one of certainty.

Biblical critics are agreed in admitting the great antiquity of the Decalogue.[26] Its opening section expresses the Israelite conception of the divinity with notable clarity:

> I am the Lord thy God, which brought thee out of the land of Egypt, out of the house of bondage.
>
> Thou shalt have none other gods before me.
>
> Thou shalt not make unto thee a graven image, nor the likeness of any form that is in heaven above, or that is in the earth beneath, or that is in the water under the earth: thou shalt not bow down thyself unto them, nor serve them . . .
>
> Thou shalt not take the name of the Lord thy God in vain; for the Lord will not hold him guiltless that taketh his name in vain.[27]

Here we must pause for a moment. Some of the essential ideas of Israelite theology have already been enunciated. In the first place, there is only one God: and with this statement Israel sets herself against the exuberant polytheism of the surrounding peoples. Secondly, God must not be represented: and this, too, offers a contrast with the ancient Oriental environment, in which the principal subject of representational art is the divinity. Finally, who, of all the other peoples of the Near East, could conceive of a God whose name was ineffable? For the God of the Israelites certainly has a name, and it can be formulated with every indication of probability as Yahweh, from the four consonants y–h–w–h which represent it in the Biblical text.[28] But the orthodox Jew will come to regard the pronunciation of that name as a contamination and a sin.

So Israel does not assimilate its God to human forms, but emphasizes his difference from them. Hence it does not attribute either sex or family to him. The ancient nomadic existence even leads to his having no fixed abode, but he is found everywhere. He manifests himself to his chosen ones, as we have seen, as a voice in the clouds, in the storm, and in fire. He follows them in their wanderings, resting on the Ark of the Covenant, which the priests carry on the march, and house in the Tabernacle at the stopping places. Only when the temple is erected at Jerusalem, in Solomon's time, will he have a fixed abode.

Now to consider the closing section of the Decalogue:

> Honour thy father and thy mother: that thy days may be long in the land which the Lord thy God giveth thee.
> Thou shalt do no murder.
> Thou shalt not commit adultery.
> Thou shalt not steal.
> Thou shalt not bear false witness against thy neighbour.
> Thou shalt not covet thy neighbour's house, thou shalt not covet thy neighbour's wife, nor his manservant, nor his maidservant, nor his ox, nor his ass, nor anything that is thy neighbour's.[29]

These words clearly express one feature which is closely associated with monotheism: morality. In two books which have been recently published and have won considerable recognition,[30] Albright has indeed maintained the thesis that ethical monotheism is the guiding thread to Israelite religious thinking from first to last. He writes:

> In essentials, however, orthodox Yahwism remained the same from Moses to Ezra. From first to last ethical monotheism remained the heart of Israelite religion, though there were many crises through which it had to pass during the slow change from the primitive simplicity of the Judges to the high cultural level of the fifth century B.C.[31]

This poses the crucial problem. It cannot be challenged that in the days of the prophets monotheism is proclaimed in its fully universal sense. But before their times? Was it monotheism then, or the cult of a national god which does not exclude the gods of other peoples? Albright admits that monotheism is explicitly affirmed only from the times of the prophets onward, but he denies that there was any substantial difference previously:

Monotheism formed an essential part of Mosaic religion from the beginning. Mosaic monotheism, like that of following centuries (at least down to the seventh century B.C.) was empirico-logical; it was practical and implicit rather than intellectual and explicit. Explicit monotheism could not fully emerge until after the dawn of the logical age about the sixth century B.C., since clear definition and logical formulation are necessary to change an implicit belief or concept into an explicit doctrine or idea.[32]

In any case, apart from the question of the time at which it was fully manifested, ethical monotheism is the dominant feature of the religion of Israel. And in the morality of God this monotheism finds another element which is at variance with the environment: the gods we have previously considered, although incomparably more powerful than mankind, had characters fundamentally similar to those of men, with loves and hates, likes and dislikes, fits of anger and caprice; on the contrary, it is a distinctive quality of Israel that it insisted on righteousness as the deity's supreme and constant characteristic:

> The Lord trieth the righteous,
> But the wicked and him that loveth violence his soul
>   hateth.
> Upon the wicked he shall rain snares;
> Fire and brimstone and burning wind shall be the por-
>   tion of their cup.
> For the Lord is righteous; he loveth righteousness:
> The upright shall behold his face.[33]

It is natural that, given the supreme power of God and the correspondingly great frailty of man, justice in the majority of cases could take no other form than that of punishment for sinful man. But God is not only righteous, he is benevolent: if there is one divine quality which is insisted upon as equal with justice, it is mercy:

> The Lord is full of compassion and gracious:
> Slow to anger, and plenteous in mercy.

> *He will not always chide;*
> *Neither will he keep his anger for ever.*
> *He hath not dealt with us after our sins,*
> *Nor rewarded us after our iniquities.*
> *For as the heaven is high above the earth,*
> *So great is his mercy towards them that fear him.*
> *As far as the east is from the west,*
> *So far hath he removed our transgressions from us.*
> *Like as a father pitieth his children,*
> *So the Lord pitieth them that fear him.*
> *For he knoweth our frame;*
> *He remembereth that we are dust.*
> *As for man, his days are as grass;*
> *As a flower of the field, so he flourisheth.*
> *For the wind passeth over it, and it is gone;*
> *And the place thereof shall know it no more.*
> *But the mercy of the Lord is from everlasting to*
> *   everlasting upon them that fear him,*
> *And his righteousness unto children's children.*[34]

This new conception of deity has one consequence of decisive significance in the ancient Oriental civilizations. This is the reaction to mythology: of the exuberant fantasies of the surrounding peoples, the legends about the loves and conflicts of the gods, only the dross remains.

We know very little concerning the priesthood in the earliest phase of Israelite history. In the days of the tribal confederation with the common sanctuary at Shiloh, the high priest must have had considerable authority, for there was no corresponding political power to counterbalance his. The establishment of the monarchy brings with it a reduction in the status of the high priest, but the situation rights itself again as soon as the monarchy falls. Sacerdotal functions are performed by the tribe of Levi; investigation shows that this tribe may also be regarded as a social class, which probably was regularly reinforced by the accession of men who dedicated themselves to the priesthood.[35]

We have already mentioned the most ancient object of the

cult, the Ark of the Covenant, which during the nomadic era was kept in a tent, and found a permanent home in the Temple at Jerusalem only from the days of Solomon onward. But in addition there were a number of other sanctuaries, often on the high places that in the past had served as sites for Canaanite worship. Here it is appropriate to mention the continuous conflict, the constant state of crisis which is characteristic of Israelite religion throughout its history: the struggle to conserve the pure and independent tradition, countervailed by the tendency to surrender to the more attractive creeds and cults of the environment. These two poles form the antithetic terms of the dialectic of Israel, a dialectic both historical and religious: in the end tradition prevails and is consolidated.

In the earliest religious festivals two chronologically different elements are found together, the one deriving from nomadism, the other from the period of settlement.[36] The Passover reveals mainly nomadic features, for the springtime offering of lambs is a link with pastoral conditions, and so is the rite of unleavened bread, traditionally associated with the flight from Egypt. On the other hand, the 'feast of weeks' (*shavuoth*) at the time of the grain harvest, and that of 'tabernacles' (*sukkoth*) at the time of the vintage, belong more to an agricultural and therefore a settled form of existence.

Outstanding among the oldest solemnities are the expiatory fast (*kippur*) on the tenth day of the new year, and the sabbatical day of rest. This latter is reflected again in the sabbatical year, every seventh year, when neither sowing nor harvesting is to take place. And seven cycles of seven years bring the Jubilee, when all lands are to return to their original owners. But this precept, which is based on the argument that there is only one absolute owner of the earth, i.e. the Lord, must have had a very restricted application, because of the exigencies of everyday existence.

In religious practice, certain dominant elements of the Near Eastern environment are greatly reduced in importance, under the impetus of the new faith. Magic, which plays an essential part in Mesopotamian, Hittite, and Egyptian ritual, is confined to occasional instances; and divination also has only a limited application, at least in the sense and the forms it has elsewhere. But seers and prophets are not lacking to tell the people, through divine inspiration, the future that is in store for them. Indeed, by force of circumstances the prophetic function becomes a dominating feature of Israel's religious history.

Although it exists from the earliest days, the prophetic movement[37] reaches its culmination only during the time of the divided monarchy, when the decadence of worship and faith brings it to constitute itself the champion of the truly authentic religious tradition. It is distinguished historically by two phases: a first, more active, and a second, more literary one. But in both cases there are the same characteristics and fundamental elements determining and typifying its existence.

First and foremost, there is the sense of vocation. This is the ancient *charisma*, the divine grace which formerly had given the Judges their sense of mission. That it came spontaneously, often unexpectedly, and sometimes undesired, is shown by accounts such as that of Jeremiah:

> O Lord, thou hast deceived me, and I was deceived . . . And if I say, I will not make any mention of him, nor speak any more in his name, then there is in mine heart as it were a burning fire shut up in my bones, and I am weary with forbearing, and I cannot contain. For I have heard the defaming of many. . . . But the Lord is with me as a mighty one and a terrible: therefore my persecutors shall stumble, and they shall not prevail: they shall be greatly ashamed, because they have not dealt wisely, even with an everlasting dishonour that shall never be forgotten. But, O Lord of hosts, that triest the righteous, that seest the reins and the heart, let me see thy vengeance on them; for unto thee have I revealed my cause. Sing unto the Lord, praise ye the Lord: for he hath delivered the soul of the needy from the hand of evil-doers.[38]

Note that the prophet does not claim to announce a new doctrine. On the contrary, his attitude is that there must be return to the ancient doctrine. This has been well brought out by Rinaldi in his recent study of the religious teaching of the prophets:

> The prophets do not mean to be the heralds and initiators of a religion, they are not innovators who bring hitherto unheard teachings; indeed they do not even intend to teach anything new; not even the greatest and oldest of them, Amos or Isaiah, or their predecessors who wrote nothing. They have no other desire than to lead the people back to the ancient religion of Israel, or to lift to the level of that religious idea the new forms of life, which had become or were judged by the prophets to be 'heretical', but, more than anything else, were steeped in selfishness, in pagan naturalism, in practical atheism. In their teaching the prophets appeal to ideas already familiar and authorities who have already spoken, to Moses, to the revelation of Israel's beginnings. Their God is the God of the fathers, of Abraham and of Jacob.[39]

The prophets' attitude to religious worship is interesting. In principle, they would have no cause for hostility. But as worship is the first religious element to yield to the pagan environment, whereas the people, despite their sinfulness, are assiduous in the external practices of their religion, the prophets react and condemn a ritual which too often lacks any genuine counterpart in life.[40] Amos makes the Lord say:

> I hate, I despise your feasts, and I will take no delight in your solemn assemblies. Yea, though ye offer me your burnt offerings and meal offerings, I will not accept them: neither will I regard the peace offerings of your fat beasts. Take away from me the noise of thy songs; for I will not hear the melody of thy viols. But let judgement roll down as waters, and righteousness as a mighty stream.[41]

A dominant feature of the prophets' preaching is the declaration that God will inflict punishment, the logical consequence of sin. From many examples we may select one from a minor prophet, Zephaniah:

The great day of the Lord is near, it is near and
hasteth greatly, even the voice of the day of the Lord;
the mighty man crieth there bitterly. That day is a day
of wrath, a day of trouble and distress, a day of waste-
ness and desolation, a day of darkness and gloominess,
a day of clouds and thick darkness, a day of the trumpet
and alarm, against the fenced cities, and against the high
battlements. And I will bring distress upon men, that
they shall walk like blind men, because they have sinned
against the Lord: and their blood shall be poured out
as dust, and their flesh as dung. Neither their silver nor
their gold shall be able to deliver them in the day of the
Lord's wrath; but the whole land shall be devoured by
the fire of his jealousy; for he shall make an end, yea,
a terrible end, of all them that dwell in the land.[42]

It is significant, however, that in their religious thought the
prophets even of the period of the kingdom go beyond simple
announcement of the crisis. When Israel has been punished,
they declare, when it has expiated its guilt, it will rise again,
the golden age will return. This golden age finds definite expression in the conception of the Messiah[43] sprung from the
root of Jesse, in other words, from the stock of David.

And there shall come forth a shoot out of the stock
of Jesse, and a branch out of his roots shall bear fruit:
and the spirit of the Lord shall rest upon him, the spirit
of wisdom and understanding, the spirit of counsel and
might, the spirit of knowledge and the fear of the Lord;
and his delight shall be in the fear of the Lord: and he
shall not judge after the sight of his eyes, neither reprove
after the hearing of his ears: but with righteousness shall
he judge the poor, and reprove with equity for the meek
of the earth: and he shall smite the earth with the rod
of his mouth, and with the breath of his lips shall he
slay the wicked. And righteousness shall be the girdle of
his loins, and faithfulness the girdle of his reins. And the
wolf shall dwell with the lamb, and the leopard shall
lie down with the kid; and the calf and the young lion

and the fatling together; and a little child shall lead them. And the cow and the bear shall feed; their young ones shall lie down together: and the lion shall eat straw like the ox. And the suckling child shall play on the hole of the asp, and the weaned child shall put his hand on the basilisk's den. They shall not hurt nor destroy in all my holy mountain: for the earth shall be full of the knowledge of the Lord, as the waters cover the sea.[44]

Messianism introduces a new element to distinguish the religious thinking of the Israelites from that of the surrounding world. No other people of the ancient Orient has left a similar vision of the future. On the contrary, elsewhere it is the tragedy of inevitable death that dominates thought. Nor is this tragedy overcome in Israel, as it is in Egypt, by a total and certain awareness of the future life; for although references to the world beyond the tomb (*sheol*) are found in the Bible, they are limited and generic, and there is no clear definition of retribution for human conduct. Instead, the prophets set the time of catharsis within the very history of the chosen people, though at its close. And — an essential point — this catharsis is a consequence of moral purification, and so is on the ethical plane characteristic of Israelite thought.

On the other hand, the moral judgement is projected backward in time to the very beginning of humanity: the Biblical account of the creation of the world and man clearly reveals the belief in a golden age, into which suffering and death enter as the consequence of sin. The Mesopotamian peoples also described a primitive golden age, and the possibilities man was offered of escaping from death: but they did not make guilt in any way responsible for the loss of such a possibility. Hence, in their thinking attention was directed rather to the actual fact of death than to its causes, or at least, to a cause involving responsibility.

The end of the political state does not connote the end of the prophetic movement. But the prediction of disaster, which now has come about, naturally vanishes from the prophets' preaching. And by a paradox peculiar to the Israelite conception of history, the foretellers of disaster become the heralds of good news and the proclaimers of renaissance. We give an example of one such announcement of revival in a passage which, from the literary aspect, is one of its finest expressions, Ezekiel's vision of the restoration to life of dry bones:

> The hand of the Lord was upon me, and he carried me out in the spirit of the Lord, and set me down in the midst of the valley; and it was full of bones; and he caused me to pass by them round about: and behold, there were very many in the open valley; and lo, they were very dry. And he said unto me, Son of man, can these bones live? And I answered, O Lord God, thou knowest. Again he said unto me, Prophesy over these bones, and say unto them, O ye dry bones, hear the word of the Lord. Thus saith the Lord God unto these bones: Behold I will cause breath to enter into you, and ye shall live; and ye shall know that I am the Lord. So I prophesied as I was commanded: and as I prophesied, there was a noise, and behold an earthquake, and the bones came together, bone to his bone. And I beheld, and lo, there were sinews upon them, and flesh came up, and skin covered them above: but there was no breath in them. Then said he unto me, Prophesy unto the wind, prophesy, son of man, and say to the wind, Thus saith the Lord God: Come from the four winds, O breath, and breathe upon these slain, that they may live. So I prophesied as he commanded me, and the breath came into them, and they lived, and stood up upon their feet, an exceeding great army. Then he said unto me, Son of man, these bones are the whole house of Israel: behold, they say, Our bones are dried up, and our hope is lost; we are clean cut off. Therefore prophesy, and say unto them, Thus saith the Lord God: Behold, I will open your graves, and cause you to come up out of your graves, O my people; and I will bring you into the land of Israel. And ye shall know that I am the Lord,

when I have opened your graves, and caused you to come up out of your graves, O my people. And I will put my spirit in you, and ye shall live, and I will place you in your own land: and ye shall know that I the Lord have spoken it, and performed it, saith the Lord.[45]

In Ezekiel, however, we find not only the prophetic vision but the procedure, for the time is at hand, and it is necessary to prescribe the course of action to be taken, the manner in which the new temple must be constructed, and the divine worship and the priesthood reorganized. Thus in Ezekiel's preaching the two opposed elements of ancient Israel come together: the prophetic ideal and the priestly law. The reorganization and codification of the law occurs precisely during the exilic period. The canon of sacred books is established. The Old Testament begins to take on the aspect which we know today.

With the return from exile the priesthood assumes the predominant position. The community must be built up anew, and provided with bonds all the more solid because the cementing element of the state is lacking. And with the predominance of the priesthood the people's nationalism is asserted at the expense of God's universality.

None the less, whatever historical vicissitudes may yet be in store for her, Israel has made her contribution to humanity. In a world which deifies nature and humanizes the gods, enveloping them in myth, Israel has separated the divine from the natural and the human, and risen superior to myth. Some authorities have maintained that this superiority is only an apparent one, since Israel has constructed her own myth, that of God manifesting himself to the people and entering into a covenant with them; and they have gone on to declare that only the Greeks overcome mythology by the force of intellect.[46] But perhaps this judgement reveals some misunderstanding. It is true that the Greeks will rise above myth in the intellectual sphere; but the Jews rise above it in the religious sphere. And it would be difficult to prove that this achievement has any lesser function or importance in the history of mankind.

IV *The Literary Genres*

The historical and religious conception of ancient Israel is expressed and documentated in the collection of books known as the Old Testament.[47] The collection consists of works by different authors, of different dates of origin, and differing content. It was completed after political independence had come to an end, with the intention of passing down the story of the nation and its faith in order to sustain and bind together the future generations.[48]

Thus the object of the collection is not literary but religious, and this accounts for the fact that a selection was made of the books to be included. Consequently the present collection is not strictly 'the' literature of ancient Israel, but so much as was deemed worthy of conservation and transmission. That other writings existed which were not included in the canon is indicated both by a number of references in the Old Testament itself and by the recent discovery of ancient Hebrew manuscripts in the desert of Judah. On the other hand, it is possible that some of the books included in the canon may originally have been of a profane nature and owe their inclusion to a religious interpretation of their content.

The order in which the collection is arranged is — always within the religious framework — more historical than systematic. In other words, the juridical prescriptions, the ethical teachings, the prophetic pronouncements are set in the context of historical events, and appear linked up with and determined by those events. Therefore the Biblical books are arranged in approximately the order of Israel's history.

It is obvious that such conditions must give rise to quite special critical problems, different from those encountered so far in ancient Oriental literature. It is true that the Israelite conception of literature approximates to that of the environment: pursuit of practical and not aesthetic aims, a scant interest in authorship, and restricted chronological evolution of the literary forms. Nevertheless there is a developing process of composition and elaboration of the texts such as we find nowhere else; and this process, culminating in the selection and closing of the canon, makes it necessary to work back, to identify the principles governing the process, to isolate its sources and to fix their periods. This is a hard task, and to achieve it we are compelled to rely upon hints and probabilities, rarely achieving certainty.

In regard to literary genres the Biblical books can be broadly classified as historical, prophetic, lyrical, and sapiential. The Old Testament also contains extensive passages of rules and regulations linked up with the people's earliest history and, together with that history, composing the group of books known as the Pentateuch. This brings us to the very heart of criticism.[49] The place of the Pentateuch in the canon is anterior to all the other books, but last century criticism divided it up according to its sources and placed it, in its final redaction, after the historical and prophetic books, the majority of which have a date of composition not long after the times to which they relate. This view can be said to be left basically unchanged by the most recent criticism; but besides entering farther into tracing the sources, this latter criticism is more and more demonstrating that the mere discovery of these sources is inadequate because of the possibility that there were successive strata and a preceding long oral tradition.[50] Consequently much of the Biblical material has been related to an earlier date, and archaeological investigation and research in allied fields has shown that this is objectively possible.

This is not the place for an examination of the sources, so we can consider the Biblical material in the genres which we now possess. First we must deal with the historical books, whose nature and contents we have already indicated. These trace the history of Israel step by step, reaching their peak of documentary amplitude and historiographic acumen in that part of the books of Samuel and Kings which relates to the undivided monarchy. They are less extended when dealing with the divided kingdom, though at the same time the commentaries and digressions of a religious nature are more accentuated. We can safely assume that this part is the work of members of the priestly class; and the same may be said of the two books of Chronicles, which repeat the history of the kingdom of Judah on similar lines. With the political crisis the consecutive historiography comes to an end; but the books of Ezra and Nehemiah provide information on the main phases of the return from exile and the work of reconstruction.

The prophetic books also have already been discussed. Beginning with the divided monarchy, they follow and comment upon events from their own special viewpoint. Besides the major prophets — Isaiah, Jeremiah, Ezekiel, Daniel — there are several minor ones, who in brief episodes repeat the admonitions to the erring people, the announcements of punishment to come, and those of the resurrection from ruin. At present the prophetic literary form is unique in the ancient Orient; although we hear of prophets among other peoples, we do not know whether their activities found expression in any literary production.

By way of premiss to the discussion of the remaining literary genres — which so far have not been considered and which will therefore be treated more analytically — reference to the environment once more raises a problem of fundamental interest. What has become of the mythological and epic literature, of those tales of gods and heroes which formed so great a part of the other Oriental literatures? In keeping with the character of the new religious thinking, these literary genres vanish, leaving only a few traces behind. Here we have the victory over myth which we have found to be peculiar to Israel.

Hebrew lyrical poetry,[51] which has as its form the customary parallelism of its verse constituents, achieves its greatest work in the book of Psalms. This consists of 150 religious poems of various authors in various epochs, some of them personal and some collective, and dedicated to prayer and the praise of God.[52] Here is a prayer raised in adversity:

> How long, O Lord, wilt thou forget me for ever?
> How long wilt thou hide thy face from me?

How long shall I take counsel in my soul,
Having sorrow in my heart all the day?
How long shall mine enemy be exalted over me?
Consider and answer me, O Lord my God:
Lighten mine eyes, lest I sleep the sleep of death;
Lest mine enemy say, I have prevailed over him;
Lest mine adversaries rejoice when I am moved.
But I have trusted in thy mercy;
My heart shall rejoice in thy salvation:
I will sing unto the Lord,
Because he hath dealt bountifully with me.[53]

And the following is a psalm of praise and thanksgiving:

It is a good thing to give thanks unto the Lord,
And to sing praises unto thy name, O Most High:
To show forth thy loving kindness in the morning,
And thy faithfulness every night,
With an instrument of ten strings, and with the psaltery;
With a solemn sound upon the harp.
For thou, O Lord, hast made me glad through thy work:
I will triumph in the works of thy hands.
How great are thy works, O Lord!
Thy thoughts are very deep.[54]

Among the Hebrew manuscripts which have recently come to light in the Judaean desert,[55] there are psalms very similar to those of the Bible in form and content. We cannot establish the date of their composition; but it is worth while considering at least one of them as an example of a literature which flourished alongside the canonical works and often dealt with remarkably similar themes. Its theme is the contrast between human pettiness and divine greatness:

For what is man? He is earth.
He was formed of dust, and to dust he returns.
What can I plan, unless thou hast desired it?
And what can I think, without thy will?
What can I achieve, unless thou hast established me?
And how can I be wise, unless thou hast planned for me?
What shall I speak, unless thou open my mouth?

And how should I reply if thou didst not make me wise?
Behold, thou art prince of gods and king of the honoured
ones,
Lord of every spirit and ruler over every work.
Without thee nothing is accomplished;
Neither is it known without thy will.
There is none beside thee,
And there is none to compare with thee in might.
There is nothing over against thy glory,
And thy power has no price.
Who among all thy wondrous great works
Is able to stand before thy glory?
What then is he who returns to his dust,
That he should prevail against thee?
For thy glory alone thou hast made all these things:
Blessed art thou, my Lord, God of mercy![56]

The transcendence, omnipotence, righteousness, and goodness of God; the frailty of man and nature: these are the
dominant themes of the Israelite faith, and we find them
coherently expressed in the literature.

Another notable work of Hebrew lyric is the Book of Lamentations, an example of a well-defined literary genre which
we know was common in the ancient Orient. When discussing
the Sumerians we referred to the lament of the goddess
Ningal over the ruins of the city of Ur. Now we cite the
Hebrew lament over fallen Jerusalem:

How doth the city sit solitary, that was full of people!
How is she become as a widow!
She that was great among the nations, and princess
among the provinces,
How is she become tributary!
She weepeth sore in the night, and her tears are on her
cheeks;
Among all her lovers she hath none to comfort her;
All her friends have dealt treacherously with her,
They are become her enemies.
Judah is gone into captivity because of affliction, and
because of great servitude;

She dwelleth among the heathen, she findeth no rest:
All her persecutors overtook her within the straits.
The ways of Zion do mourn, because none come to
      the solemn assembly;
All her gates are desolate, her priests do sigh:
Her virgins are afflicted, and she herself is in bitterness.
Her adversaries are become the head, her enemies
      prosper;
For the Lord hath afflicted her because of the
      multitude of her transgressions.[57]

The last verses are significant from the point of view of general judgement. Into the traditional literary genre the author has introduced his own distinctive conception of history: the disaster has come about because of the people's transgressions, the enemy has been the instrument of divine chastisement.

One lyric which appears to be profane in content was interpreted allegorically as having a religious meaning, and was included in the canon of Holy Scripture (we are reminded of the Sumerian hymn to king Shu-Sin, our first example of love treated allegorically): the Song of Songs in delicate accents describes the love of a young shepherd and shepherdess. The shepherdess says:

The voice of my beloved! Behold, he cometh,
Leaping upon the mountains, skipping upon the hills.
My beloved is like a roe or a young hart:
Behold, he standeth behind our wall,
He looketh in at the windows,
He sheweth himself through the lattice.
My beloved spake, and said unto me,
Rise up, my love, my fair one, and come away.
For lo, the winter is past,
The rain is over and gone;
The flowers appear on the earth;
The time of the singing of birds is come,
And the voice of the turtle is heard in our land.
The fig tree ripeneth her green figs,
And the vines are in blossom,

> *They give forth their fragrance,*
> *Arise, my love, my fair one, and come away.*[58]

As we can see, the observation of nature is acute and vivid, and recalls the scenes in Egyptian love songs. No less remarkable is the observation of man, whose motives are conveyed in typically local themes. Here is the description of the beloved shepherd:

> *My beloved is white and ruddy,*
> *The chiefest among ten thousand.*
> *His head is as the most fine gold,*
> *His locks are bushy, and black as a raven.*
> *His eyes are like doves beside the water brooks;*
> *Washed with milk, and fitly set.*
> *His cheeks are as a bed of spices, as banks of sweet herbs:*
> *His lips are as lilies, dropping liquid myrrh.*
> *His hands are as rings of gold set with beryl:*
> *His body is as ivory work overlaid with sapphires.*
> *His legs are as pillars of marble, set upon sockets of fine gold:*
> *His aspect is like Lebanon, excellent as the cedars.*
> *His mouth is most sweet, yea, he is altogether lovely.*
> *This is my beloved, and this is my friend,*
> *O daughters of Jerusalem.*[59]

And here is another admirable description of nature:

> *Come, my beloved, let us go forth into the field;*
> *Let us lodge in the villages.*
> *Let us go up early to the vineyards;*
> *Let us see whether the vine hath budded, and its blossom be open,*
> *And the pomegranates be in flower:*
> *There will I give thee my love.*
> *The mandrakes give forth fragrance,*
> *And at our doors are all manner of precious fruits, new and old,*
> *Which I have laid up for thee, O my beloved.*[60]

The Song of Songs is thoroughly artistic in the direct vividness of its inspiration and the absence of shackling conventions. Its poetry transcends the time and the environment in
which it was created, so far as their conditioning influence is
concerned: indeed, like some of the wisdom literature, it
transcends the rigid unity of thought of ancient Hebrew
literature.

Wisdom literature[61] flourishes in numerous writings more
than worthy to be set alongside the similar texts of the other
Oriental peoples, and closely linked with those texts in inspiration and themes. We begin with the book called 'Proverbs' in
the Old Testament, but which could more appropriately be
called Maxims. We select some of these with a more profound
significance:

> *As vinegar to the teeth, and as smoke to the eyes,*
> *So is the sluggard to them that send him.*[62]
> *There is he that maketh himself rich, yet hath nothing,*
> *There is he that maketh himself poor, yet hath great*
>   *wealth.*[63]
> *He that spareth his rod hateth his son:*
> *But he that loveth him chasteneth him betimes.*[64]
> *Better is little with the fear of the Lord,*
> *Than great treasure and trouble therewith.*
> *Better is a dinner of herbs where love is,*
> *Than a stalled ox and hatred therewith.*[65]
> *He that is slow to anger is better than the mighty:*
> *And he that ruleth his spirit than he that taketh a city.*[66]
> *Even a fool, when he holdeth his peace, is counted wise:*
> *When he shutteth his lips, he is esteemed as prudent.*[67]
> *The slothful will not plow by reason of the winter;*
> *Therefore he shall beg in harvest, and have nothing.*[68]
> *It is better to dwell in the corner of the housetop,*
> *Than with a contentious woman in a wide house.*[69]
> *There are four things which are little upon the earth,*
> *But they are exceeding wise:*
> *The ants are a people not strong,*
> *Yet they provide their meat in the summer;*

> *The conies are but a feeble folk,*
> *Yet make they their houses in the rocks;*
> *The locusts have no king,*
> *Yet go they forth all of them by bands;*
> *The lizard taketh hold with her hands,*
> *Yet is she in kings' palaces.*[70]

Of these Proverbs, one group (chap. xxii, 17 to xxiv, 22) reveals so close an affinity in conception and expression with the Egyptian maxims of Amenemopet that we are forced to conclude that they are literarily dependent. But in other cases the sources cannot be identified, or the background is that of typically Israelite society and its beliefs.

Besides the maxims there are counsels in the full and proper sense. Some highly significant examples are to be found in Ecclesiasticus (also referred to as Sirach, or Ben-Sira), a composition of late date, and therefore not universally included in the canon:

> *Praise no man for his beauty,*
> *And abhor no man for his appearance.*
> *Of no account among flying things is the bee,*
> *But her fruit is supreme among products.*[71]
> *Hast thou heard something? Let it die with thee;*
> *Be of good courage, it will not burst thee.*
> *A fool travaileth in pain because of a word,*
> *As a woman in labour because of a child.*
> *Like an arrow that sticketh in the fleshy thigh,*
> *So is a word in the inward parts of a fool.*[72]
> *There is no poison above the poison of a serpent,*
> *And there is no wrath above the wrath of a woman.*
> *I would rather dwell with a lion and a dragon,*
> *Than keep house with a wicked woman.*[73]

Some traces of Hebrew fable have survived as insertions in Biblical books. The most striking example is Jotham's speech to the Shechemites in the Book of Judges. Gideon's son Abimelech has slain his brethren and has had himself chosen as king of Shechem. Only Jotham has escaped. He goes to the Shechemites and tells the following fable, the meaning of which is that they, together with Abimelech, have chosen the worst part, and will quickly regret it:

> The trees went forth on a time to anoint a king over them; and they said to the olive tree, Reign thou over us. But the olive tree said unto them, Should I leave my fatness, wherewith by me they honour God and man, to go and wave to and fro over the trees? And the trees said to the fig tree, Come thou, and reign over us. But the fig tree said unto them, Should I leave my sweetness, and my good fruit, and go to wave to and fro over the trees? And the trees said unto the vine, Come thou, and reign over us. And the vine said unto them, Should I leave my wine, which cheereth God and man, and go to wave to and fro over the trees? Then said all the trees to the bramble, Come thou, and reign over us. And the bramble said unto the trees, If in truth ye anoint me king over you, then come and put your trust in my shadow: and if not, let fire come out of the bramble, and devour the cedars of Lebanon.[74]

Another type of wisdom literature, already well known to us from the Mesopotamian peoples, turns up again in Israel: the kind which centres round the problem of the Righteous Man suffering. The book of Job raises this problem, to discuss it at length:

> *Terrors are turned upon me,*
> *They chase mine honour as the wind;*
> *And my welfare is passed away as a cloud.*
> *And now my soul is poured out within me;*
> *Days of affliction have taken hold upon me.*
> *In the night season my bones are pierced in me,*
> *And the pains that gnaw me take no rest.*
> *By the great force of my disease is my garment disfigured:*
> *It bindeth me about as the collar of my coat.*
> *He hath cast me into the mire,*
> *And I am become like dust and ashes.*
> *I cry unto thee, and thou dost not answer me:*
> *I stand up, and thou lookest at me.*

Thou art turned to be cruel to me:
With the might of thy hand thou persecutest me.
Thou liftest me up to the wind, thou causest me to ride
*   upon it;*
And thou dissolvest me in the storm.
For I know that thou wilt bring me to death,
And to the house appointed for all living . . .
Did I not weep for him that was in trouble?
Was not my soul grieved for the needy?
When I looked for good, then evil came;
And when I waited for light, there came darkness.[75]

The answers to this problem recall those which were found in Mesopotamia. In the first place, how can man know what is good and what bad? How can he penetrate into God's judgements? One of Job's companions objects:

Canst thou by searching find out God?
Canst thou find out the Almighty unto perfection?
It is as high as heaven; what canst thou do?
Deeper than Sheol; what canst thou know?
The measure thereof is longer than the earth,
And broader than the sea.
If he pass through, and shut up,
And call unto judgement, then who can hinder him?
For he knoweth vain men:
He seeth iniquity also, even though he consider it not.
But vain man is void of understanding,
Yea, man is born as a wild ass's colt.[76]

The second answer brings final liberation. For all that the righteous man suffers he will in the end be rewarded, just as the wicked man will not escape chastisement. The book closes with a description of Job restored to his original prosperity:

> So the Lord blessed the latter end of Job more than his beginning: and he had fourteen thousand sheep, and six thousand camels, and a thousand yoke of oxen, and a thousand she-asses. He had also seven sons and three daughters. . . . And in all the land were no women found so fair as the daughters of Job; and their father gave

them inheritance among their brethren. And after this
Job lived an hundred and forty years, and saw his sons,
and his sons' sons, even four generations. So Job died,
being old and full of days.[77]

We close our review of the wisdom literature with the
poetry of human sorrow[78] and pessimism, which finds expression in the book of Ecclesiastes. One would not have said that
such poetry was congenial to Israel, with its just and merciful
God in whom human anxiety is appeased. But it must be
observed that this is a work of late date, and not free from
the influence of Greek thought. Moreover, for all its expression
of world-weariness, it cannot be said that the Book of Ecclesiastes is lacking in faith in God: rather does it move in a
different sphere; it ignores rather than denies, and ends by
taking refuge in deity. This provokes a number of problems
of criticism: how much of the text is original, how much
added, how much interpolated? But even addition and inter-
polation are indications of the Israelite treatment of the
philosophy of pain.

Ecclesiastes opens with a vision of the futility of human
affairs, destined to be repeated aimlessly under the sun:

> Vanity of vanities, saith the Preacher; vanity of vani-
> ties, all is vanity. What profit hath man of all his labour
> wherein he laboureth under the sun? One generation
> goeth, and another generation cometh; and the earth
> abideth for ever. The sun also ariseth, and the sun goeth
> down, and hasteth to his place where he ariseth. The
> wind goeth toward the south, and turneth about unto
> the north; it turneth about continually in its course, and
> the wind returneth again to its circuits. All the rivers
> run into the sea, yet the sea is not full; unto the place
> whither the rivers go, thither they go again. All things
> are full of weariness; man cannot utter it: the eye is not
> satisfied with seeing, nor the ear filled with hearing.
> That which has been is that which shall be; and that
> which has been done is that which shall be done: and
> there is no new thing under the sun.[79]

Wisdom is just as vain:

I the Preacher was king over Israel in Jerusalem. And I applied my heart to seek and search out by wisdom concerning all that is done under heaven: it is a sore travail that God hath given to the sons of men to be exercised therewith. I have seen all the works that are done under the sun; and behold, all is vanity and a striving after wind. That which is crooked cannot be made straight: and that which is wanting cannot be numbered. I communed with mine own heart, saying, Lo, I have gotten me great wisdom above all that were before me in Jerusalem; yea, my heart hath had great experience of wisdom and knowledge. And I applied my heart to know wisdom, and to know madness and folly; I perceived that this also was a striving after wind. For in much wisdom is much grief: and he that increaseth knowledge increaseth sorrow.[80]

These passages are among the finest in the Old Testament, and they would have to be included among those which are least in harmony with the spirit which dominates the Old Testament, if the Preacher did not reach the following conclusion:

This is the end of the matter; all hath been heard: fear God, and keep the commandments; for this is the whole duty of man. For God shall bring every man into judgement, with every hidden thing, whether it be good or whether it be evil.[81]

Is this passage an addition by a later hand? Or an alteration of the original text? Once more we are faced with the old problem, and he who seeks to resolve it must not apply his own logic, but enter into that of the environment and seek the answer thence.

A noteworthy part of Hebrew literature has a juridical content,[82] in the broad sense of laying down prescriptions of not only a legal but also an ethical and religious nature. For the purpose of comparison with the laws of the neighbouring peoples, we may divide the Hebrew material into two groups. The first, consisting of general and unconditional rules, seems original and characteristic of Israel, in both inspiration and formulation. The second group, on the other hand, is of the type usual in the ancient Orient: a series of hypothetical particular cases together with the corresponding dispositions. But their content is rather different, both because it is adapted to the special conditions of Hebrew society, and because of the ethical note, which is to be more frequently observed here than in other cases.

A characteristic example of general laws is the Decalogue. This consists of the ten great precepts which constitute the foundation of religious and moral life: to worship God, to keep the holy days, to honour one's parents, not to kill, not to steal, and so on. Some of the condemnations of sinners found in the Book of Deuteronomy are of a similar absolute character. The Levites pronounce the maledictions, and the people approve them in chorus:

> And the Levites shall answer, and say unto all the men of Israel with a loud voice,
> Cursed be the man that maketh a graven or molten image, an abomination unto the Lord, the work of the hands of the craftsman, and setteth it up in secret. And all the people shall answer and say, Amen.
> Cursed be he that setteth light by his father or his mother. And all the people shall say, Amen.
> Cursed be he that removeth his neighbour's landmark. And all the people shall say, Amen.
> Cursed be he that maketh the blind to wander out of the way. And all the people shall say, Amen.
> Cursed be he that wresteth the judgement of the stranger, fatherless, and widow. And all the people shall say, Amen.
> Cursed be he that confirmeth not the words of this law to do them. And all the people shall say, Amen.[83]

These are obviously commandments conveyed in comminatory form, that is, in the form of condemnation of those who do not keep them.

We come now to the case law, the prescription of particular solutions for particular instances. Its content will reveal the main lines of the Israelite organization of society.

First and foremost, to deal with the classes of the population. As we have seen, in Mesopotamia there were patricians, plebeians, and slaves. Here the distinction between patricians and plebeians disappears: all free citizens are equal in the eyes of the law. The condition of slaves is precarious here, as elsewhere; but religion exercises a moderating influence, as for example in prescribing that slaves are to be liberated in the seventh year:

> If thou buy an Hebrew servant, six years he shall serve: and in the seventh he shall go out free for nothing. If he come in by himself, he shall go out by himself: if he be married, then his wife shall go out with him.[84]

The head of the family is the father, as usual. Polygamy is permitted. A characteristic form of marriage is the levirate, of which we have already found a corresponding form among the Hittites. In Deuteronomy it is formulated thus:

> If brethren dwell together, and one of them die, and have no son, the wife of the dead shall not marry without unto a stranger: her husband's brother shall go in unto her, and take her to wife, and perform the duty of an husband's brother unto her. And it shall be, that the first-born which she beareth shall succeed in the name of his brother which is dead, that his name be not blotted out of Israel.[85]

As everywhere else in the Orient, divorce is allowed, with certain protective restrictions. Inheritance is through the male line, which places women in a decidedly precarious position. In this connection it must not be forgotten that for all its religious and ethical elevation ancient Israel presents a stage of development of social conditions far behind that of peoples with a long tradition of settled civilization.

Penal law is based on the Semitic principle of retaliation:

> Thou shalt give life for life, eye for eye, tooth for tooth, hand for hand, foot for foot, burning for burning, wound for wound, stripe for stripe.[86]

Nevertheless, this law is mitigated in various cases. To begin with, as in Mesopotamia it is applied only between free citizens. An offence against a slave is expiated by setting him free:

> And if a man smite the eye of his servant, or the eye of his maid, and destroy it, he shall let him go free for his eye's sake. And if he smite out his manservant's tooth, or his maidservant's tooth: he shall let him go free for his tooth's sake.[87]

Moreover, a distinction is drawn between voluntary and involuntary offences:

> He that smiteth a man, so that he die, shall surely be put to death. And if a man lie not in wait, but God deliver him into his hand; then I will appoint thee a place whither he shall flee.[88]

The ethical note which is to be observed in certain passages of Israelite law, and is associated with the conception of God as merciful and just, can be illustrated by further examples:

> And a stranger shalt thou not wrong, neither shalt thou oppress him: for ye were strangers in the land of Egypt. Ye shall not afflict any widow, or fatherless child. If thou afflict them in any wise, and they cry at all unto me, I will surely hear their cry; and my wrath shall wax hot, and I will kill you with the sword: and your wives shall be widows, and your children fatherless.
>
> If thou lend money to any of my people with thee that is poor, thou shalt not be to him as a creditor; neither shall ye lay upon him usury. If thou at all take thy neighbour's garment to pledge, thou shalt restore it unto him by that the sun goeth down: for that is his only covering, it is his garment for his skin: wherein shall he sleep? and it shall come to pass, when he crieth unto me, that I will hear; for I am gracious.[89]

And again:

> If thou meet thine enemy's ox or his ass going astray, thou shalt surely bring it back to him again. If thou see the ass of him that hateth thee lying under his burden,

and wouldest forbear to help him, thou shalt surely help
with him.[90]

Certain formulations, in particular the theme that widows
and orphans are to be protected, are already well known to
us from the legal literature of other peoples in the ancient
Orient. But others are new: for instance, the injunction to love
not only our friends but our enemies too, to help those who
hate us as well as those who love us, are presages of New
Testament themes; and in these injunctions Israelite nationalism is less exclusive and restricted. That is understandable,
since it is in this mental and spiritual world that the New
Testament has its roots.

V　The Artistic Types

If there is any one form of culture which distinctly and vividly
expresses the exclusive domination of religion which we have
noted as characteristic of Israel, it is art.[91] As we know, Israelite religion prohibits the representation of deity; and this
prohibition is sufficient to frustrate all development of the
visual arts: sculpture and painting. All that remains, in consequence, are the scanty architectural monuments and the
customary productions of minor arts, and small-scale relief
in particular. So one may well ask whether it is possible to
speak of Israelite art at all. The answer will be affirmative in
the purely superficial sense that monuments do exist; but
negative if one looks for the great impulses of artistic production, or for their characteristics and their practical realization.

One would go so far as to say that the Israelite hostility to
art extends even to the carving of inscriptions. Is it not an
outstanding and singular fact that the great kings of Israel
have left not one commemorative stele, not one victory stone?
Yet they had enterprises to commemorate and victories to
celebrate, and it was fully customary to commit them to stone
for posterity to read, as is shown by the practice of the much
less important petty kings of neighbouring states. If it is objected that it is quite by chance that we have not found any

such inscriptions, we may reply that Palestine is the most thoroughly explored region of the Near East. It is difficult to believe that the absence of inscriptions is fortuitous: there must be more profound causes for it, even if the nature of those causes remains uncertain. For what religious law forbids inscriptions?

In the architectural field, remains of fortified places have come to light in more than one spot: we may instance those in Samaria, in Lachish, and in Hazor. The walls are built according to a system which follows the Canaanite tradition. The palaces belong to the same tradition; or to put it more precisely, like the Canaanite palaces they conform to the main lines of Mesopotamian architecture. They are based on one or more courtyards, with the rooms grouped around and opening on to them. Naturally, the proportions are far more modest: as compared with the over 260 chambers of the royal palace at Mari, that of Samaria has thirteen.[92]

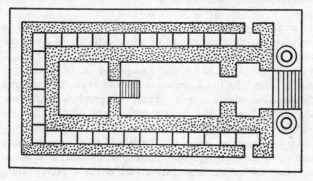

Fig. 5

Nothing has survived of the religious edifices. But the Biblical tradition completely makes up for the lack of archaeological data by providing a detailed description of the celebrated temple which Solomon built at Jerusalem[93] (Fig. 5). It consisted of a forecourt, in which stood a sacrificial altar and a great vessel for water, the 'sea of bronze'. A gate flanked by two columns, also of bronze, led to the entrance hall. Beyond it was the central hall, containing a golden altar for perfumes and a table of cedarwood for the shewbread. Finally there was the sanctuary, veiled by a curtain; it was a dark, cubical chamber in which the Ark of the Covenant was kept. It was entered only by the high priest, once a year, on the Day of Atonement. The temple was flanked on two sides and at the rear by small cubical rooms arranged in storeys.

It is easy enough to answer the question whether this temple showed any originality of structure. The Hebrews neither had nor wished to have any originality in this regard. There was no architectural tradition in their nomadic heritage. So they relied on Phoenician artisans, whom Solomon called in. The Phoenicians in turn did not have any marked artistic independence. As we have already observed, they came within the orbit of Egyptian influence. So it will occasion no surprise that Solomon's temple, with its succession of halls leading to the most remote and obscure of all, the sanctuary, repeats features already found in Egypt.

In the absence of sculpture and painting we go straight to discussion of the productions of minor arts. These consist of small scale reliefs, on seals or ivory plaques. The seals,[94] which are very numerous, are of the stamp, not the cylinder type, and usually take the Egyptian scaraboid form. The designs engraved on them consist mainly of gryphons, sphinxes, scarabs, and solar discs, always with wings: that is they are all highly characteristic of Egyptian art. We rarely find animal figures, such as lions, bulls, birds, and monkeys; and more rarely still are their representations of divinities. These are in any case of foreign importation and retain a purely ornamental value. Equally rare are representations of the human form, which are generally in an attitude of worship.

The style is static and the purpose ornamental, even down to the inscriptions with the owners' names accompanying the designs; these usually spread over two lines. Similar features are found in the small ivory plaques which are placed on the inner walls of palaces: at Samaria specimens have been found bearing a cherub (Pl. XXIX) and the Egyptian god Horus the child;[95] other specimens have been found at Megiddo, and, quite recently, by Israeli excavators at Hazor. The dominant influence of these themes is also Egyptian; and the route by which it came was probably Phoenicia. The Hebrew minor arts fall wholly within the area of Phoenician or, more generally, Syrian production; and it can be said that they possess no definite element of individuality or of independence.

Summing up Israelite civilization as a whole, we must point out how thoroughly homogeneous it is. Like the political, literary and legal forms, the artistic genres all point in the one direction, towards the religious faith. This is true to some extent of all the peoples of the ancient Orient; but only to some extent, because it is one thing for religious principles to be reflected in the forms of life and culture, and another for them to be the dominant, indeed exclusive, condition and theme of those forms. In view of the schematic simplicity of the Israelite principles, it is understandable that the features of this culture should be so individual and harmonious, in contrast to those of others, whose disparate components did not always harmonize and fuse into a single whole. In this sphere Israel lays down the foundations of its future. The religion of the people is not the religion of the state, and so it survives the state for centuries. Yet a further step can be taken, with the realization that the people itself is not necessary. That step will be taken by Christianity; Israel could not take it, because it would put an end to that very conception of history which had made her survival possible at all.

PART IV

The Synthesis

8

THE PERSIANS

I *The Synthesis and the End of an Era*

'When Cyrus entered Babylon in 539 B.C., the world was old. More significant, it knew its antiquity.'[1]

These are the opening words of Olmstead's history of the Persian empire. They are carefully chosen, and make it easier to understand that cult of antiquity which seems to take possession of the last Babylonian period. The story of the ancient Orient is drawing to its close. And yet, by a strange contrast, on the very eve of the final crisis it achieves its maximum extension, unification, and power. Up to and beyond its boundaries, fom India to Libya, a single empire[2] is built up from diverse peoples; and the synthesis which had existed momentarily under the Assyrians now becomes a stable condition, reinforced by an enlightened policy of liberality and tolerance. It is a universal monarchy, the kingdom of 'the four quarters of the earth', the conception which we saw taking shape as a will to power, and which now is put into practice in the fullness of reality. Only the west remains outside the synthesis; and so then arise the conditions for the inevitable and decisive clash.

The chief actors in this new phase of history are Indo-Europeans, known to be present long since on the Iranian plateau, but who form strong political organisms only during the first millennium, spreading with an intense energy of expansion towards the outside world. This is the second wave of Indo-European penetration into the area of the ancient Orient, and it constitutes the last ethnic force to animate the history of that area.

The periphery triumphs over the centre. The great valley civilizations are exhausted by their thousands of years of history, drained of blood by the recurrent crises to which their organisms have been subjected; and the catalysts of history, too, the peoples of the mountains and the desert, have exhausted their function, at the very moment when it achieved its end and the isolated independent states were dissolved.

The shift in the centre of gravity extends the bounds of history and diversifies its problems: the roads are opened to the Middle and Far East, while on the empire's other boundary the western frontiers are crossed at the vital point of the Bosphorus. Even before the arrival of the military crisis the ancient Orient dissolves by the obliteration of the geographical limits demarcating it and determining its history.

But the end of the ancient Oriental civilizations is distinguishable particularly in the subtle and increasing crisis of the conception of the universe which is their own. Israel has already made a deep breach in it by showing that the divine can be severed from the human and natural and set up as an autonomous moral force transcending political contingencies. Now Iran, distant in time and space, repeats the cleavage, though in a structurally different form, and reasserts the moral condition, transcending not only the political but the national limitations.

As proof of this, we shall see the religion of Zarathustra propagating itself independently of the manner in which the Persian empire is established. And if for that very reason the connection between the two paths of Iranian civilization — political and religious — becomes a problem, it is clear that henceforth the ancient Orient is capable of producing a cosmic vision not conditioned by states or peoples. This is its greatest achievement, and at the same time involves its defeat and end.

II The Historical Outlines

The prologue to the new chapter of history[3] is provided by the empire of the Medes, who are of Iranian stock and closely related to the Persians. In the seventh century B.C. they establish a powerful state and, under king Cyaxares, defeat Assyria and penetrate into Armenia and Anatolia, being checked only at the river Halys by the resistance of the Lydians. This empire is meteoric and disappears soon after its appearance. In the middle of the following century Cyrus's Persians throw off its yoke, take over the power, and set out along the open roads of expansion.

Cyrus, the founder of the Achaemenid dynasty, is the greatest conqueror in the history of the ancient Orient. In eleven years (550–539 B.C.) he thrusts on the one side into the heart of India, and on the other occupies Anatolia and Babylonia with all its territories as far as the frontier of Egypt.

Thus the greatest of the ancient Oriental empires comes into being. Why does it achieve such a sweeping success? Undoubtedly it is due in part to the youthful energies of the new conquerors, and the crisis which the ancient empires have experienced or are passing through at this time: the Hittite has fallen, the Assyrian has fallen, the Egyptian is confined within the bounds of Egypt itself, the Babylonian is undermined by internal discord. But it is certain that so extensive an empire, consisting of peoples and cultures widely differing one from another, could not have subsisted and triumphed without a political formula of its own, and a system in which the old and the new could be reconciled, the resistances and conflicts diminished, and the tendencies to union fostered and strengthened. Indeed, Cyrus's greatest achievement is precisely in this direction. Everywhere he respects local traditions and adapts himself to them. Moreover, with his distinctive view of history he presents himself as the legitimate successor to the local dynasties, which have been found wanting because of the faults of their representatives;

he takes over existing institutions without modification; he honours the gods of other peoples and makes them his own. Doubtless some of this can be attributed to propaganda and expediency;[4] but the assertion of the moral principle, the elevation of tolerance to a system, the aim at coexistence beyond the point of political necessity, all bear witness to an indubitably high ethical level and a concrete liberality, and determine the advance of practical action along the lines indicated by the theoretical premisses.

The foregoing remarks are perhaps best exemplified by the inscription which tells the story of the conquest of Babylon. Using the language of the country he has conquered, Cyrus asserts that its own god Marduk, who was despised by the local king Nabonidus, has chosen him and sent him to restore the faith:

> (Marduk) scanned and looked through all the countries, seeking a righteous ruler willing to lead him (i.e. to lead Marduk, in the annual procession). He uttered the name of Cyrus, king of Anshan, declaring him ruler of all the world . . . Marduk, the great lord, protector of his people, beheld with joy Cyrus's good deeds and his upright heart, and bade him march against his city Babylon. He made him set out on the road to Babylon, going at his side as a true friend. His huge army — its number, like that of the waters of a river, could not be counted — marched on with their weapons packed away. Without any battle, Marduk brought them into his town of Babylon, sparing it from calamity. He delivered into Cyrus's hands Nabonidus, the king, who did not worship him. All the inhabitants of Babylon as well as the entire land of Sumer and Akkad, princes and governors included, bowed to Cyrus and kissed his feet, jubilant and with shining faces because he had received the kingship. Happily they greeted him as the master by whose help they had come back to life out of death and had been spared disaster, and they worshipped his very name.[5]

Cyrus's son Cambyses (528–522 B.C.) extends the conquests farther westward: he occupies Egypt and penetrates into

Nubia and Ethiopia. These events are of great historical significance: with the disappearance of its most independent portion the ancient Orient achieves integral unity.

Whether Cambyses continued his father's enlightened policy is a problem. According to Greek sources he ridicules Egyptian religion, destroys its temples, and kills the sacred bull Apis. Is this truth or legend? If legend, on what facts is it based? We lack direct information which would provide answers to these questions.[6]

On his way back from Egypt Cambyses learns that a revolt has broken out in Persia: Gaumata the Magian has posed as the sovereign's dead brother and assumed power. Cambyses dies on his way home. But Darius, the scion of another branch of the Achaemenids, raises his standard and puts the usurper to death, re-establishing the dynasty. The lengthy inscription which records these events repeats in the sphere of internal politics the old theme of offended and restored justice; the king clearly aims at legitimizing his accession. But the inscription also contains one particularly interesting feature which raises a religious problem: Darius refers again and again to the protection accorded him by Ahuramazda, who is the god proclaimed by Zarathustra. The inscription says:

> I am Darius the Great King, King of Kings, King of Persia, King of countries, son of Hystaspes, grandson of Arsames, an Achaemenian . . .
>
> Saith Darius the King: By the favour of Ahuramazda I am king. Ahuramazda bestowed the kingdom upon me.
>
> Saith Darius the King: The kingdom which had been taken away from our family, I put in its place. I re-established it again on its foundation. As before, so I made the sanctuaries which Gaumata the Magian destroyed. I restored to the people the pastures and the herds, the household property and the houses which Gaumata the Magian took away from them. I re-established the people on its foundation, both Persia and Media and the other provinces. As before, so I brought back what had been taken away. By the favour of Ahuramazda this I did.[7]

This may suggest that it was Darius who established the

religion of Zarathustra; and as this prophet refers in the
Avesta to one of his patron's names as Hystaspes, the name
of Darius's father, it is natural that several authorities should
incline towards this hypothesis. But the question is not so
simple: although given prominence by Zarathustra, the god
Ahuramazda may have belonged to the already existing religious background; and the name Hystaspes may be a pure
coincidence. In any case, Darius also recognized other gods,
as is shown by a later passage in the inscription:

> Saith Darius the King: This is what I did; by the favour
> of Ahuramazda in one and the same year I did it. Ahura-
> mazda bore me aid, and the other gods who are.[8]

The question therefore remains obscure and complex. How
far is Zoroastrianism Darius's religion? And how can one
reconcile Zoroastrian monotheism with the Achaemenid tolerance and acceptance of foreign deities?

After achieving the throne Darius has to face a series of
revolts which break out in various parts of the state. He
quells them all with a firm hand, reconquering the empire of
Cambyses and even going farther, with offensives into India
on the east and Europe on the west. He is forced to fall back
from Europe after crossing the Danube, and in Greece he is
defeated at Marathon; but these expeditions remain as testimony to the offensive capacity of a state which has already
enlarged its bounds to an unprecedented extent.

Political organization also reaches its highest point under
Darius. The king, endowed with absolute hereditary authority, is at the summit, with a council of nobles to assist
him. The king is not deified, as elsewhere in the Orient, but
is only regarded as having divine assistance. Under him are
the satraps, the governors of the provinces into which the
empire is divided. These provinces retain their own organization and customs. The satraps are assisted in performing their
functions by the king's secretaries, who also supervise their
activities. This supervision is also exercised by inspectors,
who go round the provinces verifying the state of affairs and
sending in reports. The foundation of the state's economic life
is a perfectly organized system of taxation. Commerce is fa-

voured by an innovation of great importance: coinage is already in use in Lydia, and Darius introduces it throughout the empire. Finally, a complex system of roads, including the celebrated highway, fifteen hundred miles long, from Susa to Sardis, is created to facilitate economic life as well as military movement.

Greek sources, which describe his enormous expedition to and severe defeat at Salamis, present Darius's successor, Xerxes, as a cruel tyrant. An inscription left by the king himself, and discovered not long ago at Persepolis, shows the other side of his personality. In particular, it identifies his religious policy, in which we now indubitably find traces of Zoroastrianism. The 'wicked gods' are condemned in the following terms:

> Ahuramazda is the great god who has given us the earth, who has given us the sky, who has given being to mankind, who has given his men prosperity, who has made Xerxes king, sole king of multitudes, sole commander of others.
>
> I am Xerxes, the Great King, King of Kings, King of countries of all manner of tongues, King of this great and vast earth, the son of King Darius, the Achaemenian ...
>
> Saith Xerxes the King: After I became king, there were some of the countries mentioned above which revolted; but I crushed these countries when Ahuramazda gave me his aid; under the shadow of Ahuramazda I restored them to their former status. Furthermore, there were some among those countries who worshipped the wicked gods; but under the shadow of Ahuramazda I uprooted the temples of the wicked gods and made proclamation: no more must ye worship the wicked gods.[9]

Xerxes dies at the hand of an assassin, and his successor Artaxerxes (464–424 B.C.) passes his reign in maintaining a precarious equilibrium amid a succession of assassinations and conspiracies. Then the equilibrium breaks down. A century of internal strife follows, during which period the power of the empire is only a façade, and the foundations of the edifice are being undermined. Violence and corruption in the service of lust for power prepare the way for the end. The very conception of government is modified in a retrogressive sense: the liberality which reconciled and federated different peoples by respecting their rights is succeeded by despotic rule and intolerant repression; and then the peoples of the empire grow estranged and hostile. Thus, when the crisis does arrive, the ground for it has been prepared. Alexander the Great bursts into the Near East, and in battle after battle swiftly takes possession of the area. In 330 B.C. the process is complete. The history of the ancient Orient is finished.

But the end of a history is not the end of a civilization. We began this section with a passage from Olmstead; we close it with another passage by the same author:

> The burning of Persepolis was a symbol to the world that the great crusade had reached its destined end. Unfortunately, both symbol and crusade were equally out of date. His first conquests were organized by Alexander on the model of a Persian satrapy. In Egypt he had learned that he was son of a god and therefore himself a divine king. More and more he came under the influence of oriental beliefs, and soon he was to take over Persian pomp and circumstance. At the end he was to dream of unifying Persian and Greek peoples and cultures. The Orient had conquered its fierce conqueror.[10]

III *The Religious Structure and the Literary Genres*

An Italian scholar, Pagliaro, writes:

> The factor which had the greatest effect in shaping Iranian civilization, and in its becoming a cultural as well as a distinctive political entity for more than a thousand years, is certainly that of religion. For whereas the Iranian tribes of the plateau, who made the religion of Zarathustra their own, became an historical people, capable of establishing power on the fringe of the Greco-Roman world, the related tribes of Central Asia, who remained aloof

from that religion, were lost to view in the sea of nomadic and barbaric peoples to which the ancients gave the collective name of Scythians. Be it observed, moreover, that the self-assertion of Iranian civilization, especially on the cultural level, appears in its various developments to have a close connection with the affirmation of those religious values.[11]

These observations clearly emphasize the importance and significance of the Zarathustran religion in the Iranian world.[12] This is confirmed, with all the eloquence of history, by the fact that that religion survives the fall of the Achaemenids, and some centuries later, under the Sasanids, even becomes the official state creed, thus cementing a bond which in the ancient period was, as we have seen, frequently obscure and uncertain.

But the significance of the Zarathustran religion is not confined to the Iranian world; it extends to the whole of the ancient Orient. It forms a parallel to events in Palestine, for it asserts a monotheistic creed with a moral foundation. The differences between the two religions are profound: in Israel, faith and politics are fused into an indissoluble unity, in Iran they are distinct and different; in Israel, monotheism has a mainly emotional basis, in Iran the intellectual outlook prevails, and it would be difficult to isolate this — though it is not easy to be more precise — from the behaviour and characteristics of the Indo-European tribes which are its bearers; finally, in Israel monotheism grows more and more absolute, whereas in Iran it is attenuated as time passes. Yet in spite of these differences, and in spite of the even more obvious ones arising from the profound dissimilarity of the environment and other conditions, the two religions are linked by one essential bond: in both cases a faith breaks away into independence, and so constitutes a community — we would say, a church — independent of political conditions.

The literary patrimony of ancient Iran is substantially identical with that of its religious doctrine: it consists of a sacred book, the Avesta, which, like the sacred book of Israel, is made up of sections differing in period and content. Only part has been preserved, but even so we can identify the various literary genres of which it consists: hymns, prayers, juridical prescriptions, and ritual. The work in the form it now possesses reveals an evolution not only in time, but, concurrently, in style: the intense expression and emotion of the oldest portion — the Gathas, seventeen hymns which probably date back to Zarathustra[13] — are succeeded by a greater monotony of themes, some prolixity, and at times even less correct language. But above all there is an evolution in content: we shall consider this in detail later, but we may say now that this is not, as elsewhere, a matter simply of the natural development of ideas through time and environment, but also of alterations and of returns to elements of primitive paganism. Thus there is a clear differentiation, revealing the existence of two structurally opposed phases in the history of Zoroastrian religion.

The figure of the prophet of Iran, Zarathustra, or, in the form adapted from the Greek, Zoroaster, is still shrouded in obscurity.[14] We know very little of him from the Gathas. He says he has enemies, is persecuted:

> To what land am I to fly? Whither to turn?
> I am estranged from my family and my tribe.
> Neither the villages nor the wicked governors of the land
>   are favourable to me.
> How can I, O Lord, assure myself thy goodwill?
> I know, Lord, why I am powerless:
> It is because I have few flocks and few men.
> I direct to thee my lament: hear me, Lord,
> Coming to my aid, as a friend to a friend.[15]

Zarathustra finds hospitality and protection in a prince's court. We have already said that some authorities identify this prince with Darius's father, and in that case the prophet lived in the sixth century B.C. But others, relying on a later Iranian chronological reference, would have him living several decades earlier, while yet others have attempted to put the date back to 1000 B.C. on the ground of the archaic language of the Gathas. All this indicates the difficulty of determining Zarathustra historically; on the other hand, there is no reason to deny that he was an historical figure, as some have tried to do in former days. The indications concerning his environment given in the Gathas seem to point to the pastoral regions of eastern Iran, but it is impossible to be precise even in regard to this question.

The subject matter of his teaching can be identified quite clearly. But doubts arise when one attempts to determine its sources, or the new and distinctive elements it contains. The fact is that we know too little about the previous state of Iranian religion to be able to fix Zarathustra's position in relation to it; and an authoritative scholar, Duchesne-Guillemin, has written with a touch of irony that we are able to depreciate the prophet's contributions just as much as we like: we only need to attribute the elements of his thinking to pre-existing beliefs.[16] Consequently even the nature of his preaching is a subject of controversy: was he a sort of witch doctor,[17] or a philosopher,[18] or a social reformer?[19] All three suggestions have been advanced, but none of them seems wholly acceptable. Undoubtedly religion is the dominant motive in the prophet's activities, even if the religion in question is one dominated by intellectual factors and based on a social conception.

Zarathustra's thought centres on the affirmation of one god. The name of that god, Ahuramazda, fully conveys his character, for while Ahura, 'Lord', is already in existence as a denomination of deity, the addition of -mazda, 'wise', or even better 'the thinker', makes intellectual activity the central feature of his nature. This is a profoundly new element in the ancient Orient, where the isolation of thought and its projection on to the universal plane has not previously been achieved; it is, if anything, more in line with the recognition of reason as the law of the universe, which other Indo-European peoples are about to achieve in Greece.

The predominance of the intellectual element in the Iranian conception of the deity is confirmed by the entities which are placed alongside Ahuramazda: Justice, Good Thought, Rule, Devotion, Integrity, Immortality. These are not divinities in their own right, but attributes or aspects of the supreme god, who is their creator. In one of the oldest of the hymns the prophet defines the work of Ahuramazda in a series of rhetorical questions:

> I question thee, Lord: answer me!
> Who was at its birth the first father of Justice?
> Who assigned their paths to sun and stars?
> Who is it, if not thou, that makes the moon wax and
>   wane?
> That is what I wish to know, Wise one, and other
>   things too.
> I question thee, Lord: answer me!
> Who established heaven and earth, so that they fall not?
> Who brought forth the waters and the plants?
> Who harnessed the horses to the winds and the clouds?
> Who, Wise one, is the creator of Good Thought?
> I question thee, Lord: answer me!
> What craftsman made light and darkness?
> What craftsman sleep and wakefulness?
> Who created morning, noon and evening
> To mark his task for him who understands? . . .
> I question thee, Lord: answer me!
> Who formed Devotion, consecrated in Rule?
> Who made the son respectful to his father?
> I try so to understand thee, Wise one,
> As a holy Spirit creator of all things.[20]

Intellectual in their personifications, Zarathustra's entities also reflect a profound moral exigency: their rule over the world means simply that rectitude and justice are the hinges of society.

Placing the supreme principle in the sphere of morality does not get rid of the problem of evil in the universe; on the contrary, it dramatically raises that problem. Hence the conception of a wicked Spirit enters into Zarathustra's thought and becomes dominant, for its struggle with the good forces is the very essence of the life of the universe. Here there are elements of a dualism[21] which later speculation will develop fully, but which in Zarathustra's thought does not affect the supreme Spirit, for it is expressed in the opposition of wicked Spirit to good Spirit, who are both subordinated to the supreme principle. There is struggle, truly, and has been ever since the beginning of the world; but when men have made their choice the good will be rewarded and the evil punished, and good will reign supreme. This is Zarathustra's eschatology:

> Now will I utter for whoever will listen to the
>   instruction of the initiate
> The praises and prayers of Good Thought to the Lord,
> And the joy he will see, in the light, who will keep them.
> Hear with your ears what is the supreme good;
> Look with clear mind on the two sides,
> Between which each man must choose for himself,
> Watchful from the beginning that the great trial turn
>   in our favour.
> In the beginning the two Spirits known as twins
> Are the one good and the other evil,
> In thought, in word and in deed. And between these two
> The wise, not the foolish, can choose well.
> When these two Spirits met,
> They established from the beginning life and not-life,
> And that in the end the worse existence be for the wicked,
> And for the righteousness the Better Thought . . .
> Now, when their punishment comes to the sinners,
> Then, O Wise one, thy Rule will be granted, with Good
>   Thought,
> To those who delivered up Evil to thy Justice, Lord!
> And may it be we who renew existence!
> O Wise one, and ye other Lords, O Justice, lend your aid,
> That thoughts come together where understanding is
>   lacking.
> Then will Evil no more have success,
> And they will receive the promised reward
> In the happy dwelling of Good Thought, of the Wise one
>   and of Justice,
> Who have earned themselves good repute.[22]

Note the difficult complexity of the concepts, the intellectual concentration which characterizes them: the passage shows better than any abstract consideration the profound difference between the mentality behind this text and that which we have observed in other parts of the ancient Oriental world. The solution found to the problem of evil is connected with the position adopted by Zarathustra towards the beliefs of Iranian paganism. He denies its gods, or, rather, transforms them into wicked beings parallel with the good ones, thus, one may observe in passing, sowing other seeds of dualism for later thought. At the same time he reacts against Iranian worship, which is distinguished by the drinking of intoxicating *haoma* and by blood rites. Only one element of the preceding period remains: the adoration of sacred fire. But there are only hints in passing of this, and it is characteristically spiritualized. Says Zarathustra:

> To the question: 'Whom dost thou wish to worship?'
> I have answered: 'Thy fire! While offering him veneration
> I wish to think as much as I can of Justice.'[23]

We must make some mention of the environment to which Zarathustra speaks, doing so not so much in order to indicate the background to his teaching as in order to understand one of its essential motives, the social factor. The environment is that of shepherds, not nomadic, but settled on their pasturelands. The frequent mention of the ox to be defended from robbers, and still more the personification of its soul, make this animal the symbol of life and labour. The reformer's ideal, therefore, is not so much the reconstruction of society as its harmonious conservation.

One very well known Gatha opens with the strange lament of the ox's soul:

> For whom have you created me? Who formed me?
> Fury, violence, cruelty and tyranny bear me down.
> I have no other shepherds but you: procure for me good
> pastures![24]

And elsewhere the ox is praised as the source of plenty,

created and brought up by the supreme god in collaboration with his attendant beings:

> *Thou art the holy father of this Spirit,*
> *Which, O Wise one, has created for us the ox, source of*
>   *prosperity,*
> *And has raised up, giving us peace,*
> *To bring up this ox, Devotion, after consulting Good*
>   *Thought.*[25]

Considered as a whole, Zarathustra's religion is extremely simple in its constituent elements, and this is true not only positively, with respect to their nature, but also negatively, in regard to the repudiation, or at least the absence, of a number of factors which we have hitherto found to be integral elements of Oriental religions. There is no mythology; there is only the slightest trace of forms of worship and ritual; those forms, magic and divination, which most frequently accompany religious practice, are lacking; finally, the personnel, the priesthood, is missing.

This state of affairs is modified to some extent, after Zarathustra's death, when a profound evolution occurs, retrogressive in character, and of which traces are observable in the remainder of the Avesta. The pagan heritage and popular beliefs reappear, and monotheism is transformed, debased, and substantially dropped. In this development a great part must have been played by the priesthood, the Magians,[26] who are thought by some to have been a tribe originally, while others with more justification see their origins in a religious community.

The transformations effected are these: to begin with, monotheism is changed to dualism by identifying the good Spirit with Ahuramazda, who is thus set in opposition to an evil spirit, Ahriman, who has an analogous power in the life of the universe. Secondly, the entities assigned to the two parties, good and evil, increase in number, absorbing figures from the ancient paganism, and then evolve into independent divinities in the full sense of the word. Thus in the good camp we find the ancient Aryan god Mithras and the fertility goddess Anahita, distinctly influenced by the Mesopotamian Ishtar; in the evil camp is Indra, another typical deity of the old Iranian world. At a certain stage there is an interesting reaction to this dualism, but unfortunately we have little information concerning it, and that only of an indirect nature: we refer to Zurvanism,[27] a movement which regards the two supreme principles of good and evil as being both derived from a single element, time. This solution is more philosophical than religious in its nature, but it does reflect the aspiration after unity which was left unsatisfied by the development of Zoroastrianism.

In the new phase the eschatology is accentuated and more precisely defined.[28] The souls appear before their judges on one side of the Chinwat bridge, and their virtues and vices are weighed in the balance. The good succeed in reaching paradise, while the wicked are hurled into the infernal abyss below the bridge. But heaven and hell are both temporary: in the last judgement a sea of molten metal will purify the universe and the good will ascend to eternal life.

The ancient rites are restored to favour: the intoxicating *haoma* is again consecrated and offered; and much use is made of sacred fire in purification ceremonies.[29]

As the worship develops, there is a parallel development of the priesthood: the perpetually burning fire in particular needs a well trained personnel to look after it. This personnel has to be supported by the community, and has an ever increasing influence in its life.

Thus Zoroastrianism survives, is consolidated, and at the same time grows corrupt: strange destiny for a religion, to survive by virtue of the elements it was determined to destroy.

After this sketch of the religious history, we should bring it into relationship with the political history; but this is a very difficult and uncertain problem. It is hard to believe that Cyrus was a Zoroastrian; it is possible that Darius was, but without the exclusion of foreign gods; it is almost certain that Xerxes was a Zoroastrian. Probably, we are here still in the earliest phase of that religion: only later, in the time of Artaxerxes II, does reference to Mithras and Anahita indicate that the new phase is on the way. None the less, the comparative scission between the political and religious processes remains the essential feature. More than this can be said: the political activity is positive just as long as there is religious tolerance for foreign cults; it becomes negative when it coincides with the exclusivism of Ahuramazda. In conclusion, we would say that the relationship between the two processes is fundamentally a secondary question. The Zarathustran religion lives by its own life. In the ancient Orient it is the first religion in whose history political events have no decisive, or even prominent part.

⚹ IV   *The Artistic Types* ⚹

By a symbiosis of differing elements the community of nations which the Achaemenids weld into a single empire cooperates in creating an art which aims at being the expression of that community.[30] For although the Iranians are a new people and therefore likely to be interested in innovation, they think it an honour to gather material and artists from the most diverse parts of their empire; and it is in this combination that they express and assert its universality. Darius thus describes the construction of the palace at Susa:

> The cedar timber was brought from a mountain called Lebanon. The Assyrians brought it to Babylon; from Babylon the Carians and the Ionians brought it to Susa. The *yaka* wood was brought from Gandara and from Carmania. The gold wrought here was brought from Sardis and from Bactria. The precious stone wrought here, lapis lazuli and carnelian, was brought from Sogdiana. The turquoise wrought here was brought from Chorasmia. The silver and the ebony were brought from Egypt. The ornamentation with which the wall was adorned was brought from Ionia. The ivory wrought here was brought from Ethiopia and from Sind and from Arachosia. The stone columns wrought here were brought from a village called Abiradu, in Elam.
>
> The stone-cutters who wrought the stone were Ionians and Sardians. The goldsmiths who wrought the gold were Medes and Egyptians. The men who wrought the wood

were Sardians and Egyptians. The men who wrought the
baked brick were Babylonians. The men who adorned the
wall were Medes and Egyptians.[31]

This will to universality is truly impressive. It would seem
that on the very eve of its end the ancient Orient is attempting to achieve its last, deliberate synthesis. Certainly never
before has it expressed so explicitly the community of nations
which it now achieves.

Ancient Iranian art, then, is an official, court art, maintained not so much by the exertions of the new, victorious
people as by those of the older, conquered ones. It is an old,
not a new art, and it is grafted without apparent difficulty
into the trunk of the tradition. Its end is also the end of the
entire world of conceptions and attitudes which the Orient
has brought to expression during the preceding millennia.

The question has to be asked whether, in these conditions,
Iranian art possesses any continuity or distinctive features of
its own. We leave the answer to be given by the late Monneret
de Villard:

> There is a spiritual continuity similar, though remain-
> ing on a much lower level, to that which we see in the
> two greatest arts the world has ever known, that of Greece
> and that of China, and which is realized, perhaps, in no
> other art. This aesthetic continuity is the intense feeling
> for decoration which manifests itself in every period with
> precision, lucidity and rhythm. Not expression, therefore,
> and not pure representation, but vision subordinated to
> decoration and always realized with a technical ability
> which has rarely been surpassed. This feeling for decora-
> tion has as its foundation a precise and sympathetic ob-
> servation of reality, which materializes with a sumptuous
> vision of colour and a portentous imagination for the elab-
> oration of new forms, the whole being felt as a poetry
> which fuses everything into a sort of dream.[32]

Therefore decoration dominates over representation, and
may be said to be the distinctive element of Iranian art. It
is characteristic of that art's beginnings, and remains characteristic all its life, enduring beyond the days of the Achae-

menids right down to modern times. Thus, apart from any estimate of its good and bad qualities, this art has its own characteristic course, and it is the most distinctive in its course of all the peripheral regions of the ancient Orient.

The first architectural problem faced in Iran is the construction of the imperial palace, simultaneously the centre and the expression of the suddenly arisen political power. A like religious urgency is lacking, because of the small importance attached to worship; this explains why civil architecture greatly predominates over temple building.

The great imperial palaces of Pasargadae, Persepolis (Pl. XXX), and Susa are good examples of the principles of construction. We find a feature which we saw to be typical in Mesopotamia, namely the great artificial terrace which is erected as the platform for the main edifice. But the function of protection from flood which it possessed in Mesopotamia can be ruled out here, for this problem does not exist. Consequently this architectural feature has found a new purpose, namely that of defence.

As in Babylon, bricks for building material are in ample supply. But stone is largely, indeed chiefly used, as the nature of the terrain indicates. Supplies of stone make possible the extensive use of pillars, and here again Iran differs from Babylon. At Pasargadae the shaft is smooth, and is set on a base of disc shape; at Persepolis and Susa it is fluted, and the base is bell shaped. The capital has some original features: it has a voluted or bell-shaped section above the shaft, supporting two foreparts of horses or bulls carrying the architrave. Recent excavations at Persepolis have raised a strange problem in connection with this feature: two foreparts of gryphons were found lying abandoned by the wall; they witnessed not so much to the use of new forms as the existence of tentative divergences from tradition, which the artists, or those who directed their work, decided to abandon.[33]

The columns served a decidedly functional purpose: as many as a hundred are found supporting the roofs of the great hypostyle halls which form the main part of the palaces. Here basically Egyptian themes are worked out in an original manner, because of the height, the slenderness, and the magnificence of the columns.

Turning to religious architecture, we need mention only the small cubical edifices used for fire worship.[34] Their structure raises a complex problem involving the solution of religious questions for which we have inadequate data: are these small buildings the remains of turrets which carried altars?

The funerary architecture is more deserving of comment. Cyrus's mausoleum at Pasargadae is unique: it consists of a single chamber with gabled roof (a new feature, this) standing on a platform approached by six steps. At Persepolis and Naqsh-i-Rustam, the later Achaemenids excavated tombs in the rock,[35] which present a cruciform shape to the outside (Pl. XXXI). The cross consists of three panels in relief: the upper panel depicts the king adoring Ahuramazda, represented by a bearded bust of Assyrian type on a winged solar disc of Egyptian type; beneath it are ranks of soldiers. The middle panel, extending right across the crossbeam, has columns with a doorway in the centre, which opens to the interior of the tomb. The lower panel is usually left blank. The origin of the Persian rock tombs is difficult to decide: it is natural to relate them to the Egyptian tombs of the same type, but the Persian tombs are sited near the royal residence, and not in remote spots. Nor must we overlook the pre-Achaemenid elements which seem to indicate the existence of a native tradition.

Freestanding sculpture has not been found in ancient Iran. The nearest approach to the type are the orthostats, the great winged, human-headed bulls which support gateways, revealing Mesopotamian influence; yet there is a new quality in the features, which are much less vigorous, but more elegant and delicate even in their monumental grandeur (Pl. XXXII).

As usual, relief carving is used extensively, being applied to the outer and inner walls of palaces in the Mesopotamian manner. There are in the first place reliefs carved in stone: numerous files of tributary peoples and royal guards deployed along the sides of the staircases leading to the palaces, and in the interiors. The ethnic types and the clothing, which is accurately represented, provide first-class documentary material. But the art itself is also of great interest, for there are innovations on the Mesopotamian original in respect of both themes and treatment. One thematic innovation is the absence of war scenes, instead of which we find the processions appropriate to peace ensured by dominion; and novelty of treatment is found in the folds of the garments, which automatically bring the Greek artists to mind.

Another theme of the mural relief concerns the king: he is depicted fighting a monster, which undoubtedly owes something to the Mesopotamian motive of the hero and the wild beasts, but which may also be referred to the Iranian conception of the struggle between good and evil in the universe. In other places the king is seated on his throne: the face with its stylized beard, the posture, the attendant standing by his shoulder, all recall the Assyrian model; but the multiple files of soldiers and subjects arranged below the throne again make a local contribution.

Some of the reliefs are on brick. This type predominates at Susa, just as brick does for building material. The bricks are enamelled and painted in various colours in the later Babylonian manner, and the bas-relief accompanies the colours. The themes are fantastic animals on the Babylonian model, or files of soldiers and subjects such as have already been found carved in stone.

The art of ancient Iran includes a number of minor forms. Further proof of the high level which the artists could attain is given by the magnificent crouching lion in bronze found at Susa, and the two vase handles in the shape of winged ibexes, in which there is a closely observed reproduction of reality together with a remarkable, slender elegance. Many specimens of the goldsmith's art have also been found, and here we may note the innovation of setting an incrustation of coloured stones in a pattern of gold. The seals are noteworthy: some are cylindrical, and bear scenes of the king fighting wild beasts or evil genii, while others are flat, bearing fantastic beings, human figures in Persian attire, or the god Ahuramazda, in the semi-Assyrian, semi-Egyptian form which we have noted as proper to him. Finally, there is a new contribution to art in the coins, the most distinctive type being the daric, representing the king armed with a bow. This is a late type, and elsewhere in the ancient Orient it is represented only by imported Phoenician specimens.

Thus, at the close of the ancient Oriental world, the Iranian civilization gathers it all together and summarizes it. Among the numerous influences found in Iran the Mesopotamian is undoubtedly predominant, for which the geographical situation is sufficient explanation; but it can be said that no influence is lacking, whether great or small. These influences, however, are combined in a unity of national style which triumphs over the extensive variety of its components and is transmitted to future generations.

Certainly, the function of ancient Iranian civilization is principally historical and religious in its nature. In the historical field, the tolerant liberalism which combines different peoples into an harmonious empire has repercussions incalculable in their extent upon the maintenance of civilization. If proof of this be demanded, one has but to reflect that it is Persian liberalism that allows the reconstitution of the Hebrew religious community in Palestine, with all the consequences that follow from it. In the religious field, Zarathustra's teaching achieves the highest point of ancient Oriental intellectualism. In his conception of the universe, the forces of logic are already active. The one task remaining is to give them their own autonomous life.

THE FACE OF THE ANCIENT ORIENT

I *Oriental Isoids*

In the preceding pages we have surveyed a vast succession of events, political and social forms, religious conceptions, literary and artistic creations. But we still have to cast the balance, to bring together the threads which link up facts and ideas, and which out of a multiplicity of disparate elements create an organic whole. This is a task which has its parallel in the identification of isoglosses in linguistics; and, adopting Pisani's neologism,[1] we shall call these common elements of culture isoids.

The search for isoids is a necessary preliminary to a general appreciation of the ancient Orient, both as a distinct historical and cultural bloc, and as a centre of power irradiating elements into the surrounding world. Simultaneously this search is an indispensable prerequisite to bringing out those attitudes of thought which, seen and judged in the light of our own thought, constitute the final and most significant result of our sketch of the ancient Orient.

II *History*

Ancient Oriental history is born in the two great river valleys, where the geographical conditions first allow of settled ways of life and the formation of political groupings; and it passes, first in Egypt and then in Mesopotamia, from the fragmentary stage to that of organization, from petty city or regional states to unified kingdoms.

When this phase of the process has come to fruition, the two opposed organisms begin to expand beyond their frontiers, though in different ways; for the dominant aim of the Egyptians is control over the neighbouring peoples, whereas that of the Mesopotamians is annexation and dominion.

The meeting between the two forces comes about, after repeated skirmishes, towards the middle of the second millennium B.C., when the mountain peoples intervene from the north and east, and resolve the historical dualism into a plurality of acting forces. The Syrian strip takes on the main task of providing a meeting place for the powers, and around it gravitates an equilibrium of forces which continues unstable but substantially unchanged for some three centuries.

Then invasion from the sea by new peoples with weapons of iron destroys the equilibrium, and eliminates those who had built it up. But it cannot destroy the established reciprocal influence of the various parts of the Oriental world; and the connective function is assumed by the desert peoples, who abandon their primitive habitat and arrive to fill the gap left by the invasion, occupying the region destined to serve as a bridge.

When the roads are open again, the ancient chief actors of history, the peoples of the valleys, gradually reorganize and move on towards the encounter. But now Egypt does not get far, for her strength is exhausted; and Mesopotamia profits by this circumstance to achieve predominance over the whole of the ancient Orient for the first time.

Predominance, not dominion. This, and a durable unification of the entire area, is achieved only by the Persians, the last of the mountain peoples, who profit by the crisis in the centre to pour in from the periphery. Now the Near East confronts the West as a unity: here the clash comes, and here comes the end.

Such is the main course of ancient Oriental history, as viewed in time. Changing our viewpoint and considering it in space and in the conditions of the principal actors, the outstanding feature is the conflict between the peoples of the Fertile Crescent, the peoples of the desert, and the peoples of the mountains.[2] The logical centre of this conflict is the

Fertile Crescent, the land of the peoples engaged in settled agricultural life, the most prosperous, and the most coveted, region. Towards it press, with recurrent concentric movements, the nomadic beduin of the desert on the one side, and the nomadic horsemen and hunters of the mountains on the other. Both are moved by the prospect of freedom from want. Whenever they attain this freedom, the nomadic conditions give place to settled life, and their aspirations and policy are reversed. The settled peoples, for their part, are favoured by the geographical situation in so far as the constitution of strong states is concerned, and it is they, or the forces set up by them, that periodically determine the governing organisms of history. But it is remarkable that before the nomads they are powerless, at least to achieve a decisive success. Their operations are defensive rather than offensive; they clear the frontiers and protect their lines of communication, but their adversary always reappears, overcomes resistance, infiltrates, is assimilated — and the process begins all over again.

As a whole — to resort to an analogy from chemistry — ancient Oriental history may be regarded as a synthesis. The component elements, the reagents, are the civilizations of the valleys, Egypt and Mesopotamia, which are historically the first to establish their states and continue to have essential independence for many centuries. The substances that determine or assist the process of synthesis, the catalysts, are the peoples of the mountains and of the desert, who bring about the conjunction of the opposed forces, leading first to equilibrium, then to the domination of one side. The last of the catalysts produces the synthesis. But the elements of dissolution are already present, and the compound soon breaks down.

III *Politics*

An acute and vigorous perspective view of the history of the ancient Orient has described it as the coming into being and the progressive consolidation of an idea which is present in embryo from the very earliest period: the idea of universal monarchy.[3] The Akkadian empire of Sargon, which divides the story of the Sumerians into two parts, promotes this dominion of 'the four quarters of the earth'; and it remains a main objective during the uninterrupted evolution of political forms, until the Assyrians, the Babylonians, and above all the Persians bring it to full realization.

For all its good points, we do not consider this view satisfactory. To begin with, it covers only a portion of the time; further, and above all, it is focused upon a limited part of the ancient Orient. It is certainly true that the concept of dominion over the known world comes to the forefront during certain periods of Mesopotamian and Persian history; but it is also true that other zones and peoples share it only partially, or are completely unaffected by it. To begin with the Egyptians, we have seen that they regard relations with foreign countries more from the viewpoint of control, aiming at the security of their own frontiers, than from that of occupation and dominion. As for the Hittites, their federative system seems to us to be deliberately opposed to that of universal monarchy: far from absorbing and annihilating conquered states, it recognizes their independence and accentuates it in the juridical form of treaties.

To conclude, then, the political horizon of the ancient Oriental peoples is in our opinion more varied and changeful than has hitherto been suggested. But it is true that one constant is present: that is, not universal monarchy, but monarchy as such, the institution of single and absolute government, which prevails in both time and space, irresistibly attracting to itself everything, even what is initially ill adapted to it, such as the Sumerian city theocracies or the Hittite nobility's control over the king.

In view of the general domination of religious faith over the manifold forms of the ancient Oriental civilizations, the monarchical institution can have only a religious foundation and justification.[4] But often, quite understandably, it goes further: the two spheres of the human and divine are brought together, and the sovereign assumes the functions of a mediator between them, when he does not himself rise to the divine plane.

In this respect, there is an essential difference between the two great sources of civilization in the ancient Near East, Mesopotamia and Egypt. In Mesopotamia the king is a mediator, but a mediator who belongs to the human plane; and certain tendencies towards deification prove to be subsidiary and are not followed up. In Egypt, on the other hand, the king is a god descended among men. Hence the difference in the attitude to life: in Mesopotamia the constant anxiety, the fear lest the supreme will should remain uncomprehended and the harmony between the two spheres should be marred; in Egypt, a happy serenity, due to resignation to the predestined order which descends from on high without any break in the transmission.[5]

The relationship between monarchy and divinity, which is particularly intense in the regions with settled culture, has frequently led to the problem being viewed out of focus, concentrating only on this area. One should not underrate the different situation of the surrounding nomads, among whom the deification of the ruler and the absolute authority which it presupposes are greatly reduced. Whether he be the sheikh of tribal origin, controlled by a council of elders, or the elected leader of a restricted class of nobility, the nomad chief is very far from the ruler of a settled people. But it is a fact that the latter strongly attracts the former: for example, the Hittite sovereign of the New Empire differs from that of the Old by his adoption of the Egyptian divine symbol, and his own deification after death.

In this relationship between the divine and the human, Israel occupies a special position. The affirmation of the transcendence of the deity does not allow the king of Israel to exercise the function of mediator: what mediation can there be between two planes so distinct? Only fidelity and devotion to God are the laws of harmony. Thus the depreciation of the natural and human plane which we found proper to Israel has as its logical consequence a depression of the position of kingship also; moreover, this institution arises only out of special political circumstances, and never ceases to be regarded with aversion, or, at best, accepted only as a necessary evil.

IV Society

The progressive evolution of the historical events also marks the stages of the development of society from the most primitive conditions to those more advanced and organized.[6] In this sense, the ancient Orient is the mirror of a long and continuous transformation, with its critical moments inseparably associated with the turning points of history.

In the beginning, there is the life of the cave man, living in nomadic instability, procuring food by gathering the natural produce of the soil, and by the chase. Then the first villages make their appearance, and with them the rudimentary tools of incipient agriculture and the domestication of animals: in a word, the transition to settled forms of life.

Then the cities arise. Beyond doubt, as recent discoveries confirm, these existed in certain areas long before the beginning of history. But it is also true that in other areas the beginnings of history are definitely associated with the 'urban revolution'. The city community and the state give a collective character to the production of goods for consumption, and professional specialization takes shape: no longer are there only farmers, but merchants, officials, soldiers, priests. The theocratic monarchy is the centre towards which these categories gravitate.

But these categories are minorities. For some two thousand years, and so for the greater part of its history, the civilization of the ancient Orient comes within the copper or bronze age;[7] these metals are relatively rare and expensive, and their use, for tools or weapons, is within the reach of only a restricted political and religious upper class. The great majority of the citizens are excluded, and so do not share in the direction of social life, have few rights, and still less power. One can never insist too much on the fact that the history and the civilization of the ancient Orient are in great part the product of restricted elites, behind whom is an amorphous multitude, in whose life slavery plays a large part.

With the iron age, that is from about 1200 B.C. onward, the

use of metal spreads. Consequently the middle classes begin
to expand. When, towards the close of ancient Oriental history, coinage is introduced, a decisive stimulus is given to
trade, especially retail, and the relative class develops. At the
very end banks are set up and a financial system comes into
being. But now the classical world intervenes, and here ancient Oriental civilization comes to a close.

As we have hinted, the development of the elements and
tools of material culture has notable repercussions in the
course of history. Thus, the coming of the metal age coincides
with the beginning of history; the introduction of iron with
the invasion of the peoples of the sea; and within each phase
it is the material elements and tools, such as the Semitic bow
and arrows, or the swift war chariot of the mountain peoples, that bear decisively on the development of events. The
study of this aspect of Oriental civilizations has been no more
than outlined; but undoubtedly it will be fruitful of results,
and will set a number of facts and experiences in their proper
perspective.[8]

V *Religion*

Nevertheless, in the general run of existence, it is always the
conceptions and attitudes of a spiritual nature that seem to us
to guide the course of civilization in the ancient Orient.

First and foremost there is religion, which dominates and
interpenetrates every aspect of life. What is more, every aspect of life is shaped and motivated in accordance with the
religion. It is this unity in religious faith which again and
again appears as the dominant motive of Oriental civilizations.
This is the measuring rod of them all, to an extent unparal-
leled, it would seem, in any other civilization of ancient times:
we have to come down to the middle ages to find anything
comparable in our own world. Consider, for instance, the legal
institutions: religious and secular laws are mixed together
without distinction, and for the man of the ancient Orient
there is no sense in separating them, since they all spring from
the same authority. So, too, in regard to the sciences: astron-

omy and astrology interpenetrate, and the Oriental sees neither the need for nor any point in separating them. Similarly in respect to art: it is the handmaid of religion, and the Near East does not conceive of free artistic creation, art for art's sake. 'Render unto Caesar the things that are Caesar's, and unto God the things that are God's' is a criterion that has no place in the ancient Orient.

Even so, it would be superficial not to define more precisely, or not to make reservations with respect to, the absolute predominance of religion which has just been postulated. No one, perhaps, has put this problem better than the German scholar Schmökel, who in the course of describing Sumerian beliefs asks the questions:[9] What did the peasant think when he was continually torn from his plough and thrust into the arduous slave gangs organized for the erection of the temples of the gods? What did king Lugalzaggisi think when his conqueror Sargon put him in a cage before the temple of the very same god who previously, through his priests, had granted him rule over the Sumerians? We do not know, and probably never shall know. In other words, the religion we know is that of the restricted ruling class, the official state cult; we can penetrate very little beyond that into the religious world of the greater part of the people.

All this is true: but one might reply by pointing to the pilgrims whom Herodotus saw crowding the boats to go to the festival at Bubastis, with music and song; or the others of Papremis, who smote one another with maces, re-enacting the conflicts between the gods. The fact is that the question must be formulated differently: it is true that we do not know the degree to which individuals were attached to the religious life; but it is also true that official religion is accompanied by religion of a broadly popular nature, and that it is definitely on the traditional religious feeling of the people that the official cult is grafted and grows.

From the examination of ancient Oriental religions emerge certain aspects and conceptions which permeate and determine them from start to finish. In the first place, these religions are fundamentally naturalistic, based on the worship of cosmic forces. Heaven and earth and water are deified and given souls, and, as has been well said, are set as a 'Thou' before the 'I' which is man.[10] Divinity is also attributed to the stars, which, with time, regulate the course of life throughout the universe. The distinctive features of the divine forces are modelled on human ones: the macrocosm is adapted to the microcosm, and the gods love and hate and make mistakes. Thus the superhuman world acquires its own patrimony of events, which to a large extent are aetiological in origin, i.e. devised in order to explain the reason for everything that is in the universe, its laws and its destinies. This is the realm of mythology. We have come across various types of myth: the myth of the creation of the world; that of the origin of labour; that of the craving for immortality; that of the journey to the other world. But one towers above them all: the vegetation myth, conveyed in the figure of the god who dies and rises again, frequently with the addition of the figure of the mother goddess, symbol of the fruitful earth.[11]

But myth has no independent life in the ancient Orient. Before taking on literary form it is worship and ritual. The works of the gods are not presented as fantastic tales, but as real actions to which are joined those of men, who evoke and renew them dramatically. We can follow this interaction of myth and ritual particularly well in the two centres of ancient Oriental civilization, Egypt and Mesopotamia. Religious life is adapted to the cycle of the seasons, and its solemnities are basically those of seasonal change. The picture is dominated by fading and reflowering nature, the vegetation that dies and is revived. But between the two centres there is a profound difference, which we may call one of tone, and which directly arises out of opposing conceptions of the government of the universe. In Mesopotamia, where the king is a man, there is perhaps not one rite which does not reflect anxiety and fear, oscillation between pain and joy: because there is no certainty in the interpretation of the will of the gods and in man's conformity with that will. In Egypt, where a god is king, the rites have a basis of constant serenity: all is well, cannot be otherwise than well. Is it necessary to recall that fundamentally this difference of attitude reflects the different conditions of the two lands? Mesopotamia is open to invasion from the mountains and the desert, and depends for its life on uncertain rains and incalculable rivers; Egypt is cut off and protected by its desert, and nourished by a river whose floods never fail even though they vary in intensity and effectiveness.

Thus the essential object of all worship is the renewal and so the conservation of life. But in this respect, too, there is a profound difference between the two great valleys. In Mesopotamia the object is the life of nature, its fruitfulness, because the future of man is obscure, and the undeniable traces of a belief in survival present a predominantly unfavourable picture of the life to come as a wretched and distressful state of wandering. In Egypt, on the contrary, the life of nature and of man go together: the next life uninterruptedly continues that of this world with its peaceable and often joyous forms. The soul persists; the body is protected by mummification; the tomb is its home: it has been well said that the ancient Egyptian paradoxically denies the reality of death.[12]

Such a conception of man and the universe makes the large place occupied by divination and magic in religious life easily understandable; for when the law of existence is identified as the constant relation between the 'I' of man and the 'Thou' of deified nature — a 'Thou' which, although indeed more powerful than man, shares like characteristics with him — it is understandable that man should bend all his energies to the task of maintaining his side of that relationship, should apply his mind and the instruments which the 'Thou' itself offers him to the double purpose of comprehending and controlling its energies. Divination and magic are the extreme forms of the effort made to associate the different spheres of the universe; and it is reasonable that this effort should be greater — and the corresponding literary production more extensive — where that association is more uncertain, where distinction and uncertainty predominate.

Once more, in conclusion, we must draw attention to the circumstance that the foregoing considerations apply essentially to the principal representatives of ancient Oriental civilization. Outside their spheres, two different situations can be distinguished. To some extent there is an attitude which is

the same as — or if you will, imitated from — that of the
greater powers, but with a less accentuated degree of development, and with embryonic features because of the limited
possibilities; and there is no need to dwell on this aspect.
But to some extent we have an independent attitude, a reaction, a surpassing of the pre-existing positions. Ethical monotheism, which makes its appearance in Palestine and Iran,
overthrows the conception of the universe that prevails in the
two river valleys, severs the divine from the natural and
human plane, and attributes to it characteristics that do not
repeat but sublimate human ones, and so are opposed to
them. The nature cult declines, and the problem of cosmic
integration is absorbed into that of the superior divine will.
Even the bond of the state disappears: God in his absolute-
ness no longer knows any frontiers, cannot confine his attention to a single people, or share the government of the
universe with other deities.

At this point, religion being divorced from the state, it is
understandable that the attainment of its greatest heights is in
no way conditioned by political power. On the contrary, it
would seem that this last development of religion is in conflict
with the state, and becomes more and more an element pro-
voking crisis for it: just as Christianity, when it was established in Rome, led to Rome's crisis and fall.

VI *Literature*

The literatures of the ancient Orient present features which to
a large extent are found already formed and dominant in the
very earliest period of history. Those features are generally
valid for literature and art alike, and so for the arts in the
broad sense; this was only to be expected, since the two
activities both spring from the same spiritual realm.

The first feature is that of anonymity. Despite the great
number of works of the ancient Orient, an author's name is
known to us only in a very few and doubtful cases; and as by
comparison the copyists are mentioned more often, we must
conclude that the artist's creative personality was not accorded

the importance which it has in our own world. Next there is the relatively changeless quality of forms and themes; and since imitation and repetition are frequent from one text to another and even within the one text, and are not in any way dissimulated, we must conclude that creative originality was not the chief aim of artistic activity, as it is with us.

As we have seen, both these characteristics have their roots in a conception of art not as the subjective creation of the individual, but as the collective manifestation of the community. The artist is rather a craftsman, who works to order and must follow his model as far as possible, avoiding personal touches and innovations.

But in that case what is the object of this art? It has a practical and not an aesthetic purpose: the official expression of political power and religious faith; or rather, since in the ancient Orient the two terms are not essentially distinct, of faith in its political and religious manifestations. So there is no conception of art as an end in itself, of aesthetic striving as such, nor is art set apart as a problem in itself, as is the case in Greece.

The fact that art in our sense is nevertheless achieved is another matter; and it is also another matter that, without being explicitly aware of it, the Oriental, like the Greek artists, often feel within themselves that artistic will which is the essential motive force of creation. But this must be borne in mind if we are to understand how it is that, despite every fetter and impediment, despite the very lack of awareness, art in our sense of the word comes into being in more than one area of the ancient Near East; for certain artistic personalities are too strong to allow themselves to be constricted by traditional schemes, even with their own consent. It would seem that in the literary field this occurs above all in Egypt, for we find there more outstanding personalities, more development is to be discerned in form and subject, and even the religious unity is breached in more than one place to allow the emergence of new literary forms such as love songs and banquet songs, historical romances and tales of fantasy. It would appear that we must not regard this as a sign of a definite consciousness of art, but rather as the instinctive self-expression of an aesthetic spirit that was none the less living for not being worked out in theory.

Passing to consideration of the various literary genres, we draw attention first and foremost to the great extension of epico-mythological poetry, relating the affairs of gods and heroes. Taken as a whole, this poetry seems to have its main centre of irradiation in Mesopotamia, where it is present and flourishing from the beginning, and whence its themes spread to the outer world, especially northward to Anatolia. Mythology is present in Egypt, but for the most part it is scattered in writings of a different kind; and hero epic is entirely lacking, owing to the absence of the theme fundamental to this type of poetry: namely, the struggle with death.

The main themes of epico-mythological poetry are the creation of the world, the future life, and the vegetation cycle: in other words, the origins, ends, and laws of the universe. The solution of these problems in the realm of mythology corresponds to a general attitude of ancient Oriental thought, the characteristics and limits of which will be considered later. As for the heroes, as we have just said, the predominant theme is the problem of death. Why is man fated to die and is unable to escape this fate? The solution is given in narrative form: it is an error, a misunderstanding, within the framework of the divine will. But it is not a fault: the conception of death as the consequence of moral guilt arises only among those peoples who regard morality as the fundamental characteristic of the deity. Of course, a large quantity of epic poetry is taken up with the feats of the heroes: and above them all towers the figure of Gilgamesh, an anticipation of Hercules, who finds his way from Mesopotamia into the literatures and even more the artistic themes of the surrounding world.

Lyric poetry is another literary genre, with a strong orientation towards religious themes. As the range of subjects may easily vary in accordance with the conceptions which are formulated in each area, this type of poetry spreads extensively over the whole of the ancient Orient, and is the one form which is found everywhere. Without going into minor details, we may mention the two great categories of hymns and prayers to the gods, which include the themes of lamentation, relief, gratitude, and praise. The classification into personal and collective lyric, justly applied in the case of Israel, may be extended with advantage to other peoples. There are also lyrics dedicated to kings, whose relationship with the sphere of the divine is particularly close, though it admits of various degrees. But this does not occur where the scission between the divine and human planes is complete, i.e. in Israelite and Zoroastrian thought.

There is no lyrical poetry outside the religious sphere (apart from the controversial question of the Song of Songs) except in Egypt. Here secular themes flourish in the genres of love song and banquet song. Neither the one nor the other has any intrinsic or extrinsic religious connection: instead they exhibit an independent, extremely tolerant and varied conception of life such as one would expect from the distinctive character of the Egyptian people.

A characteristic literary composition, the lament over fallen cities, can be treated as an appendix to lyrical poetry. Examples are found in Mesopotamia and Israel. It is lacking elsewhere, and although this can sometimes be attributed to the absence of discovered texts, on other occasions the historical and political conditions hardly accord with this type of composition: it would be surprising to find it in Egypt or Iran, for instance.

The didactic or wisdom type of literature is widely developed. It is composed of a number of subtypes which may be summarized as: reflections on life, proverbs, maxims, fables, the problem of the righteous man's sufferings, the problem of human sorrow. This literature has a parallel, and so far as we can see, independent development in Mesopotamia and Egypt; it is found again in Israel; but so far it has not been found among other peoples, if we except the Ahiqar romance, of disputed origin.

A subtle question which we have already mentioned is that of the congeniality of this type of literature to local mentality. It must be pointed out that, so far as its content is concerned, part of this literature does not accord well with the conception of the universe, and especially the religious outlook, of the peoples among whom it appears. It is true that here and there adaptations and combinations have been made; but this only shifts the problem without solving it. We would rather say that the ancient Oriental mind does not seem to have felt the need to fit its reflections on life systematically into its system of religious faith; it seems instead to have given free rein to these reflections from time to time, with the result that their themes have been handed down and given more permanence in literary forms. But where the organizing activity is stronger, as in Israel, harmonization is achieved, and the expressions of doubt or scepticism are concluded by a profession of faith in the order established from above.

In the ancient Oriental literatures history is represented by lists arranged according to dynasties, sovereigns, or years; by annals; and by commemorative inscriptions. But all this is only chronicling, unsupported by an organic vision of events in terms of cause and effect. This vision — which is the basis of true history — seems to us to have been realized in only two sectors of the ancient Near East, and these neither the principal nor the oldest ones, i.e. among the Hittites and in Israel. The Hittites' attitude to historical thought is truly remarkable: first and foremost in their annals, where inquiry into cause and effect is pursued to the extent of weighing one's own intentions and those of others; and also in several texts which form a class apart and are very distinctive in their nature and value, such as the 'testament' of Hattusilis I and the autobiography of Hattusilis III. The political treaties, with their preambles, also reveal and exemplify the historical causal process. A flourishing historiography comes into existence in an entirely different form in Israel. Here the point of departure is a religious one. The new conception of political power allows a free and detached consideration and judgement of the events and chief actors in history, including the kings themselves, from the aspect of their fidelity or otherwise to the religious and moral covenant with God. From this starting point a historiography develops which at times, especially in the account of David's reign, achieves a very acute sifting of events.

It is a remarkable fact that for all the high level of their culture, neither the Egyptians nor the Mesopotamians achieved anything of this kind. In spite of the diligent search that has been made through all their varied literary production,[13] they would seem to lack an organized capacity for judging historically.

Another form of prose, namely narrative, appears in Egypt, in two forms: the tale founded on fact and the imaginative novel. The former type also exists in Aramaic, in the romance of Ahiqar; but even in this case the texts come from Egypt. This literary form is mainly secular, at least in origin, and that explains why it develops in the region which shows most independence in this field. Nevertheless, it is not easy to separate the profane from the sacred, and other peoples of the ancient Orient — namely, the Hittites and even more the Hurrians — have left works which come very close to the imaginative narrative form, though on the other hand they are connected with mythological epic.

Running rapidly over the remaining, not strictly literary production, we make a few observations, as usual, on Oriental laws. In Mesopotamia, these, though in the form of case law and not arranged according to principles, take the literary form of the legal code, and as such extend to the surrounding world. Hittite legislation is of the same type, with certain thematic innovations. Israelite legislation adopts some of this material, but colours it with its new religious outlook, and adds a series of absolute prescriptions to the case law. Finally, Egypt has no legal codes whatever, and if this is not mere chance, which it is difficult to suppose, the reason is to be sought in the living source of law represented by the god-king.

Astronomy, mathematics, medicine, and other sciences to a lesser degree, thrive in the principal centres of the area: the two river valleys. Is this phenomenon to be interpreted as exhibiting a capacity for scientific thought in the sense in which we understand the term? It is objected that astronomy and mathematics are inseparable from astrology, medicine from magical practices. But it is all a question of degree of development. Both astronomical and mathematical calculations and medical diagnoses and prescriptions undoubtedly exist: is there much point in asking whether the men who worked them out and drew them up were or were not aware that they were doing scientific work? They did it in fact, even if they had no theoretical conception of it as such. It should rather be said that it was precisely this theoretical realization that they lacked: there was thought, but no reflection on thought. For that we have to wait for Greece.

In conclusion, the literature of the ancient Orient has two principal centres of production and irradiation: Mesopotamia and Egypt. Comparing the two, we may say that Mesopotamia has more expansive force, but Egypt is less dependent on the mentality of the environment, is more original and perhaps, from the purely aesthetic viewpoint, has the greater value. As for the rest of the Near East, the Anatolian area is mainly dependent upon Mesopotamia, but has original aspects especially in the fields of history and law. The Syrian area is partly dependent and subordinate, at the meeting point of the Mesopotamian and Egyptian currents; but in Israel it achieves an independence of conceptual thought which is directly due to the new religious thinking. A similar thing happens in Iran.

VII *Arts*

Obviously, what was said above of the arts in the broad sense holds true of them in the stricter sense. Indeed, it may be said that even more than literature they exhibit the characteristics we have already indicated, of being official and public, in the service of political power and religious faith.

In this sphere also Egypt repeats and emphasizes its points of difference. The names of a few artists emerge from the general obscurity; there is a development of art, at times very noticeable, instead of the static quality which prevails elsewhere; and finally, private life enters into the range of subjects. From here it is only a short step to greater artistic value; and undoubtedly, judged by absolute aesthetic standards, the highest artistic levels in the ancient Orient are found in the Nile valley.

The fundamental problems of religious architecture are the temple and the tomb: the latter has especial importance in

Egypt, because of the greater development of the corresponding beliefs. In civil architecture the problems are the royal palace and the fortress: the latter is more important in the regions which are exposed to invasion and which retain the political form of the city state longer.

The solution of these problems is dependent primarily on the difference in materials. In Mesopotamia, especially in the south, the chief material is clay brick dried in the sun: the walls built of these bricks are unbroken and massive, without windows, which would have weakened their structure. In other regions stone is plentiful; so it becomes possible to exploit the column as a functional part of the structure, to insert windows, which have no detrimental effect on the wall, and so to achieve a less massive structure.

These being the different means available for the solution of the problems, the forms which the solution takes are various; attention may be drawn to certain fundamental ones. In Mesopotamia the plan of construction is usually the central courtyard, or more than one courtyard, with the rooms distributed around and opening on to them. In Egypt the chief form of construction is a forecourt, leading to a pillared hall and then to closed chambers; this scheme persists in its numerous variants, in so far as the more open continue to precede the more closed parts as one passes through the edifice. The form provided with an anterior hypostyle hall continues down to the religious architecture of Syria and Anatolia and even Assyria, and finally to the civil architecture of Iran.

Statuary is not always plentiful or even existent in the ancient Orient, so far as large-scale work is concerned. In Mesopotamia, in particular, it is rendered difficult by the scarcity of stone; but another reason is that for dedicatory purposes reduced proportions are sufficient. As for statuary of the human form, it must be pointed out that some regions, Anatolia, Israelite Palestine, Iran, are almost or entirely lacking in this type, at least so far as our present knowledge goes. In the case of Israel there must be a religious reason for this, but there is no such satisfactory explanation in the other cases. Only Egypt may be said to provide statuary without restriction.

The subjects of the statuary of the human form are gods and kings, the chief figures of official life. Sometimes high functionaries are included, especially in Egypt; finally, only Egypt produces statues of private persons, while Mesopotamia has only dedicatory statuettes.

In regard to the manner in which the subjects are presented, it is well to recall the principle which was brought out with respect to Egypt, but which may be applied to the rest of the Orient: sculpture, which in the Western world may be classified as predominantly 'narrative', is here 'presentative'; in other words, it does not answer the need to depict an action, but that of establishing a state. The gods and kings are represented motionless, posed in erect or seated positions, in attitudes of majestic serenity. Such a convention may easily lead to uniformity and possibly monotony. This does occur, in fact, to a greater degree in Mesopotamia, and to a lesser degree in Egypt, in conformity with the characteristics of the two areas.

As we have already pointed out, the regularity in the style of the figures is reduced to system by a geometrical canon. The masses are formed on the principle of some solid figure, in Mesopotamia chiefly the cylinder or the cone, in Egypt the cube or the parallelepiped. There is a tendency to arrange the members in this form, and for this reason, for instance, the arms remain constantly pressed against the body in the Mesopotamian statues. The canon is further favoured by the official nature of the art, which eschews non-public themes and attitudes other than poses.

Although the facial features are sometimes accurately reproduced, the human body is not subjected to analysis comparable with that which will be attained later, in Greece. The nude is most avoided or restricted. The clothing is stiff, nor is there the capacity for reproducing drapery and folds which the Greeks will achieve.

The canons governing the human figure are stricter in Mesopotamia than in Egypt, where there is a constant and lively observation of nature. Yet these canons persist, and are relaxed only in the animal figures: in this branch Mesopotamia achieves a standard in no way inferior to that of any

other area. Fantastic creatures figure largely in the animal
and semi-animal sphere. Some types are reduced to schematic
form, e.g. the sphinx in Egypt, the human-headed winged
bull in Mesopotamia. This latter figure is frequently found
in those distinctive sculptures known as orthostats, midway
between statuary and relief: set in pairs at the gates of cities
and palaces, they form one of the most typical features of
the art of ancient Western Asia.

The bas-relief is an artistic genre widely diffused in the
Near East, and in its themes it is closely allied with painting,
so far as we can judge from the remains which have survived in the latter case. In no area is relief completely absent;
and even where figurative art is avoided, in Israel, relief is
represented by the minor ornamental forms of art.

The subjects of relief carving embrace every form of political and religious public life. In particular military enterprises are largely represented, on the walls of the royal palaces
in Mesopotamia, on the walls and pillars of temples in Egypt;
and at times the representation achieves not merely decorative but properly documentary value.

Scenes of religious life are also very numerous, but this is
not the place to detail their themes. Yet we must point out
the extensive place given in Egypt to private life in the subjects of relief carving and even more of painting; this is an
unusual phenomenon, in view of the general features of
Oriental art, and all the more remarkable because it is found
especially in the tombs. The object is definitely a religious
one, but the subjects are not any the less secular and individual because of that.

As we know, in relief carving and painting the artist is
faced with the problem of representing three-dimensional
figures on a single plane surface. There is no perspective,
and so the figures are juxtaposed on the one plane, each being given the dimensions considered appropriate to it; no
reduction is made to convey the idea of distance. We have
said that this practice is associated with a 'cerebral' artistic
outlook, which presents objects as they are and not as they
appear to be. Although even in Egypt perspective is not

achieved, there a greater approximation to reality is obtained
by the restriction of figures predominantly to the one plane.
Artistic 'cerebralism' also accounts for the custom, characteristic in Mesopotamia and in the areas under its influence,
but also known in Egypt, of graduating the size of persons
in accordance with their status.

The elements of the figures are governed by strict conventions, which are adhered to with noteworthy constancy: the
face in profile, the eye and shoulders viewed frontally, the
pelvis in three-quarter view, the limbs in profile. Probably
these conventions arise from the determination to character-
ize the figure in the most efficacious fashion.

Minor arts flourish all through the ancient Orient. The
Mesopotamian seal, with its surprisingly fine workmanship,
is diffused over a wide area, and its cylindrical form prevails
over the flat stamp type found in Anatolia and Iran. The
ivories, of which the finest examples are found in Mesopotamia and Syria, are small-scale reproductions of the art of
relief. The bronzes, present all over the Near Eastern area,
attain and often surpass, even in their reduced dimensions,
the standard of the stone statuary. Wooden objects of accurate workmanship are to be found, from statues to furniture, especially in Egypt. Finally, the finest glassware is found
in Egypt and Phoenicia.

We would say, in conclusion, that in art the centres of
irradiation and the zones of influence broadly correspond to
those indicated for literature. But there are several diver-
gencies to be noted. Of the two centres which created the
new religious thought, Israel and Iran, neither has a parallel
artistic development. In the case of Israel this is the result
of an explicit refusal, while in the case of Iran it is because
in this respect she adapted herself to the models of the surrounding world, though she brings to them her capacity for
synthesis and her decorative talent. Therefore Mesopotamia
and Egypt prevail here even more than elsewhere. Moreover, Egypt is no longer closed in on herself, but exerts on
her neighbours an influence that equals and counterbalances
that of Mesopotamia.

VIII The 'Intellectual Adventure'

The complex historical, religious, literary and artistic world which we have been describing constitutes an immense bloc, existing on the very threshold of the classical age. We do not intend to go in detail into what is already well known of the connections between the two areas. It is well known that the East gave the West the very means by which culture is expressed and transmitted: namely, the alphabet. It is well known that the East was the birthplace of many of the legends and myths which have been handed on to us by Greece, and, with them, of the corresponding conceptions concerning man and his destiny. Finally, it is well known that the religious beliefs of the East, from the vegetation cycle to the Iranian dualism of good and evil, were quickly reflected in the Western world, till a religion originating in Palestine overthrew and dominated them all.

One might continue the list; but it is better to dwell on what the most recent studies reveal:[14] namely, on the one hand a literary and mythological patrimony — for instance the sources of the Hesiodic theogony — which irradiates from the East towards Greece; on the other, besides the well-known Phoenician sea route, the route of transmission which is now being traced even more to Anatolia. For here Oriental civilization, which in the Hittites summarized the vast heritage of the hinterland, was in constant contact with the Greek colonies on the coast.

Above all, there is the fact that the civilizations of the ancient Orient are more and more being revealed as a tremendous human experience, which has a value for posterity, not only through its individual contributions as such, but as an experience without which another, subsequent civilization would not be conceivable. The problem now is whether this experience can be defined, and in what manner; or, to return to our terminology, whether there is an isoid above all the many that have already been found, and if so, what it is, that sums up the thought of the ancient Orient.

The problem might seem naïve, and would be so in fact, if it were raised in terms of a search for an element common to all the Oriental world and, contrariwise, foreign to all the West. But it is not naïve if it is based on the search for the limits of one culture in face of the further development of a later culture; a search for the questions posed by one epoch, and the answers it gave them, as compared with the questions and answers of the subsequent epoch.

In any case, the problem was raised not many years ago, by a group of American scholars, in the book entitled *The Intellectual Adventure of Ancient Man*.[15] So we may take this book as our starting point, just as we have used its title as the heading to the present observations.

The authors write that Oriental thought is, to use their own word, mythopoeic, in other words, myth-making. Confronted with the universe, the Oriental regards it as animate, endowed with an intelligence and will like his own. Hence cosmic events are the meeting of two groups of wills, and the action and reaction that follow: in a word, myth. The river does not rise to its full height? It has refused to rise; it is angry at some fault man has committed, and must be appeased. Are the clouds growing blacker? A gigantic bird has covered the sky with its wings. There is no independent rational thought, there is no distinction between science and myth: the imagination veils the intellect, tinges it with fancy, will not let it conceive on its own. Only Israel reacts against myth; but it creates its own myth of its God entering into a covenant with the people. Not until the age of the Greeks does reason establish its independence.

We have already had occasion to discuss several points of this thesis; looking once more at it as a whole, we think it does not merit all the unfavourable criticism which it has undergone in certain quarters.[16] Critics have said that the extensive development of exact sciences such as astronomy, mathematics, and medicine reveals indubitable powers of ratiocination: and this is true, as we have already said, because, no matter how they were applied, positive scientific results were achieved. They have also said that rather than the natural elements themselves it was the forces that presided over those elements that were deified: the sky god rather than the god Sky, the river god rather than the god River; and this also is true in part. But in our opinion another objection is of less force, namely that the absence of metaphysical and theological writings as literary genres does not mean that these sciences did not have an extensive existence. For we think it difficult to suppose that an entire sector of intellectual activity was omitted from the written tradition, so that no trace of it has come down to us, or that the tradition itself, no matter how partial and incomplete it may be in quantity, must likewise be assumed to be incomplete in quality.

We think the problem needs to be stated differently, in accordance with the principles which we have already enunciated. The description of the Oriental mentality as myth-making seems defensible as a generalization, provided we exclude Israelite and Zoroastrian thought, which in the religious sphere unmistakably reacts against myth. But even granted this exclusion, the myth-making character is not to be understood as eliminating rational thought, but as including it in a higher unity. The Oriental is not unable to think rationally, but he feels no need to isolate reason as an independent faculty and theorize it as such.

When myth passes to Greece it does not disappear; on the contrary, it reaches its highest levels. But alongside it philosophical thought progressively takes shape as independent rational reflection on the universe. Although itself tinged in more than one point with fantasy and myth – is not Plato the best of examples? – it nevertheless attains independence in other points. This comes about on the one hand with the postulation of principles of an intellectual order in the universe – being and becoming – and on the other in epistemology and logic, the reflections which thought makes on itself. This is something really new by comparison with the ancient Orient, where the Socratic concept and Aristotelian logic would have been inconceivable.

Therefore there is not any revolution or scission between East and West, but continuity of development. And because of this continuity, at a certain point new elements make their appearance in the West, and as such these can be contrasted with the lack of them in the East. These elements are Greek philosophy and the manifold aspects of the conception of the universe appertaining to that philosophy or associated with it.

When Greek civilization comes into flower, the Near East has thousands of years of history behind it. Its cultural patrimony, and even its scientific knowledge, are crystallized in the forms of a sacred tradition. The Near East has neither the power nor the will to shatter these forms. But, while taking over the results of the culture, the Greeks, who are outsiders, do not tie themselves down to the forms in which those results are entangled, and in which the Greek mind does not see any point. They take over the elements, but do not take over the shackles. Consequently they are able to go farther, to create a civilization in which the old material is supplemented with new material and new genius. This is the 'wonder that was Greece'. No one, perhaps, has expressed it more admirably and simply than the ancient author who wrote:

'Whatever the Greeks take over from foreigners, they transform it by making it something finer.'[17]

NOTES

(*From the Tablets of Sumer,* by S. N. Kramer, as cited below, is available in the Anchor series under the title HISTORY BEGINS AT SUMER.)

CHAPTER 1

1. The story of the discovery is told by C. Virolleaud, *La légende phénicienne de Daniel,* Paris 1936, pp. 1–5. Accounts of the excavations are published from time to time in the review *Syria.*

2. Cf. the account in A. Parrot, *Mari, une ville perdue . . . ,* Paris 1945. Information on the pre-war excavations is given by C.-F. Jean, *Six campagnes de fouilles à Mari 1933–1939. Synthèse des résultats,* Tournai–Paris 1952. Reports of subsequent excavations are published from time to time in *Syria.*

3. This the the most authoritative account of the facts, as given by G. Lankester Harding in *The Times* of August 9, 1949.

4. Cf. R. de Langhe, *Les textes de Ras Shamra-Ugarit et leurs rapports avec le milieu biblique de l'Ancien Testament,* 2 vols., Paris-Gembloux 1945; C. F.-A. Schaeffer, *Ugaritica I–III,* Paris 1939–56.

5. The edition and translation of the Mari texts is being carried out by G. Dossin, C.-F. Jean, J. R. Kupper, and J. Bottéro, with the title *Archives royales de Mari;* so far they have published eight volumes of the cuneiform text (Paris 1941–57) and seven of transliteration and translation (Paris 1950–7); also a *Répertoire analytique des tomes I–V* has been issued by J. Bottéro and A. Finet (Paris 1954). A fine photographic documentation is provided in A. Parrot, *Mari. Documentation photographique de la mission archéologique de Mari,* Neuchâtel–Paris 1953.

6. Other factors, too, have contributed to the determination of the new chronology, principally the new list of the Assyrian kings found at Khorsabad: cf. P. van der Meer, *The Chronology of Ancient Western Asia and Egypt,* ed. 2, Leiden 1955. The present book follows the so-called 'short' chronology, whereby Hammurabi is dated 1728–1686 and other dates are adjusted accordingly. It must be noted, however, that the system which puts back the dating by 64 years (Hammurabi 1792–1750) also has considerable probability or even more. Cf. lastly in favour of the 'long' chro-

nology A. Goetze, *On the Chronology of the Second Millennium B.C.*, in *Journal of Cuneiform Studies*, 11 (1957), pp. 53–61, 63–73 (this article came to my notice too late for use in the present book).

7. On the scrolls cf. M. Burrows, *The Dead Sea Scrolls*, New York 1955; G. Vermès, *Discovery in the Judaean Desert. The Dead Sea Scrolls and Their Meaning*, New York 1956; T. H. Gaster, *The Dead Sea Scriptures in English Translation*, New York 1956.

8. Bibliographical indications will be found in the notes to the section of this chapter dealing with pre-history.

9. Cf. L. Woolley, *A Forgotten Kingdom*, Harmondsworth 1953, and *Alalakh*, London 1956; D. J. Wiseman, *The Alalakh Tablets*, London 1953.

10. Cf. J. Nougayrol, *Le palais royal d'Ugarit III–IV*, Paris 1955–6.

11. Cf. E. Szlechter, *Le code de Lipit-Ištar*, in *Revue d'assyriologie*, 51 (1957), pp. 57–82, 177–96; A. Goetze, *The Laws of Eshnunna*, New Haven 1956; E. Szlechter, *Le code d'Ur-Nammu*, in *Revue d'assyriologie*, 49 (1955), pp. 169–77.

12. Cf. of recent date M. E. L. Mallowan, *The Excavations at Nimrud (Kalḫu), 1956*, in *Iraq*, 19 (1957), pp. 1–25, Articles on the excavations, with fine photographs, have frequently appeared in the *Illustrated London News*.

13. Cf., for example, F. Cornelius, *Geschichte des Alten Orients*, Stuttgart–Köln 1950; W. J. Awdijew, *Geschichte des Alten Orients*, Berlin 1953.

14. So, for example, A. Scharff, A. Moortgat, *Ägypten und Vorderasien im Altertum*, München 1950.

15. Cf., for example, P. Jouguet, J. Vandier, G. Contenau, E. Dhorme, A. Aymard, F. Chapoutier, R. Grousset, *Les premières civilisations*, ed. 2, Paris 1950; H. R. Hall, *The Ancient History of the Near East. From the Earliest Times to the Battle of Salamis*, ed. 11, London 1950; A. Scharff, A. Moortgat. cit. n. 14, Ch. 1; W. J. Awdijew, cit. n. 13, Ch. 1; H. Schmökel, *Geschichte des alten Vorderasien (Handbuch der Orientalistik*, II, 3), Leiden 1957.

16. Cf., for example, L. Delaporte, *Les peuples de l'Orient méditerranéen. I. Le Proche-Orient asiatique*, ed. 3, Paris 1948.

17. Cf., for example, F. Cornelius, cit. n. 13, Ch. 1.

18. Cf. the writer's *Ancient Semitic Civilizations*, London 1957, and *Chi furono Semiti?*, Roma 1957.

19. Cf. A. Meillet, M. Cohen, *Les langues du monde*, ed. 2, Paris 1952, pp. 86–8. In the Hamito-Semitic group the independent Semitic branch is not confronted with an equally homogeneous Hamitic one, but by three branches on a like footing with regard to one another and to Semitic: Egyptian, Berber, and Cushitic.

20. On the anthropology of the Near East cf. H. Field, *Ancient and Modern Man in Southwestern Asia*, Coral Gables 1956.

21. Cf. T. Jacobsen, *The Assumed Conflict Between Sumerians and Semites in Early Mesopotamian History*, in *Journal of the American Oriental Society*, 59 (1939), pp. 485–95.

22. For a general account cf. H. Frankfort, *The Birth of Civilization in the Near East*, London 1951.

23. Cf. D. A. E. Garrod, D. M. A. Bate, *The Stone Age of Mount Carmel*, I, Oxford 1937.

24. Cf. R. J. Braidwood, *The Near East and the Foundations for Civilization*, Eugene (Oregon) 1953; L. Braidwood, *Digging Beyond the Tigris*, New York 1953. On the latest discoveries: R. J. Braidwood, *The World's First Farming Villages*, in *Illustrated London News* of April 28, 1956, pp. 410–11; R. S. Solecki, *Shanidar Cave*, in *Sumer*, 11 (1955), pp. 14–38 and 124.

25. Cf. D. A. E. Garrod, D. M. A. Bate, cit. n. 23, Ch. 1.

26. Cf. H. Frankfort (cit. n. 22, Ch. 1), pp. 35–6.

27. Cf. V. Gordon Childe, *New Light on the Most Ancient East*, London 1952, and *What Happened in History*, Harmondsworth 1954, pp. 1–112.

28. Cf. R. J. Braidwood, *The World's First Farming Villages*, cit. n. 24, Ch. 1.

29. Cf. M. Wheeler, *Walls of Jericho*, London 1956; K. Kenyon, *Digging up Jericho*, London 1957.

30. This method, which is revolutionizing archaeology, is based on the fact that a special radio-active variety of carbon, called from its atomic weight carbon 14, is present in every organic substance in a constant proportion to the ordinary carbon 12. After the death of the tissue, the carbon 14 gradually degenerates, at the rate of 50 per cent in 5,500 years approximately, into carbon 12, which remains unaltered. Consequently the proportion of carbon 14 to carbon 12 furnishes an indication of the antiquity of any substance of organic origin. This method, the invention of Dr. Libby of Chicago (cf. W. F. Libby, *Radiocarbon Dating*, ed. 2, Chicago 1955), allows datings up to 20,000 or 30,000 years back with a margin of error of scarcely 200 years. It is announced, however, that Prof. J. A. Arnold, also of Chicago, has devised an improvement which allows dating up to 44,000 years back with a margin of error of 37 years: cf. G. E. Wright, *A New Atomic Clock*, in *Biblical Archaeologist*, 17 (1954), p. 47. For a recent account of the question cf. R. Pittioni, *Der Beitrag der Radiokarbon-Methode zur absoluten Datierung urzeitlichen Quellen*, in *Forschungen und Fortschritte*, 31 (1957), pp. 357–74.

31. Cf. R. J. Braidwood, L. Lloyd, F. Safar, *Tell Hassuna*, in *Journal of Near Eastern Studies*, 4 (1945), pp. 255–89.

32. Cf. R. J. Braidwood, L. Braidwood, J. G. Smith, C. Leslie, *Matarra: a Southern Variant of the Hassunan Assemblage, Excavated in 1948*, in *Journal of Near Eastern Studies*, 11 (1952), pp. 1–75.

33. Cf. A. L. Perkins, *The Comparative Archaeology of Early Mesopotamia*, Chicago 1949; A. Parrot, *Archéologie mésopotamienne*, II. *Technique et problèmes*, Paris 1953, pp. 105–331.

34. Cf. E. Herzfeld, *Die Ausgrabungen von Samarra*, V. *Die*

vorgeschichtlichen Töpfereien von Samarra, Berlin 1930; R. J. Braidwood, L. S. Braidwood, E. Tulane, A. L. Perkins, *New Chalcolithic Material of Samarran Type and Its Implications*, in *Journal of Near Eastern Studies*, 3 (1944), pp. 47–72.

35. Cf. A. Scharff, *Die Frühkulturen Ägyptens und Mesopotamiens*, Leipzig 1941; H. Frankfort (cit. n. 22, Ch. 1), pp. 100–11; H. J. Kantor, *Further Evidence for Early Mesopotamian Relations with Egypt*, in *Journal of Near Eastern Studies*, 11 (1952), pp. 239–50.

36. P. Gilbert, *Synchronismes artistiques entre Egypte et Mésopotamie de la période thinite à la fin de l'Ancien Empire égyptien*, in *Chronique d'Egypte*, 52 (1951), pp. 225–36.

37. Cf. S. Schott, *Hieroglyphen. Untersuchungen zum Ursprung der Schrift*, Wiesbaden 1951; J. M. A. Janssen, *Hiërogliefen*, Leiden 1952. On the origin of writing in general: D. Diringer, *The Alphabet*, London 1948; J. G. Février, *Histoire de l'écriture*, Paris 1949; I. J. Gelb, *A Study of Writing*, London 1952; G. R. Driver, *Semitic Writing from Pictograph to Alphabet*, ed. 2, London 1954.

CHAPTER 2

1. On the Sumerians in general cf. H. Schmökel, *Das Land Sumer*, ed. 2, Stuttgart 1956; S. N. Kramer, *From the Tablets of Sumer*, Indian Hills 1956: French edition, *L'histoire commence à Sumer*, Paris 1957.

2. On Sumerian history: M. Lambert, *La période présargonique*, in *Sumer*, 8 (1952), pp. 57–77, 198–216; 9 (1953), pp. 198–213; 10 (1954), pp. 150–90; H. Schmökel, *Geschichte des alten Vorderasien* (cit. n. 15, Ch. 1), pp. 1–69.

3. Cf. E. A. Speiser, *The Sumerian Problem Reviewed*, in *Hebrew Union College Annual*, 23, 1 (1950–1), pp. 339–55. Speiser maintains that the Sumerians' arrival in Mesopotamia is to be dated at the end of the fourth millennium before Christ, and that they came by sea, from the east. A different view is taken by S. N. Kramer (cit. n. 1, Ch. 2), pp. 238–48: namely that the Sumerians came from the mountains of the east, and imposed themselves upon a previous Iranian-Semitic population.

4. T. Jacobsen, *Primitive Democracy in Ancient Mesopotamia*, in *Journal of Near Eastern Studies*, 2 (1943), p. 172.

5. Cf. I. M. Djakonov, *Gosudarstvennyj stroj drevnejshego Shumera*, in *Vestnik drevnej istorii*, 40, 2 (1952), pp. 13–37.

6. Cf. T. Jacobsen, *The Sumerian King List*, Chicago 1939; E. A. Speiser, *Ancient Mesopotamia*, in R. C. Dentan (ed.), *The Idea of History in the Ancient Near East*, New Haven 1955, pp. 35–76.

7. Cf. G. A. Barton, *The Royal Inscriptions of Sumer and Akkad*, New Haven 1929, pp. 2–3, to which work subsequent references will be made. The ancient Sumerian and Akkadian inscriptions have been published also by F. Thureau-Dangin, *Die sumerischen und akkadischen Königsinschriften*, Leipzig 1907.

8. A complete and up-to-date edition of the royal inscriptions of Lagash is given by E. Sollberger, *Corpus des inscriptions 'royales' présargoniques de Lagaš*, Genève 1956.

9. Cf. S. N. Kramer, *Sumerian Historiography*, in *Israel Exploration Journal*, 3 (1953), pp. 217–32.

10. Ibid., p. 217.

11. G. A. Barton (cit. n. 7, Ch. 2), pp. 80–5.

12. Cf. M. Lambert, *Les 'réformes' d'Urukagina*, in *Revue d'assyriologie*, 5 (1956), pp. 169–84.

13. G. A. Barton (cit. n. 7, Ch. 2), pp. 90–1.

14. Ibid., pp. 98–9.

15. G. A. Barton (cit. n. 7, Ch. 2), pp. 214–17.

16. Ibid., pp. 182–3.

17. Cf. E. Szlechter, *Le code d'Ur-Nammu*, cit. n. 11, Ch. 1.

18. The results of the excavations are published in the series of volumes entitled *Ur Excavations*, appearing from 1927 on, by various authors.

19. For general expositions, cf. C.-F. Jean, *La religion sumérienne d'après les documents sumériens antérieurs à la dynastie d'Isin*, Paris 1931; N. Schneider, *Die Religion der Sumerer und Akkader*, in F. König, *Christus und die Religionen der Erde*, II, Wien 1951, pp. 383–439.

20. Cf. T. Fisch, *One Aspect of the Sumerian Character*, in *Sumer*, 10 (1954), pp. 113–15.

21. Recently a new Sumerian vegetation-cycle text has been deciphered: cf. T. Jacobsen, S. N. Kramer, *The Myth of Inanna and Bilulu*, in *Journal of Near Eastern Studies*, 12 (1953), pp. 160–88.

22. Cf. A. Falkenstein, *Die Haupttypen der sumerischen Beschwörung*, Leipzig 1931, pp. 83–7.

23. Cf. F. Thureau-Dangin, *La passion du dieu Lillu*, in *Revue d'assyriologie*, 19 (1922), pp. 182–3.

24. H. and H. A. Frankfort, J. A. Wilson, T. Jacobsen, W. A. Irwin, *The Intellectual Adventure of Ancient Man*, Chicago 1943, p. 186.

25. H. Frankfort (cit. n. 22, Ch. 1), pp. 61–3. Cf. also A. Falkenstein, *La citétemple sumérienne*, in *Cahiers d'histoire mondiale*, 1 (1954), pp. 784–814.

26. An excellent general outline is that of S. N. Kramer, *Brief aperçu concernant les restes littéraires sumériens*, in *Scientia*, 86 (1951), pp. 99–109. (The various texts are examined in detail by the same author in *From the Tablets of Sumer*, cit. n. 1, Ch. 2).

27. Mention must be made of the chronological investigation of Sumerian literature initiated by Falkenstein for the later period from about 1500 B.C. onwards): cf. A. Falkenstein, *Zur Chronologie der sumerischen Literatur*, in *Mitteilungen der Deutschen Orient-Gesellschaft zu Berlin*, 85 (1953), pp. 1–13. Falkenstein presses into the service of this investigation the language, the

literary form, the style, the composition, the canonical tradition, and indications derived from the subject matter.

28. Cf. S. N. Kramer, *Sumerian Mythology*, Philadelphia 1944.

29. Cf. S. N. Kramer (cit. n. 1, Ch. 2), pp. 89–91.

30. Lines 72–83; cf. J. B. Pritchard (ed.), *Ancient Near Eastern Texts Relating to the Old Testament*, ed. 2, Princeton 1955, p. 54. In view of the recent publication of this fundamental collection of ancient Oriental texts, and its up-to-date bibliography of editions, translations, and studies, it seems best for the sake of simplicity to refer the reader to this work (henceforward abbreviated as: Pritchard, *Texts*) for all the texts here cited, which are to be found in it. This of course does not oblige us to adhere to the interpretation that has been preferred in Pritchard.

31. Lines 126–40; cf. Pritchard, *Texts*, p. 55.

32. Lines 208–13; cf. ibid., p. 56.

33. An analysis of them is given by S. N. Kramer, *From the Tablets of Sumer*, Indian Hills 1955, pp. 71–95.

34. Cf. F. M. T. Böhl, *Het Gilgamesj-Epos bij de oude Sumeriërs*, Leiden 1947.

35. Lines 21–35; cf. Pritchard, *Texts*, p. 48.

36. Lines 98–106; cf. ibid., p. 49.

37. Lines 107–11; cf. ibid.

38. Lines 33–45; cf. ibid., pp. 50–1.

39. Cf. A. Falkenstein, W. von Soden, *Sumerische und akkadische Hymnen und Gebete*, Zürich 1953, where further bibliographical information is to be found.

40. Pritchard, *Texts*, pp. 67–8.

41. Cf. ibid., pp. 115–19.

42. S. N. Kramer, H. Kizilyay, M. Çiğ, *Five New Sumerian Literary Texts*, in *Belleten*, 16 (1952), p. 361.

43. A. Falkenstein, W. von Soden (cit. n. 39, Ch. 2), p. 140.

44. Lines 269–73, 304–8; cf. Pritchard, *Texts*, pp. 460–1.

45. Cf. J. J. A. van Dijk, *La sagesse suméro-accadienne*, Leiden 1953, where further bibliographical information is to be found.

46. Cf. S. N. Kramer, *Forty-eight Proverbs and Their Translation*, in *Compte rendu de la troisième Rencontre assyriologique internationale*, Paris 1954, pp. 75–84.

47. Cf. ibid., p. 79.

48. J. J. A. van Dijk (cit. n. 45, Ch. 2), p. 8.

49. Ibid., pp. 103, 106.

50. Lines 20–5; cf. Pritchard, *Texts*, pp. 41–2; J. J. A. van Dijk (cit. n. 45, Ch. 2), pp. 67–73.

51. Lines 41–64; cf. Pritchard, *Texts*, p. 42; J. J. A. van Dijk (cit. n. 45, Ch. 2), pp. 111–18.

52. Cf. S. N. Kramer, *Schooldays: A Sumerian Composition Relating to the Education of a Scribe*, in *Journal of the American Oriental Society*, 69 (1949), pp. 199–215.

53. Lines 13–17.

54. Lines 51–60.

55. Lines 70–9.

56. S. N. Kramer, 'Man and his God'. A Sumerian Variation of the Job' Motive, in Supplements to Vetus Testamentum, III, Leiden 1955, lines 26–38, pp. 173–4, 177–8.

57. Ibid., lines 118–29, pp. 176, 180.

58. S. N. Kramer, Sumerian Mythology, Philadelphia 1944, p. 10.

59. S. N. Kramer (cit. n. 1, Ch. 2), pp. 56–60.

60. A. Falkenstein, Die neusumerischen Gerichtsurkunden, 3 vols., München 1956–7.

61. Ibid., II, No. 17, pp. 27–8.

62. Ibid., II, No. 169, lines 17–23, pp. 268–9.

63. Cf. S. N. Kramer, Brief aperçu concernant les restes littéraires sumériens (cit. n. 26, Ch. 2), p. 109.

64. On Sumerian art in general cf. C. L. Woolley, The Development of Sumerian Art, London 1935; H. Lenzen, Die Sumerer, Berlin 1948; M. M. Rutten, Arts et styles du Moyen Orient ancien, Paris 1950, pp. 39–114, passim; H. Frankfort, The Art and Architecture of the Ancient Orient, Harmondsworth 1954, pp. 1–40, 47–53.

65. Cf. E. Heinrich, Bauwerke in der altsumerischen Bildkunst, Wiesbaden 1957.

66. On the structure of the Sumerian temple cf. H. J. Lenzen, Mesopotamische Tempelanlagen von der Frühzeit bis zum zweiten Jahrtausend, in Zeitschrift für Assyriologie, 17 (1955), pp. 1–36.

67. Cf. H. J. Lenzen, Die Entwicklung der Zikkurat von ihren Anfängen bis zur Zeit der III. Dynastie von Ur, Leipzig 1941; A. Parrot, Ziqqurats et tour de Babel, Paris 1949, and The Tower of Babel, London 1955.

68. H. Frankfort (cit. n. 64, Ch. 2), p. 25.

69. M. M. Rutten (cit. n. 64, Ch. 2), p. 21.

70. Cf. H. Frankfort, Cylinder Seals, London 1939.

CHAPTER 3

1. On the Babylonians and Assyrians in general cf. B. Meissner, Babylonien und Assyrien, 2 vols., Heidelberg 1920–5; H. Schmökel, Ur, Assur und Babylon, ed. 2, Stuttgart 1956; S. A. Pallis, The Antiquity of Iraq, Copenhagen 1956.

2. The noun 'Akkadians' has not yet become so usual as has its adjective 'Akkadian' as a term for the Babylonian and Assyrian language. Its use would, however, be convenient as a general term for the Semites of Mesopotamia, nor is it any great objection that a particular dynasty, that of Sargon, is called 'of Akkad'.

3. On the history cf. B. Meissner, Könige Babyloniens und Assyriens, Leipzig 1927. For the sources: D. D. Luckenbill, Ancient Records of Assyria and Babylonia, 2 vols., Chicago 1926–7.

4. Cf. E. Weidner, *Das Reich Sargons von Akkad*, in *Archiv für Orientforschung*, 16 (1952), pp. 1–24.

5. Pritchard, *Texts*, p. 267.

6. Speiser has brought out the fact that the Gutians played only a limited part in the decadence of Sargon's dynasty: E. A. Speiser, *Some Factors in the Collapse of Akkad*, in *Journal of the American Oriental Society*, 72 (1952), pp. 97–101.

7. Cf. J.-R. Kupper, *Les nomades en Mésopotamie au temps des rois de Mari*, Paris 1957; D. O. Edzard, *Die 'Zweite Zwischenzeit' Babyloniens*, Wiesbaden 1957.

8. Cf. A. Falkenstein (cit. n. 27, Ch. 2), pp. 16–17.

9. Cf. n. 2, Ch. 1; the diplomatic rules to be gathered from the Mari archives have been studied by J. M. Munn-Rankin, *Diplomacy in Western Asia in the Early Second Millennium B.C.*, in *Iraq*, 18 (1956), pp. 68–110.

10. *Archives royales de Mari*, VI, Paris 1954, No. 54, pp. 80–1.

11. Cf. W. von Soden, *Herrscher im alten Orient*, Berlin–Göttingen–Heidelberg 1954.

12. *Archives royales de Mari*, I, Paris 1950, No. 108, pp. 182–3.

13. Ibid., II, Paris 1950, No. 106, pp. 184–5.

14. Ibid.

15. On Hammurabi: F. M. T. Böhl, *King Hammurabi of Babylon in the Setting of His Time*, Amsterdam 1946; H. A. Brongers, *Hammurabi*, Den Haag 1949.

16. For a bibliography on the Code, cf. below nn. 71, 72, Ch. 3.

17. Divine beings in Anu's service.

18. The god of Hammurabi's dynasty.

19. Sun-god.

20. Prologue, I, 1–40; cf. Pritchard, *Texts*, p. 164.

21. Epilogue, R XXIV, 31–61; R XXV, 8–14; cf. Pritchard, *Texts*, p. 178.

22. Cf. K. Balkan, *Hauptlinien der Geschichte der Kassiten*, in *Belleten*, 12 (1948), pp. 723–57; id., *Kassitenstudien I*, New Haven 1954.

23. Cf. W. von Soden, *Der Aufstieg des Assyrerreichs als geschichtliches Problem*, Leipzig 1937.

24. Pritchard, *Texts*, pp. 274–5.

25. Cf. B. B. Piotrovsky, P. N. Schultz, V. A. Golovkina, S. P. Tolstov, *Ourartou, Néapolis des Scythes, Kharezm*, Paris 1954.

26. Pritchard, *Texts*, p. 286.

27. Ibid., p. 293; cf. now R. Borger, *Die Inschriften Asarhaddons Königs von Assyrien*, Graz 1956, pp. 98–9.

28. D. J. Wiseman, *Chronicles of the Chaldaean Kings (626–556 B.C.) in the British Museum*, London 1956.

29. God of writing and wisdom, of whom we shall speak later.

30. The name of a canal.

31. Pritchard, *Texts*, p. 307.

32. On Babylonian and Assyrian religion in general: E. Dhorme, *Les religions de Babylonie et d'Assyrie*, ed. 2, Paris 1949; J. Bottéro, *La religion babylonienne*, Paris 1952; S. H. Hooke, *Babylonian and Assyrian Religion*, London 1953.

33. G. Contenau, *La magie chez les Assyriens et les Babyloniens*, Paris 1947, p. 86; further bibliography to be found there.

34. Ibid., pp. 89–90.

35. Cf. A. A. van Proosdij, *Babylonian Magic and Sorcery*, Leiden 1952.

36. G. Contenau (cit. n. 33, Ch. 3), p. 147.

37. Ibid., p. 221.

38. Ibid., p. 225.

39. G. Contenau, *La divination chez les Assyriens et les Babyloniens*, Paris 1940, pp. 220–1; further bibliography to be found there.

40. Ibid., p. 215.

41. Ibid., p. 213.

42. Cf. O. Neugebauer, *The Exact Sciences in Antiquity*, Copenhagen 1951; B. L. van der Waerden, *Science Awakening*, Groningen 1954.

43. G. Contenau (cit. n. 39, Ch. 3), pp. 331–2.

44. Pritchard, *Texts*, pp. 449–50.

45. Cf. G. Furlani, *Riti babilonesi e assiri*, Udine 1940.

46. On the literature in general: B. Meissner, *Die babylonisch-assyrische Literatur*, Wildpark-Potsdam 1928; H. A. Brongers, *De literatuur der Babyloniërs en Assyriërs*, Den Haag 1954.

47. W. von Soden, *Das Problem der zeitlichen Einordnung akkadischer Literaturwerke*, in *Mitteilungen der Deutschen Orient-Gesellschaft zu Berlin*, 85 (1953), pp. 14–26, deals with the problem of a history of Babylonian and Assyrian literature, indicating the various materials (orthographic, linguistic, onomastic, geographical, religious) which may be of use in that difficult task. An attempt to present a history of Babylonian and Assyrian literature has recently been made by G. Rinaldi, *Storia delle letterature della antica Mesopotamia*, Milano 1957.

48. Cf. A. Heidel, *The Babylonian Genesis*, ed. 2, Chicago 1954; Pritchard, *Texts*, pp. 60–72.

49. Tablet IV, lines 35–42, 89–103; cf. Pritchard, *Texts*, pp. 66–7.

50. Corresponding to Jupiter.

51. Tablet V, lines 1–10; cf. Pritchard, *Texts*, p. 67.

52. Pritchard, *Texts*, pp. 106–9.

53. Ibid., pp. 103–4.

54. Lines 77–88; cf. Pritchard, *Texts*, p. 104.

55. Cf. A. Heidel, *The Gilgamesh Epic and Old Testament Parallels*, ed. 2, Chicago 1949; F. M. T. de Liagre Böhl, *Het Gilgamesj-*

epos, ed. 2, Amsterdam 1952; Pritchard, *Texts*, pp. 72–99. On the sources: J. J. Stamm, *Das Gilgamesch-Epos und seine Vorgeschichte*, in *Asiatische Studien*, 6 (1952), pp. 9–29.

56. Tablet VI, lines 7–17; cf. Pritchard, *Texts*, pp. 83–4.

57. Tablet VI, lines 24–78; cf. ibid., p. 84.

58. Tablet X, old Babylonian version, III; cf. ibid., p. 90.

59. Tablet X, Assyrian version, VI, lines 26–9, 33–5; cf. ibid., pp. 92–3. The meaning of the concluding lines is in dispute.

60. Cf. A. Falkenstein, W. von Soden, cit. n. 39, Ch. 2.

61. Ibid., p. 321.

62. Cf. A. Falkenstein, W. von Soden, cit. n. 39, Ch. 2; Pritchard, *Texts*, pp. 390–1. The translation is controverted in several points.

63. Cf. J. J. A. van Dijk, cit. n. 45, Ch. 2.

64. Pritchard, *Texts*, p. 425.

65. Ibid., pp. 426–7.

66. Cf. C. Johnston, *Assyrian and Babylonian Beast Fables*, in *American Journal of Semitic Languages and Literatures*, 28 (1912), pp. 81–100.

67. Cf. A. Kuschke, *Altbabylonische Texte zum Thema „Der leidende Gerechte"*, in *Theologische Literaturzeitung*, 81 (1956), coll. 69–76.

68. II, lines 1–3, 23–8; cf. Pritchard, *Texts*, pp. 434–5.

69. II, lines 34–7; cf. ibid., p. 435.

70. Ibid., pp. 437–8.

71. Cf. G. R. Driver, J. C. Miles, *The Assyrian Laws*, Oxford 1935, and *The Babylonian Laws*, 2 vols., Oxford 1952–5.

72. Cf. W. Eilers, *Die Gesetzstele Chammurabis*, Leipzig 1932; A. Pohl, R. Follet, *Codex Hammurabi. Transcriptio et versio Latina*, ed. 3, Roma 1950; E. Bergmann, *Codex Hammurabi. Textus primigenius*, ed. 3, Roma 1953; Pritchard, *Texts*, pp. 163–80.

73. Art. 196–8.

74. Art. 128.

75. Art. 134.

76. Art. 218.

77. Art. 233.

78. Art. 2.

79. On Babylonian and Assyrian art in general: M. M. Rutten, cit. n. 64, Ch. 2; H. Frankfort, cit. ibid. An excellent collection of illustrations is to be found in J. B. Pritchard, *The Ancient Near East in Pictures Relating to the Old Testament*, Princeton 1954. On archaeology: A. Parrot, *Archéologie mésopotamienne*, I–II, Paris 1946–53.

80. Cf. A. Parrot, *Le temple d'Ishtar*, Paris 1956.

81. The history of the styles and motifs of Mesopotamian seals has been excellently expounded by H. Frankfort, cit. n. 70, Ch. 2.

82. Cf. W. Andrae, *Babylon. Die versunkene Weltstadt und ihr*

Ausgräber Robert Koldewey, Berlin 1952; A. Parrot, *Babylone et l'Ancien Testament*, Neuchâtel 1956.
83. Cf. R. D. Barnett, *A Catalogue of the Nimrud Ivories with Other Examples of Ancient Near Eastern Ivories*, London 1957.

CHAPTER 4

1. Pritchard, *Texts*, p. 372.
2. On Egyptian civilization in general cf. A. Erman, H. Ranke, *Ägypten und ägyptisches Leben im Altertum*, Tübingen 1923; A. Moret, *Le Nil et la civilisation égyptienne*, Paris 1926; E. Drioton, J. Vandier, *L'Egypte*, ed. 3, Paris 1952; E. Otto, *Ägypten. Der Weg des Pharaonenreiches*, Stuttgart 1953; W. Wolf, *Die Welt der Ägypter*, Stuttgart 1955.
3. J. A. Wilson, *The Burden of Egypt*, Chicago 1951, p. 145.
4. Cf. P. Montet, *La vie quotidienne en Egypte au temps des Ramsès*, Paris 1946, pp. 7–10.
5. On the history in general: J. H. Breasted, *A History of Egypt from the Earliest Times to the Persian Conquest*, ed. 2, London 1925; A. Moret, *L'Egypte pharaonique*, Paris 1932; J. A. Wilson, cit. n. 3, Ch. 4. For the sources: J. H. Breasted, *Ancient Records of Egypt*, 3 vols., Chicago 1906–7.
6. On the Egyptian royal titles, cf. H. Müller, *Die formale Entwicklung der Titulatur der ägyptischen Könige*, Glückstadt 1938.
7. Cf. W. Helck, *Untersuchungen zu Manetho und den ägyptischen Königslisten*, Berlin 1956.
8. Cf. W. Helck, *Gab es einen König 'Menes'?*, in *Zeitschrift der Deutschen Morgenländischen Gesellschaft*, 103 (1953), pp. 354–9.
9. On the formation of Egyptian culture in the Old Kingdom, cf. J. Spiegel, *Das Werden der altägyptischen Hochkultur*, Heidelberg 1953.
10. Cf. H. Frankfort, *Kingship and the Gods*, Chicago 1948.
11. On ancient Egyptian historiography cf. L. Bull, *Ancient Egypt*, in R. C. Dentan (cit. n. 6, Ch. 2), pp. 1–33.
12. On Egyptian policy in Nubia cf. T. Säve-Söderbergh, *Ägypten und Nubien*, Lund 1941; R. Herzog, *Die Nubier*, Berlin 1957. On the policy in Libya: W. Hölscher, *Libyer und Ägypter*, Glückstadt 1955.
13. Pritchard, *Texts*, pp. 227–8.
14. The term 'first illness' is that of J. A. Wilson (cit. n. 3, Ch. 4), p. 104. On the first intermediate period cf. H. Stock, *Die erste Zwischenzeit*, Roma 1949; J. Spiegel, *Soziale und weltanschauliche Reformbewegungen im alten Ägypten*, Heidelberg 1950.
15. Pritchard, *Texts*, pp. 441–2.
16. Perhaps this corresponds to Shechem.
17. Pritchard, *Texts*, p. 230. I render as 'Syrians' the Egyptian Retenu and the other names used for the people of Syria.

18. Important above all are the relations with Byblos, on which cf. P. Montet, *Byblos et l'Egypte*, 2 vols., Paris 1925.

19. Cf. A. Alt, *Die Herkunft der Hyksos in neuer Sicht*, Berlin 1954; Z. Mayani, *Les Hyksos et le monde de la Bible*, Paris 1956.

20. Pritchard, *Texts*, p. 232. An extensive supplement to this school text (the Carnarvon tablet) has recently been found: cf. Labib Habachi, *Preliminary Report on Kamose Stela and Other Inscribed Blocks Found Reused in the Foundations of Two Statues at Karnak*, in *Annales du Service des Antiquités de l'Egypte*, 53 (1955), pp. 195–202.

21. Pritchard, *Texts*, pp. 232–3.

22. Cf. G. Steindorff, K. C. Seele, *When Egypt Ruled the East*, ed. 2, Chicago 1957.

23. Cf. H. Grapow, *Studien zu den Annalen Thutmosis des Dritten und zu ihnen verwandten historischen Berichten des Neuen Reiches*, Berlin 1947.

24. Pritchard, *Texts*, p. 238.

25. Ibid., p. 374.

26. Cf. G. Lefebvre, *Histoire des grands prêtres d'Amon de Karnak*, Paris 1929.

27. On the Reform period: K. Lange, *König Echnaton und die Amarna-Zeit*, München 1951.

28. Pritchard, *Texts*, pp. 370–1.

29. Cf. C. Kuentz, *La bataille de Qadech*, Le Caire 1928–34.

30. Pritchard, *Texts*, pp. 257–8.

31. Cf. the Biblical passages 2 Kings xviii, 21 and Isaiah xxxvi, 6.

32. Pritchard, *Texts*, p. 27.

33. Expressions to be found in the Amarna letters, which we shall discuss later.

34. Cf. K. F. Kienitz, *Die politische Geschichte Ägyptens vom 7. bis zum 4. Jahrhundert vor der Zeitwende*, Berlin 1953; H. von Zeissl, *Äthioper und Assyrer in Ägypten*, Glückstadt 1955; H. de Meulenaere, *Herodotos over de 26ste Dynastie*, Louvain 1951.

35. Herodotus, Hist. ii. 37.

36. On Egyptian religion in general: A. Erman, *Die Religion der Ägypter*, Berlin-Leipzig 1934; J. Vandier, *La religion égyptienne*, ed. 2, Paris 1949; H. Frankfort, *Ancient Egyptian Religion*, New York 1948; J. Černy, *Ancient Egyptian Religion*, London 1952; H. Bonnet, *Reallexikon der ägyptischen Religionsgeschichte*, Berlin 1952; S. Donadoni, *La religione dell' Egitto antico*, Milano 1955; H. Kees, *Der Götterglaube im alten Ägypten*, ed. 2, Berlin 1956. For the sources: G. Roeder, *Urkunden zur Religion des Alten Ägypten*, Jena 1923.

37. H. and H. A. Frankfort, J. A. Wilson, T. Jacobsen, W. A. Irwin (cit. n. 24, Ch. 2), pp. 44–5.

38. This is the soundest explanation, but it is not certain.

39. On the initial period of Egyptian religion, cf. H. Junker,

Pyramidenzeit. Das Wesen der altägyptischen Religion, Einsiedeln 1949.

40. Cf. C. J. Bleeker, *Die Geburt eines Gottes. Eine Studie über den ägyptischen Gott Min und sein Fest*, Leiden 1956.

41. Cf. K. Sethe, *Amun und die acht Urgötter von Hermopolis*, Berlin 1929.

42. Cf. H. Kees, *Horus und Seth als Götterpaar*, Leipzig 1923–4.

43. Pritchard, *Texts*, pp. 8–9.

44. Cf. M. S. Holmberg, *The God Ptah*, Lund 1946.

45. Cf. H. Junker, *Die Götterlehre von Memphis*, Berlin 1940.

46. Cf. R. Anthes, *Die Maat des Echnaton von Amarna*, Baltimore 1952.

47. Cf. G. Roeder, *Volksglaube im Pharaonenreich*, Stuttgart 1952.

48. Cf. F. Lexa, *La magie dans l'Egypte antique, de l'Ancien Empire jusqu'à l'époque copte*, 3 vols., Paris 1925.

49. Pritchard, *Texts*, p. 328.

50. Ibid., p. 327.

51. Pritchard, *Texts*, pp. 12–14.

52. Cf. H. Kees, *Das Priestertum im ägyptischen Staat vom Neuen Reich bis zur Spätzeit*, Leiden-Köln 1953.

53. Cf. P. Montet, *La vie quotidienne en Egypte au temps des Ramsès*, Paris 1946, pp. 273–4. Cf. also on this point A. Moret, *Le rituel du culte divin journalier en Egypte*, Paris 1902.

54. Herodotus, Hist. ii. 60.

55. Cf. E. Drioton, *Le théâtre égyptien*, Le Caire 1942.

56. P. Montet (cit. n. 53, Ch. 4), p. 290.

57. Cf. A. H. Gardiner, *The Attitude of the Ancient Egyptians to Death and the Dead*, Cambridge 1935; H. Kees, *Totenglauben und Jenseitsvorstellung der alten Ägypter*, ed. 2, Berlin 1956.

58. Pritchard, *Texts*, pp. 34–5. On the judgement of the dead cf. J. Spiegel, *Die Idee vom Totengericht in der ägyptischen Religion*, Glückstadt 1935.

59. Cf. L. Greven, *Der Ka in Theologie und Königskult der Ägypter des alten Reiches*, Glückstadt 1952; U. Schweitzer, *Das Wesen des Ka im Diesseits und Jenseits der alten Ägypter*, Glückstadt 1956.

60. Cf. K. Sethe, *Zur Geschichte der Einbalsamierung bei den Ägyptern und einiger damit verbundener Bräuche*, Berlin 1934.

61. Herodotus, Hist. ii. 86.

62. Cf. A. Gardiner, K. Sethe, *Egyptian Letters to the Dead*, London 1928, pp. 8–9.

63. On Egyptian literature in general: A. Erman, *Die Literatur der Ägypter*, Leipzig 1923; H. Brunner, H. Grapow, H. Kees, S. Morenz, E. Otto, S. Schott, J. Spiegel, *Ägyptologie. Literatur* (*Handbuch der Orientalistik*, I, 2), Leiden 1952; S. Donadoni, *Storia della letteratura egiziana antica*, Milano 1957.

64. Cf. E. Naville, *Das ägyptische Todtenbuch der XVIII. bis XX.*

Dynastie, 3 vols., Berlin 1886; E. A. W. Budge, *The Book of the Dead*, ed. 2, London 1951.

65. Cf. T. Hopfner, *Plutarch über Isis und Osiris*, 2 vols., Prag 1940–1.

66. A cubit is about eighteen inches.

67. Pritchard, *Texts*, pp. 15–16.

68. Cf. P. Gilbert, *La poésie égyptienne*, Bruxelles 1949; S. Schott, *Altägyptische Liebslieder*, Zürich 1950.

69. Pritchard, *Texts*, p. 366.

70. S. Schott (cit. n. 68, Ch. 4), p. 41.

71. Literally 'my sister'. 'Brother' and 'sister' are used in the sense 'lover', 'beloved'.

72. Pritchard, *Texts*, pp. 468–9.

73. Ibid., p. 467.

74. Cf. R. Anthes, *Lebensregeln und Lebenweisheit der alten Ägypter*, Leipzig 1933; W. von Bissing, *Altägyptische Lebensweisheit*, Zürich 1955.

75. Pritchard, *Texts*, pp. 412–14.

76. Cf. J. M. McGlinchey, *The Teaching of Amen-em-Ope and the Book of Proverbs*, Washington 1939.

77. Pritchard, *Texts*, pp. 423–4.

78. Cf. A. Erman, *Die Literatur der Ägypter*, Leipzig 1923, pp. 224–5.

79. Cf. W. von Bissing, *Eudoxos von Knidos Aufenthalt in Ägypten und seine Übertragung ägyptischer Tierfabeln*, in *Forschungen und Fortschritte*, 25 (1949), pp. 225–30.

80. Cf. H. Jacobsohn, *Das Gespräch eines Lebensmüden mit seinem Ba*, Zürich 1952; R. O. Faulkner, *The Man Who Was Tired of Life*, in *Journal of Egyptian Archaeology*, 42 (1956), pp. 21–40.

81. Pritchard, *Texts*, pp. 406–7.

82. Ibid., p. 407.

83. Cf. G. Lefebvre, *Romans et contes égyptiens de l'époque pharaonique*, Paris 1949.

84. Pritchard, *Texts*, pp. 18–22; G. Lefebvre (cit. n. 83, Ch. 4), pp. 1–25.

85. G. Lefebvre (cit. n. 83, Ch. 4), pp. 29–40.

86. Pritchard, *Texts*, pp. 23–5; G. Lefebvre (cit. n. 83, Ch. 4), pp. 137–58.

87. Cf. O. Neugebauer, cit. n. 42, Ch. 3; B. L. van der Waerden, cit. ibid.

88. Cf. G. Lefebvre, *Essai sur la médicine égyptienne de l'époque pharaonique*, Paris 1956; H. Grapow, *Grundriss der Medizin der alten Ägypter*, 3 vols., Berlin 1954–6.

89. A. Erman, H. Ranke (cit. n. 2, Ch. 4), p. 412.

90. Cf. J. Pirenne, *Histoire des institutions et du droit privé de l'ancien Egypte*, 3 vols., Bruxelles 1932–5.

91. Cf. J. A. Wilson, E. A. Speiser, H. G. Güterbock, I. Mendel-

sohn, D. H. H. Ingalls, D. Bodde, *Authority and Law in the Ancient Orient*, Baltimore 1954, pp. 1–7.

92. Pritchard, *Texts*, p. 212.

93. Ibid., pp. 214–15.

94. On Egyptian art in general: C. Desroches-Noblecourt, *Le style égyptien*, Paris 1946; C. Aldred, *Old, Middle and New Kingdom Art*, 3 vols., London 1949–51; S. Donadoni, *L'arte egizia*, Torino 1955; K. Lange, M. Hirmer, *Ägypten. Architektur, Plastik, Malerei in drei Jahrtausenden*, München 1955. On archaeology: J. Vandier, *Manuel d'archéologie égyptienne*, 2 vols., Paris 1952–5.

95. C. Desroches-Noblecourt (cit. n. 94, Ch. 4), p. 20.

96. Ibid., p. 21.

97. On Egyptian architecture: G. Jéquier, *Manuel d'archéologie égyptienne. Les éléments de l'architecture*, Paris 1924; A. Badawi, *A History of Egyptian Architecture. I. From the Earliest Times to the End of the Old Kingdom*, Giza 1954.

98. Cf. H. Ricke, *Bemerkungen zur ägyptischen Baukunst des Alten Reiches* — S. Schott, *Bemerkungen zum ägyptischen Pyramidenkult*, Cairo 1950; W. B. Emery, *Great Tombs of the First Dynasty*, 2 vols., Cairo 1949–54.

99. Cf. P. Montet, *Les scènes de la vie privée dans les tombeaux égyptiens de l'Ancien Empire*, Paris–Strasbourg 1925.

100. On the pyramids: I. E. S. Edwards, *The Pyramids of Egypt*, West Drayton 1947; J. E. Lauer, *Le problème des pyramides d'Egypte*, Paris 1948.

101. Cf. J. Capart, *Tout-Ankh-Amon*, ed. 2, Bruxelles 1950.

102. On Egyptian materials and technique: A. Lucas, *Ancient Egyptian Materials and Industries*, ed. 3, London 1948.

103. Cf. H. G. Evers, *Staat aus dem Stein. Denkmäler, Geschichte und Bedeutung der ägyptischen Plastik während des Mittleren Reichs*, 2 vols., München 1929; W. S. Smith, *A History of Egyptian Sculpture and Painting in the Old Kingdom*, ed. 2, London 1949; B. Hornermann, *Types of Ancient Egyptian Statuary*, 3 vols., Copenhagen 1951–7.

104. Cf. E. Iversen, *Canon and Proportions in Egyptian Art*, London 1955.

105. S. Donadoni (cit. n. 94, Ch. 4), p. 34.

106. Cf. C. de Wit, *La statuaire de Tell el Amarna*, Anvers 1950.

107. Cf. S. Hassan, *The Great Sphinx and Its Secrets*, Cairo 1953.

108. Cf. A. Mekhitarian, *Egyptian Painting*, Geneva 1954.

109. Cf. G. Roeder, *Ägyptische Bronzefiguren*, 2 vols., Berlin 1956.

110. S. Donadoni (cit. n. 94, Ch. 4), pp. 113–14.

CHAPTER 5

1. Cf. A. Scharff, A. Moortgat (cit. n. 14, Ch. 1), pp. 321–31, with the reservations, however, set forth in this chapter.

2. On the Hittites in general: A. Goetze, *Hethiter, Churriter und*

Assyrer, Oslo 1938; F. Sommer, *Hethiter und Hethitisch*, Stuttgart 1947; G. Contenau, *La civilisation des Hittites et des Hurrites de Mitanni*, ed. 2, Paris 1948; O. R. Gurney, *The Hittites*, London 1952 (a second edition was published in 1954, but I have not had access to it); M. Riemschneider, *Die Welt der Hethiter*, Stuttgart 1954 (with the reservations expressed in this chapter); A. Goetze, *Kleinasien*, ed. 2, München 1957. A clarification of the meaning and the value of the term Hittites has now been effected by H. G. Güterbock, *Toward a Definition of the Term Hittite*, in *Oriens*, 10 (1957), pp. 233–9. On history in particular: A. Goetze, *Das Hethiter-Reich*, Leipzig 1928; E. Cavaignac, *Les Hittites*, Paris 1950; J. Holt, *Kilder til hittiternes historie*, København 1951. The sources are published in the series *Keilschrifttexte aus Boghazköi* and *Keilschrifturkunden aus Boghazköi*.

3. The capital of the empire, the present-day Boghazköy.

4. F. Sommer, A. Falkenstein, *Die hethitisch-akkadische Bilingue des Ḫattušili I. (Labarna II.)*, München 1938, §§ 1–3, 7, 19.

5. M. Riemschneider (cit. n. 2, Ch. 5), pp. 24–6.

6. Cf. J. Pirenne, *La politique d'expansion hittite envisagée à travers les traités de vassalité et de protectorat*, in *Revue internationale des droits de l'antiquité*, 3 (1956), pp. 11–39.

7. A. Scharff, A. Moortgat (cit. n. 14, Ch. 1), p. 351.

8. Did two dynasties exist contemporaneously? Cf. H. Otten, *Die hethitischen „Königslisten" und die altorientalische Chronologie*, in *Mitteilungen der Deutschen Orient-Gesellschaft zu Berlin*, 83 (1951), pp. 47–71; and for the contrary view, A. Goetze, *The Predecessors of Šuppiluliumaš of Ḫatti*, in *Journal of the American Oriental Society*, 72 (1952), pp. 67–72. A more recent article by the same author has been already quoted (n. 6, Ch. 1).

9. Cf. E. Cavaignac, *Subbiluliuma et son temps*, Paris 1932; and now also H. G. Güterbock, *The Deeds of Suppiluliuma as Told by His Son, Mursili II*, in *Journal of Cuneiform Studies*, 10 (1956), pp. 41–68, 75–98, 107–30.

10. Cf. A. Malamat, *Doctrines of Causality in Hittite and Biblical Historiography: a Parallel*, in *Vetus Testamentum*, 5 (1955), pp. 1–12.

11. A. Goetze, *Die Annalen des Muršiliš*, Leipzig 1933, pp. 16–21.

12. G. Furlani, *Gli Annali di Mursilis II di Hatti*, in *Saggi sulla civiltà degli Hittiti*, Udine 1939, pp. 65–140, cf. pp. 100–1.

13. Both sides claim to be victorious. Cf. C. Kuentz, cit. n. 29, Ch. 4.

14. A. Götze, *Ḫattušiliš. Der Bericht über seine Thronbesteigung nebst den Paralleltexten*, Leipzig 1925, pp. 28–31. Cf. also the same author's *Neue Bruchstücke zum Grossen Text des Ḫattušiliš und den Paralleltexten*, Leipzig 1930.

15. Cf. D. G. Hogarth, *Kings of the Hittites*, London 1926.

16. Among the many publications on this subject cf. H. T. Bossert,

Die phönizisch-hethitischen Bilinguen von Karatepe, in *Jahrbuch für kleinasiatische Forschung*, 2 (1952–3), pp. 293–339; A. Alt, *Ergänzungen zu den phönikischen Inschriften von Karatepe*, in *Die Welt des Orients*, 2 (1955), pp. 172–83.

17. On Carchemish cf. C. L. Woolley, R. D. Barnett (and others), *Carchemish*, 3 vols., London 1914–52.

18. On Hittite religion in general: G. Furlani, *La religione degli Hittiti*, Bologna 1936; R. Dussaud, *Les religions des Hittites et des Hourrites, des Phéniciens et des Syriens*, ed. 2, Paris 1949.

19. A. Scharff, A. Moortgat (cit. n. 14, Ch. 1), pp. 368–9.

20. On Hittite gods: H. G. Güterbock, *Hethitische Götterdarstellungen und Götternamen*, in *Belleten*, 7 (1953), pp. 295–317; E. Laroche, *Recherches sur les noms des dieux hittites*, Paris 1947.

21. Literally: 'the old woman'.

22. Pritchard, *Texts*, pp. 350–1.

23. Cf. A. Boissier, *Mantique babylonienne et mantique hittite*, Paris 1935; E. Laroche, *Eléments d'haruspicine hittite*, in *Revue hittite et asianique*, 12 (1952), pp. 19–48.

24. Pritchard, *Texts*, p. 497.

25. Ibid.

26. Cf. O. R. Gurney (cit. n. 2, Ch. 5), p. 151.

27. H. Otten, *Ein Bestattungsritual hethitischer Könige*, in *Zeitschrift für Assyriologie*, 12 (1940), pp. 206–24.

28. The meaning of the Hittite word, *ukturi*, is uncertain.

29. A kind of drink.

30. A kind of spoon.

31. A kind of linen.

32. Kinds of loaves, called *gug* and *al*.

33. H. Otten (cit. n. 27, Ch. 5), pp. 214–17.

34. Cf. F. Sommer, *Die Aḫḫijavā-Urkunden*, München 1932; F. Schachermeyer, *Hethiter und Achäer*, Leipzig 1935; R. Dussaud, *Prélydiens, Hittites et Achéens*, Paris 1953.

35. Cf. R. O. Gurney (cit. n. 2, Ch. 5), pp. 46–58.

36. Pritchard, *Texts*, p. 125.

37. Ibid., p. 126.

38. Cf. H. Otten, *Die Überlieferungen des Telepinu-Mythus*, Leipzig 1942.

39. Pritchard, *Texts*, p. 126.

40. Ibid.

41. Ibid., p. 128.

42. Cf. H. G. Güterbock, *Kumarbi*, Zürich–New York 1946, and *The Song of Ullikummi*, in *Journal of Cuneiform Studies*, 5 (1952), pp. 135–61; 6 (1952), pp. 8–42; H. Otten, *Mythen vom Gotte Kumarbi. Neue Fragmente*, Berlin 1950; P. Meriggi, *I miti di Kumarpi, il Kronos currico*, in *Athenaeum*, 31 (1953), pp. 101–57.

43. Pritchard, *Texts*, p. 120.

44. Cf. H. G. Güterbock, *The Hittite Version of the Hurrian Ku-*

marbi Myths: Oriental Forerunners of Hesiod, in *American Journal of Archaeology*, 52 (1948), pp. 123–34; P. Walcot, *The Texts of Hesiod's Theogony and the Hittite Epic of Kumarbi*, in *Classical Quarterly*, 6 (1956), pp. 198–206.

45. Pritchard, *Texts*, p. 122.

46. Ibid., pp. 124–5.

47. J. Friedrich, *Die hethitischen Bruchstücke des Gilgameš-Epos*, in *Zeitschrift für Assyriologie*, 39 (1950), pp. 1–82.

48. Pritchard, *Texts*, p. 397.

49. Ibid., p. 395.

50. Cf. J. Friedrich, *Staatsverträge des Ḫatti-Reiches in hethitischer Sprache*, Leipzig 1926–30; V. Korošec, *Hethitische Staatsverträge*, Leipzig 1931.

51. Pritchard, *Texts*, pp. 199–203.

52. Ibid., p. 203.

53. Ibid., p. 204.

54. Ibid., p. 205.

55. Cf. H. Zimmern, J. Friedrich, *Hethitische Gesetze aus dem Staatsarchiv von Boghazköi*, Leipzig 1922; E. Neufeld, *The Hittite Laws*, London 1951; V. Korošec, *Das hethitische Recht in seiner Stellung zwischen Osten und Westen*, in *Südostforschungen*, 15 (1956), pp. 22–40.

56. O. R. Gurney (cit. n. 2, Ch. 5), p. 91.

57. Cf. P. Koschaker, *Zum Levirat nach hethitischem Recht*, in *Revue hittite et asianique*, 2 (1932–4), pp. 77–89; A. F. Puukko, *Die Leviratsehe in den altorientalischen Gesetzen*, in *Archiv Orientální*, 17, 2 (1949), pp. 296–9.

58. Cf. O. R. Gurney (cit. n. 2, Ch. 5), pp. 101–3.

59. Art. 7–8; cf. Pritchard, *Texts*, p. 189. The translation of the expression 'pledge his estate as security' is doubtful.

60. Art. 67; cf. Pritchard, *Texts*, p. 192.

61. Cf. E. von Schuler, *Hethitische Dienstanweisungen für höhere Hof- und Staatsbeamte*, Graz 1957.

62. Translation doubtful.

63. Pritchard, *Texts*, p. 211.

64. Ibid.

65. M. Riemschneider (cit. n. 2, Ch. 5), pp. 114–21.

66. On Hittite art: A. Moortgat, *Die bildende Kunst des Alten Orients und die Bergvölker*, Berlin 1932, and *Bildwerk und Volkstrum Vorderasiens zur Hethiterzeit*, Leipzig 1934; H. Frankfort (cit. n. 64, Ch. 2), pp. 111–32; M. Vieyra, *Hittite Art*, London 1955.

67. On Hattusas cf. K. Bittel and others, *Boğazköy* I–III, Berlin 1935–57. Especially important among the neighbouring localities is Yazilikaya, on which cf. K. Bittel, R. Naumann, H. Otto, *Yazilikaya*, Leipzig 1941.

68. Cf. I. J. Gelb, *Hittite Hieroglyphic Monuments*, Chicago 1939; E. Akurgal, *Späthethitische Bildkunst*, Ankara 1949.

69. Cf. R. Naumann, *Die Architektur Kleinasiens von ihren Anfängen bis zum Ende der hethitischen Zeit*, Tübingen 1955.

70. Cf. K. Bittel, *Die Felsbilder von Yazilikaya*, Istanbul 1934.

71. Cf. E. Laroche, *Le Panthéon de Yazilikaya*, in *Journal of Cuneiform Studies*, 6 (1952), pp. 115–23.

72. Cf. O. R. Gurney (cit. n. 2, Ch. 5), p. 199.

73. Cf. P. Coussin, *Le dieu-épée de Iasili-kaïa et le culte de l'épée dans l'antiquité*, in *Revue archéologique*, 27 (1928), pp. 107–35.

74. Cf. D. G. Hogarth, *Hittite Seals*, Oxford 1920; H. G. Güterbock, *Siegel aus Boğazköy*, 2 vols., Berlin 1940–2.

75. Cf. the discussion in K. Bittel, *Nur hethitische oder auch hurritische Kunst?*, in *Zeitschrift für Assyriologie*, 49 (1949), pp. 256–90.

76. H. Frankfort (cit. n. 64, Ch. 2), p. 117.

77. On the Hurrians in general: A. Goetze, *Hethiter, Churriter und Assyrer*, Oslo 1938; I. J. Gelb, *Hurrians and Subarians*, Chicago 1944; R. T. O'Callaghan, *Aram Naharaim*, Roma 1948.

78. For the language and the sources cf. E. A. Speiser, *Introduction to Hurrian*, New Haven 1940–1.

79. On the most ancient phase of Hurrian history cf. the information collected by A. Pohl, *Ḫurriti*, in *Enciclopedia Cattolica*, VI, Città del Vaticano 1951, coll. 1511–12.

80. On religion cf. R. Dussaud, cit. n. 18, Ch. 5; J. Friedrich, *Zu einigen altkleinasiatischen Gottheiten*, in *Jahrbuch für kleinasiatische Forschung*, 2 (1952), pp. 114–53.

81. A review of the texts is to be found in H. G. Güterbock (cit. n. 42, Ch. 5), pp. 116–23. Cf. subsequent analytical studies of J. Friedrich, *Der churritische Mythus vom Schlangedämon Ḫedammu in hethitischer Sprache*, in *Archiv Orientální*, 17, 1 (1949), pp. 230–54, and *Churritische Märchen und Sagen in hethitischer Sprache*, in *Zeitschrift für Assyriologie*, 49 (1949), pp. 213–55.

82. Col. I, lines 7–17: cf. J. Friedrich, *Churritische Märchen . . .* (cit. n. 81, Ch. 5), pp. 214–15. The translation, in this and in the following passages, is often doubtful.

83. Col. III, lines 3–14: cf. J. Friedrich, ibid., pp. 220–1.

84. Col. IV, lines 21–3: cf. J. Friedrich, ibid., pp. 222–3.

85. Such pottery has been found in various localities: Nuzi, Ashur, Nineveh, Tell Billa, Tell Halaf, Tell Atchana. For bibliographical information cf. A. Parrot, *Archéologie mésopotamienne*, I, Paris 1946, under the various localities.

CHAPTER 6

1. On the Canaanites and the Aramaeans in general cf. S. Moscati, *I predecessori d'Israele*, Roma 1956; A. Jirku, *Die Welt der Bibel*,

Stuttgart 1957. On the Aramaeans in particular: R. T. O'Callaghan, cit. n. 77, Ch. 5; A. Dupont-Sommer, *Les Araméens*, Paris 1949; A. Malamat, *The Aramaeans in Aram Naharaim and the Rise of Their States*, Jerusalem 1952. On the Phoenicians: G. Contenau, *La civilisation phénicienne*, Paris 1949.

2. On Semitic irradiation cf. R. Dussaud, *La pénétration des Arabes en Syrie avant l'Islam*, Paris 1955. M. Noth's thesis, *Zum Ursprung der phönikischen Küstenstädte*, in *Die Welt des Orients*, 1 (1947), pp. 21–8, according to which the Semites were preceded by non-Semites, lacks adequate documentary support.

3. Cf. J. Gray, *Canaanite Kingship in Theory and Practice*, in *Vetus Testamentum*, 2 (1952), pp. 193–200.

4. Cf. K. Sethe, *Die Ächtung feindlicher Fürsten, Völker und Dingen auf altägyptischen Tongefässcherben des Mittleren Reiches*, Berlin 1926; G. Posener, *Princes et pays d'Asie et de Nubie. Textes hiératiques sur des figurines d'envoûtement du Moyen Empire*, Bruxelles 1940.

5. Cf. J. A. Knudtzon, *Die El-Amarna-Tafeln*, 2 vols., Leipzig 1915; C. H. Gordon, *The New Amarna Tablets*, in *Orientalia*, 16 (1947), pp. 1–21.

6. Cf. n. 9, Ch. 1.

7. Cf. nn. 4 and 10, Ch. 1.

8. The annals of Tyre, which we shall discuss later, are conserved only to a small extent and in an indirect source.

9. *Archives royales de Mari*, V, Paris 1952, No. 16, pp. 32–3.

10. Ibid., No. 20, pp. 36–7.

11. Ibid., II, No. 102, pp. 178–81.

12. Cf. M. Noth, *Die syrisch-palästinische Bevölkerung des zweiten Jahrtausends v. Chr. im Lichte neuer Quellen*, in *Zeitschrift des Deutschen Palästina Vereins*, 65 (1942), pp. 9–67.

13. J. A. Knudtzon (cit. n. 5, Ch. 6), I, No. 244, pp. 790–3; Pritchard, *Texts*, p. 485.

14. Ibid.: Knudtzon, No. 254, pp. 810–13, Pritchard, p. 486.

15. Ibid.: Knudtzon, No. 270, pp. 834–5, Pritchard, p. 486.

16. Cf. J. Bottéro, *Le problème des Ḥabiru à la 4ᵉ Rencontre assyriologique internationale*, Paris 1954; M. Greenberg, *The Ḥab/piru*, New Haven 1955; A. Pohl, *Einige Gedanken zur Ḥabiru Frage*, in *Wiener Zeitschrift für die Kunde des Morgenlandes*, 54 (1957), pp. 157–60.

17. J. Nougayrol, *Le palais royal d'Ugarit IV*, Paris 1956, pp. 35–6.

18. Cf. L. A. Stella, *Chi furono i popoli del mare?*, in *Rivista di antropologia*, 39 (1951–2), pp. 3–17.

19. Cf. O. Eissfeldt, *Philister und Phönizier*, Leipzig 1936; G. Bonfante, *Who were the Philistines?*, in *American Journal of Archaeology*, 50 (1946), pp. 251–62; C. H. Gordon, *The Rôle of the Philistines*, in *Antiquity*, 30 (1956), pp. 22–6.

20. Cf. M. McNamara, *De populi Aramaeorum primordiis*, in *Verbum Domini*, 35 (1957), pp. 129–42.

21. On Damascus: M. F. Unger, *A History of Damascus from the Earliest Times until its Conquest by Assyria*, Baltimore 1946–7, and *Israel and the Aramaeans of Damascus*, London 1957. On Hama: H. Ingholt, *Rapport préliminaire sur sept campagnes de fouilles à Hamat en Syrie*, Copenhagen 1940; P. J. Riis, *Hama*, Copenhagen 1948. On Sam'al: B. Landsberger, *Sam'al*, Ankara 1948. On Bit Adini: F. Thureau-Dangin, M. Dunand, *Til Barsip*, Paris 1936. On Bit Bakhyani: M. von Oppenheim, *Der Tell Halaf*, 3 vols., Berlin 1943–55.

22. Pritchard, *Texts*, p. 501.

23. Cf. M. Hours-Miédan, *Carthage*, Paris 1949.

24. Pritchard, *Texts*, p. 501.

25. On Canaanite and Aramaean religion: R. Dussaud, cit. n. 18, Ch. 5; T. H. Gaster, *The Religion of the Canaanites*, in V. Ferm (ed.), *Forgotten Religions*, New York 1950, pp. 111–43; R. Largement, *La religion cananéenne*, in M. Brillant, R. Aigrain, *Histoire des religions*, IV, Tournai 1956, pp. 177–99.

26. Cf. W. F. Albright, *Archaeology and the Religion of Israel*, ed. 3, Baltimore 1953, p. 71.

27. Cf. n. 4, Ch. 1.

28. Cf. O. Eissfeldt, *El im ugaritischen Pantheon*, Berlin 1951; M. H. Pope, *El in the Ugaritic Texts*, Leiden 1955.

29. Cf. A. S. Kapelrud, *Baal in the Ras Shamra Texts*, Copenhagen 1952.

30. Cf. A. De Guglielmo, *Sacrifice in the Ugaritic Texts*, in *Catholic Biblical Quarterly*, 17 (1955), pp. 196–216.

31. Cf. G. Goossens, *Hiérapolis de Syrie*, Louvain 1943.

32. Cf. A. Murtonen, *The Appearance of the Name Yhwh Outside Israel*, Helsinki 1951; J. Gray, *The God Yw in the Religion of Canaan*, in *Journal of Near Eastern Studies*, 12 (1953), pp. 278–83.

33. Cf. C. H. Gordon, *Ugaritic Manual*, Roma 1955; G. R. Driver, *Canaanite Myths and Legends*, Edinburgh 1956. A general appreciation of Ugaritic literature and of its impact on the surrounding world is J. Gray, *The Legacy of Canaan*, Leiden 1957.

34. On Aramaean literature cf. A. Dupont-Sommer, *Littérature araméenne*, in R. Quenau (ed.), *Histoire des littératures*, I, Paris 1956, pp. 631–45.

35. Cf. U. M. D. Cassuto, *The Goddess Anat*, ed. 2, Jerusalem 1953.

36. Pritchard, *Texts*, p. 140 (text 49, II, 6–14, 21–36 of Gordon's edition).

37. Ibid. (Gordon text 49, III, 10–21).

38. Cf. P. Fronzaroli, *Leggenda di Aqhat*, Firenze 1955.

39. Pritchard, *Texts*, p. 150 (text 2 Aqht, II, 8–15 of Gordon's edition).

40. Pritchard, *Texts*, p. 151 (Gordon text 2 Aqht, VI, 26–33).

41. Ibid. (Gordon text 2 Aqht, VI, 34–8).

42. Cf. J. Gray, *The Krt Text in the Literature of Ras Shamra*, Leiden 1955.

43. Pritchard, *Texts*, p. 145 (text Krt, 282–3, 288–300 of Gordon's edition).

44. Cf. R. Largement, *La Naissance de l'Aurore*, Gembloux-Louvain 1949.

45. T. H. Gaster, *Thespis*, New York 1950, p. ix.

46. Pritchard, *Texts*, pp. 428–9.

47. Ibid., p. 429.

48. Cf. J. Nougayrol, *Le palais royal d'Ugarit III*, Paris 1955.

49. Ibid., n. 16.344, p. 35.

50. Cf. A. van Selms, *Marriage and Family Life in Ugaritic Literature*, London 1954.

51. J. Nougayrol (cit. n. 48, Ch. 6), p. 32.

52. On Syrian art: H. Frankfort (cit. n. 64, Ch. 2), pp. 113–201; R. Dussaud, *L'art phénicien du IIᵉ millénaire*, Paris 1949.

53. Plentiful light is thrown on all this by the material concerning the relations between Ugarit and the Hittites, Ugarit and Egypt, and Ugarit and Cyprus, collected by C. F.-A. Schaeffer, *Ugaritica III*, Paris 1956.

54. H. Frankfort (cit. n. 64, Ch. 2), p. 168, and *The Origin of the Bit Hilani*, in *Iraq*, 14 (1952), pp. 120–31.

55. Cf. Y. Yadin, *Excavations at Hazor*, in *Biblical Archaeologist*, 19 (1956), pp. 2–11, and *Further Light on Biblical Hazor*, ibid., 20 (1957), pp. 34–47.

56. Cf. C. Decamps de Mertzenfeld, *Inventaire commenté des ivoires phéniciens et apparentés découverts dans le Proche-Orient*, Paris 1954; H. J. Kantor, *Syro-Palestinian Ivories*, in *Journal of Near Eastern Studies*, 15 (1956), pp. 153–74.

57. Cf. E. Kukahn, *Anthropoide Sarkophage in Beyrouth und die Geschichte dieser sidonischen Sarkophagkunst*, Berlin 1955.

CHAPTER 7

1. Psalm cii, 26–8. The Biblical passages are quoted according to the English Revised Version, without however reproducing its use of italics, or of capital letters as in n. 3, Ch. 7.

2. Cf. the chapter on Egypt.

3. 1 Samuel ii, 6–8. Here and in other passages the Hebrew Divine Name is rendered, in accordance with the practice of the version which we quote, 'the Lord', or 'God' (the R.V. prints: LORD, GOD); but for many reasons the proper name 'Yahweh' would have been preferable as a rendering.

4. Cf. H. and H. A. Frankfort, J. A. Wilson, T. Jacobsen, W. A. Irwin (cit. n. 24, Ch. 2), pp. 363–9.

5. As so many books exist on ancient Israel, the bibliographical indications here and in the following paragraphs will be mainly limited to general works, to which — with some exceptions — the

reader is referred for particular questions and their treatment. On history cf. R. Kittel, *Geschichte des Volkes Israel*, 3 vols., Stuttgart 1923–9; W. O. E. Oesterley, T. H. Robinson, *A History of Israel*, 2 vols., Oxford 1932; P. Heinisch, *Geschichte des Alten Testamentes*, Bonn 1950; M. Noth, *Geschichte Israels*, ed. 3, Göttingen 1956; W. F. Albright, *From the Stone Age to Christianity*, New York 1957.

6. On this subject cf. J. Obersteiner, *Biblische Sinndeutung der Geschichte*, Graz 1945; C. R. North, *The Old Testament Interpretation of History*, London 1946; G. Östborn, *Yahweh's Words and Deeds. A Preliminary Study into the Old Testament Presentation of History*, Uppsala-Wiesbaden 1952; M. Burrows, *Ancient Israel*, in R. C. Dentan (cit. n. 6, Ch. 2), pp. 99–131; E. A. Speiser, *The Biblical Idea of History in Its Common Near Eastern Setting*, in *Israel Exploration Journal*, 7 (1957), pp. 201–16.

7. On the problem of the origins cf. T. J. Meek, *Hebrew Origins*, New York 1950; H. H. Rowley, *From Joseph to Joshua*, London 1950.

8. Genesis xii, 1–4.

9. Cf. J. Hoftijzer, *Die Verheissungen an die drei Erzväter*, Leiden 1956.

10. Exodus iii, 1–10.

11. Exodus xix, 16–19.

12. M. Noth (cit. n. 5, Ch. 7), pp. 85–6. On the question of the tribes cf. the same author's *Das System der zwölf Stämme*, Stuttgart 1930.

13. Judges v, 2–5.

14. The giant Goliath.

15. 1 Samuel xviii, 6–12.

16. Cf. the fundamental study by A. R. Johnson, *Sacral Kingship in Ancient Israel*, Cardiff 1955.

17. 2 Samuel xii, 1–13.

18. 1 Kings xi, 4–11.

19. On the relations between kings and prophets cf. A. Welch, *Kings and Prophets of Israel*, London 1952.

20. Isaiah xxviii, 1–4.

21. The mountain of Jerusalem. 'Zion' and 'daughter of Zion' are also names for Jerusalem.

22. Jeremiah iv, 5–8.

23. On this period cf. E. Janssen, *Juda in der Exilzeit*, Göttingen 1956.

24. Psalm cxxxvii, 1–6.

25. On the religion of Israel in general: R. Kittel, *Die Religion des Volkes Israel*, ed. 2, Leipzig 1929; W. Eichrodt, *Theologie des Alten Testaments*, 3 vols., Leipzig 1933–9 (a new edition, of which vol. I has appeared, Stuttgart-Göttingen 1957, is being published); W. O. E. Oesterley, T. H. Robinson, *Hebrew Religion. Its Origin*

and Development, ed. 2, London 1937; B. D. Eerdmans, *The Religion of Israel*, Leiden 1947; O. Proksch, *Theologie des Alten Testaments*, Gütersloh 1949; W. F. Albright, cit. n. 26, Ch. 6; H. H. Rowley, *The Faith of Israel*, London 1956.

26. On this point cf. the important article by H. H. Rowley, *Moses and the Decalogue*, in *Bulletin of the John Rylands Library*, 34 (1951), pp. 81–118.

27. Exodus xx, 2–7.

28. On the name of the God of Israel cf., of recent date, H. Reisel, *The Mysterious Name of Y.h.w.h.*, Assen 1957.

29. Exodus xx, 12–17.

30. W. F. Albright, cit. n. 5, Ch. 7 and n. 26, Ch. 6.

31. Ibid. (cit. n. 26, Ch. 6), p. 175.

32. Ibid., p. 177.

33. Psalm xi, 5–7.

34. Psalm ciii, 8–17.

35. W. F. Albright (cit. n. 26, Ch. 6), p. 109.

36. On the nomad heritage in Israel: S. Nystrom, *Beduinentum und Jahwismus*, Lund 1946.

37. Recent studies on prophecy: S. Mowinckel, *Prophecy and Tradition*, Oslo 1946; G. Widengren, *Literary and Psychological Aspects of the Hebrew Prophets*, Uppsala 1948; H. H. Rowley (ed.), *Studies in Old Testament Prophecy*, Edinburgh 1950; T. H. Robinson, *Prophecy and the Prophets in Ancient Israel*, ed. 2, London 1953; A. C. Welch, *Prophet and Priest in Old Israel*, Oxford 1953; A. Néher, *L'essence du prophétisme*, Paris 1955; C. Kuhl, *Israels Propheten*, Bern 1956. On the relations between prophecy and the cult: A. R. Johnson, *The Cultic Prophet in Ancient Israel*, Cardiff 1944; A. Haldar, *Associations of Cult Prophets Among the Ancient Semites*, Uppsala 1945.

38. Jeremiah xx, 7–13.

39. G. Rinaldi, *I profeti minori*, I. *Introduzione generale. Amos*, Torino 1953, pp. 46–7.

40. Cf. ibid., pp. 58–9.

41. Amos v, 21–4.

42. Zephaniah i, 14–18.

43. On messianism cf. the recent studies: S. Mowinckel, *He That Cometh. The Messianic Hope in the Old Testament and in the Time of Jesus*, Oxford 1956; J. Klausner, *The Messianic Idea in Israel*, New York 1955.

44. Isaiah xi, 1–9.

45. Ezekiel xxxvii, 1–14.

46. H. and H. A. Frankfort, J. A. Wilson, T. Jacobsen, W. A. Irwin (cit. n. 24, Ch. 2), pp. 369–70.

47. Histories of Hebrew literature: J. Hempel, *Althebräische Literatur*, Potsdam 1934; A. Lods, *Histoire de la littérature hébraïque et juive des origines à la ruine de l'état juif*, Paris 1950. Among the

most recent and authoritative introductions to the Old Testament: R. H. Pfeiffer, *Introduction to the Old Testament*, London 1952; A. Bentzen, *Introduction to the Old Testament*, ed. 2, Copenhagen 1952; C. Kuhl, *Die Entstehung des Alten Testaments*, Bern–München 1953; O. Eissfeldt, *Einleitung in das Alte Testament*, ed. 2, Tübingen 1956; A. Robert, A. Feuillet, *Introduction à la Bible*, I, Tournai 1957. For the individual books, in view of the large range of studies, the reader is referred to the most recent and authoritative commentaries: *The International Critical Commentary*, under the editorship of S. R. Driver, A. Plummer, C. A. Briggs, Edinburgh 1910 onwards; *Handbuch zum Alten Testament*, edited by O. Eissfeldt, Tübingen 1934 onwards; *La Sainte Bible*, edited by L. Pirot, A. Clamer, Paris 1935 onwards; *La Sacra Bibbia*, edited by S. Garofalo and G. Rinaldi, Torino 1947 onwards; *Die Heilige Schrift in deutscher Übersetzung, Echter Bibel*, edited by F. Nötscher, Würzburg 1947 onwards; *Das Alte Testament deutsch*, edited by V. Herntrich, A. Weiser, Göttingen 1949 onwards; *The Interpreter's Bible*, edited by G. A. Buttrick, New York–Nashville 1952 onwards. A bibliography and a review of existing studies on the various books is given by H. H. Rowley (ed.), *The Old Testament and Modern Study*, Oxford 1951.

48. On the canon cf. G. Östborn, *Cult and Canon. A Study in the Canonisation of the Old Testament*, Uppsala–Leipzig 1950.

49. Among the more recent studies cf. M. Noth, *Überlieferungs-geschichte des Pentateuch*, Stuttgart 1948; C. A. Simpson, *The Early Traditions of Israel*, Oxford 1948; O. Eissfeldt, *Die älteste Traditionen Israels*, Berlin 1950; G. Hölscher, *Geschichtsschreibung in Israel*, Lund 1952; I. Lewy, *The Growth of the Pentateuch*, New York 1955.

50. On oral tradition: E. Nielsen, *Oral Tradition. A Modern Problem in Old Testament Introduction*, London 1954.

51. On Hebrew poetry cf. T. H. Robinson, *The Poetry of the Old Testament*, London 1947.

52. For a more thorough classification of Psalm-types, cf. G. Castellino, *Libro dei Salmi*, Torino 1955.

53. Psalm xiii.

54. Psalm xcii, 1–6.

55. Cf. n. 7, Ch. 1.

56. Cf. M. Burrows (cit. n. 7, Ch. 1), pp. 412–13.

57. Lamentations i, 1–6.

58. Song of Songs ii, 8–13.

59. Song of Songs v, 10–16.

60. Songs of Songs vii, 11–13.

61. On wisdom literature cf. H. Ranston, *The Old Testament Wisdom Books and Their Teaching*, London 1930; W. Baumgartner, *Israelitische und altorientalische Weisheit*, Tübingen 1933; O. S. Rankin, *Israel's Wisdom Literature*, Edinburgh 1936; M. Noth, D.

W. Thomas (ed.), *Wisdom in Israel and in the Ancient Near East*, Leiden 1955.

62. Proverbs x, 26.

63. Proverbs xiii, 7.

64. Proverbs xiii, 24.

65. Proverbs xv, 16–17.

66. Proverbs xvi, 32.

67. Proverbs xvii, 28.

68. Proverbs xx, 4.

69. Proverbs xxi, 9.

70. Proverbs xxx, 24–8.

71. Ecclesiasticus (Sirach) xi, 2–3. This passage and the two following ones are quoted in Charles's translation (R. H. Charles, *The Apocrypha and Pseudepigrapha of the Old Testament*, I. Apocrypha, Oxford 1913).

72. Ecclesiasticus (Sirach) xix, 10–12.

73. Ecclesiasticus (Sirach) xxv, 15–16.

74. Judges ix, 8–15.

75. Job xxx, 15–26.

76. Job. xi, 7–12.

77. Job xlii, 12–17.

78. On the problem of suffering cf. J. Scharbert, *Der Schmerz im Alten Testament*, Bonn 1955.

79. Ecclesiastes i, 2–9.

80. Ecclesiastes i, 12–18.

81. Ecclesiastes xii, 13.

82. On Hebrew law: A. Alt, *Die Ursprünge des israelitischen Rechts*, Leipzig 1934. On Hebrew society in general: J. Pedersen, *Israel. Its Life and Culture*, 4 vols., London–Copenhagen 1926–47.

83. Deuteronomy xxvii, 14–26.

84. Exodus xxi, 2–3.

85. Deuteronomy xxv, 5–6.

86. Exodus xxi, 23–5.

87. Exodus xxi, 26–7.

88. Exodus xxi, 12–13.

89. Exodus xxii, 21–7.

90. Exodus xxiii, 4–5.

91. On Hebrew art in general: A. Reifenberg, *Ancient Hebrew Arts*, New York 1950.

92. On Samaria cf. A. Parrot, *Samarie capitale du royaume d'Israël*, Neuchâtel 1955.

93. On the Temple of Jerusalem cf. A. Parrot, *Le temple de Jérusalem*, Neuchâtel 1954.

94. Cf. A. Reifenberg, *Ancient Hebrew Seals*, London 1950.

95. Cf. J. W. Crowfoot, G. M. Crowfoot, E. L. Sukenik, *Early Ivories from Samaria*, London 1938.

CHAPTER 8

1. A. T. Olmstead, *History of the Persian Empire*, Chicago 1948, p. 1.

2. On ancient Iran in general: C. Huart, L. Delaporte, *L'Iran antique, Elam et Perse et la civilisation iranienne*, Paris 1952; R. Ghirshman, *Iran*, Harmondsworth 1954; H. H. von der Osten, *Die Welt der Perser*, Stuttgart 1956.

3. On the history of the Persians, in general: G. G. Cameron, *History of Early Iran*, Chicago 1936; A. T. Olmstead, cit. n. 1, Ch. 8. For the sources: F. H. Weissbach, *Die Keilschriften der Achaemeniden*, Leipzig 1911; R. G. Kent, *Old Persian. Grammar, Texts, Lexicon*, New Haven 1950 (I am informed that a second edition appeared in 1953, but have not had access to it).

4. Cf. G. G. Cameron, *Ancient Persia*, in R. C. Dentan (cit. n. 6, Ch. 2), pp. 77–97.

5. Pritchard, *Texts*, pp. 315–16.

6. Recent studies reveal the attempt made by Cambyses to 'legitimate' himself in Egypt: cf. K. M. T. Atkinson, *The Legitimacy of Cambyses and Darius as Kings of Egypt*, in *Journal of the American Oriental Society*, 76 (1956), pp. 167–77.

7. R. G. Kent (cit. n. 3, Ch. 8), pp. 116–20; §§ 1, 5, 14.

8. Ibid., pp. 129, 132; § 63.

9. Pritchard, *Texts*, pp. 316–17.

10. A. T. Olmstead (cit. n. 1, Ch. 8), p. 522.

11. A. Pagliaro, *Persia*, in *Enciclopedia Cattolica*, IX, Città del Vaticano 1952, col. 1206.

12. On the religion of Zarathustra: G. Messina, *Der Ursprung der Magier und die zarathustrische Religion*, Roma 1930; H. Lommel, *Die Religion Zarathustras nach dem Avesta dargestellt*, Tübingen 1930; H. S. Nyberg, *Die Religionen des alten Iran*, Leipzig 1938; G. Widengren, *Hochgottglaube im alten Iran*, Uppsala–Leipzig 1938; A. Carnoy, *La religion de l'Iran*, in M. Brillant, R. Aigrain, *Histoire des religions*, II, Tournai 1954, pp. 219–71; A. Bausani, *Testi religiosi zoroastriani*, Milano 1957.

13. On the Gathas: J. Duchesne-Guillemin, *The Hymns of Zarathustra*, London 1952; D. F. A. Bode, P. Nanavutty, *Songs of Zarathustra*, London 1952.

14. Cf. E. Herzfeld, *Zoroaster and his World*, Princeton 1947; J. Duchesne-Guillemin, cit. n. 13, Ch. 8; W. B. Henning, *Zoroaster Politician or Witch-Doctor?*, Oxford 1951.

15. Yasna 46, 1–2.

16. J. Duchesne-Guillemin (cit. n. 13, Ch. 8), p. 137.

17. Cf. H. S. Nyberg, cit. n. 12, Ch. 8.

18. Cf. G. Messina, *Le religioni dell' Iran*, in N. Turchi, *Le religioni del mondo*, Roma 1946, pp. 150–1.

19. Cf. E. Herzfeld, cit. n. 14, Ch. 8.

20. Yasna 44, 3–7.

21. Cf. J. Duchesne-Guillemin, *Ormazd et Ahriman*, Paris 1953.

22. Yasna 30.

23. Yasna 43, 9.

24. Yasna 29, 1.

25. Yasna 47, 3.

26. Cf. E. Benveniste, *Les Mages dans l'ancien Iran*, Paris 1938; R. C. Zaehner, *The Teachings of the Magi*, London 1956.

27. Cf. R. C. Zaehner, *Zurvan*, Oxford 1955.

28. Cf. J. D. C. Pavry, *The Zoroastrian Doctrine of the Future Life*, ed. 2, New York 1929.

29. Cf. S. Wikander, *Feuerpriester in Kleinasien und Iran*, Lund 1946.

30. On Persian art in general: A. U. Pope, P. Ackerman, *A Survey of Persian Art*, I, IV, Oxford 1938; H. Frankfort (cit. n. 64, Ch. 2), pp. 202–33; U. Monneret de Villard, *L'arte iranica*, Milano 1954. On Persepolis cf. E. F. Schmidt, *Persepolis I–II*, Chicago 1953–7.

31. R. G. Kent (cit. n. 3, Ch. 8), pp. 143–4; § 3 g–k.

32. U. Monneret de Villard (cit. n. 30, Ch. 8), pp. 11–12.

33. Cf. A. Godard, *The Newly Found Palace of Prince Xerxes at Persepolis, and Sculptures which the Architects Rejected*, in *Illustrated London News*, January 2, 1954, pp. 17–19.

34. Cf. K. Erdmann, *Das iranische Feuerheiligtum*, Leipzig 1941.

35. Cf. F. Sarre, E. Herzfeld, *Iranische Felsrelief*, Berlin 1910.

CHAPTER 9

1. Cf. V. Pisani, *Introduzione alla linguistica indoeuropea*, Torino 1949, p. 41.

2. Cf. A. Scharff, A. Moortgat (cit. n. 14, Ch. 1), pp. 204–5.

3. Ibid., passim.

4. C. J. Gadd, *Ideas of Divine Rule in the Ancient East*, London 1948; H. Frankfort, cit. n. 10, Ch. 4.

5. Cf. H. Frankfort (cit. n. 10, Ch. 4), pp. 3–4.

6. Cf. V. Gordon Childe, *New Light on the Most Ancient East*, London 1952, and *What Happened in History*, Harmondsworth 1954; R. J. Forbes, *Studies in Ancient Technology*, I–V, Leiden 1955–6.

7. Cf. J. Lur'e, K. Ljapunov, M. Mat'e, B. Piotrovskij, N. Flittner, *Ocherki po istorii tekhniki drevnego Vostoka*, Leningrad–Moskva 1940.

8. There are many recent studies on this subject by Russian authors. A list of them will be found in W. J. Awdijew (cit. n. 13, Ch. 1), pp. 492–524.

9. H. Schmökel (cit. n. 1, Ch. 2), pp. 122–3.

10. Cf. H. and H. A. Frankfort, J. A. Wilson, T. Jacobsen, W. A. Irwin (cit. n. 24, Ch. 2), p. 4. On the position and the conception

of man, cf. C. J. Bleeker (ed.), *Anthropologie religieuse*, Leiden 1955.

11. Cf. A. Moortgat, *Tammuz*, Berlin 1949.

12. H. Frankfort (cit. n. 10, Ch. 4), p. 5.

13. Cf. R. C. Dentan, cit. n. 6, Ch. 2.

14. Cf. especially R. Dussaud, *Prélydiens, Hittites et Achéens*, Paris 1953. On the relations between Egyptians and Pre-Hellenes cf. J. Vercoutter, *Essai sur les relations entre Egyptiens et Préhellènes*, Paris 1954; C. H. Gordon, *Homer and the Bible*, in *Hebrew Union College Annual*, 26 (1955), pp. 43–108; S. S. Weinberg (ed.), *The Aegean and the Near East*, New York 1956.

15. H. and H. A. Frankfort, J. A. Wilson, T. Jacobsen, W. A. Irwin, cit. n. 24, Ch. 2.

16. S. N. Kramer's review in *Journal of Cuneiform Studies*, 2 (1948), pp. 39–70, is of fundamental importance.

17. (Pseudo-)Plato, *Epinomis*, 987d.

INDEX

ANCHOR BOOKS

HISTORY

Aa

ANCHOR BOOKS

Due